Preparation for IELTS Academic

IELTS Target 6.5

Course Book and Workbook

Chris Gough

Garnet
EDUCATION

Published by
Garnet Publishing Ltd
8 Southern Court
South Street
Reading RG1 4QS, UK

ISBN 978 1 90757 510 5

British Library Cataloguing-in-Publication Data
A catalogue record for this book is available from
the British Library.

Production
Project manager: Clare Roberts
Editorial: Kate Kemp, Karen Kinnair-Pugh, Alison Ramsey,
Clare Roberts
Design and layout: Neil Collier, Mike Hinks
Illustration: Doug Nash
Photography: Alamy, Clipart, Corbis, Getty Images,
iStockphoto, Shutterstock.
Audio recorded and produced by Silver Street Studios.

Printed and bound
in Lebanon by International Press: interpress@int-press.com

Contents

Book map

Unit 1   Life and death
Speaking	exchanging personal information / talking about stages and events
Vocabulary	stages of life and life events
Listening	listening for gist
Reading	skimming for gist
Writing	different types of figure / describing figures

Unit 2   Nature or nurture
Speaking	nature or nurture? / talking about background and upbringing
Vocabulary	in the family
Listening	listening for specific information
Reading	scanning
Writing	understanding the task / deciding what to say / organizing your points

Unit 3   Boys and girls
Speaking	changing roles / agreeing and disagreeing
Vocabulary	characteristics
Listening	listening for paraphrased language
Reading	scanning for paraphrased language
Writing	interpreting and describing line graphs / dealing with more information / deciding what to include in your report / writing your report

Unit 4   Past and present
Speaking	memories / describing memories
Vocabulary	looking back / idioms
Listening	listening to label pictures and diagrams
Reading	making sure that information is given in a text
Writing	understanding the task / deciding what to say / writing a balanced composition

Unit 5   Work and play
Speaking	work hard and play hard / talking about your free time
Vocabulary	busy or free / prefixes / free time
Listening	listening to complete a summary
Reading	paragraphs and topic sentences
Writing	interpreting a simple bar chart / interpreting a simple pie chart / comparing and contrasting information

Unit 6   Home and away
Speaking	what are holidays for? / comparing and contrasting
Vocabulary	confusing words
Listening	maps and plans / noticing how information is repeated
Reading	using topic sentences to predict
Writing	organizing paragraphs and using topic sentences

Unit 7   Kill or cure
Speaking	lifestyle / giving yourself time to think
Vocabulary	health and fitness / health issues and minor accidents
Listening	listening to complete a table
Reading	unknown words and phrases in context / working out meaning from context
Writing	describing a flow chart

Introduction

How this course works

IELTS Target 6.5 is aimed at students who are currently at intermediate level (IELTS 5.0), but who want to achieve a score of 6.5 in the IELTS Academic exam. It is especially helpful for students who need support and guidance with some or all of the various tests that make up the exam. Carefully scaffolded tasks aim to orientate and prepare you, rather than throw you directly into challenging exam practice. Frequent reflective exercises encourage you to think about how you approached an exam task, why you performed well or not as well as you'd hoped, and how to go about performing better next time. The course aims to help you develop your all-round English, as well as to prepare you specifically for the exam.

The course consists of 12 units and develops in terms of challenge, to take you from an intermediate level through to an advanced level. In the earlier units, language is graded and texts and recordings are simplified to guide you and give you confidence. By the end of the course, you will be tackling texts and working with language at an advanced level that you will deal with in the exam.

Each unit consists of five modules, which are briefly summarized below.

Speaking and Vocabulary

The focus is on speaking exam practice and the aim is to prepare you for the type of interaction you can expect with the examiner. There is frequent practice of understanding and answering appropriately the type of questions the examiner is likely to ask. The vocabulary selected is the vocabulary that you are most likely to need during the interview. You are also encouraged to record and revise vocabulary that is particular to your interests, and that you will need to remember in order to talk fluently about your life. There are frequent reflective tasks that allow you to assess your progress and talk about concerns you may have.

IELTS Target 6.5 doesn't have a grammar syllabus. Grammar is dealt with mainly as revision, as it is assumed that you will be studying grammar on a general English course at the same time as you work through this course. Some major grammar points are dealt with a little more thoroughly, but, generally, the aim is to develop your ability to use grammatical structures to communicate or to recognize them when you are reading texts.

The *Grammar checks* in each unit focus attention on key grammar points as they arise. If you feel that you need further practice with a particular grammar point, you should use an appropriate grammar resource in your own time or ask your teacher to help you in the lesson.

The speaking part of each unit focuses attention on a key pronunciation point. Sometimes this involves practising difficult individual phonemes, and sometimes it involves working with features of connected speech, stress and intonation. These points are there to help improve your pronunciation in the Speaking test.

Listening

The Listening Module is roughly divided into two sections. The first section aims to engage you in a topic, pre-teach key vocabulary and then focus on a key skill or particular IELTS exam technique. The second section aims to practise the skill or technique, and then encourage you to reflect and develop. Each unit focuses on a different skill or technique, but those skills and techniques are revised as the course progresses. All listening tasks are just like the ones you will tackle in the exam.

Reading

The Reading Module is designed like the Listening Module. Earlier units focus on a number of short texts and practise general reading skills, while later units deal with longer texts and provide practice with specific exam techniques.

Both the Listening and Reading Modules end with a focus on *Key vocabulary in context*. The aim here is to focus on the semi-formal vocabulary that you are likely to meet in the recordings and texts which make up the IELTS exam. Sometimes you are encouraged to select vocabulary from a text that you think will be particularly useful to you and that you should record and revise.

Writing

The Writing Module focuses equally on the two parts of the Academic Writing test. Each unit provides analysis of and practice with a particular writing skill or technique that is required for the exam. There is a focus on step-by-step guided writing and there are model compositions and reports for all of the writing tasks.

Consolidation and Exam Practice

This is divided into two parts. The first part revises the speaking focus and vocabulary presented in the first module. Occasionally, a speaking skill will be developed and there might be a new focus. The second part practises listening, reading or writing skills under exam-type conditions. Each unit practises one skill – reading, listening or writing – so over the 12 units, each skill is practised four times.

Exam tips and Question-type tips

These tips occur all the way through the course. They are there to help you know how to approach the various tasks that make up the exam and to provide advice on how to go about getting the highest score possible in the exam. They also give advice that will help you to improve your all-round level of general English.

Reviews

There is a review at the end of each of the three sections. The aim is not simply to revise language that has been learnt, but to reflect on what has been achieved and what subsequently most needs work. There are exercises that encourage you to revise the vocabulary you have learnt independently and to reflect on which of it is most useful to you.

Workbook

There are Workbook exercises for each of the first four modules in the Course Book units. You might complete these exercises in class if your teacher feels that you need further practice with a point, or complete them for homework. At this level, the aim is both to revise and develop. The speaking and vocabulary exercises in particular aim to develop and expand your vocabulary, and often introduce language that helps you improve your general English, such as idioms and phrasal verbs. In the Course Book reading modules, direct reference is made to the Workbook exercises because the exercises specifically focus on the content of that particular module.

As you work through the course, you will learn more about the exam and what you have to do in each of the tests. By the end of the course, you will know everything about every part of the exam and what is expected of you. When you have finished this course, you will be ready to either sit the Academic exam or to take a short post-advanced course that will prepare you to achieve an even higher score in the exam.

1 Life and death

'Life is what happens while you are busy making other plans.'
John Lennon

Speaking 1: exchanging personal information

A Match the questions 1–8 with the answers a–h.

1. What's your name?
2. Where are you from?
3. What are you studying?
4. What do you do for a living?
5. Have you got brothers and sisters?
6. Are you married?
7. Have you got children?
8. What do you do in your free time?

a. No, I'm an only child.
b. Psychology.
c. Not yet, but I am engaged.
d. I play golf most of the time.
e. Orlaith.
f. Yes two, one of each.
g. Well, originally from Bangor.
h. I'm in film production.

B Now match each of these follow-up comments to the exchanges in Exercise A.

i. Are you? My family's huge. There are eight of us!
ii. Sorry, is that in Wales or Ireland?
iii. Oh, how glamorous. I wish I could do something like that.
iv. That's pretty. It's Irish isn't it?
v. That's nice. What are their names?
vi. Oh, how interesting. What do you want to do in the future?
vii. Do you? I play a bit myself now and again.
viii. How lovely. Have you set a date?

C 🎧 Listen to the complete exchanges and check your answers.

> **Pronunciation check**
> When a word ends in a consonant sound and the next word begins with a vowel sound, you hear the consonant sound at the beginning of the second word, rather than at the end of the first word. Look at the phrases below and then practise saying the phrases with a partner.
> 1. I'm an only child. /aɪm ən əʊnli: tʃaɪld/
> 2. one of each /wʌ nə viːtʃ/
> 3. eight of us! /eɪ tə vəs/
> 4. It's Irish isn't it? /ɪt saɪrɪ ʃɪzən tɪt/

D Add four more personal information questions to the eight questions in Exercise A. Then walk around the class, asking and answering the questions.

Vocabulary 1: stages of life and life events

A Mark each word or phrase in the box (S) if it is a stage or period of somebody's life and (E) if it is a single event in somebody's life.

> infancy __   childhood __   changing school __   adolescence __   moving house __
> leaving school __   leaving home __   graduating from university __   18th birthday __
> starting work __   wedding __   marriage __   pregnancy __   birth of a child __
> divorce __   middle age __   retirement __   old age __   funeral __

B Match some of the events from the box in Exercise A with the pictures below.

C Match the feelings below with the pictures. There is more than one option in some cases and you may not want to use all the feelings.

| joy | apprehension | grief | excitement | sadness | anxiety | pride | fear |

D In pairs, discuss how to form adjectives from some of the nouns in the box in Exercise C.

Speaking 2: talking about stages and events

A Talk with a partner about stages and events in your life. Follow the steps below.

1. Choose two stages and two events from the box in Vocabulary 1A.
2. Plan what you want to say about each. Think about how you felt, especially about the events.
3. Exchange information with your partner.

> *I was feeling very anxious.*

> *I was filled with anxiety.*

Exam tip: In the Speaking test, Part 1, the examiner will ask you questions about your life. These will be questions about home, work or studies and other familiar topics. Practise and make sure you can talk confidently about various aspects of your life.

B Check any unknown words or phrases in these questions and think about how you would answer each question.

1. Where did you grow up?
2. What important decisions have you made recently?
3. Who influenced you as a child?
4. Do you have regrets about any choices you've made?
5. Tell me about a turning point in your life.
6. Do you ever worry about growing old?

C 🎧 Listen to some students answering the questions in Exercise B. For each question, tick the student that gives the better answer.

1. Student A ☐ Student B ☐   2. Student A ☐ Student B ☐   3. Student A ☐ Student B ☐
4. Student A ☐ Student B ☐   5. Student A ☐ Student B ☐   6. Student A ☐ Student B ☐

D In pairs, ask and answer the questions in Exercise B.

Grammar check

Look at these questions from the section. Talk with a partner about which tense is used in each and why.

1. What do you do in your free time?
2. What are you studying?
3. Where did you grow up?
4. What important decisions have you made recently?

Watch out!
typical errors

What are you doing in your free time? ✗

What important decisions did you make recently? ✗

1

Listening 1: listening for gist

A Look at the pictures below and talk to a partner about what is happening in each.

B   Listen to four extracts and match them with the pictures. Write the number of the extract in the box.

C Complete each sentence of advice about listening for gist. Then compare with a partner.
1. When you listen for gist, you listen to understand the ...
2. You are not listening for ...
3. You don't need to understand ...
4. Understanding the gist of a conversation or talk will make it easier to understand ... as well.

D Talk in pairs. What helped you to understand the gist of each extract that you listened to?

Exam tip: When you listen for gist, predicting what you will hear is very important. In the exam, you won't have photos, but a map, a diagram or a table will help you predict. You can also predict by looking at headings and questions and noticing key words and phrases. You will have 30 seconds to read the questions for each listening section.

E Look at the four images below. You will hear a short extract for each. What can you predict about each extract?

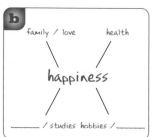

c (c): The Roman Baths
The communal baths were at the heart of (22) _____.

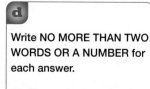

d Write NO MORE THAN TWO WORDS OR A NUMBER for each answer.

10. The student's project is going to be about the life of _____.

F 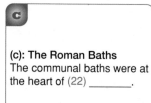 Listen to the four extracts and match them with the images in Exercise E.
1. ___   2. ___   3. ___   4. ___

Listening 2: practise listening for gist

A You will listen to four extracts from typical exam listening tasks. Read options a–c for Extracts 1–4 below and make predictions about what you could hear.

Extract 1 ___
a. A couple discuss moving home.
b. A couple's children have problems at school.
c. A couple discuss their children's friends.

Extract 2 ___
a. A woman talks about the importance of travel.
b. A woman gives advice about finding balance in life.
c. A woman recommends a family health programme.

Extract 3 ___
a. Some students compare cities in Britain.
b. Some students discuss where they want to go to university.
c. Some students agree on which course they should apply for.

Extract 4 ___
a. A lecturer talks about disease in Africa.
b. A lecturer compares Africa with Afghanistan.
c. A lecturer emphasizes that people die early in Africa.

B 🎧 Listen to Extracts 1–4 and choose the correct summary a, b or c, for each extract.

Exam tip: Understanding the gist of a talk or conversation is an essential step towards understanding details and answering questions.

C 🎧 Listen again and complete the sentences. Use NO MORE THAN TWO WORDS for each answer.

1. In Extract 1, the man wants his children to be able to play in _____.
2. In Extract 2, the woman says that people who work very _____ put their health at risk.
3. In Extract 3, the male student has considered applying to a university in _____ or _____.
4. In Extract 4, the lecturer says that in many parts of Africa, people cannot expect to live for more than _____.

D Check the key on page 263. How many questions did you answer correctly?

E Tick the sentences about the Listening task that are true for you and think about how you can answer more questions correctly next time.

- [ ] 1. Reading the questions and making predictions helped me to understand the gist of each extract.
- [ ] 2. It was quite easy to choose the correct summary from listening to the extracts.
- [ ] 3. Understanding the gist helped me to understand detail.

Key vocabulary in context

Look at these sentences and then look again at the key words in the tapescripts. Circle the correct option.

1. Your **lifestyle** is the *way you live your life / clothes you like to wear*.
2. Your **life expectancy** is how *much you enjoy life / long you are likely to live*.
3. **Fulfilment** is a sense of *disappointment / satisfaction*.
4. If one thing is **in conflict with** another, *everything is fine / there is some sort of problem*.
5. If something **interferes with** your life, it has a *positive / negative* effect on it.
6. If you are **uprooted**, your location and situation *improves / changes dramatically*.

WB See *Vocabulary development* on Workbook page 210.

1

Reading 1: skimming for gist

A Check that you understand these words and phrases.

> life expectancy   infant mortality   longevity

B Answer these questions in small groups.

1. What factors determine life expectancy in any country or region?
2. What factors contribute to a high infant mortality rate in any country or region?
3. Is there a reason that some people live to a very old age or is it just luck?

C Read these three headings and make predictions about the content of the extract to which each relates.

1. Infant mortality and poverty link undeniable
2. Social and economic status may lower life expectancy
3. Searching for the secret of longevity

D Read the extracts quickly (90 seconds) and match them with headings 1–3 in Exercise C. Some key words and phrases closely linked to the theme are blocked out.

A

Centenarians – people who live past ▮▮▮▮▮▮▮ – may help researchers find the key to ▮▮▮▮▮▮. Scientists who study this elite group claim that centenarians may possess genes that protect them from disease into ▮▮▮▮.

One in every 10,000 individuals in the U.S. reaches the ▮▮▮▮▮. There are currently an estimated 60,000 centenarians in the US with around 70 beyond the ▮▮▮▮▮. For the past decade, researchers have wondered at these individuals, who often live independently and free from major disability.

To better understand their exceptional ▮▮▮▮▮, scientists have recruited centenarians for extensive physical and genetic screening. Of particular interest to researchers is that some of these people have a history of obesity or heavy smoking, but remain healthy up to the last few months of their lives.

B

There is a definite correlation between ▮▮▮▮ and ▮▮▮▮▮▮ according to speakers at a recent major conference. Data research reveals that the more deprivation in an area, the very much higher the percentage of neonatal deaths.

With nearly three million people now living in relative ▮▮▮▮ and the UK seventh in the world's 'league of shame', the problem is described as 'absolutely massive'. The impact of parental occupation or unemployment on ▮▮▮▮ levels cannot be ignored.

C

People who live in areas with lower household incomes are far more likely to die because of their personal and household characteristics and their community surroundings, according to research conducted at Virginia Commonwealth University.

Researchers analyzed census data and vital statistics from Virginia counties over 15 years. They demonstrated that one in four deaths would have been averted if the mortality rates of Virginia's five wealthiest counties had existed across the whole state. In some of the most disadvantaged areas of the state, nearly half of the deaths would have been averted.

E Talk in pairs. What helped you to understand the general idea of each extract? Highlight some key words and phrases.

F Cover all the extracts. With a partner, summarize the main point of each.

G Talk in pairs. Why is skimming for gist an important reading skill? How does skimming for gist well help you in the IELTS exam?

Exam tip: Being able to skim a text for gist successfully is a very important reading skill. There are tasks such as matching headings to paragraphs, for which you don't need to understand everything, and good skimming skills are essential. Understanding the general idea of a text will also help you decide what to read again more carefully when tasks do require more in-depth comprehension.

Reading 2: practise skimming for gist

A Look at the maps and pictures. What do you think the link between these four places is?

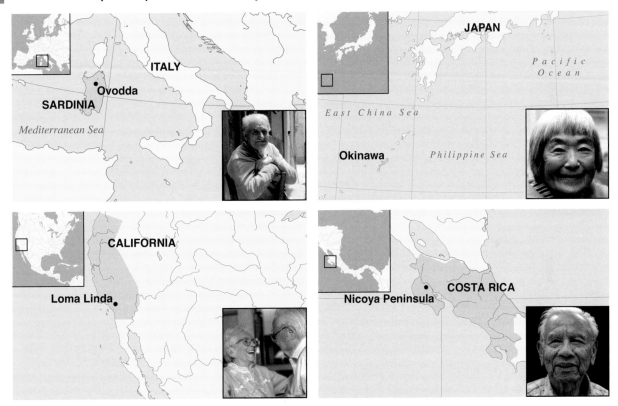

B Read the first part of a text about the four places and check your ideas.

So-called *Blue Zones* are pockets in the world where people live longer, many surpassing the average life expectancy by several years. It is this phenomenon that links Ovodda, a small town in the mountains of Sardinia, Okinawa, a remote Japanese island, Loma Linda, a city in the hills of California and the Nicoya Peninsula, a neck of land on the coast of Costa Rica.

C Look at these possible reasons for such longevity. In the first column, tick four that you think will be given in the text.

1. eating healthily ☐ ☐
2. not eating too much ☐ ☐
3. belonging to a gym ☐ ☐
4. working hard to an old age ☐ ☐
5. not smoking or drinking alcohol ☐ ☐
6. placing emphasis on spirituality ☐ ☐

D Skim the whole text quickly and tick the reasons that are given in the second column.

Still dancing at 100 in the Blue Zones

A So-called *Blue Zones* are pockets in the world where people live longer, many surpassing the average life expectancy by several years. It is this phenomenon that links Ovodda, a small town in the mountains of Sardinia, Okinawa, a remote Japanese island, Loma Linda, a city in the hills of California and the Nicoya Peninsula, a neck of land on the coast of Costa Rica. In fact, in these four otherwise unrelated places, people have three times the chance of living to 100 than they do anywhere else the world, and what is more, they are still active and content with life.

Researcher Dan Buettner wanted to understand. He worked in conjunction with the National Institute on Ageing to investigate the connection between the four zones. The people and cultures in question could not be more disparate, but once the prevailing lifestyles are analyzed, it is not difficult to recognize common lifestyle choices which contribute to the longevity experienced.

B Ovodda has a population of only around 1,700, but it is home to several centenarians. A typical Sardinian diet consists of wholegrain bread, beans, vegetables, fruit and pecorino cheese. Meat consumption is infrequent, reserved for Sundays or special occasions. People drink goat's milk, and enjoy red wine in moderation. Life is uncomplicated in this sheep-herding community, where men walk seven or eight kilometres a day over mountainous terrain. Women may not be quite so active, but they are far from sedentary. Communities have strong family values and ensure every member of the family is cared for. In Ovodda, elders are respected and celebrated, and grandparents play an important role, providing childcare, wisdom, financial help and ties to traditions.

C Okinawa can boast that of its one million inhabitants, 900 are centenarians. That is a longevity rate 25% higher than most other parts of the world. Here, as in Ovodda, diet appears to be central to the equation. Okinawans enjoy a plant-based intake, consisting of stir-fried vegetables, sweet potatoes, tofu and other soy-based fare. Also common is *goya*, a bitter melon, high in antioxidants. Pork is on the menu, but only occasionally and in very small quantities.

Perhaps, more importantly, Okinawans practice *hara hachi bu* – an ancient Japanese tradition that means eat until you are 80% full. These people never over-indulge and, all in all, consume 20% fewer calories each day than westerners do. Older Okinawans remain active and regularly exercise. They embrace *ikigai* – a purpose for living, which they can readily articulate. They have clearly defined roles and responsibilities well into their senior years. Family and community bonds are strong.

D Nowhere else in the United States do people live as long as they do in Loma Linda, and here longevity may be connected with faith. The small community is home to America's largest population of Seventh-Day Adventists. As in the other zones, these people eat healthily. They also renounce caffeinated drinks and alcohol. Of more significant impact, however, could be the spiritual side of life. Adventists encourage members to volunteer well into old age. It provides a sense of purpose and an opportunity to socialize. Adventists also take a weekly 24-hour break for the Sabbath to focus on God, family, friends and nature. They spend most of their time with those who share their values, and they support one another in times of need.

E Costa Rica's Nicoya Peninsula has the world's lowest middle-age death rate. Here, a traditional diet is tortillas, beans, rice and a variety of fruits and vegetables. Meat and dairy products are less common. The water is calcium rich, and people consume a great quantity. For the majority of inhabitants, demanding physical labour is the norm. Even the elderly take pleasure and pride in completing their everyday chores. Older Costa Ricans have a keen sense of purpose and place within the community. They have social traditions that have protected them from stress, and they are cared for into old age by their devoted families.

F So what does this mean for people who do not live in one of the *Blue Zones*? Buettner has distilled the lifestyle principles so that they can be emulated and adopted by all. Firstly, sustainable, moderate-level exercise is essential. Secondly, a restriction of calorie intake and more time taken over meals is hugely beneficial. Frequent consumption of fruit and vegetables and a limit on meat is ideal. Finally, a sense of purpose reduces stress and the risk of disease. All of the Blue Zone centenarians are, or were, part of a faith community. Regardless of the religion, worship of one kind or another appears to aid longevity.

 Exam tip: Some tasks involve skimming a whole passage while others involve skimming each paragraph to identify its purpose or the point made in it.

E Read the text again and answer the questions.

For questions 1–4, say if the information given below agrees with information given in the text. Write (T) true, (F) false or (NG) not given, if there is no information on this.

1. In all four places, people are living longer than other people in their countries. ___
2. All four places are similar in every respect. ___
3. What people eat in all four places is mentioned. ___
4. People in other parts of the world are copying the people in these four places. ___

For questions 5–10, match the headings below with the sections A–F. Write the letter of the section as your answer.

5. The benefits of constraint ___   6. Hard work is healthy ___
7. A simple but energetic way of life ___   8. Why the similarities? ___
9. Can lessons be learnt? ___   10. The power of religion ___

F Check the key on page 263. How many questions did you answer correctly?

G Tick the sentences about the Reading task that are true for you and think about how you can answer more questions correctly next time.

☐ 1. Making some predictions before I read helped me understand the general theme of the text.
☐ 2. I skimmed the whole text quickly to answer questions 1–4.
☐ 3. I skimmed each paragraph to match them with the headings in the second task.
☐ 4. I identified key lines and key words and phrases that helped me match.
☐ 5. I didn't worry about understanding everything in the text.
☐ 6. I'm pleased with how quickly I did the task.

H Answer these questions with a partner or in small groups.

1. Do you think more and more people will live to be 100 years old or more?
2. What are the advantages and disadvantages of living to 100 years old or more?
3. Do you ever think about the age you might live to? Is it important?

Key vocabulary in context

A There are a number of synonyms (words with a very similar meaning) in the text. Delete the one word in each list that is different from the others.

1. link / connection / choice   2. unrelated / common / disparate
3. consumption / intake / moderation   4. sedentary / active / energetic
5. faith / religion / purpose

B Write the correct dependent preposition into space below. Then check in the text.

1. He worked _____ **conjunction** _____ the National Institute on Ageing …
2. … lifestyle choices which **contribute** _____ longevity.
3. A typical Sardinian diet **consists** _____ wholegrain bread …
4. … diet appears to be **central** _____ the equation.
5. It provides **a sense** _____ **purpose**.

WB See *Vocabulary development* on Workbook page 210.

WB For focus on reading skills, go to Workbook page 211.

Writing 1: different types of figure

Exam tip: The Writing test consists of two writing tasks. For Task 1, you have to write a report based on data. You must write 150 words. The data that you have to interpret is usually presented in the form of a graph, chart or table. You may also have to describe a picture, such as a flow chart or diagram, or describe changes shown on a pair of related diagrams. In this book, you'll practise interpreting and describing data from all these sources. To write well, you need to plan well and interpret the information before you start to write.

A Check the highlighted phrase and answer these questions with a partner.

1. How do you think life expectancy in developed countries has changed since 1900?
2. Do you know what age a child born today is likely to live to?

B Look at Figure 1 below. Answer the questions with a partner.

1. What do we call a figure like this?
2. What does the vertical axis show?
3. What does the horizontal axis show?
4. What important information is illustrated here?
5. Does any information surprise you?

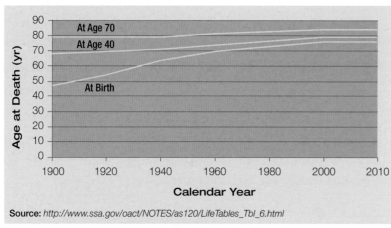

Source: http://www.ssa.gov/oact/NOTES/as120/LifeTables_Tbl_6.html

Figure 1: *Expected Age at Death (EAD) in the U.S*

C Answer these questions with a partner.

1. What are the differences between typical causes of death in developed and developing countries?
2. Which one cause of death do you think could be far more common in the developing world?

D Look at Figure 2 opposite and check *communicable* and *non-communicable*. Then answer the questions with a partner.

1. What do we call a figure like this?
2. What do we call the various coloured parts of a figure like this?
3. What important information is illustrated here?
4. Does any information surprise you?

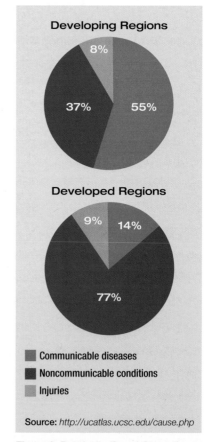

Source: http://ucatlas.ucsc.edu/cause.php

Figure 2: *Deaths by Broad Cause Group*

Discuss these questions with a partner.

1. What do you think are the most common causes of death in most developed countries? Write some causes below.

_____

_____

2. Are there any differences between the most common causes of death for men and women?

F **Look at Figure 3 below and check any causes of death that you don't understand. Then answer the questions with a partner.**

1. What do we call a figure like this?
2. What does the vertical axis show?
3. What does the horizontal axis show?
4. Why is the figure divided into two parts?
5. What important information is illustrated here?
6. Does any information surprise you?

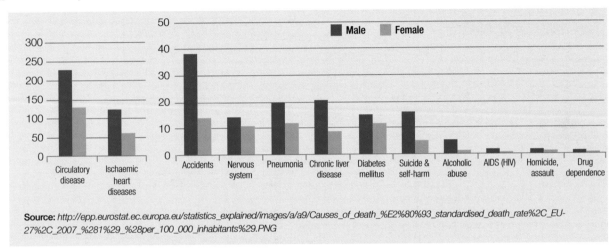

Source: http://epp.eurostat.ec.europa.eu/statistics_explained/images/a/a9/Causes_of_death_%E2%80%93_standardised_death_rate%2C_EU-27%2C_2007_%281%29_%28per_100_000_inhabitants%29.PNG

Figure 3: *Causes of death – standardized death rate, EU-27, 2010 (per 100,000 inhabitants)*

G **Cover the figures in the table below and look only at the heading and list of countries on the left. Discuss these questions with a partner.**

1. Do you think most countries in Europe now have a similar infant mortality rate?
2. Which countries in the list have a relatively high infant mortality rate?
3. In which countries in the list has the infant mortality rate fallen most dramatically?

H **Look at the table and check your answers in Exercise G. Does any information surprise you?**

	1965	1970	1975	1980	1985	1990	1995	2000	2005	2010
Belgium	23.7	21.1	16.1	12.1	9.8	8.0	6.0	4.8	3.7	3.5
Bulgaria	30.8	27.3	23.1	20.2	15.4	14.8	13.3	10.4	8.6	9.4
France	22.4	18.2	13.8	10.0	8.3	7.3	4.9	4.5	3.8	3.6
Germany	24.1	22.5	18.9	12.4	9.1	7.0	5.3	4.4	3.9	3.4
Greece	34.3	29.6	24.0	17.9	14.1	9.7	8.1	5.9	3.8	3.8
Italy	35.0	-	20.8	14.6	10.5	8.2	6.2	4.5	3.8	3.4
Norway	14.6	11.3	9.5	8.1	8.5	6.9	4.0	3.8	2.7	2.8
Portugal	64.9	55.5	38.9	24.2	17.8	11.0	7.5	6.5	3.5	2.5
Romania	44.1	49.4	34.7	29.3	25.6	26.9	21.2	18.6	15.0	9.8
Spain	29.4	20.7	18.9	12.3	8.9	7.6	5.5	4.4	3.8	3.2
Turkey	-	-	-	-	-	-	-	28.9	23.6	13.6
United Kingdom	19.6	18.5	18.9	13.9	11.1	7.9	6.2	5.6	5.1	4.3

Source: http://epp.eurostat.ec.europa.eu/tgm/table.do?tab=table&init=1&language=en&pcode=tps00027

Figure 4: *Infant mortality rate (per 1,000 live births), in selected European Countries, 1965–2010*

I Check the highlighted words and phrases and answer these questions.

1. Have you learnt how to give first aid?
2. Do you know what to do if somebody is choking?

J Look at Figure 5 below. Check any words and phrases that you don't know. Then answer these questions with a partner.

1. What do we call a figure like this?
2. What process does this figure demonstrate?
3. What is the purpose of the arrows?
4. Did you know this information, or is it new to you?

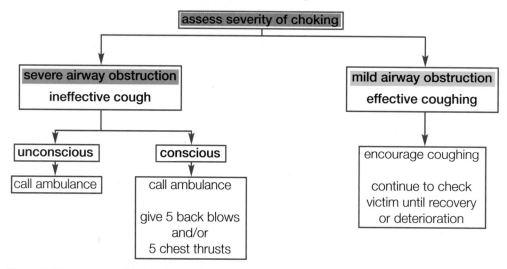

Figure 5: *Management of foreign body airway obstruction (choking)*

Writing 2: describing figures

A Below are extracts from reports written about each of the figures in the module. Match the reports with Figures 1–5. Words and phrases that give away the answers are blocked out.

A The ▉ demonstrates what action to take if somebody is ▉. It shows what to do in both very severe and milder cases.

B The ▉ is divided into two separate figures because some causes of ▉ are so much more common than others. The vertical axis in the ▉ on the left shows numbers of ▉ from 0–250, climbing in 50s, while ...

C The ▉ shows that ▉ has not increased that noticeably once people have reached 40 years of age. What has changed dramatically is how long people can expect ...

D The ▉ illustrates that over the last 40–50 years, the ▉ has decreased in all the countries shown, but that it has decreased more drastically in some countries than in others.

E It is clear from what the ▉ shows that ▉ are still far more common in ▉ countries than in the ▉ world.

B Work with a partner. Choose one of the figures and write some more about the information shown. You don't need to write a complete report.

WB Go to Workbook page 212 for the Writing task.

Speaking

A Answer these questions about Part 1 of the Speaking test with a partner.

1. How long does the Speaking test, Part 1 last?
2. What will the examiner ask you when you first meet him or her?
3. Do you recognize different ways that people greet each other? Are you confident about what to say?
4. What topics will you talk about with the examiner? What kind of questions will the examiner ask?

B Complete each of these questions with the correct question word.

1. _____ are you learning English?
2. _____ do you hope to achieve over the next ten years?
3. _____ in the world would you most like to spend a year studying or working?
4. _____ do you usually travel around your hometown or city?
5. _____ do you think of as your best friend?
6. _____ was the last time you made a wrong decision?

C Ask and answer the questions with other students in the class.

Vocabulary

A Match words from Box A with words from Box B to make six common two-part nouns.

A
life   infant   *mortality*
lifestyle HOUSEHOLD   calorie

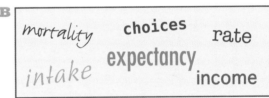

B
mortality   choices   rate
intake   expectancy   income

B Cover Exercise A. How many of the two-part nouns can you remember?

C Fill each gap with a root word made from one of the words in the box.

1. My parents have had a long and happy _____.
2. My whole family came to see my _____ ceremony.
3. Children begin their education when they are still in their _____.
4. If women smoke, they usually give it up during _____.
5. Many people worry that the _____ side of life is being forgotten.
6. _____ in life means different things to different people.

infant
spirit
graduate
marry
pregnant
fulfil

Errors

A There are grammatical errors in all of these sentences. Correct them.

1. My family is very big. There are seven of them.   2. That's a Scottish name, doesn't it?
3. Did you make any important decisions recently?   4. I don't let it interfere in my life.
5. Knowing what action to do can save lives.   6. What are the advantages in becoming older?

Listening

A You will hear two friends talking about why it is a good idea to belong to a gym. Make some predictions about reasons they will give.

> *I think they'll mention losing weight.*

B Read the questions below and make some predictions about how the conversation will develop.

C 🎧 Listen and answer the questions.

For questions 1 and 2, choose the correct answer a, b or c.

1. Tina …
   a. has had a bad experience recently.
   b. needs a change in her life.
   c. is worried about an illness.

2. Tina's friend …
   a. doesn't really understand what Tina's problem is.
   b. is very worried about Tina.
   c. thinks that Tina is selfish for being unhappy.

For questions 3–6, choose FOUR answers from A–H. The order is not important. Which of the following reasons does Tina give for not belonging to a gym?

> A   She wouldn't use it frequently enough.
> B   She doesn't know how to use the machines.
> C   She doesn't want to spend more than an hour exercising.
> D   She wouldn't meet people.
> E   Other people there are very fit and look good.
> F   She doesn't like the idea of men and women using the same gym.
> G   The opening times don't suit her.
> H   It costs too much.

3. ___   4. ___   5. ___   6. ___

For questions 7–12, complete the notes. Write NO MORE THAN TWO WORDS OR A NUMBER for each answer.

> Annual membership – (7) £_____
> The monthly rate – (8) £_____
> Each individual visit – (9) £_____ does not include use of the (10) _____
> or (11) _____
> Monthly bill can be paid (12) _____

D You will hear a talk in which the speaker claims that there are seven habits that people can develop to improve their lives. Can you guess any of the habits?

E Read the questions and notice key words and phrases that will help you predict more.

F 🎧 Listen and answer the questions.

For questions 13–22, complete the notes a student has made about the talk. Write **NO MORE THAN THREE WORDS OR A NUMBER** for each answer.

Life-changing habits

seven habits – people should choose
(13) _____ to develop over a few months

1. positive thinking – keystone habit – will
   (14) _____ people to implement other habits
   negative thoughts mean failure!

2. regular (15) _____ – reinforces positive
   thinking – relieves stress – provides thinking time

3. single-tasking – being (16) _____ by other tasks means things don't get done

4. focus on one goal – people don't have enough (17) _____ for too many tasks

5. eliminate the non-essential – identify what is (18) _____ in life

6. kindness – people will (19) _____ you differently; progress from small acts of kindness
   to bigger things, e.g., help people (20) _____

7. (21) _____ – start and end day in same way – make good start and end the day
   getting ready for (22) _____

2 Nature or nurture

'Give me a child until he is seven and I will give you the man.'
Jesuit motto

Speaking 1: nature or nurture?

A Look at the pictures and answer these questions with a partner.

1. Who are the famous people in each picture?
2. What do the children (or some of the children) in the pictures have in common?

B Check the highlighted words and phrases in these questions. Then answer the questions in small groups.

1. What will the adopted children in the pictures above inherit from their biological parents?
2. In what ways will the adopted children take after their biological parents? In what ways will they take after their adoptive parents?
3. Will the adopted children's characters be more influenced by their genes or by their upbringing?

Vocabulary 1: in the family

A Answer the questions about the highlighted words below with a partner.

1. Why do you think people usually now say *birth parents* or *biological parents*, rather than *real parents*?
2. What is the difference between *look like somebody* and *take after somebody*?
3. What is the difference between *pick something up from somebody* and *pass something on to somebody*?
4. What is the difference between your *education*, your *upbringing* and your *family background*?
5. When we say *where you grew up* and *where you were brought up*, does it mean more or less the same thing?

> **Pronunciation check**
> When the form of a word changes, the stress usually falls on a different syllable in the word.
> The verb is *educate*. /ˈedʒuːkeɪt/ The noun is *education*. /edʒuːˈkeɪʃn/
> 🎧 Listen and mark where the stress falls in these related word pairs.
> 1. biology / biological /baɪˈɒlədʒiː/ /baɪəˈlɒdʒɪkl/
> 2. character / characteristic /ˈkærəktər/ /kærəktəˈrɪstɪk/
> 3. parent / parental /ˈpeərənt/ /pəˈrentl/
> Listen again and notice how the syllables that are not stressed are often produced as weak forms. Practise saying the phrases with a partner.

B Talk in pairs. Can you explain what the expressions below mean? Do you have similar expressions in your own language?

1. I've got my father's hair and my mother's eyes.
2. All my brothers and sisters are artistic. It runs in the family.
3. Julie and Mel are twins. You can't tell them apart.
4. You wouldn't think Sam and Jake were brothers. They're like chalk and cheese.
5. I want to be a doctor. I'm going to follow in my father's footsteps.

Grammar check

Transitive verbs (verbs that are followed by a direct object) can be used in the passive voice.
Intransitive verbs (verbs that are not followed by an object) cannot.
I was brought up in the country / brought up by my grandparents.

Some transitive verbs are very frequently used in the passive voice because they are more likely to describe what **happens to** somebody than what somebody **does**.
I was raised / brought up in Manchester.
Where were you educated?

Watch out!
typical errors
Where did you brought up? ✗
I was grown up in London. ✗

Speaking 2: talking about background and upbringing

A Use vocabulary from Vocabulary 1A and B to tell a partner about you and your family.

Exam tip: In the Speaking test, Part 2, you have to talk about a topic for about two minutes. The examiner will give you a task card with the topic and some points to think about. You have a minute to prepare and write notes if you wish. You can ask the examiner about anything that you don't understand.

B Here are two typical task cards for Part 2 of the Speaking test. Work with a partner – one of you is A, the other is B. Think about the topic for a minute and make notes.

A

Describe a person you know well.
Say ...
- who the person is.
- who he/she looks like.
- who he/she takes after.
- how his/her upbringing has determined his/her character.

B

Talk about a famous person who is very successful, despite a difficult background.
Say ...
- who the person is.
- how or why his/her background was difficult.
- in what he/she is successful.
- how you feel about this person.

C Before you start talking, listen to two students talking to the examiner. Which student do you think performs better? Why?

D Take turns to speak about what's on your task card for about two minutes.

2

Listening 1: listening for specific information

A Look at the picture and answer the questions with a partner.

1. What do we call a school like this for very young children?
2. Did you go to a school like this before starting primary school?
3. If you did, what do you remember about it?

B Look at the gaps in the sentences a–l and answer the questions 1–3 with a partner.

1. What kind of information do you think is missing in each case?
2. In which gaps can you write a figure as your answer?
3. In which answers do you need to use capital letters?

a. The children will go to the nursery school _____ a week.
b. The mother is called _____.
c. There are _____ at the nursery school.
d. There is one other child on the _____.
e. The mother wants her children to start at the nursery school on _____.
f. The children are called _____ and _____.
g. The mother and children's family name is _____.
h. Both children are nearly _____ old.
i. The family live at _____.
j. The mother can be contacted on _____.
k. The daily cost of sending a child to the nursery school is normally £____.
l. If there are two children at the school, the daily cost is £____ for each child.

C Listen and fill in the missing information.

> **Exam tip:** Listening test, Section 1 is a conversation between two speakers and you often need to fill in very specific information, such as names, numbers and dates.

Listening 2: practise listening for specific information

A Answer these questions with a partner.

1. What is the difference between the twins in the two pictures?
2. Do you remember what the mother said about identical twins on the recording?
3. What else do you know about twins?
4. Do you know any twins?
5. If you do, are they different from other brothers and sisters in any way?

> **Exam tip:** It is very important that you learn to listen for gist. However, most listening tasks demand that you understand more specific information the first and only time you listen. It is essential that you look at the questions carefully and predict as much about what you will hear as possible.

B You will listen to a talk about twins. Read through the questions and make predictions about what you will hear.

C 🎧 Listen and complete the notes a student made. Use NO MORE THAN THREE WORDS OR A NUMBER for each answer.

Talk March 13 – Twins
identical (monozygotic) twins – single fertilized egg splits (1) _____
fraternal (dizygotic) twins – (2) _____ fertilized separately
about (3) _____ are identical – twice as many are fraternal
possible category – hybrid/half-identical (check website at www. (4) _____ .com)
identical twins – always same gender and (5) _____ / share all genetic markers
fraternal twins share (6) _____ of genetic markers
Reason for twin births
identical twins – not known
fraternal twins – older mothers (over (7) _____) / fertility treatment
Development of identical twins – not exactly the same
connection to placenta can be better – (8) _____ can differ as they age –
different (9) _____ and interests – want to have own (10) _____
research into twinning might tell us more about (11) _____ / autism
identical twins – like two (12) _____ cooked from the same recipe or the two
sides of (13) _____ – very similar, but not the same!

✋ **Question-type tip:** In the Listening and Reading tests, the instructions for some tasks tell you how many words you can write for your answer. If you go over the limit, your answer will be marked as wrong.

D Check the key on page 263. How many questions did you answer correctly?

E Tick the sentences about the Listening task that are true for you and think about how you can answer more questions correctly next time.

☐ 1. Reading the questions and making predictions helped me to understand the gist.
☐ 2. Understanding the gist helped me to understand detail.
☐ 3. I predicted the type of answer I needed to write successfully.
☐ 4. I used the correct number of words and capital letters when necessary.

Key vocabulary in context
Find the nouns of these verbs and adjectives in the tapescript and write them in the spaces.

1. different _____
2. treat _____
3. similar _____
4. likely _____
5. develop _____
6. connect _____
7. fertile _____
8. individual _____

WB See *Vocabulary development* on page 213 in the Workbook.

2

Reading 1: scanning

A The title of the unit is *Nature or nurture*. What do you now understand that to mean?

B Skim the first three paragraphs of a text about nature or nurture and tick the summary below that is most accurate.

- ☐ 1. It is now clear that what people inherit through their genes shapes their personality.
- ☐ 2. What people experience as they go through life makes them who they are.
- ☐ 3. Whether nature or nurture has a bigger influence on our personality is open to debate.

You inherited curly hair from your father and your dazzling blue eyes from your mother, but where did you acquire your carefree personality and a talent for ball sports? Did these develop as your parents brought you up or were they pre-determined by your genes? While it has always been clear that physical characteristics are hereditary, the genetics is a little more of a grey area when it comes to an individual's behaviour, intelligence and personality. The old argument of nature versus nurture has never really been won. We do not yet know how much of who we are is determined by our DNA and how much by life experience. What we do know is that both play a part.

It has been suggested that the use of the terms *nature* and *nurture* as a convenient catchphrase to describe the roles of heredity and environment in human development goes back as far as 13th-century France. Some scientists believe that people behave as they do according to genetic predispositions – a sort of animal instinct, if you like. This is known as the *nature theory* of human behaviour. Other scientists have concluded that people think and behave in certain ways because they are taught to do so. This is known as the *nurture theory* of human behaviour.

As understanding of the human genome keeps increasing, it is becoming clear that both sides are partly correct. Nature endows us with inborn abilities and traits; nurture takes these genetic tendencies and moulds them as we develop and mature. However, nobody is satisfied with this compromise and the *nature versus nurture* debate rages on.

C For questions 1–3, find the answers to these questions in the text as quickly as possible. Use NO MORE THAN THREE WORDS for each answer.

1. According to the text, what might your mother pass on to you? _____
2. What have people always understood to be hereditary? _____
3. In which country might the term *nature or nurture* have originated? _____

For questions 4–6, decide if the information given below agrees with the information given in the text. Write (T) true, (F) false or (NG) not given, if there is no information on this.

4. People are more likely to inherit curly hair from their father than from their mother. ____
5. People have talked about *nature versus nurture* for over a thousand years. ____
6. Scientists know more about the human genome than ever before. ____

Question-type tip: In the Reading test, you sometimes need to write short answers to questions. The instructions will say how many words you can use. Sometimes, you will also need to decide whether statements about the passage are true or false or say that information is not given. Questions will always be in the same order as information is given in the passage.

D Answer the following questions about reading skills with a partner.

1. What different reading skills did you apply to Exercises B and C?
2. If skimming is reading for gist, what do we call reading to find specific information?
3. Why is this skill important and how will it help you in the IELTS exam?

Exam tip: In the Reading test, you should first read a text quickly to understand the gist. You will then save a lot of time if you can scan efficiently to find the answers to specific questions without reading everything again. Practise scanning exercises and try to do them more quickly as your English improves.

Reading 2: practise scanning

A Check the words and phrases below in a dictionary and decide if each is (NA) more related to nature or (NU) more related to nurture.

conditioning ___	modify and control behaviour ___	innate ___
inborn ___	inherited temperament ___	moulding ___

B Skim the text quickly (about three minutes) and put the following ideas into the order in which they are mentioned.

___ a description of research that proved that nature was also important in human development
___ the fact that, historically, scientists have disagreed about roles of nature and nurture
___ the suggestion that nurture affects nature and nature affects nurture
___ a description of research that supported the nurture theory

Products but Not Prisoners of Our Past

A Throughout the 20ᵗʰ century, students of human development debated the relative significance of various determinants of human personality and behaviour. The larger debate centred on the question: Is it nature or nurture that determines the character and actions of the person? Decade after decade, the pendulum has swung back and forth from one viewpoint to the other as scientists from every sphere have jumped into the debate with their own sets of data.

B In the 1930s, Dr B. F. Skinner and his pioneering studies of behaviour and conditioning had a huge impact. Building on the ideas of earlier behaviourists, he demonstrated the potential of conditioning to modify and control behaviour. Although controversial even in his own day, Skinner's work illustrated the power of environment and experience to modify behaviour in animals as well as humans.

C The essential implication of behaviourism is straightforward: if an observer (a parent, teacher, or researcher) likes a given behaviour, he or she rewards it. If the observer does not like the behaviour, he or she punishes it or withholds a reward. Rewarded behaviour continues and dominates, while punished or unrewarded behaviour begins to disappear. Observation confirmed that behaviour modification worked. So, nurture obviously played a part in human behaviour. Skinner and those that followed him took this principle to an extreme and claimed that all behaviour was primarily determined by the nurture applied to it.

D In the last few decades of the 20th century, research revealed that human behaviour was far more complex than the behaviourist model indicated. In child development circles, there was an increasing dialogue about the concept of temperament, the concept that certain aspects of a person's personality are innate or inborn, rather than learnt.

E Dr Stella Chess and Dr Alexander Thomas pioneered studies of temperament that illustrates the complexity of human drives and the interaction between the forces of nature and nurture. In the early 1950s, they began work on a huge project which came to be known as the 'New York Longitudinal Study'. They selected 133 infants at birth. These selected infants were carefully observed in the newborn nursery and various characteristics of activity and responsiveness to the environment were noted. Chess and Thomas observed that, as newborns, the infants had unique traits and distinct ways of reacting. No two were exactly alike. The key finding of these researchers was the stereotypical and reproducible nature of the infants' reactivity.

F Drs Thomas and Chess did not end their study at this point, however. They continued to observe the growing children throughout infancy, childhood, adolescence and into adulthood. Among the findings was that the temperamental style exhibited by each infant in the nursery persisted, to varying degrees, throughout the growing years. In fact, this innate temperament continued to influence various aspects of the individual's behaviour into adulthood. It was clear that nature (these inborn characteristics) affects behaviour and personality in significant ways.

G These studies, along with many others, affirmed that both nature and nurture affected behaviour in critical ways. The data showed that inherited temperament and talents (genetically determined) interact with the environment and produce a dynamic interplay between the two. It became clear that this interplay determined the final product: the unique character and behaviour of the child and the adult he or she becomes. The actions of parents, teachers, therapists and others do make a difference. We now know that these nurturing influences are moulding forces long at work in the individual.

H These conclusions are not the end of the story, however. By the 1990s, the issue of behaviour had become even more complex. Fresh understanding developed as high-tech tools allowed scientists to 'see' the brain in action. Instruments such as Magnetic Resonance Imaging (MRI), Positron Emission Tomography (PET) and fMRI (functional MRI), provided a way for the newly emerging field of neuroscience to correlate brain activity and brain anatomy with action and behaviour.

I This complex area of study has helped us understand that the brain from birth is in the process of remoulding itself. At birth, the baby's brain holds about 100 billion neurons (about as many functional brain cells as there are stars in the Milky Way). At birth, the brain contains all the brain cells it will ever have. At first, the majority of these cells are isolated. Maturity in all of its forms – physical, mental, emotional and spiritual – is the process of these cells becoming connected and forming trillions of functional networks. This process is gradual, but deliberate. At the same time that networks are forming, another process is occurring. The brain is steadily discarding neurons (brain cells) that are not used and apparently not needed.

J So, it now seems that the nurture the individual receives (the environmental stimulation) determines which neurons are deleted and which ones form permanent connections with other neurons. At the biological, micro-anatomy level, nurture affects nature. However, nature (inborn temperament) to a great degree determines how the person reacts to the environment and so affects the feedback received. So nature and nurture work together in a recycling feedback loop. As one eminent scientist has pointed out, asking whether nature or nurture is more important to human development is like asking whether length or width is more important to a rectangle.

C Scan the passage to answer the following questions.

For questions 1–5, answer the following questions with words from the text. Use NO MORE THAN TWO WORDS AND OR A NUMBER for each answer.

1. What is the ever-changing common view of nature and nurture compared with in the first paragraph? _____

2. Whose ideas did Dr B. F. Skinner develop in the 1930s? _____

3. During research into behaviourism, what does the researcher refuse to give when behaviour is not good? _____

4. How many children were involved in the 'New York Longitudinal Study'? _____

5. Which aspect of personality remained from birth through to adulthood according to Drs Thomas and Chess's research? _____

For questions 6–12, decide if the information given below agrees with the information given in the text. Write (T) true, (F) false or (NG) not given, if there is no information on this.

6. Parents, teachers and therapists influence what already exists in each individual. ___

7. In the 1990s, new technology helped scientists to measure intelligence. ___

8. The number of brain cells a human has increases with age. ___

9. Brain cells connect quickly during the first years of human development. ___

10. As people develop, they do not need all their brain cells. ___

11. If people grow up in a positive environment, more of their brain cells will connect. ___

12. It is useful to understand whether length or width is more important in defining the quality of a rectangle. ___

D Check the key on page 263. How many questions did you answer correctly?

E Tick the sentences about the Reading task that are true for you and think about how you can answer more questions correctly next time.

☐ 1. Learning some key words before reading helped me understand the text.
☐ 2. I skimmed the whole text quickly to answer the questions in Exercise B.
☐ 3. I'm pleased with how quickly I skimmed the text and how well I did Exercise B.
☐ 4. Skimming the text first helped me know where to look when I answered questions 1–12.
☐ 5. I didn't try to read the whole text again in order to answer questions 1–12.
☐ 6. I could answer questions 1–12 without understanding every word in the text.
☐ 7. I'm pleased with how many of questions 1–12 I answered correctly.

F Talk in small groups. What have you learnt about the nature or nurture debate?

Key vocabulary in context

Answer these questions about words used in the text. The paragraph number is given in brackets.

1. Which adjective means *new and fresh and likely to make others want to follow*? (2) _____
2. Which adjective means *likely to upset some people and cause arguments*? (2) _____
3. Which adjective means *simple and uncomplicated*? (3) _____
4. Which verb is the opposite of *rewarded*? (3) _____
5. Which noun is the opposite of *simplicity*? (5) _____
6. Which adjective means *not the same as anything or anyone else*? (5 & 7) _____
7. Which verb means *show that two things are connected*? (8) _____
8. Which adjective means *alone and unconnected*? (9) _____
9. Which noun means *the state of being fully grown or developed*? (9) _____

WB See *Vocabulary development* on Workbook page 213.

WB For focus on reading skills, go to Workbook page 214.

Writing 1: understanding the task

A Look carefully at the instructions for a typical IELTS Writing task.

Write about the following topic:

The most up-to-date research suggests that the characteristics we inherit at birth have more influence on our personality and development than what we experience during our lives.

Do you believe this to be the case?

Give reasons for your answer and include any relevant examples from your own knowledge or experience.

Write at least 250 words.

B Now tick the comment below that is true for you.

1. ☐ a. I understand all the words and phrases in the statement and question.
   ☐ b. I don't know some of the words and phrases in the statement and question.
2. ☐ a. I understand all the words and phrases in the instructions and know what to include in my answer.
   ☐ b. I'm not sure about some of the words and phrases in the instructions so I don't know what I must include in my answer.

C Look at the instructions again and the notes that a student has made on them.

most recent

Write about the following topic:

get from our parents

The most up-to-date research suggests that the characteristics we inherit at birth have more influence on our personality and development than what we experience during our lives.

Do you believe this to be the case? ——— *to be true*

Give reasons for your answer and include any relevant examples from your own knowledge or experience.

Write at least 250 words.

I must say why I think something.

Mention things that I know from what has happened in my life.

'relevant' – say only things connected with the topic

Exam tip: For Writing Task 2, the instructions will be like this or very similar. Make sure you know what the words and phrases highlighted in purple mean.

Writing 2: deciding what to say

A Now that you understand the task shown in Writing 1, tick the comment below that is true for you.

☐ 1. I don't know what to say about this topic. I couldn't write about it even in my own language.

☐ 2. I know what I want to say, but it's very difficult to say in English.

☐ 3. I can say what I want to say about this topic quite easily in English.

Exam tip: In Writing Task 2, you need to express your views on a topic like this one. You don't need to be an expert on the topic, but you must have something to say. Think about how you'd answer the question in your own language first.

B Work in pairs. Look back at the Listening and Reading Modules of this unit and note points you can use in your composition. Then add some points of your own.

C 🎧 Listen to some British students discussing the Writing task and answer the questions below.

1. Which student seems to be more confident about writing the composition?
2. What is the male student worried about at the beginning of the discussion?
3. What does the female student say to make him feel more confident?
4. Why does the female student feel that writing about the history of the *nature or nurture* debate is not a good idea?
5. What does the female student mean when she talks about *challenging the statement*?
6. Do they decide to mention studies with twins to support the nature theory, the nurture theory or both theories?
7. What does the female student do when the male student suggests mentioning inheriting physical characteristics?
8. What does the female student give as an example of the nature only theory making people prisoners?
9. What examples of personal experience do the students discuss?
10. Which part of the composition does the male student think will be easy?

D Now read the composition that the female student wrote. Does it include all the points that she and her partner discussed?

These days, modern science and research into genetics strongly influences what we believe about mental development and human behaviour. We understand much more about what can be passed on through genes and about how we inherit certain characteristics. However, we also appreciate even more about how our environment and what we experience shapes who we are. The question of nature versus nurture is very much alive.

Research has shown that identical twins, even those that have grown up apart, can have very similar personalities and even lifestyles. Other twins can be quite different, though, and it seems that characteristics inherited at birth need the right environment and circumstances to develop. What we experience in life is varied and often unexpected. Events can have such impact that they become more important than what we might have started out with.

I have two cousins that are twins. When they were children they were very similar and liked the same things. Now they are teenagers, they are quite different. The experiences they have had have gradually changed them. I think that they have even tried to be different and that would not have been possible if everything had been fixed at birth. I think that what we inherit and what we experience interacts all the time to make us who we are. Our nature determines some experiences we might have and those experiences in turn change our nature. If that was not the case, we would be like prisoners. We would not be able to shape our own destiny.

E 🎧 Listen to the students in Exercise C again. Highlight the points in the composition as you hear them.

F How has the student answered the question? Choose one option from below.
1. She has said that the statement is true and given evidence to say why.
2. She has said that the statement is not altogether true and given examples to show why she thinks that.
3. She has balanced her argument and said that she does not really know if the statement is true or not.

Writing 3: organizing your points

A Put the stages into the order in which they appear in the student's composition.

___ She says that she understands why some people would believe the statement to be true.

___ She summarizes what she believes to be in the conclusion.

___ She ends by making a powerful point that she hopes will make people agree with her.

___ She gives evidence to support the fact that she does agree with the statement.

___ She shows that she understands the statement and topic generally – by expanding on the statement.

___ She provides an example from her own experience to support her opinion.

 Exam tip: However you answer the question, it is essential that you organize points logically. The examiner must be able to follow your argument easily.

WB Go to Workbook page 215 for the Writing task.

Speaking

A Answer these questions about Part 2 of the Speaking test with a partner.

1. How long does Part 2 of the Speaking test last?
2. What does the examiner give you to look at?
3. What do you do before you talk to the examiner?
4. What can you ask the examiner before you start talking?
5. What do you think the examiner will listen for while you are talking?

B 🎧 Here are two typical task cards for Part 2 of the Speaking test. Look at the cards and then listen to two students doing the exam. Which words do they check?

A

Talk about a person you know that has several siblings.
Say ...
- who the person is.
- how having a large family affects him/her.
- in what way(s) he/she is similar to his/her siblings.

B

Talk about a person you know that is an only child.
Say ...
- who the person is.
- if you think he/she would be happier with siblings.
- how being an only child affects him/her.

C Work with a partner – one of you is A, the other is B. Think about the topic for a minute and make notes. Then take turns to speak for about two minutes.

Vocabulary

A Complete each sentence with the correct form of a phrasal verb from the box.

1. Katy really _____ her mum. They've both got red hair.
2. Do you think David will _____ his sense of humour _____ to his children?
3. Julie _____ her dad. They both live for sport.
4. I _____ by the sea and I never want to move too far away from it.
5. Lisa and Jack have _____ their children _____ to be kind and polite.
6. I _____ a few strange habits when I was in the army.

| grow up |
| pick up |
| look like |
| take after |
| pass on |
| bring up |

Grammar check

When phrasal verbs are transitive, they can be separable or inseparable. If a phrasal verb is separable, the object can come before or after the particle.
He passed on his good looks to his son. / He passed his good looks on to his son.
If the object is a pronoun, however, it must come between the verb and the particle.
pass it on ✓ pass on it ✗
If a phrasal verb is inseparable, the object must come after the particle.
Simon looks just like his mother. ✓ Simon looks just his mother like. ✗

Watch out!
typical errors

Do you take your father after? ✗
Where did you pick up it? ✗

B 🎧 Mark the main stress on these words. Then listen and check. Practise saying the words.

biological   behaviour   parental   significance   likelihood   maturity   complexity   individuality

Errors

A Correct the errors in these expressions.

1. Being successful in business runs through our family.
2. I can't say Mark and Liam apart.
3. I want to follow along my grandfather's footsteps.
4. They're like cheese and chalk.

Reading

A Talk in pairs. Look at the pictures and answer the questions.

1. What do the pictures show about the advantages and disadvantages of being an only child?

2. Do you think that only children are less happy than children with siblings or are the disadvantages exaggerated?

3. Is it becoming more usual to have only one child in your country, or are bigger families still the norm?

4. Will the concept of being an only child change if being an only child becomes more common?

A The number of single child families is increasing all over the world. In China, this is happening largely due to the government's one-child policy. The policy officially restricts the number of children married urban couples can have to one. In Europe, the United States and other wealthier parts of the world, the change is probably more related to people starting families later in life and a range of economic and financial considerations. As the number of smaller families grows, the debate about whether only children are disadvantaged or deprived of opportunity is fiercer than ever.

B A recent survey of only children (men and women aged between 18 and 45) conducted in South India brought into focus some interesting factors. With the single-child family increasingly becoming the norm in India, the questionnaire was aimed at exploring the situation from the perspective of a person growing up without siblings.

- 88% said that their sense of responsibility towards ageing parents weighed heavily on them.
- 96% said being the single child had forced them to make some hard choices in life.
- 88% felt smothered by excessive parental care.
- 72% missed sharing life experience with a non-adult family member.
- 38% missed a sibling for practical reasons as well as for the emotional bonding.
- 80% said they felt anger, probably because they have had to internalize feelings, not wanting to upset their parents.
- 80% said they were addicted to social networking on the Internet.
- 100% said they were now opposed to the concept of a single child family.

Interestingly, only children who grew up in extended or joint families in rural areas said they had never felt different from those children with siblings until they moved with their parents to cities for purposes of education and employment.

C Back in the 1800s, the father of child psychology, G. Stanley Hall, labelled being an only child *a disease in itself*. Since then, these children have been variously stereotyped as selfish, self-absorbed, aggressive, bossy, lonely and even maladjusted. Though hundreds of research studies have shown that only children are no different from their peers, the question of whether the single child syndrome is a myth or a reality continues to be debated the world over.

D It is generally assumed that parents lavish far more attention on an only child than they would a child with siblings. This results in the child being self-centred, dependent and lacking discipline and interpersonal skills. They lose out on being able to interact with others close to their age in the home and they miss out on daily social interactions that can help to properly socialize them. Only children often are stereotyped as spoilt, which may later hinder the success of friendships.

E Research, however, shows that only children actually become very independent and accept responsibility at an early age. They are inclined to take on more than they can manage and rarely ask for help. Trying to please parents and live up to expectations is known to weigh them down, though, in most cases, these expectations are theirs rather than imposed.

F The desire to succeed, mainly for self-fulfilment, is predominant in single children. Studies show that they are focused, preferring things to be simple and straightforward. They tend to complete one task at a time and generally prefer their lives uncluttered. A landmark 20-year study shows that increased one-on-one parenting produces higher education levels and higher achievement motivation.

G An important facet of being an only child was highlighted by women. In Asia particularly, the female only child is burdened with the responsibility of being the sole carer of ageing parents. She will often hesitate to move away from the family home and will struggle to live her own life. If she marries, she becomes part of what is known as the *sandwich generation*. She is needed by husband, children and in-laws on the one side, and ageing parents on the other. In Asian cultures, married women are often expected to be more committed to their in-laws than to their parents. It is common for daughters without siblings to turn inward and suffer depression.

H Current lifestyles are redefining family norms and offering fresh choices all over the world. It could be that families will continue to decrease in size, in which case, being an only child will surely lose some of the negativity currently attached to it. If, in the end, there are as many only children as there are children with siblings, their personalities and behavioural traits will be seen as equally normal.

C Read the passage and answer the questions.

For questions 1–6, answer the following questions with words from the passage. Use NO MORE THAN THREE WORDS OR A NUMBER for each answer.

1. What is the name given to the system in China that limits the number of children born?

    _____

2. What sort of decisions are people now making about family size in wealthy countries?

    _____

3. In which country was the survey that the text is written about conducted?

    _____

4. What percentage of those surveyed felt that their mothers and fathers gave them too much attention?

    _____

5. What percentage of those surveyed worried about looking after a mother or father in the future?

    _____

6. What percentage of those surveyed felt they had protected their parents by not telling them how they felt about being an only child?

    _____

For questions 7–10, choose the correct answer a, b, c or d.

7. The survey reveals that a large percentage of only children go online to …
    a. find out more about what it's like to have siblings.
    b. trace their birth parents.
    c. find work.
    d. meet people and make friends.

8. The survey reveals that …
    a. a number of only children choose not to have children of their own.
    b. many only children will probably have only one child themselves.
    c. only children do not want their children to also be only children.
    d. most only children are not concerned about how many children they have themselves.

9. Which group of only children felt no different from other children with siblings?
    a. those that grew up in the country with only a mother and father
    b. those that grew up in the country with cousins and friends
    c. those that grew up in big cities with only a mother and father
    d. those that grew up in big cities surrounded by other families

10. What did the psychologist G. Stanley Hall believe in the 1800s?
    a. that children without siblings were at a disadvantage
    b. that only children were often sick
    c. that children without siblings were no less happy than children with siblings
    d. that many only children would be successful in later life

For questions 11–12, choose two letters a–e. The order of your answers is not important.

According to the text, which of these statements are often considered to be true of only children?
a. Their parents do not give them enough attention.
b. They behave badly.
c. They frequently need other people to help them.
d. They enjoy being with children of their own age.
e. They make friends easily.

11. ___   12. ___

For questions 13–14, choose two letters a–e. The order of your answers is not important.

According to the text, what does research show to be true of only children?
a. They often try to do things are too difficult for them.
b. Their parents push them too hard.
c. They have a strong desire to do well.
d. They are good at dealing with a number of problems at the same time.
e. They are more intelligent than children of the same age with siblings.

13. ___   14. ___

**For questions 15–18, complete the following sentences with words from the passage.
Use NO MORE THAN TWO WORDS for each answer.**

15. In Asia, a female only child may have _____ that need her care.
16. She may remain close to the _____, rather than do what she wants to do.
17. Women who are torn between the needs of their own parents and their husband's family are called the _____.
18. _____ is not an unusual condition among female only children as they grow older.

3 Boys and girls

'Women like the simple things in life, like men.'
Graffiti

Speaking 1: changing roles

A Talk in pairs. What do the pictures show about the changing roles of men and women in various areas of society?

B Think about the following questions for a few minutes and then discuss them with a partner.

1. What do you think are the most important differences between men and women?
2. Do you think there are some things that men are naturally better at than women?
3. Are there some things that women are naturally better at than men?
4. Are differences between men and women determined by nature or nurture?

Vocabulary 1: characteristics

A Check the highlighted words and phrases in the statements below. Use a dictionary or discuss them with a partner.

1. Men think more rationally and logically than women. ___
2. Women are more sensitive and emotional than men. ___
3. Women are more thoughtful and considerate than men and make better listeners. ___
4. Women express their feelings better than men do. ___
5. Men are more determined to succeed than women. ___
6. Men are more competitive than women. ___
7. Men are naturally more aggressive and potentially violent than women. ___
8. Women are more easily hurt by criticism than men. ___
9. Men are more decisive than women. ___
10. Men are more stubborn than women. ___
11. Women are naturally more cautious and take fewer risks than men. ___
12. Women are vainer than men and worry about their physical appearance more than men do. ___
13. Men have natural leadership qualities and make better leaders than women. ___
14. Women are naturally more protective and make better carers than men. ___

Speaking 2: agreeing and disagreeing

A Mark each statement in Vocabulary 1A like this: (SA) I strongly agree, (A) I tend to agree, (D) I tend to disagree or (SD) I strongly disagree.

B Talk in groups of three. Compare how you have marked the statements. Try to give examples from your own experience to support your views.

C 🎧 Listen to some native speakers and decide which statement they are discussing. Write the number of the statement for each answer.

Conversation 1 ___   Conversation 2 ___   Conversation 3 ___

D 🎧 Listen and complete these sentences from the conversations.

1. _____ being better than someone else _____ matters.
2. _____ makes me really angry _____ attitudes like this in the workplace.
3. _____ that drives me crazy about my wife _____ her inability to make choices.

Grammar check

The sentences in Exercise D are called cleft sentences. These sentences are used to focus attention onto the main message of what is being expressed. In spoken language, they make the message more emphatic. Look at these conventional sentences and compare them with the sentences in Exercise D above.

1. *Being better than someone else matters.*
2. *Attitudes like this in the workplace make me really angry.*
3. *My wife's inability to make choices drives me crazy.*

Using each of the three structures above, rewrite the sentences below so that they are more emphatic.
1. Men who think they are more intelligent than women make me furious.
2. The amount of time women need to get ready drives me crazy.

🎧 Listen and check your answers.

> **Watch out!**
> **typical errors**
>
> It's men who think they are more intelligent than women what really makes me cross.   ✗

Pronunciation check

🎧 Listen to all the emphatic sentences from Exercise D and the *Grammar check*.

Notice how the appropriate stress and intonation is essential to the message. Notice also how the speaker pauses slightly before delivering the important part of the message. Practise saying each sentence two or three times with a partner.

E Discuss these questions with a partner. Use the emphatic structures you have learnt, if appropriate.

1. How have traditional male and female roles changed in your country in the last 20 years?
2. Should women stay at home to look after the house and care for children?
3. Is it a man's responsibility to earn a living and look after his family financially?
4. Do you think women still face inequality in the workplace?
5. Will women in sport ever be taken as seriously as men in sport?
6. Should parents encourage boys to play with traditionally male toys like guns, and girls with traditionally female toys like dolls?

 Exam tip: In Part 3 of the Speaking test, the examiner will expand the topic (from the task card) in Part 2. He or she will ask you to express your opinion on related topics. The topics will be more abstract and possibly more controversial.

3

Listening 1: listening for paraphrased language

A In pairs, answer the questions below.

1. Do you think men and women should compete against each other in sport?
2. In which sports do you think women could compete with men at the highest level?
3. In which sports will women never be able to compete against men at the highest level?

B Look at the pictures. What do they say about the changing role of women in sport?

C Listen to four extracts and match them with the pictures.

1. ___   2. ___   3. ___   4. ___

D Listen again and complete the sentences. There are two sentences for each extract. Use NO MORE THAN TWO WORDS OR A NUMBER for each answer.

1. In 2005, Hayley Turner rode out her claim. She could ride against _____ as an equal.
2. In one season, Turner rode _____ winners.
3. In darts, the _____ between men and women doesn't matter.
4. Many _____ still think women should play in women's competitions.
5. In the Indianapolis 500, Danica Patrick finished 3rd, which was the highest final position ever for a _____.
6. There is still prejudice. People don't think she has the ability to participate in _____.
7. In 2003, Annika Sorenstam played in a men's event, but the experience was _____ than she thought it would be.
8. Michelle Wie is over _____ tall and may be physically the equal of men.

E Answer these questions about the Listening task you have just done with a partner.

1. Did you hear the exact words that you needed to write as answers on the recording?
2. Did you hear the words you needed to write as answers used in sentences that are exactly the same as those in the written questions?

 Exam tip: In the Listening test, you always hear the words that you need to write as answers. However, those words will not be exactly the same as those in the written questions. You need to listen for clues and language that is paraphrased – words and phrases that mean the same as those in the question.

F Listen again as you read the tapescript. Notice examples of paraphrased language as you read.

Listening 2: practise listening for paraphrased language

A 🎧 You will hear a talk given to students studying gender studies about women in sport. Listen and answer the questions.

For questions 1–4, choose the correct letter a, b or c.

1. The speaker says that it is difficult for women to compete in sport with men because …
   a. men are too good.   b. of male attitudes.   c. they don't have enough experience.
2. The speaker says that, in horse racing, females are …
   a. given less important jobs than men.
   b. asked to ride in too many races at meetings.   c. expected to win big races.
3. The speaker says that when it comes to contact sports, some people worry that …
   a. women are hurt more easily   b. men will be too aggressive.
   c. men and women will not want to touch each other.
4. The speaker suggests that girls might be able to play football as well as boys because they …
   a. are strong at an early age.   b. can run fast.   c. are skilful.

For questions 5–11, complete the notes. Use NO MORE THAN THREE WORDS OR A NUMBER for each answer.

Tennis: men + women (5) _____ equally hard now.
      1970s: female player beat (6) _____ easily.

Golf: top female player not (7) _____ in men's event (2003).
      said M Wie as good as any male, but her (8) _____ has not been realized.

Should women always want to compete with men?
Serena Williams (tennis world no. 1) would be ranked much lower – would beat men, but probably not win (9) _____. Would not be so famous / would have won much less (10) _____.
Maybe better to encourage people to take women's sport more (11) _____.

B Check the key on page 263. How many questions did you answer correctly?

C Tick the sentences about the Listening task that are true for you and think about how you can answer more questions correctly next time.

☐ 1. Reading the questions and making predictions helped me to understand better.
☐ 2. I recognized paraphrased language and that helped me answer questions.
☐ 3. I am pleased with how many questions I answered correctly.

D Talk in small groups. What do you think now about men and women competing together in sport?

Key vocabulary in context

In the sentences below, nouns from the tapescripts are used incorrectly. Correct the sentences.

1. If you have promise of something, you know about it and understand it.
2. If you show prejudice or awareness, you are likely to develop and achieve something in the future.
3. If there is potential, people believe something that is unreasonable, often based on dislike or fear.

▶ WB See *Vocabulary development* on page 217 in the Workbook.

3

Reading 1: scanning for paraphrased language

A Talk in pairs. In the USA, what percentage of the people doing each of the jobs in the box do you think are women?

> lawyers   pilots   surgeons   engineer

B Read the extracts and check your ideas in Exercise A.

A
We do not have enough women engineers in the US. When I look around the undergraduate classes I teach, I don't see many female faces. Why? Certainly, there are influences from home, school and peers. There are negative stereotypes like dolls that say, 'I hate Maths.' There is little general public understanding of what engineers do. Engineering in high school is thought of as a vocational option, rather than an academic one. No wonder women have made up only about 20% of the undergraduate engineering population in colleges for the last ten years.

B
Over the past 25 years, women have flocked to study law. By 2006, they comprised over 50% of law school graduates. In the last decade, however, women have been leaving the profession, at two to three times the rate of their male counterparts and now only around 25% of lawyers are women. Patricia Blocksom, a senior partner with a leading law firm, suggests several reasons for the exodus. She claims there is a 'lack of accommodation for women for child-bearing responsibilities, a lack of mentoring and a dominant male culture.'

C
Women make up about 6% of the total number of pilots in the United States or about 36,000 of the 600,000 pilots currently flying. Of that, there are over 7,000 with Commercial pilot certificates and over 5,000 with Airline Transport Pilot certificates. Becoming a pilot is actually no harder for a female, but in most schools it is unusual for girls to meet with encouragement if considering a future as a pilot. Cultural and gender stereotypes still dictate what most young girls aspire to.

D
Recent research has gained entry into the closely guarded world of surgeons to examine how women fulfil their dreams of practising a profession in which 95% of their colleagues are men. It reveals that being a woman does not guarantee a traditionally feminine approach to patient care. Some female surgeons are caring and nurturing, while others are cold and slightly aggressive.

C Scan the four texts and use the highlighted parts to answer these questions. Write the number of the text in the space. Which text:
1. says that more than half the students who gained a qualification were female? ___
2. suggests that people in a certain profession do not talk about it much? ___
3. suggests that children's toys affect the attitudes that girls have? ___
4. claims that a certain job is no more difficult for a woman than for a man? ___

Exam tip: In some scanning tasks, you need to look quickly for parts of the text that mean the same as the words and phrases in the question. You will not find the exact words and phrases from the question in the text.

D Scan the text again to answer these questions in the same way. Highlight the parts of the text that provide the answer. Which text:

1. accuses employers of not being supportive when women have babies?   ___
2. suggests that working women do not always behave in a typically womanly way?   ___
3. claims that people underestimate the importance of a certain profession?   ___
4. says that girls' ambitions are influenced by traditional thinking?   ___

Reading 2: practise scanning for paraphrased language

A In pairs, answer the questions below.

1. How many reasons for women not entering a profession or leaving a profession can you remember from the extracts in Reading 1?
2. Can you think of any more reasons?

B Read this text about women working in academic medicine and answer the questions on the next page.

Stereotypes Keep Women from Academic Achievement

A Women in academic medicine who aspire to leadership positions often find their opportunities limited by gender bias, unequal pay and lack of mentors. This is certainly the view of Leah Dickstein, M.D., a Professor of Psychiatry and Associate Dean at the University Of Louisville School Of Medicine. 'When women psychiatrists are not considered for leadership positions for which they are qualified, they often hear such comments as "I didn't think your husband would be willing to move" or "I heard that you had several children, so I didn't think you could take on this new responsibility"', she claims.

B Dickstein also suggests that female staff over the age of 50 may face age bias, 'We are viewed as too old and over the hill to assume new leadership responsibilities. Yet men in academic medicine in their 60s and 70s are offered new positions as deans and presidents of academic institutions and provided with senior academic leadership opportunities.'

C Gender-biased assumptions combined with lower salaries, a lack of effective mentoring and being given a higher number of clinical assignments than male colleagues add up to frustration for women who are attempting to advance their careers. These barriers have kept the number of women who are full, associate or assistant professors low, compared with male professors. Of the nation's 125 medical schools, only five have permanent deans who are women physicians, and none is a psychiatrist. Women make up 8% (206) of all permanent department chairs, and only five are psychiatrists.

D Studies on salaries and gender in academic medicine have found that women in some specialties and at some institutions earn up to 30% less than their male counterparts. Dickstein blamed women's lack of progress in academic medicine on too many stereotypes and a lack of courage on the part of male colleagues to mentor and recommend qualified women for leadership positions.

E 'The dearth of female faculty staff in the top ranks means fewer role models, mentors and networking opportunities for aspiring women physicians', said Dickstein. It seems that mentors can provide valuable information about promotion criteria and salaries. However, mentors tend to give this advice to other men. Women, especially those with children, sometimes feel so grateful when they are offered an academic position that they don't think about negotiating salaries or checking the research time and support staff that will be available to them.

F The rules for promotion in academic medicine were developed by men, so it is not surprising that women in academia sometimes feel like a square peg trying to fit into a round hole. For example, promotion committees measure outstanding performance by the number of papers published in journals. The problem with this yardstick is that women in nonsurgical specialties may be assigned more clinical duties and more complex patients than their male colleagues. This leaves women with less time to conduct research and write papers.

G Marion Goldstein, M.D., an Assistant Professor and Director of the Division Of Geriatric Psychiatry at the State University of New York at Buffalo, recalled a painful lesson she learnt during her research career. She said that her NIH grant wasn't renewed because she didn't have time to publish several papers. 'I was directing an 18-bed geriatric inpatient unit, teaching residents and rotating coverage for five other psychiatrists,' she explained.

H Dickstein would like the academic promotion criteria changed to reflect women's strengths. 'There should be less emphasis on research qualifications for leadership positions, with the exception of vice deans or chairs of research, and more emphasis on excellence in administration, education and in fostering student development,' she said. 'Women with fewer published research papers than their male colleagues often have larger citation indexes and write more comprehensive papers,' she observed.

I Women in the workplace often receive mixed messages about how they are expected to behave. They may be expected to take risks, but not to make mistakes; to be tough, but also to be feminine; and to be ambitious, but not to expect equal treatment. It appears that women who desire power fear a loss of approval and abandonment by others. Those who act in their own interests are viewed as selfish and destructively aggressive. Many women who don't see themselves as powerful feel that they are inadequate. This self-devaluation can lead to the belief that success is due to luck or chance, rather than ability.

For questions 1–6, identify the paragraph which contains the following information. Write the correct letter A–I in the space.

1. men earning a third more than women do in some workplaces   ___
2. women feeling unsuited to roles that men have designed for them   ___
3. the idea that women take jobs without knowing enough about them   ___
4. contradictory information about what is expected of women   ___
5. the assumption that women have family commitments   ___
6. anger that pay is low, little advice is given and work is too hard   ___

For questions 7–14, decide if the information given below agrees with the information given in the text. Write (T) true, (F) false or (NG) not given, if there is no information on this.

7. A man's age seems to matter less than a woman's age.   ___
8. There are no women currently working as psychiatrists.   ___
9. Male mentors tell other men about good jobs that are available.   ___
10. Women often have a heavier workload and more difficult patients to deal with.   ___
11. Marion Goldstein's grant wasn't renewed because she was too busy to do some writing.   ___
12. Leah Dickstein believes that the criteria for academic promotion are fair.   ___
13. When women feel unsatisfied at work, they are more likely to make mistakes.   ___
14. Women continue to have faith in their ability even when faced with inequality.   ___

C Check the key on page 263. How many questions did you answer correctly?

D Tick the sentences about the Reading task that are true for you and think about how you can answer more questions correctly next time.

☐ 1. It helped to know what the text would be about before I read it.
☐ 2. I didn't feel that I had to understand every word of the text to complete the tasks.
☐ 3. It was difficult to answer some questions because I didn't know words or phrases.
☐ 4. I recognized paraphrased language in order to complete questions 1–6.
☐ 5. I'm pleased with how quickly I scanned the text in order to complete questions 1–6.
☐ 6. I didn't try to read the whole text again in order to answer questions 7–14.
☐ 7. I recognized paraphrased language in order to complete questions 7–14.

E Talk in small groups. Do you think the experience of the women described in the text is unique to their situation or is a situation that exists in many institutions?

Grammar check

Passive forms are used more frequently in written language than in spoken language, and even more frequently in academic written texts.

Complete these examples of passive forms from the text. Use the verb and grammatical structure provided.

1. Men in their 60s and 70s _____ (offer) new positions as deans and presidents. (present simple)
2. The rules for promotion in academic medicine _____ (develop) by men. (past simple)
3. ... a lack of effective mentoring and _____ (give) a higher number of clinical assignments than male colleagues add up to frustration. (an ~*ing* form)
4. They may _____ (expect) to take risks, but not to make mistakes. (an infinitive + past participle)

Check your answers in the text. Discuss with a partner why a passive rather than an active form is used in each example.

Key vocabulary in context

A Look at these sentences and then look again at the key words in the text (the paragraph is provided in each case). Highlight the correct option.

1. If there is **bias** (A/B), *everyone is treated fairly / some people are treated better than others*.
2. A **barrier** (C) *gets in the way of something / allows something to happen*.
3. A **counterpart** (D) is *somebody doing the same thing / something quite different*.
4. If there is a **dearth** (E) of something, there is *very little or very few / a large number*.
5. **Mentors** (A/E), are *responsible for paying employees / experienced people who give advice*.
6. If somebody or something is **outstanding** (F), it *is especially good / takes a long time to do*.
7. If you **foster** (H) something, you *look after and help it succeed / get in the way*.
8. If somebody is **inadequate**, he or she is *sad and lonely / not good enough*.

B Cover the text. Complete these phrases with the correct preposition.

1. women who **aspire** _____ leadership positions
2. gender-biased assumptions **combined** _____ lower salaries
3. less **emphasis** _____ research qualifications
4. a lack of courage _____ **the part of** male colleagues

WB See *Vocabulary development* on Workbook page 217.

WB For focus on reading skills, go to Workbook page 218.

3

Writing 1: interpreting and describing line graphs

A Cover the graph below and talk in pairs. Complete each statement with your own ideas.

1. In 1948, around ___% of women in the United States worked.
2. In 2009, around ___% of women in the United States worked.
3. Between 1948 and 2009, the percentage of women working in the United States increased by around ___%.

B Look at the simple line graph below and check your ideas in Exercise A.

Percentage of Women 16+ in Workforce (US 1948–2009)

Source: *(2009) Bureau of Labor Statistics, Current Population Survey, Labor Force Statistics.*

C Talk in pairs about your own country. Has the number of women that work increased significantly since around the middle of the last century?

D Make sure you understand all the verbs in the box. Then tick the verbs that can be used in the statement below about the line graph in Exercise B.

| increased   decreased   rose   fell   grew   dropped   remained steady   fluctuated |

Between 1948 and 2009, the percentage of women working in the United States …

E Check you understand the two verbs in the statement below and choose the correct option.

Between 1948 and 2009, the number of women that worked almost doubled / trebled.

Writing 2: dealing with more information

Exam tip: When you are interpreting and describing graphs and charts in Writing Task 1, you will be given more than one source of information. You will have to compare and contrast information.

A Look at the graph below. What information does it compare?

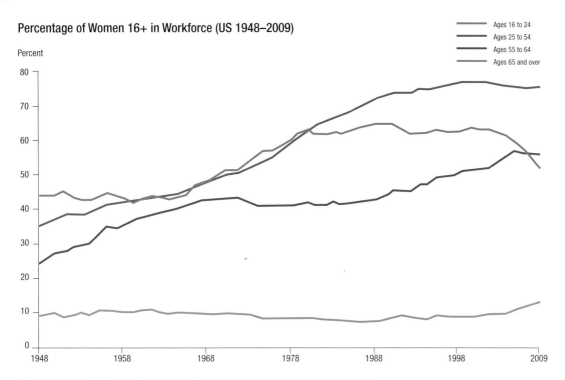

Percentage of Women 16+ in Workforce (US 1948–2009)

— Ages 16 to 24
— Ages 25 to 54
— Ages 55 to 64
— Ages 65 and over

Source: *(2009) Bureau of Labor Statistics, Current Population Survey, Labor Force Statistics.*

B In pairs, look at these instructions for a typical IELTS Writing task and answer the questions below.

> *The line graph shows the percentage of the women of various ages that were in full-time work in the United States between 1948 and 2009.*
>
> *Summarize the information by selecting and reporting the main features, and make comparisons where relevant.*
>
> Write at least 150 words.

1. What must you do before you start writing about the graph?
2. What should you say in the opening sentence of your report?
3. How do you decide what information to include in your report?
4. Do you need to explain information – for example, say why more women worked from home in 2009?
5. Is there a conventional style that you should use to write a report like this?
6. Should you divide your report into paragraphs?
7. How should you end your report?
8. What will the examiner look for when he or she marks your report?

Exam tip: You must spend time looking at the information and planning what to say before you start writing. You cannot describe everything the chart shows in 150 words, so choose information that stands out. Don't try to explain information.

C Why are each of the opening sentences below inappropriate? Compare ideas with a partner.

1. The line graph shows the percentage of the women of various ages that were in full-time work in the United States between 1948 and 2009.
2. The line graph shows that the percentage of women between 16 and 24 that worked in full-time jobs in the United States decreased between 1988 and 2009.
3. The line graph shows that, as women in the United States were emancipated in the second half of the 20th century, the percentage of those working in full-time jobs increased.
4. The line graph shows that the percentage of women between 55 and 64 who worked in full-time jobs in the United States increased steadily between 1988 and 2009, but that the percentage of women between 16 and 54 stopped increasing after around 2000.

Exam tip: Your first sentence should show that you understand the information given – don't just repeat what it says in the instructions and don't try to describe too much.

D In pairs, write an appropriate opening line.

Writing 3: deciding what to include in your report

A Talk in pairs. Identify information that you think should be included in a report of the graph.

B Look at the comments a student has made on the graph. Does she identify the same things as you?

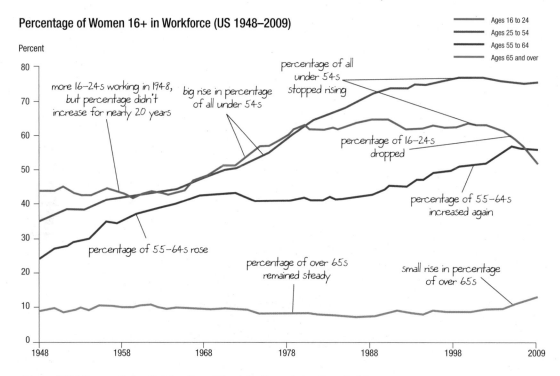

Percentage of Women 16+ in Workforce (US 1948–2009)

Source: *(2009) Bureau of Labor Statistics, Current Population Survey, Labor Force Statistics.*

Writing 4: writing your report

A Check the highlighted phrases below and complete each sentence with a year from the horizontal axis on the graph.

1. Between _____ and 1968, the percentage of women aged 55–64 working increased steadily.
2. Between 1968 and _____, the percentage of women aged 16–54 working rose noticeably/sharply.
3. Between _____ and 2009, the percentage of women aged 25–54 working fell slightly.
4. Between 1954 and _____, there was a dramatic rise in the percentage of women aged 55–64 working.
5. Between 1998 and _____, there was a gradual fall in the percentage of women aged 16–24 working.

Grammar check

Adjectives describe nouns – *a dramatic increase / a steady fall.*
Adverbs modify adjectives – *rose sharply / decreased noticeably.*
Notice these spelling rules for adverbs: *sharp – sharply / noticeable – noticeably / dramatic – dramatically.*

B Rewrite the noun phrases 1–5 as verb phrases and the verb phrases 6–10 as noun phrases.

1. a sharp increase   *increased sharply*
2. a steady decrease   _____
3. a noticeable rise   _____
4. a dramatic fall   _____
5. a slight drop   _____

6. decreased gradually   *a gradual decrease*
7. increased sharply   _____
8. rose slightly   _____
9. fell steadily   _____
10. dropped dramatically   _____

C Complete the report below with your own ideas. Use one or two words in each space. Then check the model on pages 263 and 264.

The line graph shows that the percentage of women of working age in employment in the United States increased between 1948 and 1998, but fell slightly between 1998 and 2009. The percentage of women over 65 working changed _____.

In 1948, there were more women aged 16–24 working than women of _____ age. However, the percentage of young women working did not increase for 20 years. In _____, the percentage of women aged 25–54 in work _____ in that period. The percentage of women aged 16–24 in work rose _____ between 1966 and 1978, but _____ between 1978 and 2009.

Between 1998 and 2009, the percentage of women under 54 working _____. However, the percentage of women aged 55–65 working rose once again. In the last two or three years shown, there was a _____ in the percentage of women over 65 in work. The percentage of older women working continues to rise while the percentage of _____ falls.

D Look at the Exam Practice Module on page 51 for the Writing task.

Speaking

A Answer these questions about Part 3 of the Speaking test with a partner.

1. How does Part 3 of the Speaking test develop from Part 2?
2. How are the questions in Part 3 of the Speaking test different from those in the first part?
3. Does the examiner expect you to know a lot about the topic he or she asks about?
4. Is it better to answer questions as quickly as possible or to take a moment to think about your answer?
5. What should you do if you don't understand a question or the meaning of a particular word in a question?
6. What will the examiner listen for when you're answering questions?

B Look again at this question from the unit. Can you remember how you answered it?

How have traditional male and female roles changed in your country in the last 20 years?

C 🎧 Listen to some students answering the question. Mark each speaker (✓) for a good answer or (✗) not a good answer.

Speaker 1 ___   Speaker 2 ___   Speaker 3 ___   Speaker 4 ___

D 🎧 Listen again and make notes about each speaker's answer. Then compare notes with a partner.

Vocabulary

A Fill each gap with a root word made from one of the words in the box.

1. I think women have the same _____ qualities as men.
2. People shouldn't make _____ about people they don't know.
3. The scheme needs the boss's _____ before it can go ahead.
4. As a parent, you have more _____ than when you're single.
5. People miss opportunities when they are not _____.
6. Most people find it hard to take _____ from somebody at work.

| approve |
| decide |
| assume |
| critic |
| lead |
| response |

B There were a number of synonyms (or near synonyms) in the unit. Delete the word in each line that is different from the other two.

1. emotional / considerate / thoughtful
2. prejudice / bias / dearth
3. logical / rational / determined
4. exceptional / aspiring / outstanding
5. potential / criteria / promise
6. foster / realize / fulfil

C Look again at these expressions from the unit. Discuss what they mean with a partner.

1. a level playing field
2. over the hill
3. a square peg in a round hole
4. mixed messages

Errors

A There are errors in all of these sentences. Correct them.

1. The thing what makes me really cross is his attitude.
2. Been given too much work is common.
3. Doctors are expect to work long hours.
4. There should be more emphasis in teamwork.
5. Most people aspire in something better in life.
6. Numbers rose steady last month.

Writing

A Talk in pairs. What are the major causes of heart disease?

B Highlight the option in each statement below that you think is correct. Then compare with other students.

1. In the United States, people are more likely to die of heart disease / cancer.
2. In the United States, more men / women die each year from heart disease.
3. Men / Women are more likely to die after suffering a heart attack.
4. Women are more / less likely than men to have a second heart attack after an initial heart attack.
5. In the United States, men / women are more likely to be treated quickly if they have chest pain.

C Look at the line graph below. What does it show? Does any of the information surprise you?

D Look at the instructions for a typical IELTS Writing task. Choose five or six points that you want to make about the information shown and make notes. Then compare with a partner.

The line graph shows the number of deaths related to heart disease for both men and women in the United States between 1979 and 2008.

Summarize the information by selecting and reporting the main features, and make comparisons where relevant.

Write at least 150 words.

Heart Disease Mortality Trends

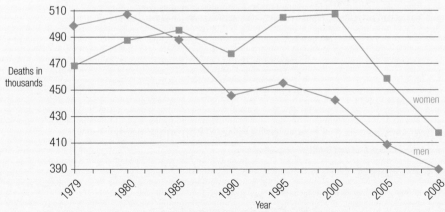

Source: *http://circ.ahajournals.org/content/125/1/e2/F26.expansion.html*

E Check all the Exam tips in the Writing Module again and then write your report. Check the model on page 264.

4 Past and present

'Don't let yesterday use up too much of today.'
Cherokee Indian Proverb

Speaking 1: memories

A In pairs, answer the questions below.

1. What is your earliest memory?
2. Are you sure that you really remember it or have you just heard people talking about it?
3. When you think back to your early childhood, which of the senses is most important – what you saw, what you heard, what you smelt and tasted or what you felt?

B Look at the pictures and follow the steps below.

1. Think about which pictures bring back particular memories.
2. Decide if they bring back good memories or bad memories.
3. Think about what you want to say about any memories the pictures bring back and check any key words you need.
4. Talk about the memories with a partner.

C 🎧 Listen to people talking about the pictures. Match each speaker with a picture. Then listen again and make notes.

Speaker 1 ___   Speaker 2 ___   Speaker 3 ___   Speaker 4 ___

Vocabulary 1: looking back

A Check the highlighted words and phrases in the sentences below. Then mark each sentence (T) true or (F) false. Compare answers with a partner.

1. Forget means the same as not remember. ___
2. Remember and recall always mean the same thing. ___
3. If one thing reminds you of another thing, the two things are very different. ___
4. A recollection is the same as a memory. ___
5. If you reminisce, you think back about unhappy experiences. ___
6. If you regret something or have regrets about something, you wish you hadn't done it. ___
7. If you have fond memories of a period in the past, it is painful to think about it. ___
8. If something makes you feel nostalgic, it makes you think about the past. ___

B Complete the phrasal verbs in these sentences with the correct form of the verbs in the box. Use one of the verbs twice.

go
bring
take
look

1. We had great fun at school. I _____ back to that time with a smile.
2. These photos really _____ me back. I feel quite nostalgic.
3. 'Do you remember Steve Morris?'
   'Goodness, you're _____ back a while now, but yes I do.'
4. I don't like to talk about that period. It _____ back some painful memories.
5. Debbie and I _____ back a long way. We were at primary school together.

C Talk again about some of your earliest memories using the new vocabulary.

Grammar check

Some verbs can be followed by an infinitive or an ~ing verb to mean different things.
I remember playing cowboys and Indians. / Did you remember to lock the door?
(Note that you can *remember to do something* ✓ but NOT *recall to do something* ✗).

I will never forget meeting Jim. / Oh dear, I forgot to phone Claire.
I wish and *if only* can be used to express regrets about the present or the past.
To talk about the present, we use a past verb. *I wish I had more money. / If only I were 20 years younger.*
To talk about the past, we use the past perfect. *I wish I'd taken that job. / If only I hadn't been driving so fast.*

Watch out!
typical errors

I remember to go to school in shorts. ✗
Oh no, I forgot turning off the lights. ✗
If only I didn't lose my passport. ✗

Pronunciation check

🎧 Listen and write the sentences you hear. Underline the syllables that are most heavily stressed.
Example: *I <u>wish</u> I wasn't so <u>bu</u>sy all the time.*
Listen again as you check the tapescript. Practise saying all the sentences with a partner. Then talk about your own life using *I wish* and *If only*.

Vocabulary 2: idioms

A Complete each idiomatic expression with a key word from the box.

milk
clock
kick
regret

1. I can't believe I did that. If only I could turn back the _____.
2. You have to stop worrying. It's no use crying over spilt _____.
3. I wish I'd taken that job now. I could _____ myself.
4. If you leave school now, you'll live to _____ it.

B Talk in pairs. What do the expressions mean? Do you have the same expressions in your language?

Speaking 2: describing memories

A Here are two typical task cards for Part 2 of the Speaking test. Work with a partner – one of you is A, the other is B. Think about the topic for a minute and make notes.

A

Describe an event in your childhood that you remember well.
Say ...
- how old you were.
- where you were.
- what happened.
- how you felt and why you remember it.

B

Talk about a period in the past that brings back fond memories.
Say ...
- how old you were.
- where you were.
- what you especially remember.
- why you were happy.

B Take turns to speak about what's on your card for about two minutes.

4

Listening 1: listening to label pictures and diagrams

A In pairs, answer these questions about the pictures a–h.

1. Do you know what each object is or was called?
2. Do you know what all of the objects are or were for?
3. Do any of the objects bring back memories for you?

B Listen to some people talking about some of the objects. Match each speaker with an object.

Speaker 1 ___   Speaker 2 ___   Speaker 3 ___   Speaker 4 ___   Speaker 5 ___

C Listen to a father talking to his daughter about two more of the objects in the pictures. Match the words 1–6 below with the letters a–f on the diagrams.

1. carriage ___   2. arm ___   3. keytop ___
4. ribbon ___   5. turntable ___   6. stylus ___

1. _____

2. _____

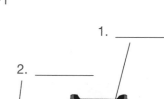

D Now listen to the father and daughter talking about an old telephone. Fill in the missing information on the diagram. Use NO MORE THAN TWO WORDS for each answer.

E In pairs, answer these questions about Exercises C and D.

1. When you listen to label a diagram, what must you do before you listen?
2. What must you then do while you are listening?
3. Do you need to know about the topic or what is shown in a diagram?
4. Did you find Exercise C or Exercise D easier to do? Why?

3. _____

4. _____

 Exam tip: You might need to label a diagram for questions in any part of the Listening test. Section 4 is often an academic lecture given by one speaker, and labelling diagrams is common. If the words that you need to listen for are common words, you might need to write them onto a diagram. If the words are more unusual, perhaps technical, you will probably need to match them with parts of a diagram.

Listening 2: practise listening to label pictures and diagrams

A 🎧 You will hear three parts of a talk about the history of the bicycle. Listen and answer the questions.

For questions 1–3, listen to the introduction and choose three answers from A–F. Which of these does the speaker mention?

> A cars replacing bicycles
> B the importance of bicycles in some parts of the world
> C the adaptation of the basic design to serve various functions
> D significant changes to the basic design
> E improvements made possible by technology
> F the low cost of running a bicycle

1. ___   2. ___   3. ___

For questions 4–8, fill in the missing information on the diagram in Figure 1. Use NO MORE THAN TWO WORDS for each answer.

For questions 9–12, match the words and phrases with the letters a–d on the diagram in Figure 2.

9. cogset ___   10. shock absorber ___
11. spokes ___   12. seat post   ___

Penny-farthing 1880

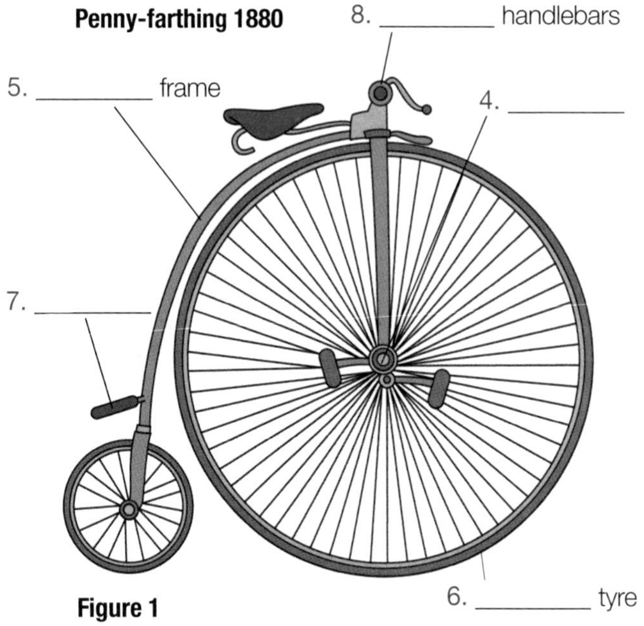

8. _____ handlebars

5. _____ frame

4. _____

7. _____

6. _____ tyre

Figure 1

Modern mountain bike

a

c

d

b

Figure 2

B Check the key on page 264. How many questions did you answer correctly?

C Tick the sentences about the Listening task that are true for you and think about how you can answer more questions correctly next time.

- [ ] 1. Looking at the diagram and reading through the questions helped me to predict content.
- [ ] 2. I didn't need to know about the topic to answer questions correctly.
- [ ] 3. Specialist vocabulary was not a problem and my spelling was correct.

Key vocabulary in context

Look at the tapescript and check how the key words below are used in context. Then discuss the meaning of each with a partner.

> recreation   advent   components   defunct   assembly   adjusted   compresses   tension

WB See *Vocabulary development* on Workbook page 221.

4

Reading 1: making sure that information is given in the text

A In the Speaking and Vocabulary Module of this unit, you learnt the word *nostalgic*. Check it again and answer these questions with a partner.

1. What is *nostalgia*? How is a feeling of nostalgia different from having concrete memories?
2. Can you feel nostalgic about the recent past or only the more distant past?
3. Are feelings of nostalgia always positive? Is it possible to feel nostalgic about a time when you were unhappy?
4. Does nostalgia have a purpose?

B You will read a short extract about nostalgia. Before you read, put the points below into what you think is a logical order.

___ give examples of who might benefit from nostalgia

___ define nostalgia and give some examples of what makes people feel nostalgic

___ explain why feeling nostalgic might be beneficial

C Skim the extract quickly and check your answers in Exercise B.

Sweet Remembrance

A For one person it might be a bite of a dessert that was a common school lunch, for another it might be a few notes of a popular Beatles song. For you it could be the sight of a little boy stacking plastic bricks or playing with a catapult that suddenly takes you back years into the past. In the right environment, the tiniest trigger can bring back a flood of memories, even for the least sentimental of us.

B Such reminiscing might be healthier than you think. Despite the fact that we are frequently told to live for the moment and not to dwell on the past, research suggests that the occasional trip back in time can give your spirits a much needed lift. In fact, just half an hour spent each day contemplating fond memories can make people more cheerful and more contented with their current situation.

C Most people spontaneously reminisce when they feel lonely or miserable. This suggests that we see pleasant memories as an antidote to sadness. A new arrival in a big city will think about friends back home, while a college student struggling with an assignment will bolster his confidence by reliving high school glories. Nostalgia can motivate people and make them feel they are rooted, rather than being blown around by the vagaries of everyday life.

D Read the extract again more carefully and answer the questions. For questions 1–3, choose the correct answer a, b or c according to the text.

1. Memories can come flooding back because of …
   a. something very small.   b. a song.   c. a favourite game.
2. Most people are led to believe that they should think about …
   a. the past.   b. now.   c. the future.
3. A college student struggling with an assignment thinks about …
   a. being happy at high school.   b. how difficult high school was.   c. what he achieved at high school.

For questions 4–8, decide if the information given below agrees with information given in the text. Write (T) true, (F) false or (NG) not given, if there is no information on this.

4. Everybody feels nostalgic when they think about school lunches. ___
5. Only very sensitive and emotional people are affected by nostalgia. ___
6. People can feel better about the life they live now if they sometimes think about the past. ___

7. Thinking about the past can make sadness less painful. ___

8. People who do not think about the past much have little direction in life. ___

E 🎧 Before you check the answers to Exercise D, listen to some students talking about them. Which student gives the correct answer to each question? Write (M) male or (F) female.

1. ___ 2. ___ 3. ___ 4. ___ 5. ___ 6. ___ 7. ___ 8. ___

Exam tip: When tasks in the Reading test are multiple choice or T/F/NG tasks, do not use your own knowledge of the topic or assume that an answer is obvious. You must find the answer in the text. Remember that questions will sometimes include words from the text that make you think an answer is true when it is not.

Reading 2: practise making sure that information is given in the text

A You will read a longer text about nostalgia. Before you read, guess why the words and phrases in the box below are mentioned. Compare ideas with a partner.

> a spell in hospital or prison   a record collection   the Greek language
> a neurological disorder   self-esteem   film sequels   advertising

B Read the text and answer the questions that follow. Check your ideas in Exercise A as you do so.

Looking for the Purpose of Nostalgia

A *Nostalgia* is one of those words which everyone understands and uses quite freely, but which is almost impossible to clearly define. What exactly is nostalgia? There is not yet a great deal of scientific literature on nostalgia, but there are a few fascinating studies that have attempted to identify its essence, and the reasons that we feel that warm glow when reminiscing.

B People appreciate that nostalgia is all about memories and that these recollections are generally of important events, people we care about or who have influenced us, and places in which we have spent time. What perhaps people realize less is that nostalgia is almost always associated with positive emotions, even when the trigger for recalling a particular memory is something negative. Research suggests that a negative memory can evoke feelings of nostalgia as long as the period or situation to which the feeling relates was eventually overcome. Some individuals report feeling nostalgic about generally painful schooldays, a job they loathed or even a spell in hospital or prison.

C Smell and touch are the senses that tend to most readily prompt nostalgia, perhaps due to the processing of these stimuli first passing through the amygdala, the emotional seat of the brain. This may explain why environments like primary school or hospital bring back vague but fond recollections, rather than concrete memories of fear or dislike. Music is also known to be a strong trigger, perhaps explaining why most record collections or MP3s are full of songs from bygone eras listened to more for old times' sake than for their timeless quality.

D So, what is the point of nostalgia? Does nostalgia serve a purpose? The brain is incredibly energy-intensive, on average using more glucose each day than do muscles. It goes without saying that the brain rarely does something without a good reason. It should be noted that the word *nostalgia* is the foundation of two Greek words, *nostos*, meaning 'homecoming', and *algos*, meaning 'pain'. However, the word was first used popularly among 18th-century medics, who were still determined that they would find a nostalgia *bone* or *organ* somewhere in the body. During the American Civil War, soldiers suffering from severe homesickness were temporarily relieved of their posts and treated as though they had a tangible physical condition.

E For much of the 19th century, though no longer considered a neurological disorder, nostalgia continued to be associated with homesickness and depression. It was only when it became clear that people could clearly distinguish between *homesickness*, a negative feeling of loss or yearning, and *nostalgia*, a warm feeling of past comfort, that the more modern usage of the term became widely understood.

F A recent report *Nostalgia: Content, Triggers, Functions* (Wildschut, Sedikides, Arndt & Routledge), suggests that nostalgia does indeed have a purpose and is in fact of great benefit. Remembering past times improves mood, increases self-esteem, strengthens social bonds and gives meaning to life. Clay Routledge explains, 'Most of our days are filled with routine activities with no significance, like travelling to and from work or shopping for groceries. Nostalgia is a way of tapping into meaningful past experiences that confirm that our lives are worthwhile, that we are happy with our relationships and that our existence has a purpose.' It seems that nostalgia may serve as a sort of natural antidepressant, something to motivate us and help us through difficult times. However, as Tim Wildschut points out, 'It is not possible to say whether nostalgia becomes more frequent as people's lives become more challenging. We are talking about a fundamental human emotion, not something that changes overnight.'

G These findings might also explain why we should avoid revisiting or attempting to relive the past. There is nothing quite like the disappointment of meeting an old school friend only to find he or she is nothing like the person you remember. A journey back to a place that has been the source of many wistful memories can be disastrous when it becomes clear that those recollections have always been viewed through rose-coloured spectacles. Film sequels can be equally damaging. A movie remade 20 years after the much-loved original often turns out to be nothing more than an attack on our fondest memories. We can come away from the cinema feeling hurt and insulted.

H Whatever the benefits of nostalgia, it is clear that nobody should use it as an excuse to live in the past. The idea that things were 'better in the good old days' is generally a myth. Because we tend to focus on fond memories, we edit out what we do not want to remember. People who grew up in the 1950s might remember Elvis Presley and drive-in movies, but they have probably forgotten all about sexual and racial inequality. Advertising does not help either. Companies have known for a long time that nostalgia sells and it is far easier to tap into past memories than to create a whole new association with a product. It is not surprising then that so many people feel that their current lives are mundane and unfulfilling compared with how they believe things were once upon a time.

For questions 1–5, identify the paragraph which contains the following information. Write the letter of the paragraph in the space.

1. the belief that nostalgia was an illness   ___
2. the mistaken belief that things used to be better   ___
3. people feeling nostalgic about something that made them unhappy   ___
4. spoiling fond memories by trying to bring them back to life   ___
5. the suggestion that much of our lives is spent doing boring things   ___

For questions 6–9, decide if the information given below agrees with information given in the text. Write (T) true, (F) false or (NG) not given, if there is no information on this.

6. Not many books have been written about nostalgia.   ___
7. People rarely feel nostalgic about what they see and hear.   ___
8. Getting through a difficult time can mean thinking more positively about it later.   ___
9. Most people only listen to music that they think is especially good.   ___

For questions 10–11, choose the correct answer a, b, c or d.

10. According to the text, the brain …
     a. has a number of unnecessary functions.   b. uses a lot of energy.
     c. is like a large muscle.   d. is used mainly to think about the past.

11. In the 18th century, some soldiers were taken off duty …
     a. because they were physically injured.   b. in order to retrain.
     c. because they thought only about going home.   d. to spend time at home.

For questions 12–14, choose three answers from A–F. What does the recent report suggest is the purpose of nostalgia?

A It can make people feel better about themselves.
B It helps people relate better to others.
C It is mainly connected with routine events.
D It helps us understand why we exist.
E It often makes people feel depressed.
F Its nature is constantly changing.

12. ___   13. ___   14. ___

For questions 15–16, choose the correct answer a, b, c or d.

15. Paragraph G suggests that …
     a. it is good to meet up with old school friends.
     b. revisiting a loved place is usually enjoyable.
     c. we often have an unrealistic view of how things used to be.
     d. not many people go to see remakes of old movies.

16. Why do some people choose to live in the past?
     a. They were happier then.
     b. They remember only the good parts.
     c. They see too much advertising.
     d. They have nothing to live for now.

C Check the key on page 264. How many questions did you answer correctly?

D Tick the sentences about the Reading task that are true for you and think about how you can answer more questions correctly next time.

☐ 1. Making some predictions before I read helped me understand the text.
☐ 2. I skimmed the text to get a general idea before I looked at the questions.
☐ 3. I found the information that provided answers and I didn't need to guess.
☐ 4. I am happy with the time it took to answer the questions and how many I answered correctly.

E Talk in small groups about something that makes you feel nostalgic.

Key vocabulary in context

A Look at these sentences and then look again at the key words in the text (the paragraph letter is provided in each case). Choose the correct option.

1. The **essence** (A) of something is *the most important part of it / where it came from*.
2. If something **evokes** (B) an emotion, it *brings the emotion out / represses the emotion*.
3. If you **loathe** (B) something, you *like it very much / hate it*.
4. If we **tap into** (F/H), something, we *pretend it doesn't exist / use and benefit from it*.
5. A **myth** (H) is something people *rightly believe to be untrue / wrongly believe to be true*.

B Cover the text. Complete these phrases with the correct preposition.

1. be associated _____   2. distinguish _____   3. serve _____

WB See *Vocabulary development* on Workbook page 221.

WB For focus on reading skills, go to Workbook page 222.

4

Writing 1: understanding the task

 A Look at the pairs of pictures below and answer these questions with a partner.

1. What do the pictures show about how life has changed in the last 50 years?
2. Do you think the changes have made life better or worse in each case?

Exam tip: Writing Task 2 will often involve comparing a situation in the past with a situation now. You will need to identify advantages and disadvantages of each situation and usually balance your argument.

B Talk in pairs. Think of a typical IELTS Writing task for each pair of pictures.

C Look at the instructions for three typical IELTS Writing tasks. Match them with the pairs of pictures above.

A

Write about the following topic:

For various reasons, many people – children in particular – are eating less healthily than they did 20 or 30 years ago. People consume more pre-cooked food, more frozen food and more fast food than ever before.

How much of a problem do you think this is, what are some of the causes and what can be done to address it?

Give reasons for your answer and include any relevant examples from your own knowledge or experience.

Write at least 250 words.

B

Write about the following topic:

Computers are now used in almost every area of both business and everyday life and society is becoming increasingly dependent on them. Some people say that we rely on computers too much and that they are having a negative effect on the way we live.

What are your views on this issue?

Give reasons for your answer and include any relevant examples from your own knowledge or experience.

Write at least 250 words.

C

Write about the following topic:

Traffic congestion and the pollution it causes, especially in the biggest cities, is one of the biggest problems we face. Governments must act now to reduce the number of motor vehicles and offer alternative transport.

Do you agree there is a problem? What solutions are there?

Give reasons for your answer and include any relevant examples from your own knowledge or experience.

Write at least 250 words.

D Read all the instructions again carefully and answer these questions in small groups.

1. Do you understand all three tasks and know what you have to write about?
2. Which task would you find easiest to answer?
3. Which task would you least like to answer? Why?

Writing 2: deciding what to say

A Choose ONE of the tasks in Writing 1C and make a list of points you want to make. Think in your own language about the issue first if it helps.

B Compare your list of points with other students.

1. Compare your list with a student who chose the same task as you.
2. Compare your notes with students who chose the other two tasks.

C 🎧 Listen to some people talking about the topics in the three tasks. Match each speaker with one of the tasks A, B or C.

1. ___   2. ___   3. ___   4. ___   5. ___   6. ___   7. ___   8. ___   9. ___   10. ___

D Read the tapescript on pages 287 and 288. Do any of the people make the same points that you made or discussed with classmates?

Writing 3: writing a balanced composition

A A student has decided to answer Task B. Look at this page from their notebook and notice how they have organized points to help them plan their composition.

computers at work / school +	computers at work / school −	computers at home +	computers at home −
quicker / save time	people don't talk	Internet / games	families stop talking
learn about the world	sometimes crash	shop / book holidays	Internet safety

B Copy the table in Exercise A into your notebook. Then add points of your own to the correct column.

C Below are the possible stages of the composition. Put them into a logical order. There isn't necessarily one correct order.

___ Describe the benefits of having computers at home.
___ Show that you understand the question and introduce the argument.
___ Describe the disadvantages of using computers at work and at school.
___ Express your own opinion and conclude the argument.
___ Describe the disadvantages of having computers at home.
___ Describe the benefits of using computers at work and at school.

D Read the composition and check the order of the stages above.

Computers are everywhere nowadays. Everyone uses a computer at work and children are using them increasingly at school. Computers are used in shops and hospitals and to drive trains. Most families have a computer at home and perhaps a laptop too. So, do we rely on computers too much and is that having a negative effect on how we live? Many people think the answer is 'yes'.

In the workplace, computers do everything quickly and efficiently. It is difficult to imagine going back to pen and paper. E-mailing is more convenient than making phone calls. In schools, children can learn with interesting interactive programmes about the world and its history. However, all this could mean that people communicate less. In offices, people stare at a screen instead of talking to each other and, at school, children work less in groups to solve problems.

People love having a computer at home. They can find information online immediately and use the Internet to shop and book holidays. Young people enjoy playing computer games and making friends in chat rooms. However, there are disadvantages here too. Families communicate less and perhaps do not go out so often. Some Internet sites are inappropriate for children and parents have to check that they are safe.

Personally, I think the advantages far outweigh the disadvantages. Computers make life more convenient and enjoyable. Information is at our fingertips instead of having to search through books. Of course, people should not sit at a computer all day every day, whether at work, at school or at home, but as long as they are used sensibly, computers should be seen as a great benefit.

E Highlight some aspects of the composition that you like. Compare with a partner.

F Go to Workbook page 224 for the Writing task.

Speaking

A Complete this advice about using vocabulary in the Speaking test. Use ONE WORD in each space.

When you're speaking with the examiner, he or she will listen and make a _____ of the vocabulary you use. However, you shouldn't _____ about this. You can only use words and phrases you know and you shouldn't try to impress the examiner. If you try too hard to use words and phrases that you don't really know, you'll use them incorrectly or inappropriately and you won't sound _____. At the same time, you don't want your language to be too _____. After the interview, you might regret that you didn't use a word or phrase that you know was _____ for the situation. Listen to what the examiner says and _____ for a moment before you speak.

B 🎧 Listen and check your answers.

C Look at the answers that some students give to questions below. Which words and phrases from the unit would be better than the highlighted words and phrases the students use?

1. Examiner: Would you say that you were happy at school?
   Student: Yes, I have some very good … erm … things that I remember of school.
2. Examiner: What was your favourite time of year as a child?
   Student: Winter. When it's winter now I always have strong feelings. I mean, it takes me back to my childhood.
3. Examiner: Is there a danger that people end up living in the past?
   Student: Mm, I don't think so. Everyone likes to sit and … er … you know, think about the past occasionally.
4. Examiner: Do you have regrets about leaving university so early?
   Student: Oh yes. Now I wish I had my degree. If only I could go back in the past.

D 🎧 Listen to the same students using the more appropriate words and phrases. Check your ideas.

E In pairs, ask and answer the questions about past events that your teacher will give you. Think about what you want to say and the vocabulary you want to use before you speak.

Vocabulary

A Fill each gap with a root word made from one of the words in the box.

1. Racial and sexual _____ is still an issue in some workplaces.
2. My first day at school is one of my earliest _____.
3. A tablet computer is simply an _____ of a laptop.
4. People tend to live in the past if their lives are _____.
5. Research shows that nostalgia can _____ social bonds.

equal
fulfil
adapt
collect
strong

B 🎧 Mark the main stress on these words. Then listen and check. Practise saying the words.

recollection   reminisce   associate (v)   association   fundamental   spontaneously

Errors

A There are errors in all of these sentences. Correct them.

1. I'll never forget to drive a car for the first time.
2. I hope you remembered phoning your mum.
3. I wish I would have more money.
4. If only I didn't listen to what they said.
5. I regret to take the job now.
6. It's no use to worry about the past.

4

Listening

A Look at the pictures below and answer these questions with a partner.

1. What do the two houses have in common?
2. What are the biggest differences between the two houses?

B 🎧 You will hear two parts of a lecture about houses. Listen and answer the questions.

For questions 1–3, listen and choose the correct answer a, b, or c.

1. People started to build houses …
   a. during the Stone Age.
   b. during the Iron Age.
   c. at various times.

2. During the Palaeolithic era, people …
   a. did not have a permanent base.
   b. lived in caves.
   c. built strong houses.

3. During the Neolithic era, people started to settle due to …
   a. building materials.
   b. farming.
   c. hunting.

For questions 4–8, listen and match the words with the letters a–e on the diagram.

4. flint ___   5. plaster ___   6. doorway ___   7. beams ___   8. hearth ___

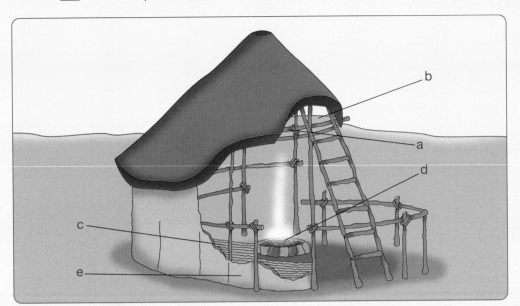

For questions 9–11, listen and complete the notes. Use NO MORE THAN TWO WORDS for each answer.

Smart houses – called 'smart' because intelligent

Advanced systems inside house

can share (9) _____

Systems operated from outside house

turn on and off lights / contact you (tell you (10) _____ have

called and let them in)

(11) _____ (police station / supermarket) connected

For questions 12–16, fill in the missing information on the diagram. Use NO MORE THAN TWO WORDS for each answer.

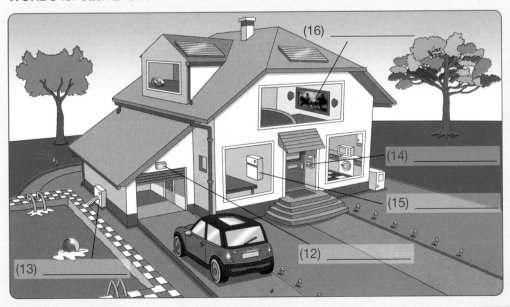

Review 1

Speaking and Vocabulary

A In pairs, answer these questions about the IELTS Speaking test.

1. How many parts are there to the Speaking test, and how long does each last?
2. What happens in each part of the Speaking test? What sort of questions will you answer?
3. Do you feel confident about the Speaking test? Is there a part you prefer or a part you have concerns about?

B Look at some comments made by students studying for the IELTS exam. Tick three that you most agree with.

☐ 'I prefer the first part, when the examiner asks about my life and what I'm interested in. It's more difficult to talk about a topic on a card or answer questions about an issue that you don't know much about.'

☐ 'I prefer the second part because reading the card gives you ideas and you can plan what to say and how to say it.'

☐ 'The third part of the Speaking test is the part I worry about. You don't know what the examiner will ask and questions might be about quite a serious topic.'

☐ 'I find the third part of the Speaking test inspires me. It's the most challenging part, but I prefer to express opinions rather than just tell somebody about me and my hobbies.'

☐ 'I guess accuracy is important, but I think talking fluently and using the right vocabulary will impress the examiner more. I learn vocabulary that will help me talk about typical IELTS topics.'

☐ 'To tell the truth, I worry more about my pronunciation than about my grammar or vocabulary. If the examiner can't understand me, the other aspects don't matter.'

C Write two more comments of your own. Then compare with other students in your class.

D Write important words and phrases that you have learnt so far under each heading.

life – stages and events
_____
_____
_____

families and upbringing
_____
_____
_____

nature and nurture
_____
_____
_____

characteristics
_____
_____
_____

(**my words and phrases**)

men and women
_____
_____
_____

memories
_____
_____

past and present
_____
_____

Listening

A Complete these sentences about the IELTS Listening test. Use one or two words or a number in each space.

1. There are _____ sections to the Listening test.
2. In total there are _____ questions to answer.
3. In the first section, _____ people speak in a _____ situation.
4. In the second section, _____ speaks about a non-academic topic.
5. In the third section, two, three or four people have a discussion related to _____.
6. In the final section, one person gives a talk or lecture of an _____ nature.
7. The Listening test gradually becomes more _____. The _____ section is the longest section.

B What different listening tasks have you practised so far?

C In pairs, answer these questions about the Listening test.

1. Which of the following comments is truer for you?
   a. 'I understand the gist of a talk or conversation, but don't always catch important points or details.'
   b. 'I often hear specific points and details, but don't understand what the people are talking about.'
2. Do you find it easier to listen to one person giving a talk or two or more people exchanging information or opinions?
3. Do you ever find it difficult to read options when you're trying to listen at the same time?
4. Do you ever find it difficult to write answers at the same time that you're trying to listen?
5. Do you find it difficult to complete notes and spell words correctly while you're listening?
6. Do you find diagrams, maps or tables helpful or do they complicate things?

Reading

A Correct six words in this information about the IELTS Reading test.

In the IELTS Academic Reading test, there are four texts that gradually become less challenging in terms of content and density of language. In total, there are 30 questions to answer in an hour and a half. The texts come from books and articles in newspapers, magazines and journals, and are light-hearted in nature. The language used in the texts is generally fairly informal.

B What different reading tasks have you practised so far?

C Talk in pairs. Explain the meaning of each word below as it relates to reading skills.

> skim gist prediction paraphrasing
> scan vocabulary in context

D Give yourself a score out of 5 for the progress you are making with each of these reading skills.

skimming / reading for gist	___
scanning / reading for specific information	___
general reading speed	___
understanding new words and phrases in context	___
recognizing paraphrased language	___

Remember! There are some listening and reading tasks that you haven't practised yet.

Writing

A In pairs, answer these questions about the IELTS Writing test.

1. What are some of the figures you might describe for the Writing Task 1?
2. What sort of composition do you have to write for the Writing Task 2?
3. How many words do you have to write for Writing Task 1?
4. How many words do you have to write for Writing Task 2?
5. How long do you have to write the two tasks?
6. Do you think you should split your time equally between the two compositions?
7. Which aspects of Writing Task 1 do you find challenging?
8. Which aspects of Writing Task 2 do you find challenging?

B When you write, you must consider all of the points below. However, there are two points that are absolutely essential if your compositions are to achieve a reasonable score. Tick them.

☐ 1. You must answer the question and make points that are relevant.
☐ 2. You must make sure that what you write is grammatically correct.
☐ 3. You must use a range of vocabulary and choose the right words and phrases.
☐ 4. You must organize your composition so that the examiner can read it easily and understand what you want to say.
☐ 5. You must use appropriate linking words and phrases.
☐ 6. You must use an appropriate style for the composition you are writing.
☐ 7. You must make sure that all your spelling is correct.
☐ 8. You must make sure that all your punctuation is correct.

C Is your writing improving? Tick the aspects of your writing that you feel have improved recently.

☐ understanding the question and knowing what is required
☐ having something relevant to say
☐ organizing ideas
☐ using paragraphs
☐ linking ideas together
☐ using the right register
☐ using a wider range of vocabulary
☐ spelling
☐ punctuation

What next?

You've only completed a third of the course, so don't worry if you haven't improved all aspects of your English. There is plenty of time to learn more and practise the skills and tasks that you find difficult. Here are some things that you should do now. Decide which you'd like to do first. Number them.

☐ Find as many opportunities to speak English as possible. If you have friends or relatives who speak good English, practise with them. Practise with other students in your class when you have a break or after the lesson. Practise talking about typical IELTS exam topics. If you know anyone who has taken the IELTS exam, ask them what the examiner talked about and what questions he or she had to answer.

☐ If you find the Listening test difficult, ask to borrow CDs and listen outside school. Listen to English that is at your level to give you confidence, but also listen to English that is more challenging so that your ability develops. Listen to extracts which have a tapescript, so that after you listen, you can read and check what you didn't understand and why you didn't understand it. When you listen, try to identify key words and phrases that you don't know. Then check them in a dictionary or in the tapescript.

☐ Read as much as you can. Borrow books and read articles in magazines and newspapers. Read any information related to your studies or your job that you're sent or that you find in documents. Read texts that challenge you, but not texts that are so difficult that you don't enjoy them. When you read, notice how the text is organized. Look at how the paragraphs facilitate the reading process and how words and phrases are used to introduce and summarize ideas. Get used to reading without a dictionary so that you can guess the meaning of new words and phrases in context.

☐ You should learn vocabulary that is important to you so that you can talk about yourself and your interests, but also the typical vocabulary that you know occurs frequently in the IELTS Academic exam. Note down new vocabulary and make sure you revise it. Make sure that you learn phrases, fixed expressions and idioms as well as single words, and focus on words you know used in new ways as well as words that are completely new to you.

☐ Think about which aspects of your writing you most need to improve and concentrate on those. You will probably not have time to keep writing whole reports and compositions, so practise writing short extracts that focus on specific elements of written language. Practise introducing the theme of a report or introducing and concluding an argument. Practise organizing and linking ideas within an extract or whole composition. Practise writing more complex sentences that will improve your grammatical accuracy, spelling and punctuation. Do the tasks in the Course Book and Workbook and ask your teacher to give you more writing tasks if you need more practice. Make a list of typical topics for Writing Task 2 and start thinking about what you would say about them.

Go on to the next section of the Course Book. Make sure you practise all aspects of your English, but focus on what you are having problems with. Don't worry if you don't make progress in all areas at the same time. Remember, it is much easier to learn English if you enjoy it!

5 Work and play

'All work and no play makes Jack a dull boy.'
English proverb

Vocabulary 1: busy or free

A Mark each of the words and phrases below (B) if they relate to being busy or (F) if they relate to having free time and relaxing.

1. It's always hectic. ___
2. I need to just chill out sometimes. ___
3. I'm on the go all day. ___
4. I'm usually rushed off my feet. ___
5. I need to let my hair down. ___
6. It's great to let off steam. ___
7. It's pretty much non-stop. ___
8. It's great to recharge the batteries. ___

B Work in pairs. Discuss what each expression in Exercise A means and say if you have a similar expression in your own language.

Speaking 1: work hard and play hard

A Look at the pictures and talk to a partner. What do the pictures show about work time and leisure time? Use the words and phrases from Vocabulary A when appropriate.

B In pairs, answer the questions below.

1. How much time each week do you spend studying or working?
2. How much leisure time do you have?
3. Do you spend time thinking about your social life when you're studying or at work?
4. Do you spend time worrying about studies or work during your free time?
5. If you had more free time, how would you spend it?

Vocabulary 2: prefixes

A Talk in pairs. How do the highlighted prefixes below affect the meaning of each root word?

1. It's pretty much non-stop.
2. It's great to recharge the batteries.
3. Too many people feel that they're overworked and underpaid.
4. Too many people working too many hours is antisocial.
5. Staff working too many hours can be counterproductive.
6. Working too hard can demotivate people.

B Use the prefixes from Exercise A to complete these phrases.

1. ____ stabilize the economy
2. ____ loaded with work
3. a ____-smoker
4. ____ live the past
5. ____ act negative effects
6. take ____biotics

Vocabulary 3: free time

A Work in pairs. Copy the table and add some more examples to the columns below.

outdoor pursuits	sports	extreme sports	hobbies & pastimes	social activities	games & puzzles
hiking	football	paragliding	photography	singing in a choir	chess

B Complete the highlighted phrases in these sentences with the correct preposition.

1. I'm very interested _____ literature. I read all the time.
2. I'm keen _____ most ball sports, but I especially like tennis.
3. I'm absolutely mad / crazy _____ horses. I go riding twice a week.
4. I get a lot of pleasure / enjoyment _____ running. It helps me think.
5. I really look forward _____ swimming after school on Tuesdays.

Speaking 2: talking about your free time

A 🎧 Guess the missing word in each of these examiners' questions. Then listen and check.

1. So, how do you _____ your free time?   2. Tell me about the free-time _____ you enjoy.
3. Have you _____ up any hobbies in the last few years?   4. Do you have a very active _____ life?

B 🎧 Listen to some students answering the questions. Complete the sentences below with ONE word in each space.

1. I'm really _____ painting.   2. I guess my _____ is martial arts.
3. I'm a bit of a health _____.   4. I never was a _____ _____.

C In pairs, ask and answer the questions in Exercise A.

Exam tip: In the Speaking test, Part 1, it is likely that the examiner will ask about studies, work or what you do in your free time. Make sure you can talk about these areas of your life confidently using a range of vocabulary.

Grammar check

When verbs follow prepositions, they are ~ing forms.
I look forward to playing golf.
When *like* means *enjoy*, it is followed by verb + ~ing.
I like dancing.
Sometimes *like* is followed by an infinitive.
I like to keep fit.
Here *like* doesn't mean *enjoy*. It means *This is my routine. / I think this is a good thing to do.*
The expression *spend time* is followed by verb + ~ing.
I spend a lot of time painting.

Watch out!
typical errors

I'm interested in visit new places. ✗
I spend my time to read. ✗

5

Listening 1: listening to complete a summary

A Talk in pairs. What do the pictures show about various aspects of student life?

B 🎧 Listen to some students talking and tick each picture as you hear it mentioned.

C Tick the statement below that best summarizes the conversation.

- [ ] 1. Some students are discussing how well their parents did at university.
- [ ] 2. Some students are arguing about how much money the government should give them to live on.
- [ ] 3. Some students are discussing how hard they work and whether or not it is appreciated by others.

Exam tip: In Section 3 of the Listening test, there is a conversation between at least two, and up to four speakers. The conversation is always related in some way to education or training.

D 🎧 Listen to the first part of the conversation again and complete the summary. Use NO MORE THAN TWO WORDS in each space. Do not check the answers yet.

Some students are cross because some newspaper (1) _____ claim that they do not work hard. The reporters claim that students attend very few (2) _____ and prefer (3) _____ doing very little. The students think that the real aim is (4) _____ copies of newspapers and not to report what is (5) _____ to their community.

Question-type tip: You've practised completing sentences or notes. Sometimes you have to complete a short summary of a recording or part of a recording. The words you write as answers will always be words you hear, but the words around those words won't be exactly as they are on the recording. You need to look at the words before and after the space to make sure that your answers fit logically and grammatically.

E Look at a student's attempt to complete the summary below. All of her answers are wrong. In pairs, discuss why each answer is wrong.

> Some students are cross because some newspaper (1) _storys_ claim that they do not work hard. The reporters claim that students attend very few (2) _lectures a week_ and prefer (3) _to sit around_ doing very little. The students think that the real aim is (4) _for selling_ copies of newspapers and not to report what is (5) _the truth_ to their community.

F Check the correct answers on page 265. Did you make any similar mistakes?

Listening 2: practise completing a summary

A Read the summary below. Think about the type of word or phrase that goes into each space.

B 🎧 Listen to the complete conversation again and complete the summary.

> The students believe that, in the past, (1) _____ were more generous and students then did not have to worry about being (2) _____ when they finished studying. They complain that the (3) _____ does not appreciate how hard they work. The students think that when their parents were students, a lot of time was spent going to (4) _____ and watching (5) _____ play. They suggest that their parents were more interested in (6) _____ than in studying. The students feel that it is unfair that they will be (7) _____ what they owe for the first few years that they work and do not understand why the financial help they get has been (8) _____.

C Check the key on page 265. How many questions did you answer correctly?

D Tick the sentences about the Listening task that are true for you and think about how you can answer more questions correctly next time.

- ☐ 1. I read through the summary carefully before I listened.
- ☐ 2. I could predict the type of word or phrase that I needed for most spaces.
- ☐ 3. I understood the speaker and knew which words to write in the spaces.
- ☐ 4. I spelt my answers correctly and made sure they fitted grammatically.
- ☐ 5. I am happy with how many questions I answered correctly.

Key vocabulary in context

Complete each of the phrases from the conversation with the correct verb.

1. _____ attention
2. _____ the impression that
3. _____ research
4. _____ something seriously

WB ▶ See *Vocabulary development* on Workbook page 225.

5

Reading 1: paragraphs and topic sentences

A Answer the questions below in groups of three.

1. Do you think people work too hard these days?
2. Do you think most people find a balance between work or study and leisure time?
3. Do you think there should be a reduction in the typical working week?
4. What is the best way of relaxing and relieving stress if you are feeling overworked?

B You will read an article about working too hard. Sentences a–e below are the first lines from each of the five paragraphs in the article. Read the sentences and then, in pairs, follow the steps below.

1. Discuss how reading the sentences helps you understand how the article will be organized.
2. Make predictions about what else the article will say.
3. Make predictions about the content of each paragraph.

a. People often become tired with work and daily domestic duty because of the pressure they feel they are under from society.
b. Jobs with excessive workloads or high levels of responsibility can lead to stress and anxiety.
c. For many, an annual salary is the standard way to measure success.
d. Parents can feel especially pressured …
e. Taking a holiday, ideally far away from any temptation to work, is the best way of relieving stress and anxiety.

C Read the article and check your ideas.

The Need for Balance

People often become tired with work and daily domestic duty because of the pressure they feel they are under from society. They find themselves constantly worrying about their job and other aspects of their daily routine. It is essential that everyone recognizes their limitations and understands that relentlessly trying to achieve more than is possible is potentially dangerous to both mind and body.

Jobs with excessive workloads or high levels of responsibility can lead to stress and anxiety. People must remember that they ultimately work for one of two reasons, either to utilize knowledge and skill acquired during education and training, or to earn enough money on which to live. Many individuals lose sight of the reason they work and feel that they are never achieving quite enough.

For many, an annual salary is the standard way to measure success. People feel pressured not just because of the work they do, but because they feel that they are not earning what they should be or advancing to a position where they will. They become more concerned with society's opinion of them than with what makes them happy.

Parents can feel especially pressured because they have to balance earning enough to look after their family with performing all the other duties that being a mother or father brings. Faced with a seemingly endless demand on their time and energy, some actually work even harder and risk becoming workaholics, unable to ever switch off from the need to produce and achieve.

Taking a holiday, ideally far away from any temptation to work, is the best way of relieving stress and anxiety. Research shows that a period of at least two weeks away from daily responsibility, both job-related and domestic, re-energizes and rebuilds a sense of perspective in terms of the real meaning and purpose of duty.

D Cover the text and look at the sentences a–e in Exercise B again. In pairs, use the sentences to discuss the main idea of each paragraph in your own words.

Exam tip: The first sentence of a paragraph is referred to as the *topic sentence*. This means that it tells the reader what the rest of the paragraph will be about. Sentences in the rest of the paragraph usually support the topic sentence. If a sentence is not related to the topic sentence, the writer should start a new paragraph.

Reading 2: practice with paragraphs and topic sentences

A Read the text below about overwork. Put the topic sentences 1–7 into the correct place at the start of each paragraph.

1. Labour economists may be celebrating an increase in productivity, but employees are suffering.
2. Statistics aside, many workers would agree that they work hard, but that there is little reward for their labour.
3. So what should companies do?
4. When was the last time you arrived home full of energy with a sense of accomplishment that you had fully completed your work for the day?
5. And what should employees do?
6. Over the past 25 years, jobs have become more demanding of workers' time.
7. Overwork is defined as negative outcomes that occur when individuals are required to work more hours than they want to work.

Overwork
Higher Production but at What Cost?

A ___ When did you last return from a holiday and not have to work extra hours dealing with a vast backlog of e-mails? If you have a job that means being on call, when did you last turn off that excruciating hand-held beeper?

B ___ The average dual-earner couple works a combined 82 hours per week today, compared to 70 hours 25 years ago. Technology adds to the blurring of any division between work and non-work time, and employees complain of interruptions that prevent them from focusing properly on their work. People are mired in a culture of instant responses, where contacts expect an immediate reply to an e-mail, a text message or a voicemail.

C ___ Research conducted by the Economic Policy Institute in the United States illustrates that despite workers' increased efforts, salaries are declining. Productivity has increased by 16.6% over the last five years, but income has fallen by 2.7%. To put it simply, we are producing more but earning less. One in three employees is chronically overworked, according to a study conducted by the Families and Work Institute in New York.

D ___ It has become a trend, in part, as a consequence of cutbacks and lay-offs and it has a huge impact on the well-being of employees' and their families. Not surprisingly, heavy workloads and long working hours increase employee stress levels, burnout and health care costs. This in turn results in lower employee productivity, reduces aspirations and leaves less time to spend with family and friends and to engage in leisure pursuits and exercise. Ironically, what is lost is exactly what replenishes energy and reduces symptoms associated with stress.

E ___ This begs the question, what impact do these trends have on employers? The American Institute of Stress estimates that U.S. companies lose an estimated $300 billion annually from costs associated with absenteeism, high staff turnover, poor morale and insurance fees related to stress. When employees are exhausted, there is also a greater likelihood of mistakes and generally poor work.

F ___ The causes of chronic overwork are complex and vary across organizations. There is no one solution that will reduce overwork and its ill effects. Nonetheless, the first step to reducing workloads is to understand what factors are causing employees to overwork. Once causes are identified, organizations can develop solutions that benefit everyone. The most frequently stated practices that create overwork include: conflicting demands from different managers, a lack of guidance and support, unnecessary additional responsibilities, staff cutbacks and insufficient sickness and holiday cover.

G ___ As a short-term solution, stress management techniques are critical. Rest, exercise and meditation are proven ways of reducing stress and workers must find time to take a proper lunch break away from their desk. People should assess their situation and ask themselves if their job really requires them to work such long hours or if it is partly their choice. If indeed overwork is a condition of the job, employees must demand that their employer engages in discussion and looks for a solution. To some degree, it is the employee's responsibility to persuade the employer that overwork benefits nobody.

Exam tip: Reading and understanding the topic sentence will help you to read more quickly. When you read for gist, you can sometimes skip the rest of the paragraph if the topic sentence is clear. When you are doing the Reading test, understanding the topic sentence will help you to know where to look back to find answers.

B Read the text again and answer the questions.

The passage has seven paragraphs labelled A–G. For questions 1–6, choose the correct heading for paragraphs B–G from the list of headings in the box. You do not need to use all the headings.

i. A damaging cycle
ii. Less clear distinction
iii. An attack on basic rights
iv. Employees protecting themselves
v. Improvements being made
vi. Financial implications
vii. More output – lower pay
viii. A shorter working week
ix. Solutions from the top

1. Paragraph B ___   2. Paragraph C ___   3. Paragraph D ___
4. Paragraph E ___   5. Paragraph F ___   6. Paragraph G ___

Question-type tip: A common task is matching headings with paragraphs or sections of the text. This requires both skimming and scanning skills. Sometimes a heading will relate to the overall message expressed by the whole paragraph, and sometimes a heading will relate to one key sentence within a paragraph. Headings are often short and concise and you have to look for words, phrases and whole sentences that paraphrase the idea expressed in them. Instructions can be quite complicated – you may have letters, numbers and Roman numerals to look at.

For questions 7–10, choose FOUR letters A–G. Which of the following are mentioned as effects of overwork?

> A people becoming unwell
> B employees feeling less positive about the future
> C the break-up of families
> D higher energy levels
> E employees taking time off work
> F people frequently changing jobs
> G a better quality of work produced

7. ___   8. ___   9. ___   10. ___

For questions 11–14, decide if the information given below agrees with the information given in the text. Write (T) true, (F) false or (NG) if there is no information on this.

11. Knowing why people overwork is the start of solving the problem.   ___
12. Managers giving unclear instructions is a cause of stress.   ___
13. Not having sufficient staff numbers is often a reason for overwork.   ___
14. Overwork is always down to the excessive demands of an employer. ___

C Check the key on page 265. How many questions did you answer correctly?

D Tick the sentences about the Reading task that are true for you and think about how you can answer more questions correctly next time.

- [ ] 1. Reading the topic sentence at the start of each paragraph helped to me read more quickly.
- [ ] 2. Reading the topic sentence helped me understand the purpose and content of each paragraph.
- [ ] 3. Reading the topic sentences helped me to look back and match the headings with the paragraphs.
- [ ] 4. Reading the topic sentences meant I knew which paragraphs to look back to answer questions 7–14.
- [ ] 5. I am happy with how many I answered correctly.

Key vocabulary in context

It's often difficult to know whether compound nouns are written as one complete word, a hyphenated word or as two separate words. Native speakers are often unsure and even dictionaries occasionally disagree.

A Match the word parts in Box A with the word parts in Box B to make compounds from the passage. Write the words as compounds, checking the passage to see how they should be written.

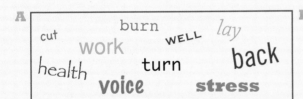

B In pairs, discuss what each compound means from the context in which it is used in the passage. Use a dictionary to check if the context is not clear.

C In pairs, discuss what the phrases with compounds from the passage mean.

a **hand-held** bleeper   a **short-term** solution   reduce its **ill effects**

WB See *Vocabulary development* on Workbook page 225.

WB For focus on reading skills, go to Workbook page 226.

Writing 1: interpreting a simple bar chart

A In pairs, answer the questions below.

1. Do you think that people in different countries work more or less the same number of hours or are there differences between countries?
2. Have you heard that people in some countries tend to work long hours? Which countries are they?
3. Do you think people in your country work long hours?

B The simple bar chart opposite shows how many hours annually the average worker works in a number of selected countries. In pairs:

1. discuss exactly what the horizontal axis shows.
2. try to guess the missing countries.

C Talk in pairs. Does any of the information surprise you?

D Complete these sentences about the information in the bar chart with the words and phrases below.

| fewer   far more   the fewest   nearly as |
| the highest   less   as many   the lowest |

1. People in Mexico work _____ hours annually than people in Germany do.
2. People in the Netherlands work _____ hours annually than people in the United States do.
3. People spend _____ time working in Germany than anywhere else.
4. People in Germany work _____ hours annually.
5. _____ number of hours worked annually is in Mexico.
6. _____ number of hours worked annually is in Germany.
7. People in Spain do not work _____ hours annually as people in Mexico do.
8. In Germany, people do not work _____ many hours annually as people in South Korea.

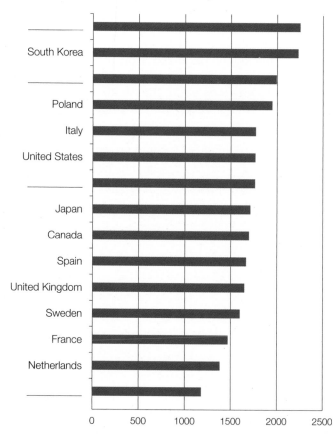

Annual work hours per worker

South Korea
Poland
Italy
United States
Japan
Canada
Spain
United Kingdom
Sweden
France
Netherlands

0   500   1000   1500   2000   2500

Source: *OECD. (2009) Average annual hours actually worked per worker [Data set]. Retrieved from* http://www.oecd-ilibrary.org/ http://www.oecd-ilibrary.org/employment/average-annual-working-time_20752342-table8

Grammar check

We use *more* with both countable and uncountable nouns.
more hours / less time
We use *fewer* with countable nouns and *less* with uncountable nouns.
fewer hours / less time

We use *not as many (as)* with countable nouns.
not as many hours
We use *not as much (as)* with uncountable nouns.
not as much time

When there is a big difference:
We can use *much more* or *far more* and *much less* or *far less* with uncountable nouns.
much more time / far less work
We can use *far more* and *far fewer* with countable nouns.
far more hours / far fewer people
We can use *not nearly as* with both *much* and *many*.
not nearly as much time / not nearly as many hours

We use *the number of* with countable nouns and *the amount of* with uncountable nouns.
the number of hours / the amount of time

E Write some more sentences comparing the countries in the bar chart.

Writing 2: interpreting a simple pie chart

A In pairs, make a list of reasons why people take time off work.

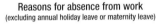

Reasons for absence from work
(excluding annual holiday leave or maternity leave)

B Look at the pie chart. Check any words and phrases in a dictionary if necessary. Does the information shown reflect your ideas in Exercise A?

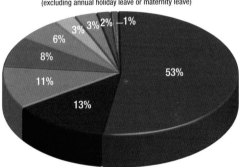

■ sickness (less than three days – no doctor's certificate)
■ sickness (over three days – doctor's certificate)
□ caring for sick child / older relative
■ visit to doctor / dentist
□ long-term disability

□ stress / exhaustion
■ accidental injury
■ other emergencies / urgent event (e.g., funeral)
■ jury service

C Match the two halves of the sentences about the pie chart above. Check that you understand the highlighted phrases first. One ending goes with two beginnings.

1. **The majority of** time taken off work is
2. **A small minority of** time taken off work is
3. **Just over half of** all time taken off is
4. **Around a tenth of** all time taken off is
5. **Around one in seven** days are taken off

a. to do jury service.
b. due to illness that needs a doctor's certificate.
c. due to sickness for less than three days.
d. to care for a sick child.

Grammar check
We generally use *the* with *majority* and *a* with *minority*.
the majority of the time / a (small) minority of people

D Write these fractions or percentages as phrases.

1. a third   <u>around one in three</u>
3. three quarters   _____

2. 25%   _____
4. 90%   _____

Writing 3: comparing and contrasting information

 Exam tip: Remember that in the IELTS test, you will have to compare at least two sources of information.

A In pairs, look at the bar chart and discuss what it shows.

Sickness absence rates in the United Kingdom, 2008

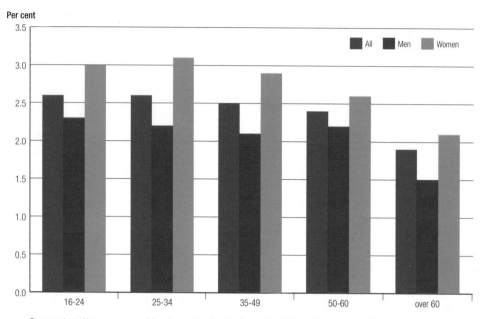

Source: *http://www.ons.gov.uk/ons/search/index.html?pageSize=50&sortBy=none&sortDirection=none&newquery=Sickness+absence+rates+in+the+United+Kingdom*

B Look at the instructions for a typical IELTS Writing task below. Then follow the steps 1–4 in pairs.

1. Decide what information is relevant – what stands out.
2. Decide what comparisons you could make.
3. Write an introductory sentence that paraphrases the first line of the instructions and shows that you understand the information shown.
4. Write three sentences that you would include in a report.

> *The bar chart shows the percentage of time taken off work annually due to sickness by male and female employees in various age groups in the United Kingdom.*
>
> *Summarize the information by selecting and reporting the main features, and make comparisons where relevant.*
>
> Write at least 150 words.

C Read a student's report below. In pairs, discuss how the report could be improved.

> The bar chart shows the percentage of time taken off work each year due to sickness by male and female employees in various age groups in the United Kingdom. The first thing to say is that women take more time off work than men. I think this may be because they must look after sick children sometimes. Also younger employees take off more time from work than older ones and I am surprised. In fact, workers over 60 take less time off than any other age. Women between 25 and 34 are most likely to have time off work because they are sick.

D Read the model report on page 265 and check your ideas in Exercise C.

E In pairs, look at the pie charts below and discuss what they show.

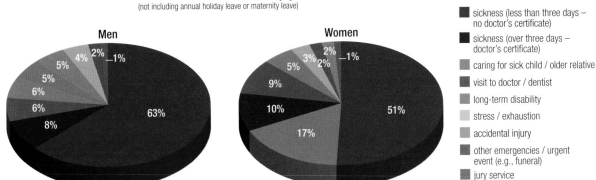

Reasons for absence from work by gender
(not including annual holiday leave or maternity leave)

Men
2% 4% 1%
5%
5%
6%
6%
8%
63%

Women
2% 3% 2% 1%
5%
9%
10%
17%
51%

- ■ sickness (less than three days – no doctor's certificate)
- ■ sickness (over three days – doctor's certificate)
- caring for sick child / older relative
- visit to doctor / dentist
- long-term disability
- stress / exhaustion
- accidental injury
- other emergencies / urgent event (e.g., funeral)
- jury service

F Look at the instructions for a typical IELTS Writing task below and, in pairs, follow steps 1–4 in Exercise B.

The pie charts show the reasons why male and female employees are absent from work.

Summarize the information by selecting and reporting the main features, and make comparisons where relevant.

Write at least 150 words.

G Complete the report below with your own ideas. Use one or two words in each space. Then check the model on page 265.

The pie charts show the various reasons why men and women take time off work as percentages. Although there _____, there are some noticeable differences too.

The most common reason for absence for both men and women is a short period of sickness. Nearly _____ of time taken off by men is due to this, _____ for women it is just over half. Time taken off for more serious illness is about _____ for men and women.

Women are _____ to take time off to care for a child or older relative. At 17%, this is _____ most common reason for women to be absent. Caring for another person accounts for only 5% of time taken off by men.

Absence due to long-term disability or stress is similarly likely for both men and women _____ is a visit to the doctor or dentist. Men, however, are more than _____ as likely to take time off due to accidental injury.

H In pairs, answer the questions below about how information can best be shown.

1. Is it always possible to show the information from a pie chart on a bar graph? Why / why not?
2. Is it always possible to show the information from a bar graph on a pie chart? Why / why not?

I In pairs, design a bar chart that shows the information from the two pie charts.

WB Go to Workbook page 228 for the Writing task.

Speaking

 Exam tip: In the Speaking test, you want to sound as natural as possible. Native speakers frequently use follow-up comments to clarify or emphasize something they have said.

A Match each statement 1–5 with a follow-up comment a–e.

1. I get a lot of pleasure from cycling.
2. I probably work harder than I should.
3. I usually go dancing somewhere at the weekend.
4. To tell you the truth, I like staying in more than going out these days.
5. Frankly, I'm thinking about looking for a new job.

a. I really need to let my hair down.
b. I've never really been a party animal.
c. It helps me think.
d. I'm overworked and underpaid where I am.
e. I'm on the go all day.

B 🎧 Listen and check your answers.

C Practise saying the complete sentences as you heard them on the recording.

Vocabulary

A In each line below, two words have a very similar meaning and one word is different. Delete the word that is different.

1. stress / anxiety / enthusiasm
2. underpaid / hectic / non-stop
3. duty / guidance / responsibility
4. pleasure / temptation / enjoyment
5. recognize / appreciate / replenish
6. lay-offs / reductions / cutbacks

B Complete each phrase below with the correct dependent preposition.

1. be keen _____ something
2. be crazy _____ something
3. look forward _____ something
4. get _____ debt
5. feel _____ pressure
6. lose sight _____ something
7. a lack _____ support
8. engage _____ an activity

C Look again at these expressions from the unit. Discuss what they mean with a partner.

1. rushed off my feet
2. let off steam
3. a health fanatic
4. Joe Public

Errors

A There are grammatical errors in all of these sentences. Correct them.

1. I look forward to swim after work.
2. Do you spend much time to listen to music?
3. Now I work, I've got less friends.
4. I can't believe the amount of people who overwork.
5. Much fewer men take time off work.
6. I try not to take it too serious.

Reading

A Read only the title of the article below. Tick what you think is the correct summary of the article below.

☐ 1. Small children do not benefit from trying to learn too much too soon.
☐ 2. It is important that children learn to read and write as early as possible.
☐ 3. People who do not work hard as children suffer later in life.

B Answer the questions below in groups of three.

1. Did you go to nursery school, a pre-school or kindergarten before you started at primary school?
2. Do you know if you spent your time playing or if you started learning to read, write or add numbers?
3. Do you think very small children benefit from directed learning?

C Read the topic sentences from four of the seven paragraphs in the passage. In pairs, make predictions about what the rest of each paragraph will tell you.

Paragraph B: Dyson feels that the very young are not encouraged to use their imagination enough.
Paragraph C: While Dyson does see some value in teaching the ABC to pre-school children, she thinks that trying to accelerate learning actually works against a child's development.
Paragraph E: So what can caring mothers and fathers do to stimulate their children?
Paragraph F: Dyson also feels that parents worry too much about what television or online shows their children watch.

D The text includes the word *edutainment*, which is a new word made from two existing words. In pairs, answer the questions below about the word.

1. Which two words do you think *edutainment* is made from?
2. What do you think it means?
3. Why is it used in the article?

E Before you read the passage, spend some time looking at the questions. In pairs, discuss what more you can predict about the content of the article.

All Work and No Play Spells Trouble in Early Education

A Parents and educators who favour traditional classroom-style learning over free, unstructured playtime in pre-school and kindergarten may actually be stunting a child's development instead of enhancing it, according to a University of Illinois professor who studies childhood learning and literacy development.

Anne Haas Dyson, a professor of Curriculum and Instruction at the university, says playtime for children is a 'fundamental avenue' for learning, and attempts by parents and educators to create gifted children by overloading them with information, though well-intentioned, is ultimately counter-productive. 'That approach doesn't appreciate the role of play and imagination in a child's intellectual development,' Dyson claims. 'Play is where children discover ideas, experiences and concepts and start to think about their consequences. This is where literacy and learning really begins.'

B Dyson feels that the very young are not encouraged to use their imagination enough. This may be influenced by what some critics have called 'Baby Genius Edutainment' a whole range of mind-enriching products developed specifically for infants and toddlers and marketed to anxious parents who want to maximize their children's early learning. 'I see this "Baby Einstein" trend as more about fulfilling parents' needs than children's needs,' Dyson said. 'Children learn the way we all learn: through engagement and construction. They have to make sense of the world, and that's what play or any other symbolic activity does for children.'

C While Dyson does see some value in teaching the ABC to pre-school children, she thinks that trying to accelerate learning actually works against a child's development. She believes that kindergarten and pre-school should be environments in which children experience play as intellectual inquiry, before they are oppressed by the inevitable process of assessment and testing. 'I'm certainly not opposed to literacy early on,' Dyson said, 'but the idea that we can eliminate play from the curriculum just doesn't make sense. Kids don't respond well to sitting still in their desks and listening at that age. They need stimulation.'

D Dyson feels that having an early-childhood curriculum reduced to isolated test scores or other measurable pieces of information doesn't take into account a child's interests or an ability to imagine, problem-solve or negotiate with other children, all of which are essential social and intellectual qualities. 'Tests simply tell us how many letters and how many sounds young children know,' she explains. 'I think there should be far more debate about what children find intellectually motivating and exciting.'

E So what can caring mothers and fathers do to stimulate their children? 'I think parents have to engage with their children,' Dyson emphasizes. 'Follow the child's interests in people, objects, places and activities, and talk about those things with them. It's social interaction that creates a link between the child and an ongoing activity. Adults have to help children to learn how to articulate themselves and participate in the world.'

F Dyson also feels that parents worry too much about what television shows their children watch or what online games they play. She feels that parents should be attentive and make judgements about the appropriateness of the material, but that they shouldn't try to control it. What is more important is to talk with children about what they engage in and why they enjoy it. 'We want children to grow up media-literate,' Dyson explains, 'but we often end up dismissing the source of their pleasure because it doesn't appeal to our adult sensibilities. What today's children know about is largely learnt through the media, and it can be very informative. Knowledge of media plays a part in social bonding between children too. Kids who normally wouldn't have much in common communicate when they watch the same shows.'

F **Read the passage and answer the questions.**

The passage has six sections labelled A–F. For questions 1–6, choose the correct heading for each section from the list of headings in the box. You do not need to use all the headings.

i. Toys for brilliant babies!
ii. Putting children's interests first
iii. Growing up too fast
iv. Pushing them forward or holding them back?
v. The only way to make a friend
vi. Motivation rather than assessment is required
vii. Still a place for the basics
viii. Back to school
ix. Much to learn from popular culture

1. Section A   ___   2. Section B   ___   3. Section C   ___

4. Section D   ___   5. Section E   ___   6. Section F   ___

For question 7–10, choose the correct answer a, b, c or d.

7. Parents and educators sometimes push children because …
    a. they know it will benefit them.
    b. they want to do what is right.
    c. that's what happened when they were children.
    d. they know little about what children need.

8. According to the article, why may children not be encouraged to use their imagination enough?
    a. Their parents only do what is best for themselves.
    b. Their parents are too anxious to allow them freedom.
    c. There are too many toys that make them think in a certain way.
    d. Their parents don't think they are ready for it.

9. Anne Haas Dyson believes that at pre-school and kindergarten …
    a. children should spend all their time playing.
    b. children should learn to read and write.
    c. there should be balance between learning and playing.
    d. children should learn to sit still.

10. What does Anne Haas Dyson think about tests for very young children?
    a. They have limited value.
    b. Children find them motivating.
    c. They tell educators a lot about development.
    d. They are an essential part of the education process.

For questions 11–14, complete the notes below with words from the passage. Use NO MORE THAN TWO words for each answer.

Role of Media

Parents
- worry about children watching TV and going (11) _____
- must make sure content is appropriate but not (12) _____
- should talk to children about what they watch
- should encourage children to become (13) _____ by allowing some freedom

Children
- learn a great deal through TV, etc.
- bond with others when they have interests (14) _____

G Answer the questions below about the article in groups of three.

1. Do you agree with some of what Anne Haas Dyson believes?
2. Do you think children benefit from going to pre-school or kindergarten or should they be at home with their parents before they start at primary school?
3. Would you change the age at which children start primary school in your country?

6 Home and away

'The world is a book, and those who do not travel read only a page.'
St Augustine

Speaking 1: what are holidays for?

A Look at the questions below and spend a few minutes planning what you want to say. Check the highlighted words and phrases if necessary. Then discuss the questions in groups of three.

1. How often do you get away for a week or more?
2. Do you usually go abroad on holiday or do you visit new places in your own country?
3. Do you go on holiday to relax and unwind or do you look for discovery and adventure?
4. Do you usually buy a package holiday or do you travel independently?
5. Do you usually go to popular holiday resorts or do you look for somewhere off the beaten track?
6. What was the best holiday you ever had?
7. Are you planning to go on holiday in the near future?

B Check that you understand each type of holiday in the box. Then in your group, answer the questions below.

1. What do people want from each type of holiday?
2. Which of the holidays most appeal to you?
3. What type of holiday was your last holiday?

| beach / sun and sea   city break / sightseeing |
| organized coach tour   camping   skiing |
| theme park   safari   cruise |

C Check any words you don't know in the list of holiday features below. Then use the prompts to tell a partner about your last holiday.

1. where you went
2. how you got there
3. where you stayed
4. what you did (days/evenings)
5. the weather
6. places of interest / sights / monuments / excursions
7. local traditions / festivals
8. local people / other holidaymakers
9. traditional food and drink
10. local products / souvenirs / gifts you bought

Vocabulary 1: confusing words

A In pairs, discuss the difference in meaning and usage between the words in each pair.

Travel is uncountable and is more of a concept. A *journey* is a concrete thing and is countable.

1. holiday / festival
2. travel / journey
3. journey / tour
4. trip / excursion
5. adventure / expedition
6. sights / sites
7. reach / arrive
8. gift / souvenir

B 🎧 Listen to two students speaking in the exam and write answers to the questions.

1. How does the first speaker explain the word he can't remember?
   '… *you know,* _____ ,'
2. Do you know the word that the second student doesn't know? _____ .

C Talk with a partner about an aspect of travel that you don't know the correct word for. Explain what you mean.

> *I usually book my holidays online now but I still look at, you know, those magazines you get in travel agents.*

Speaking 2: comparing and contrasting

A 🎧 Listen to some more students talking with an examiner. Complete the sentences below with ONE WORD ONLY in each space.

1. Oh, it was _____ better than I hoped it would be.
2. Well, Paris wasn't _____ as nice as I thought it would be.
3. However, it was _____ more beautiful than I imagined.
4. … it was very exciting and not _____ as polluted as I expected.

Grammar check
We often use adverbs to modify comparative structures, especially in spoken language.
We use *much / a lot* and *far* to make affirmative structures more extreme.
much more than / a lot bigger than / far more interesting than

We use *quite* and *nearly* to modify negative structures.
not quite as nice as / not nearly as good as

We use *even* with both affirmative and negative structures.
even more beautiful than I hoped / not even as nice as my town

We can use *by far* with superlatives
It's by far the biggest city I've ever visited.

Watch out!
typical errors

It wasn't nearly as nice than I hoped. ✗

It's far more big than … ✗

Pronunciation check
🎧 Listen again to the exchanges in Exercise A. Notice how the modifying adverbs are stressed to make the message clear.

1. Practise saying the sentences 1–4 in Exercise A.
2. Practise reading the exchanges from the tapescript. One of you is the examiner, the other is the student.

B Choose five or six places (countries, cities or famous sites) you have visited and follow the steps below.

1. Write the names of the places on a piece of paper ready to give to a partner.
2. Plan what you want to say about the places using the comparative structures with modifying adverbs from the *Grammar check*.
3. Exchange lists of places with a partner.
4. Ask and answer questions: *So, what did you think of / Did you like …?*, etc.

C Here is a typical task card for the Speaking test, Part 2. Spend a minute planning what you want to say and make notes. Then talk to at least two other students.

A

Compare a city you have visited with your hometown or city.

Say …
- when and why you went there.
- what you liked or disliked about it.
- how it is different from your hometown or city.

6

Listening 1: maps and plans

A Look at the maps and plans below. In pairs, discuss what sort of information you expect to hear.

B 🎧 Listen and match the extracts with the maps and plans.

Extract 1 ___   Extract 2 ___   Extract 3 ___

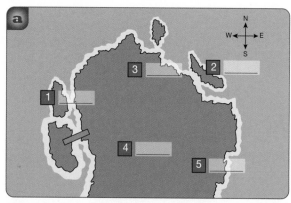

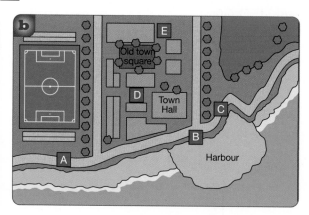

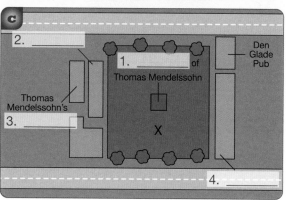

C 🎧 Listen to the first extract and circle *Las Gaviotas* (A, B, C, D or E) on the map.

D 🎧 Listen to the second extract and label the plan with ONE WORD in each space.

E 🎧 Listen to the third extract and label the map. Choose from the box below and write five letters A–I next to the labels 1–5.

A boathouse	B lighthouse	C garden centre	D road bridge	E wildlife park
F bird sanctuary	G castle	H farm	I manor house	

Listening 2: noticing how information is repeated

⏳ **Exam tip:** When you are you listening for specific information like names of people and places, the speaker will often repeat information that you need to answer a question. If you don't catch a word or phrase for an answer, listen carefully to see if the speaker repeats the word or phrase that you need.

A 🎧 Listen again. Notice examples of a speaker repeating information.

B Look at the tapescript on pages 293 and 294 and highlight examples of a speaker repeating information.

Listening 3: practice with maps and plans

A You will hear a holiday rep talking to some guests as they arrive at a hotel. Look at the hotel plan below and make some predictions about what you will hear. Compare ideas with a partner.

B 🎧 Listen and answer the questions.

For questions 1–8, label the plan below. Choose from the box and write eight letters A–J next to the numbers 1–8.

A sauna / jacuzzi	B stable	C towel collection	D children's pool	E restaurant
F money exchange	G main bar	H stage	I showers	J shop

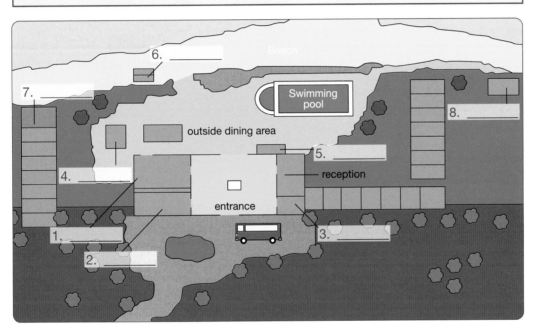

C Check the key on page 266. How many questions did you answer correctly?

D Tick the sentences about the Listening task that are true for you and think about how you can answer more questions correctly next time.

☐ 1. Looking at the plan and reading through the questions helped me to predict content.

☐ 2. I heard the speaker repeat some of the information I needed.

Key vocabulary in context

Fill each space with the correct preposition.

1. There are four islands _____ the coast.
2. The larger island is home _____ Old Finkley.
3. Next to the restaurant just here _____ the left is the main bar.
4. There's a separate children's pool _____ one end.

▶ **WB** See *Vocabulary development* on Workbook page 229.

6

Reading 1: preparing to read

A Read the title of the short article opposite and then, in pairs, answer these questions.

1. What benefits does tourism bring to a region?
2. What are the damaging effects of increased tourism?

Reading 2: using topic sentences to predict

A In the last unit, you learnt about topic sentences. In pairs, answer the questions below.

1. Which sentence in a paragraph is usually the topic sentence?
2. What is the purpose of a topic sentence?
3. What should the other sentences within the paragraph do? What do we call these sentences?
4. When should the writer begin a new paragraph?

B Below are the topic sentences from six paragraphs in a text about tourism. Read them and then, in pairs, answer the questions that follow.

Paragraph 1: The sheer scale of tourism and the impact it has on local communities worldwide is almost inconceivably huge.

Paragraph 2: The primary economic benefit of tourism is the income it brings to the local and regional area.

Paragraph 3: There are many accounts of tourism being responsible for the destruction of the environment.

Paragraph 4: The cultural effects of tourism are patently clear.

Paragraph 5: The growth of tourism in a region usually means a range of employment opportunities for local people.

Paragraph 6: It is claimed that as tourism grows and the world shrinks, the gap between cultures and religions diminishes.

1. Do you get a clear idea of what the text will be about from reading only the topic sentences?
2. Can you see how the text will be organized from looking at the topic sentences?
3. Can you predict what supporting information will be in each paragraph?
4. In which of the paragraphs will each of the supporting ideas in the box below be?

the conservation of an area of beauty ___	people becoming more tolerant ___
local people doing menial work ___	the cost of maintaining a tourist industry ___
the need for debate about tourism ___	unique customs and lifestyles changing ___

WEIGHING UP THE BENEFITS OF TOURISM

The sheer scale of tourism and the impact it has on local communities worldwide is almost inconceivably huge. So huge, in fact, that any debate over whether its effects are generally positive or largely damaging ends up being little more than a game of verbal tennis. However, this ongoing debate is necessary if sustainable tourism policies are ever to be developed.

The primary economic benefit of tourism is the income it brings to the local and regional area. However, in order to construct and then maintain a tourism industry, the community will bear an enormous financial burden. The development of tourism creates opportunities for outside operations to intrude and provide services to wealthy travellers, diverting the lion's share of profit away from locals.

There are many accounts of tourism being responsible for the destruction of the environment. Although vast numbers of travellers can disrupt or destroy habitats and ecosystems, tourism can also be the impetus for the conservation of an area of unspoiled beauty which might otherwise fall victim to development.

The cultural effects of tourism are patently clear. For the visitor, the experience of unique customs and lifestyles far removed from their own is hugely rewarding. Tourism by nature, though, is an invasive process that propels traditional communities into the modern world, threatening their distinct way of life and changing completely the way they go about their daily business.

The growth of tourism in a region usually means a range of employment opportunities for local people. While that may be a benefit, locals often find themselves doing menial work, such as cleaning or serving in restaurants, while westerners are given managerial roles. Families frequently become dependent on income from tourism while traditional industries, like fishing, die out.

It is claimed that as tourism grows and the world shrinks, the gap between cultures and religions diminishes. People become more tolerant and understanding. In many cases, however, the extreme difference in wealth between locals and visitors causes distrust and conflict. In very popular destinations, the inappropriate behaviour of tourists can aggravate tension between them and those in the community.

Exam tip: Remember that when you are doing the IELTS Reading test, understanding the topic sentences will help you to know where to look back to find answers.

D Cover the text and look again at the topic sentences in Exercise B. Use the sentences to talk in your own words about the effects of tourism.

Reading 3: practise using topic sentences to predict

A You will read an online blog about package holidays. Before you read it, answer the questions below. Check the highlighted words if necessary.

1. Why do people choose to go on package holidays?
2. What are the possible disadvantages of a package holiday?
3. Do you think some people can be snobbish about holidays and travel? Do people who travel independently look down on people who buy package holidays?

B Read only the topic sentences highlighted at the beginning of each paragraph in the passage and think about:

1. what the whole text will be about.
2. how the text will be organized.
3. what supporting information will be in each paragraph.

C Read sentences 1–5 below and predict which paragraph the information will be found in.

D Read the passage and answer the questions.

The passage has six paragraphs, A–F. Which paragraph contains the following information? For questions 1–5 write the correct letter A–F into the space. You will not need to use one letter.

1. independent travel not necessarily being expensive   ___
2. feeling uncomfortable with people who claim to be superior   ___
3. the writer admitting that she is part of the exploitation   ___
4. people doing what they have always done   ___
5. tourists not understanding the impact that their choices have   ___

THE PROBLEM WITH PACKAGE HOLIDAYS

A **I had a discussion with my parents recently about their plans for their upcoming retirement and travel was very high on the agenda.** As the conversation developed, it struck me that though both my mother and father are interested in and curious about other countries and cultures, they have always elected to buy package holidays, and seemed to have no intention of changing their habits. Whether they have bought a cheap trip to Spain or ventured further afield to Mauritius or Bali, they have always opted for the *never need to leave the hotel type* deals rather than chance the slightest degree of independence. It's a concept I find hard to relate to. As far as I'm concerned, those packages are not just damaging to the country or region visited, they also exclude any opportunity for discovery and adventure and minimize the likelihood of learning anything about the culture and customs of the local community.

B **The irony of all this is that I have always prided myself on not being a travel snob.** I loathe it when hardened travellers and adventurous young backpackers look down on anyone whose particular holiday option they feel is somehow less worthy than their own.

Yet on this occasion I found myself trying to explain to my parents why I disapproved of their preferences and how I felt that their style of travel was based on ignorance.

C **When I look at package tourism, I see people who don't want to make an effort and who care very little about what they experience as long as they get some good holiday snaps and come home with a suntan.** The vast majority of any profit made at large chain hotels is sent back to the United States or the wealthier European countries while local employees are paid a pittance. I understand that people who opt for these holidays seek a bit of luxury or escapism from a dull 9 to 5 back home, but I don't think half of them ever stop to think about the people who cleaned their room, cooked their food or drove them around. These people probably earn less in a year than the tourists do in a week. They don't realize that by buying an all inclusive deal and relying on their hotel for every meal and all their entertainment they are contributing even less to the local economy. Even those who are aware seem unwilling to make a few simple changes that would help to make their travel more sustainable.

D **In saying all of this, I realize I am not the perfect traveller.** Although I have never booked a package holiday, I often stay in upmarket hotels, I occasionally eat in western style chain restaurants and frequently rely on people who have almost certainly had a far less privileged education than mine to speak my language – English. I'm sure there is far more I could do support sustainability, but I'd like to think that I'm learning and that I'm keen to know more. I want to travel in a way that contributes to a local economy and in a way in that is respectful to the local communities I pass through.

E **I realize that the attraction of these package deals is that they offer incomparable value for money.** People on low incomes have the opportunity of a cheap break in a warm climate that they would otherwise simply not be able to afford. However, other options are available. I like many others have travelled in the past on a shoe-string budget, and had memorable experiences. A holiday might take a little more time and effort to plan and there might be more uncertainly involved, but a culturally rewarding experience that respects the local community is possible.

F **Perhaps, after all, I am rather snobbish when it comes to travel.** I wouldn't go so far as to say that package tourism is ruining the planet, but it certainly isn't doing a great deal to protect it. I don't see people who opt for a package holiday as inferior to me in any way, but I can't pretend that I like the choice they're making. I think it's important to look beyond the convenience of these deals and see what is really happening. I would urge anyone planning to book one of these holidays to look at the alternatives. There are a thousand adventures out there waiting to be had.

Source: www.runawayjane.com

For questions 6–12, decide if the following statements reflect the claims of the writer in the reading passage? Write:

- **(Y) YES** if the statement reflects the claims of the writer.
- **(N) NO** if the statement contradicts the claims of the writer.
- **(NG) NOT GIVEN** if it is impossible to say what the writer thinks about this.

6. People who go on package holidays learn less than people who travel independently. ___
7. Most young backpackers are very snobbish. ___
8. People who go on package holidays mainly want to take photos and lie in the sun. ___
9. Local people employed in tourism earn good money. ___
10. Better quality hotels are more comfortable than cheaper options. ___
11. People who earn little can only afford to buy package holidays. ___
12. More travellers should choose adventure holidays. ___

Question-type tip: When a passage largely consists of the writer's point of view, tasks sometimes require you to answer *yes*, *no* or *not given* instead of *true*, *false* or *not given*. The two task types are very similar and you can approach them in a similar way. Remember that you should not use your own knowledge of the topic and you must take into consideration that the writer's opinion may not be what most people would assume is true or false.

E Check the key on page 266. How many questions did you answer correctly?

F Tick the sentences about the Reading task that are true for you and think about how you can answer more questions correctly next time.

- ☐ 1. I understand better how topic sentences make a paragraph easier to read.
- ☐ 2. I could make predictions about what would be in each paragraph from reading the topic sentences.
- ☐ 3. I appreciate that reading and understanding the topic sentence helps me to know where to locate information that I need to answer questions.
- ☐ 4. I located the information that provided answers quickly.

Key vocabulary in context

In both texts, there are a number of words that have either a strong positive or negative connotation. Mark the words below (P) positive or (N) negative. The words are in the order in which they appear.

Text 1:
1. burden (n)	___	2. intrude (v)	___	3. disrupt (v)	___
4. impetus (n)	___	5. unspoiled (adj)	___	6. rewarding (adj)	___
7. menial (adj)	___	8. distrust (n)	___	9. conflict (n)	___

Text 2:
1. disapprove (v)	___	2. pittance (n)	___	3. luxury (n)	___
4. upmarket (adj)	___	5. privileged (adj)	___	6. uncertainty (n)	___
7. ruin (v)	___	8. inferior (adj)	___

WB See *Vocabulary development* on Workbook page 229.

WB For focus on reading skills, go to Workbook page 230.

Writing 1: preparing for the task

A Look at the pictures. What do they say about tourism in poor countries?

B Look at the instructions for a typical IELTS Writing task below and start thinking about how you would approach it.

> Write about the following topic:
>
> *In many of the world's poorest countries, tourism is a huge industry. However, the profit made from tourism rarely benefits the poorest people living in the local community.*
>
> *What are some of the reasons for this situation and what are some possible solutions?*
>
> Give reasons for your answer and include any relevant examples from your own knowledge or experience.
>
> Write at least 250 words.

C Look back at Writing 1 in the Writing Module of Unit 2 (page 30).

1. Look again at how a student made notes on the task.
2. Make notes on the Writing task here in the same way.

Exam tip: Writing Task 2 will sometimes ask you to suggest some reasons for a problem and then to list some possible solutions. Making notes is an especially important step in deciding what you have to say and organizing your ideas. You don't have to be an expert on the issue, but your suggestions must be relevant and make sense – the issue will be an issue that everyone knows at least something about.

D Work in pairs and follow the steps below.

1. Decide if this is a task that you would feel confident about writing.
2. Think of three reasons why the poorest people in a community do not benefit from tourism.
3. Think of three possible solutions to the problem.

E Below are some notes a student made before writing the composition. Write ONE WORD ONLY into each space to complete the notes. Use a dictionary to check any words you don't know.

Reasons:
1. biggest _____ owned by companies in wealthy countries
2. too many _____ businesses (shops / bars / restaurants, etc.)
3. tourists spend money in their hotel – don't support _____ businesses
4. better-paid _____ go to westerners (they speak English) / locals do _____ work
5. local produce and handicrafts replaced by _____ marketed brands

Solutions:
1. government should _____ number of foreign businesses allowed
2. govt could give _____ to local businesses
3. local people need better _____ – need English to get better jobs in tourism
4. govt must encourage businesses to _____ local people
5. govt should encourage _____ to support local businesses

F In pairs, discuss:

1. how each line could be expanded into a fuller point.
2. whether there are any other important points that you'd prefer to make.

Writing 2: organizing paragraphs and using topic sentences

A You have decided that the logical approach is to organize your composition into five paragraphs. In pairs, discuss what each of the five paragraphs will include.

B Read the composition below and compare it with your ideas in Exercise A. Don't worry about the missing lines for now.

___. Local communities welcome tourism because it brings in money and provides employment. However, the huge profit made from tourism benefits the rich companies that fly people to the destination and provide their accommodation and food. Very little of the income goes to the poorest local people.

___. Firstly, constructing a tourist industry is very expensive, so many hotels and other large tourist facilities are owned by companies in the wealthiest countries. Businesses that grow up around the initial development are also foreign. Of course, these businesses give managerial and better jobs to their nationals because they speak English. Local people usually do the most menial work, like cleaning or serving food. The very poorest people are not employable.

___. They spend their money in their hotels and support the foreign businesses because they are familiar. They buy globally marketed brands instead of local produce and handicrafts.

___. Governments could limit the number of foreign businesses allowed in an area and could provide subsidies to local businesses to help them start up and survive. They could also encourage or force foreign businesses to employ local people in better jobs.

___. They especially need to learn English. At the same time, tourists must be made aware of the situation and encouraged to support local businesses and buy more locally made products.

C Make sure Exercise D below is covered. In pairs, write an appropriate topic sentence for each paragraph on the lines provided.

Paragraph 1: _____
_____

Paragraph 2: _____
_____

Paragraph 3: _____
_____

Paragraph 4: _____
_____

Paragraph 5: _____
_____

D Put the topic sentences below into the correct place at the beginning of each paragraph in the composition. Write just the number of each sentence.

1. Tourists are also responsible for the problem.
2. Perhaps the most important change would be to give the local people better education.
3. Tourism is a multi-million dollar industry and is growing especially fast in developing countries.
4. It will not be easy to resolve this problem and ensure that more money goes to the people who need it, but there are measures that can be taken.
5. There are several reasons for this situation.

E Compare the topic sentences with your own ideas.

F Go to the Exam Practice Module on page 99 for the Writing task.

Speaking

A Work in pairs. One of you is A, the other is B. Use a dictionary to look up the words and phrases in your box. Then explain them to your partner.

A | stopover   jabs   full board |

B | half board   turbulence   sand dunes |

B Look again at Speaking 2 from this unit on page 87. Remember how you answered the question on your card.

C In pairs, ask and answer these follow-up questions.

1. What attracts visitors to a town or city these days?
2. What might put visitors off visiting a foreign destination?
3. How has international travel changed in recent years?
4. What sort of holidays do you think people will go on 50 years from now?

Vocabulary

A Match the verbs 1–7 with their definitions a–g.

1. intrude   a. get smaller
2. disrupt   b. put in danger
3. threaten   c. enter or become involved when not wanted
4. divert   d. allow to exist and develop
5. sustain   e. make something worse
6. shrink   f. cause difficulties / prevent something form running smoothly
7. aggravate   g. make something go in a different direction

B Fill each gap with a root word made from the word in brackets.

1. It was an especially _____ holiday because I met my husband there. (memory)
2. Independent travellers seem to _____ of people who buy package holidays. (approve)
3. There are still some _____ beaches in that region. (spoil)
4. These days, everyone is talking about _____ tourism. (sustain)
5. I like to have everything well-planned when I travel. I don't like _____. (certain)
6. Many tourists are _____ to change their habits. (will)
7. Travel is like other forms of entertainment. It's all about _____. (escape)
8. Local people are not frequently offered _____ positions. (manager)

Errors

A There are errors in all of these sentences. Correct them.

1. The travel from the airport to the hotel was quick.
2. We arrived to Sydney at lunchtime.
3. What time will we reach to the coast?
4. The hotel wasn't quite as big than I expected.
5. It's by much the nicest city in my country.
6. Venice was more beautiful even than I hoped.

Writing

A The pictures below show different ways in which increased tourism can spoil a destination.

1. In pairs, discuss the problem that each picture shows.
2. Suggest some possible solutions to each problem.

B Look carefully at the instructions for this Writing task. Highlight the key words and make sure you understand what you have to do.

Write about the following topic:

As the tourist industry develops, travellers look to visit ever more remote parts of the world. The problem is that increased tourism can spoil these places and make them less appealing to visit.

What are some examples of this problem and what are some possible solutions?

Give reasons for your answer and include any relevant examples from your own knowledge or experience.

Write at least 250 words.

C In pairs, make notes like the notes in Writing 1E.

1. Make a list of four of five examples.
2. Make another list of positive solutions.
   - Suggest solutions to the general problem of increased tourism.
   - Suggest solutions to the specific problems you mention.

 Exam tip: When you do Writing Task 2, you may feel that you don't have enough to write, so make sure you write a solid introduction. The introduction to the model on page 266 is 69 words. When you read the model, notice how, in the introduction, the writer paraphrases language in the task instructions.

D Write your composition. Remember – you don't need to include all the points you discussed or listed. Then check the model on page 266.

7 Kill or cure

'The greatest wealth is health.'
Virgil

Speaking 1: lifestyle

A Look at the pictures below and talk in pairs.

1. Discuss what each image says about what is a healthy or an unhealthy lifestyle.
2. Discuss which images reflect aspects of your lifestyle and which you can relate to.

Vocabulary 1: health and fitness

A Answer the questions below in pairs. Use a dictionary to check the highlighted words and phrases if necessary.

1. What is the difference in meaning between being healthy and being fit?
2. If somebody is in good shape or likes to stay in shape is he/she healthy or fit?
3. If somebody complains that he/she is out of condition, what does he/she mean?
4. If somebody says 'I like to look after myself', what does he/she mean?
5. If somebody says 'I have a balanced diet', what does he/she mean?
6. If somebody often feels under the weather, what does it mean?

B With your partner, ask and answer questions using the words and phrases in Exercise A.

> Would you say that you're in good shape?

Pronunciation check

How is *th* pronounced in the two words below? Is it the same in both words?

healthy   weather

🎧 Mark the words below /θ/ or /ð/ depending on how *th* is pronounced. Listen and check. Practise saying the words in pairs.

bath   bathe   breath   breathe   truth   clothes   teeth   teething

Vocabulary 2: health issues and minor accidents

A Check that you understand the highlighted words and phrases in the activity below. Use a dictionary if necessary.

Find somebody who …

- has an allergy to a certain type of food.
- suffers from hay fever.
- usually gets seasick.
- has poor eyesight (and wears contact lenses).
- has needed stitches in a wound or bad cut.
- has had his/her arm or leg in plaster.

- has been put under anaesthetic.
- has had an electric shock.
- has been the victim of food poisoning.
- has been stung by a jellyfish.
- has been bitten by a dog.
- has burnt himself/herself recently.

B Walk around the classroom. Find at least one person who answers *yes* to each question.

Grammar check

Remember that we use the passive when we want to focus on what **happened to** somebody rather than who or what **did** the action. This is very common when talking about health issues and accidents. Sometimes who or what did the action is also important, so we put it at the end of the sentence and use *by*.
Have you ever been stung by a jellyfish? NOT *Has a jellyfish ever stung you?*
The second question is not wrong, but it isn't very natural.

Reflexive pronouns are used when the object of a sentence is the same as the subject.
I hurt myself. / He cut himself.
Each personal pronoun (*I*, *you*, *he*, etc.) has its own reflexive form. Write the reflexive forms of these personal pronouns.

1. I = _____
2. you (singular) = _____
3. you (plural) = _____
4. he = _____
5. she = _____
6. it = _____
7. we = _____
8. they = _____

Watch out!
typical errors
I burnt me. ✗
We saw ourself. ✗

Speaking 2: giving yourself time to think

A The questions below are typical of the Speaking test, Part 3. Think about how you would answer each question.

1. Do you think your generation has a healthier lifestyle than your parents' generation?
2. What do you think about alternative approaches to health care, like acupuncture or aromatherapy?
3. Does the government of a country have a responsibility to promote healthy lifestyle options?
4. Is an ageing population placing too much of a health care burden on taxpayers?

B 🎧 Listen to some students answering the questions. How do they give themselves time to think?

C 🎧 Listen again and fill the gaps.

1. Mm, I haven't really _____ before.
2. Mm, _____. It's not a topic …
3. That's _____ question.
4. I don't know if _____ that in a few words. It's _____ question.

 Exam tip: If the examiner asks you a difficult question, you need time to think. Rather than saying nothing, try to use expressions that show you are thinking before you give an answer.

D Talk in pairs. Ask and answer the questions in Exercise A, using strategies that give you time to think.

E Ask each other questions of your own about health and fitness and practise giving yourself time to think before answering.

7

Listening 1: preparing to listen

A You will hear a talk to a class of medical students. Look at the pictures. What do you think the topic of the talk will be?

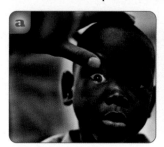 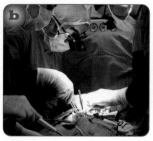  

B Try to answer the questions below in groups of three.

1. Which human organs have been successfully transplanted? Make a list.
2. What was the first successful transplant of a human body part?
3. What have been some more recent developments in transplant surgery?

C Listen to the introductory part of the talk. Answer the questions below in pairs.

1. What does the speaker want the students to do after the lecture?
2. How does the speaker define a *transplant*?
3. Why is the Chinese physician's operation not a real example of a transplant?

Listening 2: listening to complete a table

Question-type tip: In both the Listening and Reading tests you will sometimes need to complete information in a table.

A Look at the table below and, in pairs, discuss why having information presented in a table might help you in the Listening test.

B Listen to the first part of the talk and complete the table. Use NO MORE THAN TWO WORDS OR A NUMBER for each answer.

Date	Organ transplanted	Details
(1) _____	cornea	damaged cornea replaced by donated tissue.
1954	(2) _____	operation performed on (3) _____
1966	pancreas	patient suffered from (4) _____ –
		immediate fall in (5) _____ levels

C Compare your answers with a partner. Did the table format help you understand more?

Exam tip: Having a table helps you because you can predict how the talk will be organized and divided into parts. When you listen, you know when the speaker is going to go from one topic to another because you can follow the squares on the table.

Listening 3: practise listening to complete a table

A 🎧 Listen to the rest of the talk and answer the questions.

For questions 1–15, complete the table. Write NO MORE THAN TWO WORDS OR A NUMBER for each answer.

Date	Organ transplanted	Details
1967	(1) _____	patient survived (3) _____ after operation – several previous attempts failed
	(2) _____	man in S. Africa – now (4) _____ transplants annually
(5) _____	heart and lung	operation in 1963 – patient died after (6) _____
		heart + lung machine + drugs enabled (7) _____
1998	(8) _____	many failed attempts – first in (9) _____
		transplant not total success – patient did not follow (10) _____ of rehabilitation
2005	(11) _____ face	donor transplant – woman in (12) _____ attacked by (13) _____ part of donor's (14) _____ + (15) _____ grafted onto victim of accident
2010	full face	man in Spain / 30 doctors

B Check the key on page 266. How many questions did you answer correctly?

C Tick the sentences about the Listening task that are true for you and think about how you could answer more questions correctly next time.

☐ 1. I looked at the table carefully before I listened.
☐ 2. The table helped me predict the type of word or phrase that I needed for most spaces.
☐ 3. I spelt my answers correctly and used capital letters when necessary.
☐ 4. I am pleased with how many questions I answered correctly.

Key vocabulary in context

In pairs, define each of the highlighted words below using your own words.

1. the donor
2. the recipient
3. a surgical procedure
4. failed to sustain life
5. the prescribed programme
6. was grafted onto
7. her immune system

▶ **WB** See *Vocabulary development* on Workbook page 233.

Reading 1: unknown words and phrases in context

A Look only at the highlighted words in the extracts below. Do you know what any of them mean?

> Parts of Europe and North America are beginning to see cases of West Nile disease, which, as the name suggests, has previously only thrived in tropical and subtropical areas. Rising temperatures result in mosquitoes that carry and spread the disease roaming further north.

> Ever since it was first suggested that the Earth might be experiencing widespread climate change, there have been concerns about the resulting possibility of a spread of arboviruses – viruses carried by arthropods such as mosquitoes, midges and ticks. Changes in temperature and rainfall are important factors in a new territory becoming hospitable to an arbovirus.

> A recent report from the Wildlife Conservation Society warns that climate change may hasten the spread of diseases that can move from wild animals to humans. The report lists 12 deadly animal-carried diseases which may spread as temperatures rise around the globe.

B The three extracts are all about the same issue. Read the extracts and summarize the content.

C Read the extracts again and, in pairs, try to explain what each of the highlighted words means.

 Exam tip: When you read, don't worry about the meaning of every word. However, some words are vital to understand the text or a paragraph, or to answer a question correctly. You will not have a dictionary in the exam so it is important that you learn to work out the meaning of words from the context – from the other words around the word that you don't know. Sometimes you can work out new words from parts of the word that you already know.

D In pairs, answer the questions below about the highlighted words.

1. Which of the highlighted words are verbs, which are nouns and which are adjectives? How do you know?
2. Which words can you guess because they are items in a list which includes another word you know?
3. Which of the words can you understand from parts of it that you already know?
4. What other aspects of the context help you to work out the meaning of each word?

E Work out what the words and phrases below mean from parts of the word or phrase that you already know. Then compare with a partner.

| heart-stopping | bloodless | jet lag | fighting fit | my feet are killing me |

Reading 2: preparing to read

A You will read a complete passage about the relationship between global warming and disease. Before you read, match the technical terms 1–4 with the definitions a–d.

1. pathogen
2. parasite
3. virus
4. vector organism

a. creature that lives in or on another creature and feeds on it
b. insect or small animal that carries disease between larger animals and humans
c. bacteria or virus that causes disease
d. tiny living thing (smaller than bacteria) that enters the body and causes disease

B In pairs, write five questions that you would like answered in the passage.

Reading 3: working out meaning from context

A Look at the highlighted words and phrases, but do not check them in a dictionary. You will need to guess their meanings to answer the questions.

B Read the passage.

1. See if any of the questions you wrote are answered.
2. Check the meanings of the highlighted items more carefully in context. Think about:
   - the general context – the other words around the highlighted word or phrase.
   - the part of speech – if the highlighted word or phrase is a noun, verb, adjective, etc.
   - parts of the highlighted word or phrase that you already know.
   - if you know another (probably more basic) meaning of the word or phrase.

Climate Change
and the Spread of Disease

Climate change will affect the frequency and spread of disease because of its impact on the population size and range of hosts and pathogens, the duration of the transmission season and the timing and intensity of outbreaks. Warmer temperatures and increased moisture will result in the geographical range of vector organisms such as insects, rodents and snails extending, and the period in which they are active lengthening. The potential transmission zone for many vector-borne diseases, among them malaria, yellow fever and dengue, will expand. Extreme weather events like storms and droughts often prompt disease outbreaks, especially in poor areas where prevention measures and treatment are inadequate.

Mosquitoes are particularly sensitive to temperature. The mosquitoes that carry malaria rarely develop or breed at temperatures below 15°C, and the variety that transmits dengue is restricted by winter temperatures below 10°C. Mosquito survival also decreases at their upper temperature threshold, about 40°C. With sufficient moisture, warmer temperatures will cause an increase in mosquito abundance and activity level, and will speed up the incubation of the parasites and viruses within them.

Warmer global temperatures will allow an expansion of the geographic range within which both the mosquito and parasite could survive in sufficient numbers to result in sustained transmission. Model predictions indicate that a 3°C global temperature rise by 2100 could increase the number of annual malaria cases by 50–80 million. The most extreme changes will occur in areas neighbouring current high-risk areas at both higher altitudes and latitudes. In these regions, a temperature increase could convert an area that is malaria-free into an area that suffers seasonal epidemics. The affected populations would frequently have little or no immunity, so high levels of sickness and death would be the norm.

Recent disease outbreaks are consistent with model projections. Mosquito-borne diseases are being reported at higher elevations than in the past in parts of Asia, Central Africa and Latin America. In the summer of 1999, an outbreak of encephalitis claimed three lives in New York City and necessitated widespread pesticide spraying. Experts have identified the West Nile virus, transmitted by mosquitoes that feed on infected birds, as being responsible. Encephalitis had not been previously recorded anywhere in the Western hemisphere, occurring primarily in the late summer or early autumn in temperate regions, but year-round in milder climates.

Diseases carried by mammals, particularly rodents, may also be affected by climate change. A recent study found a 60% rise in human plague cases in New Mexico following wetter than average winters and springs. Plague has only existed in New Mexico since the 1940s, but a large increase in per capita cases occurred in the 1970s and 1980s associated with wetter than normal conditions. The increased precipitation apparently enhances food resources for small mammals that serve as hosts for infected fleas. The moister climate may also encourage flea survival and reproduction. The study notes that if future climate conditions become more favourable for reproduction and survival of either wild mammal populations or their flea populations, the probability of human infection via animal-flea-human contact will almost certainly increase.

Climate change will also have an impact on diseases of plants and animals, and could lead to significant population declines or even the extinction of endangered species. Climate change has been implicated, for example, in the emergence and spread of marine diseases. This happens because the range of hosts and pathogens change, because stress brought on by warming can lower disease resistance and because contaminant input from terrestrial sources increases due to run-off from heavy rainfall. Higher sea surface temperatures, for example, increase the stress on corals, increasing susceptibility to infection. Forests and agricultural crops are susceptible to the spread of pathogens, especially following droughts and floods.

The disproportionate warming at night and during the winter can allow destructive insects and pathogens to invade forests at higher latitudes from which they are now excluded.

C Read the passage again and answer the questions.

For questions 1–3, complete the sentences with words taken from the passage. Write NO MORE THAN TWO WORDS for each answer.

1. _____ of disease could become more frequent and more intense due to rising temperatures.
2. Vector organisms will exist in places where they previously did not and they will be _____ for longer.
3. In poor areas, disease will spread quickly because there are insufficient _____.

For questions 4–10, complete the notes with words taken from the passage. Write NO MORE THAN THREE WORDS OR A NUMBER for each answer.

Mosquitoes
Sensitive to temperature
Malaria mos. – (4) _____ too cold / (5) _____ too hot
Dengue mos. – (6) _____ too cold
Warmer and wetter weather = higher numbers of active mos. + (7) _____ will incubate more quickly
Mos. could operate in wider (8) _____, increasing number of malaria cases
Areas most at risk – those closest to existing (9) _____
Areas now (10) _____ could be hit by epidemics – many deaths

For questions 11–13, complete the flow chart with words taken from the passage. Write **NO MORE THAN TWO WORDS OR A NUMBER** for each answer.

IMPACT OF CLIMATE CHANGE ON SMALL MAMMALS

(11) _____ improve in wetter environments.

↓

(12) _____ live longer and multiply.

↓

Any (13) _____ between humans and animals spreads disease.

For question 14–15, choose TWO letters A–E. According to the passage, how does or will climate change affect plants and animals

A Many more species of animal will become endangered.
B Some living organisms find it more difficult to fight infection.
C Heavy rain washes poisonous matter into the sea.
D More people swimming in the sea will damage coral.
E Crops fail due to higher incidence of floods and droughts.

14. ___   15. ___

D Check the key on page 266. How many questions did you answer correctly?

E Tick the sentences about the Reading task that are true for you and think about how you can answer more questions correctly next time.

☐ 1. I could guess the meaning of most highlighted words and phrases in context.   ___
☐ 2. I worked out the meaning of some unknown words from words I already knew.   ___
☐ 3. Guessing unknown words and phrases helped me to answer the questions.   ___
☐ 4. I found the information I needed to answer questions quite quickly.   ___
☐ 5. I didn't worry about understanding everything in the text.   ___

Key vocabulary in context

Complete each sentence with a word formed from the root word in brackets at the end.

1. The _____ of disease is facilitated by warmer temperatures. (transmit)
2. Tourists in some countries will have to deal with an _____ of mosquitoes this year. (abundant)
3. Warmer conditions reduce the _____ period. (incubate)
4. Some parts of the world will face _____ epidemics. (season)
5. People most at risk are those with no _____. (immune)
6. These weather conditions are _____ for a good day's fishing. (favour)

WB ▶ See *Vocabulary development* on Workbook page 233.

WB ▶ For focus on reading skills, go to Workbook page 234.

7

Writing 1: preparing to write

A Look carefully at the advertisement below and talk in pairs.

1. What exactly is being advertised?
2. What are the benefits of the service?
3. What are the risks?
4. What more would you like to know?

B Talk in pairs. Do you get the impression that medical tourism, or health tourism, as it is also called, is a good thing?

C 🎧 Listen to a doctor talking. Compare what she says with your ideas in Exercise B.

D 🎧 Listen again and make notes. Then compare your notes with a partner.

E In pairs, discuss the meaning of the words and phrases from the recording below.

joint replacement	convalescing	waiting list	be frowned on	queue-jumping	expertise

Writing 2: describing a flow chart

A Complete the extract below about flow charts with ONE WORD in each space.

Flow charts show the stages in a (1) p_____. They help you understand how something happens and sometimes why it happens. Flow charts usually show cause and (2) e_____. They demonstrate how one event can be the (3) r_____ for another. Flow charts are usually designed with arrows that show you the (4) d_____ of the sequence of events.

B Cover the flow chart below. Look at the instructions for a typical IELTS Writing task below and, in pairs, make predictions about the stages that will be part of the process.

> The flow chart shows the typical stages of medical tourism provided by a private company in Thailand.
>
> Summarize the information by selecting and reporting the main features.
>
> Write at least 150 words.

C Look at the flow chart and compare it with your ideas in Exercise B.

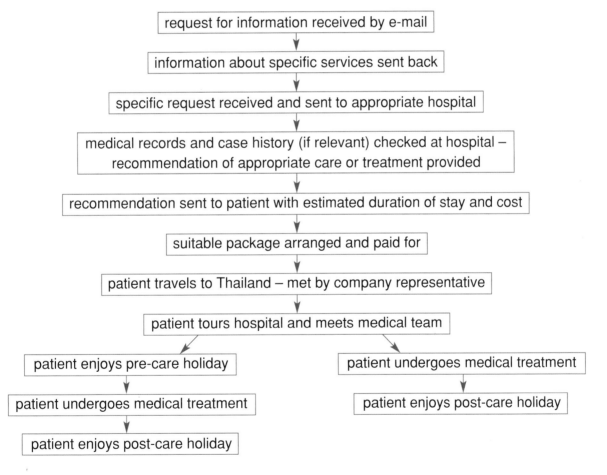

request for information received by e-mail
↓
information about specific services sent back
↓
specific request received and sent to appropriate hospital
↓
medical records and case history (if relevant) checked at hospital – recommendation of appropriate care or treatment provided
↓
recommendation sent to patient with estimated duration of stay and cost
↓
suitable package arranged and paid for
↓
patient travels to Thailand – met by company representative
↓
patient tours hospital and meets medical team
↓
patient enjoys pre-care holiday   patient undergoes medical treatment
↓   ↓
patient undergoes medical treatment   patient enjoys post-care holiday
↓
patient enjoys post-care holiday

D In pairs, answer these questions about the Writing task.

1. Do you need to know a lot about the process described to answer the question?
2. Do you need to add your own ideas to make your description more interesting?
3. Which grammatical structures will you need to use to describe different parts of the process?

E Read a student's report below.

1. Put the verbs in brackets (1–14) into the correct form in the spaces provided.
2. Delete the incorrect linking word or phrase in each pair of options.

The diagram shows the stages in the process of medical tourism (1) _____ (arrange) by a private company. It shows what happens from when an initial request for information (2) _____ (received), to when the patient (3) _____ (enjoy) a post-care holiday.

At the beginning / First of all, when there is a request, information about specific services (4) _____ (send back). **When / As** a specific request is received, it is sent to the hospital that the company (5) _____ (think) appropriate. **At this point / In this time**, the patient's medical records (6) _____ (check) at the hospital and a recommendation of what treatment is appropriate (7) _____ (provide). This is sent to the patient, together with an estimate of the duration of their stay and what the treatment (8) _____ (cost). A suitable package (9) _____ (arrange) and the bill (10) _____ (pay).

The patient travels to Thailand, **where / which** he or she (11) _____ (meet) by a company representative. The patient can tour the hospital and meet the medical team that will provide the treatment or perform the operation.

If the patient (12) _____ (choose) a pre-care holiday, he or she can **now / then** enjoy that before the treatment. If not, the patient (13) _____ (undergo) the medical treatment directly. **Finally / In the end**, the patient can enjoy a post-care holiday before (14) _____ (return) home.

Grammar check

Remember that we use the passive when we want to focus on what happens, rather than who or what does the action. Passive forms are very frequently used to describe a process.
A request for information is received. / Medical records are checked.

Sometimes who or what did the action is also important so we put it at the end of the sentence and use *by*.
The patient is met by a representative of the company.

Passive forms are usually reduced when they are part of a relative clause.
medical tourism arranged by a private company NOT *medical tourism that is arranged by a private company*

 Exam tip: If Writing Task 1 involves describing a process, you will need to use passive forms. Many of the most common verbs in English are irregular. Make sure you know the past participle form of all common verbs.

F Highlight some aspects of the composition that you like. Compare with a partner.

G Talk in groups of three. What do you think about medical or health tourism? Would you ever consider it if you needed treatment?

WB Go to Workbook page 236 for the Writing task.

Speaking

A Look at this typical task card for Part 2 of the Speaking test. Is it easy to talk about?

> **Describe a time that you were hurt or injured.**
> **Say ...**
> • where you were and what you were doing.
> • what happened.
> • what you or other people did to deal with the situation.

B 🎧 Listen to a student talking and answer the questions.

1. Where was she and what was she doing when she was hurt?
2. What happened?
3. What did another person do?

C In pairs, decide if the student spoke well and how she could have done better.

D 🎧 Listen to the same student speaking again. What does she do better the second time?

E Talk in pairs about what's on the task card.

Vocabulary

A Complete the phrases in the sentences below with the correct preposition.

1. I think it's important to **stay** _____ **shape**.
2. I always feel a bit _____ **of condition** after the Christmas festivities.
3. Going to the gym is a good way of **looking** _____ **yourself**.
4. I've been feeling a bit _____ **the weather** over the weekend.
5. How long was her leg _____ **plaster** after the accident?
6. Quite a few people are **allergic** _____ cat hair.
7. There were several **attempts** _____ this surgery before it was successful.
8. Warmer weather means that new territories become **hospitable** _____ vector organisms.
9. Small children and old people are more **susceptible** _____ disease.
10. Paying for health care is **frowned** _____ in some circles.

B Match words from Box A with words from Box B to form common two-part phrases.

A endangered balanced immune food JOINT climate liver queue

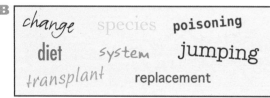

B change species poisoning diet system jumping transplant replacement

Errors

A There are grammatical errors in all of these sentences. Correct them.

1. Have you ever chased by a bull?
2. Most people like to think of theirselves as tolerant.
3. I think we should do it ourself.
4. When a request is received it is sent to the hospital.
5. In this point, medical records are checked.
6. She arrived in China where she met the medical team.

7

Listening

A You will hear three students discussing health care and the precautions they should take when travelling abroad. In pairs, look at the pictures and make some predictions about what they will say.

B Look at the Listening task below. In pairs:

1. think about what the students might say at the beginning of their conversation.
2. think about how the table helps you to predict what they say about various dangers.
3. make further predictions about the content of the talk based on what you can see in the questions.

🎧 **Listen and complete the tasks.**

For questions 1–5, complete the summary of the first part of the conversation below using words from the box.

The students talk about that fact that one of them is planning to travel soon. The student that is travelling has arranged (1) _____, but is apprehensive. His friends say that (2) _____ might be prevalent in the regions in which he plans to travel. One friend suggests that there is more than one way to protect against (3) _____. The other friend is surprised that there is a (4) _____ charge for medical products of this type. They all agree that travel insurance is a necessity, especially for anyone who already suffers from (5) _____.

A hygiene	B ill-health	C medicine	D prescription	E typhoid
F pills	G treatment	H payment	I vaccination	J hospital
K malaria	L immunity	M disease		

For questions 6–17, complete the table. Write NO MORE THAN TWO WORDS OR A NUMBER for each answer.

danger	cause and effect	precaution
food / drink	sickness and diarrhoea caused by: consumption of (6) _____ water and poorly cooked (7) _____ drinks containing (8) _____ fruit and salad	drink only (9) _____ (10) _____ fruit / avoid salad
bites	mosquitoes (15) _____ are dangerous	(11) _____ provided in some rooms use insect repellent / cream / spray keep (12) _____ closed avoid wearing (13) _____ / wear socks to protect (14) _____ keep your distance
sun and heat	skin cancer is long-term risk (16) _____ possible when unaccustomed to high temperature	(17) _____ to heat should be gradual

D Read the tapescript and highlight useful words and phrases.

E In pairs, discuss the meaning of these expressions that the speakers use.

1. go down with   2. cough up   3. the bottom line

8 Bricks and mortar

'Architecture should speak of its time and place, but yearn for timelessness.'
Frank Gehry

Speaking 1: impressive architecture

A Look at the buildings in the pictures and think about the immediate impression each has on you.

B Discuss your thoughts in groups of three.

Vocabulary 1: describing buildings

A Categorize the words and phrases below into three groups. Use a dictionary to check any items you don't know.

magnificent	hideous	peculiar	spectacular	weird	a monstrosity	ghastly	splendid
imposing	unsightly	eccentric	an eyesore	grand	quirky	a blot on the landscape	

B Discuss how you have categorized the words and phrases with a partner.

C Talk about the buildings in the pictures again using the new words and phrases.

D Is there one building in the world that you especially like? Compare your thoughts with other students.

Pronunciation check

In the word *architecture, ch* is pronounced as /k/ rather than /tʃ/. Decide how *ch* is pronounced in the words below, /k/, /tʃ/ and /ʃ/ as you practise saying them in pairs.

1. technology
2. attachment
3. machine
4. chimney
5. character
6. parachute

Speaking 2: construction in your country / expressing obligation

A In pairs, answer the questions below.

1. Are there any especially famous buildings in your town or city?
2. What do you think is the most impressive building in your capital city?
3. Are there any buildings that are considered especially ugly in your capital city?
4. Are there any cities in your country that you think have grown too big or have become ugly?

B Look at an examiner's question below. Think about how you would answer it.

'Do you think there should be restrictions on the level of construction in certain places?'

C 🎧 Listen to three students answering the question and make notes for each exchange.

D 🎧 Listen again and then, in pairs, discuss the meaning of the words and phrases below.

| green belt | two or three storeys | brownfield sites | derelict |

E 🎧 Listen one more time as you read the tapescript and check your answers in Exercise D.

Grammar check

Obligation can be expressed in various ways. As your level progresses, you need to be able to use structures other than *must* and *can't*. Look at the options below.

Buildings **have to** *be under ...*
Buildings **are not allowed to** *be over ...*
It is **forbidden to** *build ...*
Buildings over ... **are not permitted**.
Buildings over ... **are forbidden / banned**.

Watch out!
typical errors

It is banned to build ... ✗
It is not allowed to build ... ✗

F Talk in pairs using some of the structures from the *Grammar check*.

1. Answer the examiner's question in Exercise B.
2. Compare any regulations or restrictions that apply to construction in your country.

8

Listening 1: identifying key words that you don't know

A In pairs, discuss what you think is happening in each of the pictures below.

B Listen to three extracts. Match each with a picture from Exercise A. Write the letter in the space.

Extract 1 ___   Extract 2 ___   Extract 3 ___

Exam tip: When you are listening, there will sometimes be one key word or phrase that you don't know. You may need to work out the meaning from the context so that you can answer a question.

C Listen again and choose the correct letter a, b or c.

Extract 1: The estate agent starts by selling the virtues of …
a. the front garden.   b. the front of the house.   c. the inside of the house.

Extract 2: The health and safety inspector …
a. has good first impressions of the site.   b. is lost.   c. speaks to the wrong person.

Extract 3: The salesman is selling something related to …
a. the roof.   b. doors and windows.   c. finance.

D What were the key words or phrases in each extract? Compare with a partner. Try to pronounce them.

Exam tip: In the Listening test, any words that you need to write as answers will usually be quite simple words. Occasionally, you might need to write a word that you don't know as an answer. You will need to listen carefully and guess the spelling.

E Listen again and write the key words and phrases in the spaces. You may need to guess the spelling.

1. The house is surrounded by _____ and bushes.
2. The estate agent thinks the _____ looks especially good.
3. The inspector is concerned about the _____.
4. The inspector should really be talking to the _____.
5. The salesman wants the customer to consider _____.
6. The customer has recently bought roof _____.

Listening 2: practise identifying key words

A In pairs, answer the questions below.

1. What are the advantages of buying an old house that needs a lot of work?
2. Make a list of some work that needs to be done when an old house is renovated and modernized.

B 🎧 Listen to a couple talking about buying an old house and check your ideas in Exercise A.

C 🎧 Listen again and answer the questions.

For question 1, identify the house on the map. Write the correct letter as your answer.

1. ___

For questions 2–14 complete the notes. Use NO MORE THAN TWO WORDS OR A NUMBER for each answer.

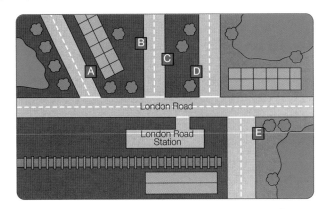

Abbey Road

Rooms
(2) _____ house - 4 bedrooms - one with (3) _____ (view of garden)
space for bedroom 5 in (4) _____
large (5) _____ needs attention

Heating / plumbing / electrics
House has (6) _____ but v. old - needs overhaul / all new radiators
electrics in poor state - whole house needs (7) _____

General condition
(8) _____ falling off in places - hall worst
strip & treat floors / replace some (9) _____
damage to (10) _____ but roof OK / all (11) _____ needs replacing
needs new (12) _____
on for (13) £_____,000 - but will probably lower (14) _____

D Check the key on page 266. How many questions did you answer correctly?

E Tick the sentences about the Listening task that are true for you and think about how you can answer more questions correctly next time.

☐ 1. I identified key words that I didn't know.
☐ 2. I could answer questions by guessing the meaning of new words in context.
☐ 3. I could guess the meaning of some new words and phrases from words I already knew.
☐ 4. I spelt most of my answers correctly.

Grammar check
The verb *need* can be followed by an ~*ing* form to have similar meaning to a passive form.
The whole house needs rewiring. / Some of the floorboards need replacing.

Key vocabulary in context

Look at the tapescript carefully and highlight words and phrases related to houses and buildings that are useful to you. Compare ideas with a partner.

WB See *Vocabulary development* on Workbook page 237.

Reading 1: understanding the general idea

A Look at the picture and answer the questions below.

1. Do you know the word for areas of large cities like this?
2. What characterizes these settlements?
3. What characterizes the people who live in these settlements and what sort of problems do they face?
4. Is simply clearing settlements like these a solution to the problems that exist in them?

B Read the text below and check your answers to the questions in Exercise A. Highlight key words and phrases that relate to the questions.

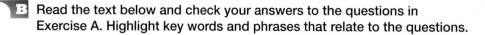

Slum Population Is Growing

The United Nations defines a slum as a run-down area of a city characterized by substandard housing and squalor. Residents have no security in terms of ownership of property. The term once referred to areas that were relatively affluent, but which deteriorated as the original dwellers moved on to newer and better parts of the city, but has come to include the vast settlements found in cities in the developing world.

The percentage of the developing world's urban population living in slums reportedly dropped from 47% to 37% between 1990 and 2005; though, due to the rising population, especially in urban areas, the actual number of slum dwellers is rising. Two billion people worldwide will almost certainly live in slums by 2030.

Although their characteristics vary between geographic regions, slums are usually inhabited by the very poor or socially disadvantaged. Slum buildings vary from primitive shacks to more permanent, well-maintained structures. Most slums lack clean water, electricity, sanitation and other basic necessities. A lack of garbage collection may allow rubbish to accumulate while narrow alleys may not allow access to vehicles like ambulances and fire engines. On top of all this, informal settlements often face the brunt of natural disasters, such as earthquakes, landslides and tropical storms.

The people inhabiting slums are characterised by poverty, illiteracy and unemployment. They are commonly affected by social problems such as crime, drug addiction, alcoholism, high rates of mental illness and suicide. In poor countries, they are prone to high rates of disease due to unsanitary conditions, malnutrition and lack of basic health care. Many slum dwellers employ themselves in the informal economy, doing domestic work or street vending, but can often be drawn into drug dealing or prostitution. In some slums, people recycle trash, selling either the odd usable item or stripping goods for parts or raw materials.

Recent years have seen a dramatic growth in the number of slums as urban populations have increased in the developing world. An additional 50 million people have joined the world's slums in just the past two years. The number of people living in slums in India has more than doubled in the past two decades and now exceeds the entire population of Britain. The number of people living in slums is projected to rise to close to 100 million by 2015, 8% of the population.

Governments have attempted to solve the problems of slums by clearing old, substandard housing and replacing it with modern accommodation. The displacement of slums is made easy by the fact that many are squatter settlements and property rights are not a consideration. Critics argue that slum clearance ignores the root social problems and simply redistributes poverty. Where communities have been moved to newer housing, social cohesion can be lost. If the original community is moved back into newer housing after it has been built in the same location, residents of the new housing are still poor and powerless.

C Work out the meaning of each word and phrase below from the context. Discuss them in pairs.

| affluent | slum dwellers | shacks | alleys | prone to | trash | displacement | squatter |

D Cover the text. In pairs, answer the questions in Exercise A again using information and language you have learnt.

Reading 2: completing a summary

Question-type tip: As well as completing sentences or notes, you will sometimes be instructed to complete a summary.

A Look at the task below. In pairs, discuss some strategies that will ensure you do the task well.

Complete the summary of part of the text below. Use NO MORE THAN TWO WORDS from the text for each answer.

Slums in different parts of the world have different (1) _____, but all are inhabited by the poorest people. Slums sometimes consist of reasonably well-built units, but are usually made up of (2) _____. Slums lack basic amenities and services and are frequently the communities hit hardest by (3) _____. Slum dwellers are poor, illiterate and unemployed. A range of (4) _____ are likely to impact on their lives. The lack of sanitation and health care means that (5) _____ can flourish. Many people make a living by selling what they can salvage from (6) _____.

B Do the task and then compare answers with a partner. Check the key on page 266 and think about why you made any mistakes.

Exam tip: When you complete a summary, skim the summary – ignoring the spaces – to understand the general meaning. Identify which part(s) of the passage is/are summarized (very occasionally it is the whole passage) – don't waste time re-reading what's not relevant. Look at each space, think about what part of speech the missing item is likely to be. Scan the passage to find the words you need. The language around the key word or phrase will be paraphrased, so you need to look for language that means the same as language used in the summary.

C Look at the task below and talk in pairs. How is it different from the task you have just done and what different strategies will you need to use?

Question-type tip: Some summary completion tasks involve choosing words from a list to fill spaces. There are more words in the list than there are spaces in the summary and the words in the list are not usually words from the passage.

Complete the summary using the list of words A–L below. Write the correct letter as your answer.

In the developing world, slum populations grow as people move to (1) _____. The number of slum dwellers in India is (2) _____ what it was 20 years ago. One obvious solution is the clearance of slums and the (3) _____ of superior housing. The fact that slum inhabitants have no rights over the (4) _____ they live on facilitates this option. However, clearance fails to address the real issues and the poorest people are simply moved to new places where there is less (5) _____ to their community.

A control	B buildings	C cities
D twice	E extra	F land
G transition	H structure	I construction
J shelter	K half	L villages

D Do the task and then compare answers with a partner. Check the key on page 266 and think about why you made any mistakes.

Exam tip: When there is a list of words to choose from, the summary is often of a larger part of the passage. You need to identify which part of the passage is relevant and continue to look at the list as you read again. Words in the list that you don't need are often similar in meaning to words that you need. Be careful not to choose a word quickly because you think you remember a synonym in the passage. Sometimes the words in the list are all the same part of speech and the task checks overall comprehension. Alternatively, the words in the list are different parts of speech and the task tests your grammar too. Always read the summary carefully and look at what comes before and after a space so you know what part of speech to use.

Reading 3: practise completing a summary

A Look at the picture and the title of the passage below. In pairs, make predictions about what the passage will say about the following features of these slum dwellings in Hong Kong.

| space   furniture and facilities   heat / ventilation   cleanliness |

B Read the text below and on the next page quickly and check your ideas in Exercise A.

Hong Kong's 'cage homes' reveal wealth gap

Seventy-year-old Fai Po-cheng has made the most of the tiny space he inhabits. He hangs the plastic bag of vegetables he has just bought to the bottom of his bed, next to the damp towel he has just finished with. His meagre collection of clothes is stuffed under his pillow. He sleeps in the top bunk in what is rather optimistically referred to as a 'bed space'. To say that conditions are cramped in this 18-square-foot portion of an apartment that Fai shares with 20 other men is something of an understatement.

Fai's home is one of Hong Kong's infamous 'cage dwellings' – small, dimly-lit apartments that have been subdivided into even smaller units in which there is no room for anything much apart from a bed. Here people live in cages, roughly constructed from rusty steel mesh with a sliding door at one end that allows them to crawl in and out. There are no windows; for ventilation he relies on the draught from holes between the walls and ceiling. The filthy communal kitchen has a wet, broken concrete floor.

Chinese rule was reinstated to Hong Kong well over a decade ago, but behind towering office blocks and plush shopping malls, the city's poorest residents have been abandoned by the economic boom. Some of Asia's richest individuals may be residents of this international hub, and the city boasts commercial and retail establishments that rival Paris and New York, but out of a seven million population, an estimated 1.25 million people live well below the poverty line.

Hong Kong has had a rough economic ride over the past 15 years since the end of the colonial era, and the cage dwellings are just one example of worsening deprivation. Only 35% of the 3.4 million working population pays income tax, and the top 100,000 earners contribute 60% of salary tax. The vast 50-year-old building which houses the cages was built in the 1940s to accommodate a wave of Chinese refugees fleeing the civil war on the mainland. Apartments were partitioned into smaller and smaller units to meet the demand. Around 100 cage homes remain, and are home to some of the city's poorest and most downtrodden. Apart from the astonishing lack of space, residents – frequently elderly and in many cases physically or mentally ill – must tolerate extreme temperatures and relentless filth. They share their living quarters with rats, lizards and cockroaches.

The cages are a feature of Hong Kong that more affluent city-dwellers prefer to ignore, perhaps even deny, shamed that the economic downturn has forced so many vulnerable people into such unacceptable hardship. Recent statistics suggest that a small but significant percentage of the cage-dwellers are new tenants. These people may have jobs but their salaries are low, and they are often referred to as 'the working poor'. Closer integration with China has resulted in more Hong Kong companies moving to the mainland to tap into the rapid growth and cheap labour. The city is left with fewer jobs, and workers are being forced to accept lower wages.

The absence of a minimum wage policy compounds the problem. The jobs market is shrinking, but more workers are without minimum wage protection. Stories of people working upwards of 60 hours a week for the paltry sum of 6,000 Hong Kong dollars a month are rife. With no sign of the slump ending, the future looks bleak for those at the very thinnest end of the wedge.

C Read the passage again and answer the questions.

For questions 1–6, complete the summary below. Use NO MORE THAN TWO WORDS from the text for each answer.

It is 15 years since Hong Kong came under (1) _____ and the city is home to some of Asia's richest people. However, the (2) _____ has not touched the lives of the city's poorest residents, some of whom live in desperate conditions. One example is the 50-year-old building which houses the notorious cage-dwellings. This was originally built when the war on mainland China created large numbers of (3) _____. The (4) _____ in which they were accommodated became increasingly tiny. (5) _____ members of Hong Kong's community seem reluctant to accept the existence of these dwellings, but they do not look like disappearing just yet. Research shows that (6) _____ are arriving to take up accommodation.

For questions 7–12, complete the summary using the list of words A–O below. Write the correct letter as your answer.

Hong Kong's tiny cage dwellings provide just enough space for a bed and a few (7) _____. They are hot and dirty and there is very little (8) _____. The (9) _____ kitchen is unfit for humans use. Other parts of the city may have an air of (10) _____, but more than a seventh of the population are extremely poor. Many of those who live in the cages are either old or in (11) _____. They must endure extreme temperatures, filth and the typical (12) _____ that frequent such old buildings.

A security	B poor health	C property
D poverty	E fresh air	F pests
G danger	H structures	I water
J belongings	K abandoned	L luxury
M pain	N shared	O disease

D Check the key on page 266. How many questions did you answer correctly?

E Tick the sentences about the Reading task that are true for you and think about how you can answer more questions correctly next time.

☐ 1. Did you understand the gist of each summary before you started filling spaces?
☐ 2. Did you quickly identify the parts of the passage to which each summary related?
☐ 3. Did you find it difficult to read the passage and the summary at the same time?
☐ 4. Did you check that answers fitted grammatically as well as logically?
☐ 5. Which of the summary tasks did you find easier?

Key vocabulary in context

In your notebook, add words and phrases from the passage that are used to paint a negative picture of conditions in the cage dwellings to the list below.

damp / meagre / stuffed under his pillow / cramped …

WB See *Vocabulary development* on Workbook page 237.

WB For focus on reading skills, go to Workbook page 239.

8

Writing 1: preparing to write

A In pairs, look at the pictures and answer the questions below.

1. Are the images typical of cities that you know well?
2. Do you feel that the appeal of a historic part of a city is lost if modern buildings are constructed close to old buildings?
3. Should old historic buildings ever be pulled down to create space for new buildings?

B Look at these instructions for a typical IELTS Writing task. Is it a topic you want to write about?

Write about the following topic:

In cities all over the world old, historic buildings are being destroyed and replaced with modern buildings.
Do you feel this is the right course of action?

Give reasons for your answer and include any relevant examples from your own knowledge or experience.

Write at least 250 words.

Writing 2: style and register

A Read the composition a student wrote below. Make notes about what you like and what you don't like. Then compare with a partner.

All over the world, beautiful old houses and public buildings are being destroyed to make way for ugly new buildings and I find this really shocking. Many of these new buildings are not examples of innovative architecture – they're built quickly and cheaply using basic materials. Frankly, the biggest of these constructions are complete eyesores!

If we preserve historical buildings and monuments, we pass our history on to the next generation. It's terrible that children must be surrounded by ugly modern monstrosities. They learn nothing about tradition and heritage. Destroying a building that a great architect has designed is an insult to his work too.

Money generated from tourism will be lost if too many old buildings are pulled down. Tourists don't want to look at office blocks or rows of modern apartments. If no tourists come, there'll be no money to build new buildings anyway.

Some new buildings are necessary and there are modern buildings that I really like, but they don't have to be in old, historical parts of a city and old, historical buildings don't need to be pulled down for them.

I'd say that town planners must be stupid to make decisions about knocking down beautiful old buildings. Maybe they are corrupt and take money from developers!

B A teacher has read the composition and made some comments below. In pairs, mark each comment (F) if you think it is fair and (U) if you think it is unfair.

1. The composition is difficult to follow. I don't know what you are trying to say. ___
2. You need a separate introduction. You express your opinion too early. ___
3. Quite a lot of what you say is not relevant to the question. ___
4. You haven't planned and the composition is disorganized. ___
5. The style you've adopted is sometimes not suitable for a composition like this. ___
6. You express your opinions too forcefully using informal words and expressions. ___
7. You need to write topic sentences that introduce the ideas within each paragraph. ___
8. You need to introduce some of your opinions with conventional phrases. ___
9. There are quite a few grammatical and spelling mistakes. ___
10. Contractions are not appropriate in a composition like this. ___

C Find at least one example of each fair comment in the composition.

D Read a second version of the composition. In pairs, discuss the improvements that have been made.

As towns and cities grow, there is an ever greater need for new housing, office buildings and public facilities – like cinemas and leisure centres. Unfortunately, there is not always sufficient space for these new constructions and old buildings often have to be destroyed. Many people accept that this is necessary, but many others find it deeply regrettable, especially when the building pulled down is of architectural or historical interest.

Personally, I find it sad when an interesting old building is destroyed and I think it should always be the last option. Preserving historical buildings and monuments is one way of passing our history on to the next generation. Children learn from visiting these buildings and develop an interest in and respect for the past. Perhaps when we pull down a magnificent old building, we show a lack of respect for the architect and his work.

Importantly, much tourism revolves around sightseeing and historical buildings and monuments. Visitors to cities expect to see old buildings, especially in the city centre. If too many are destroyed, the income generated by tourism may be lost. That would mean less money being available for fresh construction.

I admit that new buildings are necessary and there are certainly some fabulous examples of modern architecture in most cities. However, I am not convinced that old buildings have to be destroyed.

In conclusion, I would stress that town planners must consider very carefully before deciding that a new building is to be constructed where an old building once stood.

Writing 3: introducing opinions

A In pairs, discuss how the highlighted introductory words and phrases in the composition are used.

B Look at the alternative introductory phrases below.

1. Decide which introductory phrase in the composition could be replaced by each phrase below. Note that the phrases do not have to mean exactly the same thing.
2. Write the phrase from the composition in the space provided.

1. In my opinion   _____
2. Of course   _____
3. Sadly   _____
4. Significantly   _____
5. To sum up   _____
6. Possibly   _____
7. To my mind   _____
8. Regrettably   _____
9. All in all   _____
10. Crucially   _____
11. It goes without saying _____

Exam tip: You will need to express your opinion in Writing Task 2, but you shouldn't express it too forcefully or aggressively. Introduce opinions with conventional introductory phrases that soften them.

C Complete each sentence with your own ideas about the issue of destroying old buildings. Then compare answers with a partner.

1. Unfortunately, _____ .
2. It goes without saying that _____
   _____ .
3. To my mind, _____ .
4. Crucially, _____ .
5. Perhaps, _____ .
6. All in all, I would say _____
   _____ .

Grammar check

Remember, we use the passive when we want to focus on what *happens* rather than *who* or *what* does the action. Look at these examples of complex passive structures from the composition.

That would mean less money being available for fresh construction.
I am not convinced that old buildings have to be destroyed.
... before deciding that a new building is to be constructed.

In pairs, discuss the form of the passive in each example.

Watch out!
typical error

A new school is to build ... ✗
It means more houses been built. ✗

WB Go to Workbook page 241 for the Writing task.

Speaking

A 🎧 Look at these exchanges between an examiner and some students. Listen to the students answering the questions. What do you think about the students' answers?

1. Examiner: So, tell me about a part of your city that you like.
   Student: I don't like any part of my city. It's a horrible city.
2. Examiner: So, Paris must be a lovely to place to study. You're very lucky.
   Student: No, it's overrated. Everything's too expensive for a student like me.
3. Examiner: What do you think of that amazing new museum they've just built?
   Student: I hate it. It's a blot on the landscape.

B 🎧 Listen to the students answering the questions again. How are their answers better?

 Exam tip: When speaking – as when you're writing – you shouldn't express opinions, especially negative opinions, too forcefully or aggressively. Introduce your comment with a phrase that tells the examiner you're going to express a strong opinion or even disagree with something he or she said.

C 🎧 Look at the tapescript and listen again. Highlight expressions you want to use.

D Practise the exchanges with a partner.

Vocabulary

A In each line below, two words have a very similar meaning and one word is different. Delete the word that is different.

1. magnificent / splendid / unsightly
2. weird / imposing / peculiar
3. forbidden / permitted / banned
4. plush / substandard / inadequate
5. downturn / slump / boom
6. rusty / humid / damp

B Complete each phrase below with the correct dependent preposition.

1. be prone _____ something
2. partitioned _____ smaller units
3. have / allow access _____ somewhere
4. rely _____ something / somebody
5. be drawn _____ something
6. be eligible _____ something

C Fill each gap with a root word made from the word in brackets.

1. _____ is a common problem in the poorest towns. (literate)
2. The poorest people have always been _____. (power)
3. The figure has _____ dropped. (report)
4. It's certainly a _____ piece of architecture. (spectacle)
5. The dreadful conditions are totally _____. (accept)

Errors

A There are errors with grammar or punctuation in all of these sentences. Correct them.

1. It is not allowed to smoke in the office.
2. It is forbidden speak during the exam.
3. These windows need replaced.
4. The rooms are divided in cages.
5. The children have to be collect at 7 p.m.
6. That would mean changes been made.

Reading

Exam tip: Summary completion tasks are often applied to passages that contain a lot of factual or technical information. Some of the words you need to use will be words related to a very specific area and you won't recognize them. The task directly assesses your ability to understand those words from the context.

A Look at the title of the passage on the next page and the pictures below. In pairs, answer the questions below.

1. What do you think a wattle and daub method of building involves?
2. What were the advantages and disadvantages of the method when it was widely used?
3. What is the appeal of wattle and daub in modern times?

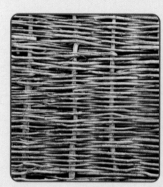 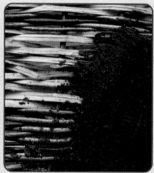  

B Use a dictionary to check the words in the box below if necessary. Then use each word to complete the topic sentences from each paragraph of the passage.

> movement   infills   damage   timber   limewash   gables   panels

1. The wonderful irregularities of wattle and daub walls and the undulations of a distorted roofline are much of the attraction of a medieval _____-framed building.
2. Wattle and daub is one of the most common _____, easily recognizable by the appearance of irregular and often bulging panels that are normally plastered and painted.
3. The strength of wattle and daub is that it is able to accommodate even the most severe structural _____.
4. Traditional infill _____ in timber-framed buildings can perform extremely well if properly constructed and maintained.
5. Where timber framing was not plastered over, it was normal practice to _____ it each spring.
6. In some cases, weatherboarding or tile hanging may have been added over the infill panels, particularly on exposed _____, to protect them from the weather.
7. Through the passage of time, buildings may become neglected and some _____ is inevitable.

C Has reading the topic sentences helped you to predict more about the style and content of the passage? Discuss in pairs.

Wattle and daub

The wonderful irregularities of wattle and daub walls and the undulations of a distorted roofline are much of the attraction of a medieval timber-framed building. The walls gain their character from the timber frame which forms the load-bearing structure of the building, leaving open areas between that need to be filled in to keep the weather out. The type of infilling varies according to the function and status of the building, its location within the country and the locally available materials. It is probably fair to assume that if a material was readily available and could be adapted for use it would have been used as an infill to a timber-framed building at sometime, somewhere.

Wattle and daub is one of the most common infills, easily recognizable by the appearance of irregular and often bulging panels that are normally plastered and painted. Wattle is the arrangement of small timbers which form a matrix to support a mud-based daub. The timbers normally fall into two groups, the primary timbers or staves, which are held fast within the frame and the secondary timbers or withies, which are nailed or tied to the staves. Arrangement and sizes of panels vary from area to area, as does the orientation of the staves. The daub was applied simultaneously from both sides, pressed into and around the wattle in order to form a regular mass. Once the daub had hardened, the surface was dampened to receive a lime plaster covering. The surface plaster was usually made of lime and sand or other aggregates reinforced with animal hair or plant fibre. The plaster was finished flush, or in some cases, it would continue across the panels and timbers alike. This would allow less important timbers to be concealed and only principal timbers to be visible.

The strength of wattle and daub is that it is able to accommodate even the most severe structural movement. It is usually well sprung into the timber frame and offers support to weakening timbers that other forms of infill may not. Wattle and daub is not lightweight or flimsy. Its weight is not dissimilar to bricks, but its insulation is better and from a security point of view it can be far more difficult to break through than brick. Although wattle and daub is porous and moisture is absorbed when it rains, moisture levels are kept low because the daub acts like blotting paper to disperse the moisture and because of the high rate of evaporation from its surface. In moderate, sheltered conditions and if maintained, a wattle and daub panel should last indefinitely. Seven hundred-year-old examples are known to exist.

Traditional infill panels in timber-framed buildings can perform extremely well if properly constructed and maintained. Although in some areas of the country it was normal for infill panels to have protective plaster coatings which extended over the timber frame, it has become fashionable to remove plaster to expose timbers. This is likely to compromise the performance of the building and accelerate the decay of the previously protected structure. It is unreasonable to expect to have a timber frame exposed on both sides and not have draughts and some water penetration.

Where timber framing was not plastered over, it was normal practice to limewash it each spring. This was partly for hygienic reasons since fresh limewash acts as a mild disinfectant, but it also had the benefit of filling minor cracks caused by seasonal movement. Medieval buildings would have looked quite different from the more recent black and white interpretation that we see so often today.

In some cases, weatherboarding or tile hanging may have been added over the infill panels, particularly on exposed gables, to protect them from the weather. Removing the protective covering can lead to the recurrence of old problems. It would be wise to learn from our ancestors' experience and consider alterations only for specific reasons, rather than on purely aesthetic grounds. Decay is often caused by the introduction of hard cement into new renders and repairs, and by the use of modern impervious paints. Cement-based renders are brittle and often crack, especially at the junction with the timber frame. When it rains, water runs down the face of the panels because both the cement and the modern paints are impervious, soaking into the wall behind wherever a crack appears. The daub will become wetter and wetter over time, leading to the decay of the timber frame and wattles, as well as soggy, unstable daub. Only soft, porous and flexible finishes such as haired lime plaster and lime wash should be applied to daub.

Through the passage of time, buildings may become neglected and some damage is inevitable. Knowing whether a damaged panel should be repaired or replaced, even with experience, requires careful consideration, weighing up many factors such as age, importance, rarity, position and function within the building, condition and cost. Although cost has deliberately been placed at the end of this list it will, in many cases, be the deciding factor. Age, importance and rarity can be difficult to define without research, but all elements of ancient fabric are important and its loss erodes our heritage.

For questions 1–10, complete the summary. Use NO MORE THAN TWO WORDS from the text for each answer.

The building method known as wattle and daub is what gives the walls of many old buildings (1) _____. A vast range of (2) _____ can be used to fill in the panels between large timbers. Wattle is a (3) _____ of small timbers, which is covered by daub. It usually consists of two sizes of timbers, the larger of which are called (4) _____ and the smaller of which are known as (5) _____. Both sides of the wattle were covered in daub, to which (6) _____ was then applied. All but the largest timbers were usually (7) _____ by the finished panels. Wattle and daub is flexible and is not affected by (8) _____. It supports older timbers. It is also strong and provides greater (9) _____ than brick. The walls of these old buildings are porous, but wattle and daub absorbs and disperses water in the same way that (10) _____ does. In the right conditions, a wattle and daub panel should last forever.

For questions 11–16, complete the summary using the list of words A–O below. Write the correct letter as your answer.

There are various strategies when it comes to maintaining and protecting wattle and daub. Exposed timbers benefit from a regular wash with lime, which both cleans and addresses any slight (11) ___. Panels higher on the building will be exposed to (12) ___ and any structures designed to prevent attack should be left in place. It is best to deal only with what is necessary and not try to improve the (13) ___ of old buildings. Using the wrong materials on panels can be disastrous. Where there are (14) ___, hard cement will crack easily, while modern paints allow (15) ___ to penetrate daub and cause decay. Over time, there will be deterioration, especially when an old building lacks (16) ___, but restoration is a process that must be treated sensitively.

A value	B holes	C heat
D condition	E treatment	F wind and rain
G sunlight	H joints	I damage
J patches	K complications	L appearance
M attention	N support	O moisture

For questions 17–20, choose the correct answer a, b, c or d.

17. The attraction of old buildings built using wattle and daub is that they ...
    a. come in all shapes and sizes.
    b. do not look perfectly regular.
    c. are clearly very strong.
    d. they have cost a lot of money to construct.

18. The secondary timbers or withies, which were part of the wattle ...
    a. were held in place by large timbers.
    b. were held in place by daub.
    c. could move around freely.
    d. were attached to slightly larger timbers.

19. Exposing larger timbers by removing panels of wattle and daub ...
    a. has never become popular.
    b. protects wood from decay.
    c. will speed up deterioration.
    d. keeps cold air out of the building.

20. Which of the following is not mentioned as a consideration when it comes to repairing wattle and daub?
    a. how long the work will take
    b. whether there are many other examples of the building
    c. what the building is used for
    d. how expensive the work will be

E **Answer the questions below in small groups.**

1. Are there old wattle and daub buildings in your country?
2. Do you think money spent restoring an old building is money well spent or should it be spent on building modern housing?
3. Would you prefer to live in an old house with character or a modern house built with the most up-to-date materials?

Review 2

Speaking and Vocabulary

A Answer these questions with a partner.

1. Do you know what kind of questions the examiner will ask you in each part of the interview?
2. Do you feel more confident about answering questions and developing a conversation?
3. Do you feel that your speaking has improved over the last few weeks?

B The questions below practise the topics that you learnt in Units 5–8. Work in pairs. One of you is A, the other is B. Ask and answer the questions with your partner.

> **Student A**
> 1. Do you feel there is a balance between work or study and leisure time in your life?
> 2. What sort of things do you look forward to?
> 3. Is it important that people travel responsibly and think about the environment?
> 4. Which country would you most like to visit? Why?
> 5. What do you do to stay in shape?
> 6. What is architecturally the most impressive town or city you have visited?

> **Student B**
> 1. What would you do with more free time if you had it?
> 2. What is the best way to deal with stress?
> 3. How do you think tourism will develop in the future?
> 4. What is the best way for older people to remain active and healthy?
> 5. Are young people in your country generally fit and healthy?
> 6. Which building in the word would you most like to go and see? Why?

C Write important words and phrases that you have learnt in Units 5–8 under each heading.

hard work / stress
_____
_____
_____
_____

free time / relaxation
_____
_____
_____
_____

travel and tourism
_____
_____
_____
_____

buildings / architecture
_____
_____
_____
_____

my words and phrases

ailments / injuries
_____
_____
_____
_____

healthy / unhealthy lifestyles
_____
_____
_____
_____

Listening and Reading

The thoughts below are from the Exam tips in the Reading and Listening Modules of Units 5–8.

A Complete each sentence about the Listening test, using one word only.

1. The _____ section of the Listening test is always related to education. There is a conversation between at least _____ people and sometimes more.

2. Typical tasks include completing sentences, notes or a short _____ of the recording or part of it.

3. The words I need to write as _____ will always be words I hear on the recording. However, what I hear will not all be the same as what is written. Language around the space I need to fill will be _____.

4. It is important that answers in gap-filling tasks fit logically and _____ and that I don't use too many words.

5. When I'm listening for specific information, the speaker will often _____ information needed to answer a question.

6. A table that accompanies a Listening task helps to predict how the talk will be _____ and divided into parts. The segments of the table signpost when the speaker is going to move to a new _____ within the talk.

7. Sometimes I will need to work out the meaning of a key word or phrase from the _____. I might have to guess the _____ of a new word if it is part of an answer.

B Complete each sentence about the Reading test, using one word only.

1. Understanding the _____ sentence, usually at the beginning of each paragraph, will help me decide what is important in a text and to locate important information. Sometimes it is not necessary to read _____ information if it does not relate to any of the questions.

2. A common task is matching _____ with paragraphs or sections of the text. This assesses both skimming and scanning skills as a _____ may relate to the overall message expressed in a whole paragraph or to one key sentence within a paragraph.

3. When a passage largely consists of the writer's _____, *yes*, *no* or *not given* tasks are often used instead of *true*, *false* or *not given* tasks. It is essential that I don't rely on my own _____ of a topic to answer question like this.

4. Worrying about the _____ of every word in a passage will slow me down. It is essential to work out new words and phrases from the context or to guess from parts of the word I already know.

5. There two types of summary task. One involves taking words from the _____, while the other involves choosing words or phrases from a _____. A summary usually relates to part of a passage and it is important to read only the _____ part again.

6. When completing a summary, I should read the whole summary quickly before trying to fill any spaces. It is a good idea to start thinking about what part of _____ will be needed for each answer.

C In pairs, answer these questions about listening and reading skills.

1. Do you feel more confident about doing tasks in the Listening and Reading tests?
2. Are there certain task types that you find easier or more difficult than others?
3. Which aspects of your listening skills have improved recently?
4. Which aspects of your listening skills do you need to work on?
5. Which aspects of your reading skills have improved recently?
6. Which aspects of your reading skills do you need to work on?
7. Do you feel that you are dealing better with words and phrases that you don't know?
8. Are you happy with the number of correct answers you are achieving in the tasks?

Writing

You will hear an interview with an IELTS examiner. She talks about marking writing tasks.

A 🎧 Look at the interviewer's first question and then listen to the first part of the interview. Mark the statements below (T) true, (F) false or (NG) not given.

'Do students tend to do better in Writing Task 1 or 2?'

1. Many students gain better marks for Task 1 than for Task 2.   ___
2. Students often don't write enough for Task 2.   ___
3. Some students find Task 2 easier than Task 1.   ___

B 🎧 Listen to the second part of the interview about Writing Task 1 and complete the notes below. Use NO MORE THAN TWO WORDS for each answer.

Task 1
important to report what is (1) _____
report writing formulaic – not (2) _____
like a driving test – very difficult without (3) _____
(4) _____ the figure before writing essential – information can be selected
only use (5) _____ structures if confident
not necessary to (6) _____ information

C 🎧 Put the points into the order in which you hear them.

'What do you look for when you mark an IELTS Writing task?'

___ organizing points
___ using the appropriate style and register
___ using the right number of words
___ planning what to say
_1_ answering the question
___ using reference words and linking devices
___ using vocabulary and grammar
___ getting plenty of practice
___ using paragraphs and topic sentences

D 🎧 Listen again as you read the tapescript.

E Give yourself a mark out of ten for how much your writing has improved since the last Review unit.

0 ——————— 5 ———————10

My writing has not
really improved at all.

My writing is much better
than it was at the beginning
of the course.

What next?

You've now completed two thirds of the course. You've practised most of the task types for each test. You should feel more confident about taking the exam, but don't worry if there are still parts that you find challenging. There is plenty of time to practise those parts and to deal with any problems you are having. Here are some things that you should do now.

☐ Continue to take every possible opportunity to speak English. You know what sort of things the examiner will ask you in the spoken exam, so practise exchanges of that nature. Concentrate on both fluency and accuracy and try to use new words, phrases and expressions you've learnt recently. Practise using grammatical structures that you have difficulty with like mixed past tenses or conditionals. Go online and find clips of students in the IELTS interview.

☐ Continue to listen to both English that you understand quite effortlessly and English that stretches you. Watch the news once each day on an international TV channel rather than in your own language, or go online to listen to news items and stories. Watch other types of TV programme and listen to radio programmes in English if possible. Watch films in English whenever you get the chance. Occasionally, stop and replay parts that you didn't understand or that you want to listen to again. There are all sorts of websites that have short clips with people speaking English. Continue to borrow CDs if you need extra practice with the Listening test of the exam.

☐ Continue to read as much as you can. You should now be able to cope with English newspaper stories and magazine articles. There are an infinite number of websites in English and you can always find something that you are especially interested in. Whatever you read, continue to look at how the text is organized and how paragraphs are introduced by topic sentences. Note down new vocabulary that you think will be useful. Think about joining a chat room where people communicate in English. This will develop both reading and writing skills. Choose something you are really interested in – a site for fans of your football team, for example – so that you forget you're trying to use another language.

☐ The texts you are reading on this course contain a lot of new vocabulary and you may feel that you want to learn and remember more than is realistic. Make sure you learn and revise vocabulary that is useful and that you'll use to talk about what interests you. As well as single words, you should learn words that you already know used in new ways. You should learn how words go together to form common phrases and expressions. When you learn a new word, make a note of its various forms. If you learn a verb, for example, check what the noun and adjective is. Make a note of any nouns that typically collocate with the verb.

☐ Practise writing reports and discursive compositions. Write whole compositions, but also concentrate on individual parts that you have difficulty with like introductions and conclusions or topic sentences. Make sure that you check and revise the spelling of any new words you are likely to use. Continue to look at as many model answers to exam questions as possible. This will further familiarize you with typical IELTS writing tasks and the typical content of a good answer.

Go on to the next section of the Course Book. Make sure you practise all aspects of your English, but focus on what you are having problems with. Don't worry if you don't make progress in all areas at the same time.

9 Words and pictures

*'The sole substitute for an experience which we have
not ourselves lived through is art and literature.'*
Alexander Solzhenitsyn

Speaking 1: books and paintings

A Look at the book covers and paintings. In pairs, discuss what you know about each one.

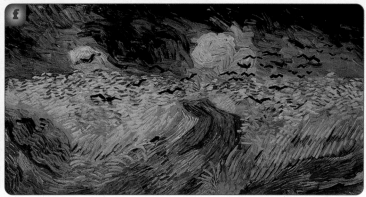
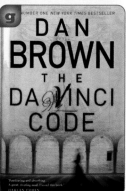

B Choose two more books and paintings that you especially like. Discuss them in your pair.

Vocabulary 1: art and literature

A Mark each word below (A) if it is related to art and (L) if it is related to literature. You
may feel that some words can relate to both.

> novel ___   landscape ___   character ___   abstract ___   surreal ___   plot ___   best-seller ___
> portrait ___   exhibition ___   fiction ___   poetry ___   chapter ___   watercolour ___
> play ___   classic ___   sketch ___   biography ___   paperback ___   masterpiece ___

B In pairs, discuss the meanings of any words from Exercise A that you are not sure of.
Decide which of the words can apply to any of the books and paintings in Speaking 1A.

C Use some of the words to talk about yourself with a partner.

> *I usually read a couple of paperbacks while I'm on holiday.*

> *I don't see the point of surreal art!*

Speaking 2: likes and dislikes

A Below are various ways of expressing likes and dislikes. Can you complete each expression with one key word?

1. I absolutely _____ …   ___
2. It's not really my _____   ___
3. I'm very _____ on …   ___
4. It doesn't _____ much for me.   ___
5. I don't know what they _____ in him.   ___
6. I've gone _____ him.   ___
7. I couldn't put it _____   ___
8. I'm a huge _____ of …   ___

B 🎧 Listen and check your answers. Then mark each expression (L) like or (D) dislike.

> **Pronunciation check**
>
> Stress and intonation are very important when expressing opinions and talking about what you like and don't like. Stressing key words and using rising intonation will make you sound enthusiastic, while a flatter intonation will help you sound less enthusiastic without sounding too negative.
> 1. 🎧 Listen again to the exchanges and focus on the speakers' pronunciation.
> 2. In pairs, look at the tapescript and practise the exchanges. Read the examiner's question and the first line of the student's response in each case.

C In pairs, answer the questions below.

1. Are you keen on biographies or accounts of historical events, or do you prefer fiction?
2. Is there an artist, writer or musician that you used to like, but have now gone off?
3. Whose work are you a huge fan of?
4. Can you say 'I couldn't put it down' about a book you have read in the last year?
5. Is there a writer, artist, poet or musician that you can say you love, adore or even worship?

D Look at some paintings painted by the following artists: René Magritte, Frida Kahlo, Andy Warhol, John Constable, Damien Hirst and Leonardo da Vinci. Work in pairs.

1. Describe them using vocabulary you've learnt in the module.
2. Express your views about them using expressions from Exercise A.

> **Grammar check**
>
> The perfect participle is formed with *having* + past participle.
> Perfect particle clauses can be used simply to sequence events in the past.
> *Having read two chapters of my book, I went to sleep.*
> They are more frequently used to express cause and reason.
> *Having written two best-sellers, Tom no longer needed to work.*
> = *Because he had written two best-sellers … / Tom had written two best-sellers so …*
>
> In the same way, they can be used to the link the past with the present.
> *Having studied art for three years, I know quite a lot about painting and drawing.*
> The perfect participle has a passive form – *having* + *been* + past participle.
> *Having only been given the homework on Friday, I didn't manage to hand it on Monday.*
>
> In spoken language, perfect participle clauses often introduce an assumption.
> *Having studied so much Shakespeare, I guess he's one of your favourites?*
>
> Complete each of these sentences logically. Then, in pairs, compare ideas.
> 1. Having worked hard on her novel for a year, Tina finally …
> 2. Having sold a painting for £100,000, James …
> 3. Having met so many famous artists, I suppose you …

> **Watch out!**
> **typical errors**
>
> Having wrote my essay, I … ✗
> Learning French at school, she can … ✗

Listening 1: preparing to listen

A The picture shows three sisters who were all writers. Their novels are considered to be masterpieces of literature. Can you answer the questions below about them?

1. What was their family name?
2. What were the names of the three sisters?
3. What were the titles of their most famous novels?
4. Do you know anything else about them?

B 🎧 Listen to the introduction of a talk and check your answers.

C What additional information did you learn from the introduction?

Listening 2: matching features

A 🎧 Look at the statements 1–8. Listen and match each statement with the correct sister A, B or C.

> A Charlotte
> B Emily
> C Anne

1. She was a pupil of her elder sister. ___
2. She understood why her older sisters had died. ___
3. There are records of early creativity. ___
4. She was close to her mother's sister. ___
5. She lost a job for not doing it well. ___
6. She was angry about the discovery of some of her writing. ___
7. Her first novel was not published. ___
8. Her first novel had less impact than the work of her sisters. ___

B In pairs, answer these questions about the task you have just done.

1. What feature of the recording was in the same order as the information on the page?
2. What was referred to in a different order from what is on the page?
3. How did the order in which points were made affect the way you did the task?

Question-type tip: Some listening and reading tasks require you to match features of a recording or text to statements on the page. The task type usually applies when the recording or text is about a number of clearly distinguishable themes – the three Brontë sisters, for example. In the task above, the speaker talked about the sisters in the order in which they appear on the page but, of course, didn't refer to the statements in the same order. Make sure you know what you have to do and read carefully while you are listening.

Listening 3: practise matching features

A 🎧 Look at the statements 1–8 about four of the Brontë sisters' novels. Then listen to a continuation of the talk and match each statement with the correct title A, B, C or D.

> A *Jane Eyre*
> B *Villette*
> C *Wuthering Heights*
> D *The Tenant of Wildfell Hall*

1. Initially, critics had differing opinions about it. ___
2. It was not reprinted even though it was very popular. ___
3. What happens at the end is not totally clear. ___
4. Good and bad conduct is a central theme. ___
5. It is an intense story, which appears not to mirror the writer's own experience. ___
6. Events are very similar to those experienced by the writer. ___
7. Its reputation as a great novel increased over time. ___
8. It shocked a lot of people. ___

B 🎧 Listen to the part of the talk about *Jane Eyre* again. Complete the sentences below. Use NO MORE THAN THREE WORDS for each answer.

9. The novel was described as an influential feminist text because it explored the strength shown by a _____.
10. Because it follows a character through her life, it can be considered a _____ novel.
11. Charlotte Brontë's _____ clearly had a great influence on the events in the story.

C Check the key on page 267. How many questions did you answer correctly?

D Tick the sentences about the Listening task that are true for you and think about how you could answer more questions correctly next time.

☐ 1. I understood the instructions for the matching task easily.
☐ 2. I needed time to read all the statements before I was ready to listen.
☐ 3. Looking at all the statements as I listened was quite challenging.
☐ 4. I am happy with how many questions I answered correctly.

E Which of the Brontë sisters' novels would you like to read? Why? Compare with other students.

F What are some other well-known rites of passage novels?

> ## Key vocabulary in context
> Find the words and phrases below in the tapescripts. Discuss the meaning of each with a partner, using the context to work it out.
>
> 1. pseudonym   2. blossomed   3. prolific   4. a household name
> 5. stern   6. inseparable   7. traumatic   8. ahead of its time
> 9. charismatic   10. ambiguous   11. thwarted   12. sheltered
>
> **WB** See *Vocabulary development* on Workbook page 242.

Reading 1: preparing to read

A In pairs, look at the famous art exhibits and answer the questions below.

1. Do you consider these exhibits to be works of art? If not, why not?
2. Is any one exhibit more a work of art than another?
3. Do you have strong opinions about any of the exhibits?

 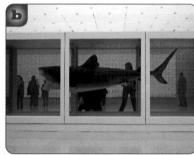 

B Read the comments on an online forum and decide which you agree with.

Responses to *What do you think of modern art?*

Dom says:
June 23, 2011 at 10:20 a.m.

The history of art can be traced back to 15,000 BCE when people painted on the walls of caves. Over centuries, the basic principles of drawing and painting remained the same. Then, suddenly, a very small number of people decided that it was ideas that mattered and not artistic ability. For the last 60 years, so-called artists have been throwing paint at a canvas, constructing pointless 'environments' or trying to persuade people that a chair they found on the beach is a piece of art!

Debbie says:
June 23, 2011 at 10:43 a.m.

I'm an art student and it saddens me that so many people hate conceptual art. What people don't understand is that conceptual art emerged because artists felt that there was nothing left to say by drawing or painting – artists had been doing it for centuries and had said everything. I know I can't paint like Michelangelo so why should I try? What modern artists CAN do is have brilliant ideas that they express in some sort of visual form.

Jill says:
June 23, 2011 at 10:57 a.m.

My problem with conceptual art is that I can't just enjoy what I'm looking at. The concept has to be explained before I can appreciate the point of it all. It seems to me that contemporary art is now about a group of pretentious wannabes explaining their pretentious concepts to a tiny elite of even more pretentious art critics, who wield far too much power.

Toby says:
June 23, 2011 at 11:24 a.m.

People have always said they don't like what they don't understand. Thank goodness there are a few people who appreciate and welcome change. Those who criticize conceptualism are just stuck in the past!

Reading 2: facts and opinions

A Decide if the following sentences from the forum express (F) fact or (O) opinion.

1. The history of art can be traced back to 15,000 BCE. ___
2. For the last 60 years, so-called artists have been throwing paint at a canvas. ___
3. It saddens me that so many people hate conceptual art. ___
4. Conceptual art emerged because artists felt that there was nothing left to say by drawing or painting. ___
5. The concept has to be explained before I can appreciate the point of it all. ___
6. People have always said they don't like what they don't understand. ___

Exam tip: When you read authentic texts in English, it's essential that you recognize what is fact and what is opinion. You need to be able to distinguish between what is a stated fact and what the writer expresses as his or her personal opinion. You need to appreciate the writer's overall viewpoint from opinions expressed. You've already seen that when a passage is largely the writer's opinion, a Y/N/NG task is often applied instead of a T/F/NG task. Matching tasks might ask you to match opinions with people mentioned in the passage.

B Match the opinions below with the names on the forum. Write the name as your answer. Highlight the part of the comment that provides the answer.

1. It became difficult for artists to express new ideas. _____
2. There are people who think they are more important than they are. _____
3. Some people have outdated ideas about art _____
4. Not all people who claim to be artists really are artists. _____

Now decide if the following statements reflect the opinions of the forum contributors. Write (Y) yes, (N) no or (NG) not given as your answer.

5. Dom thinks that a chair found on the beach is a valid piece of art. ___
6. Debbie feels that she paints badly. ___
7. Jill thinks that a very small number of art critics have too much influence. ___
8. Toby thinks that people who criticize today's art world are out of touch. ___

C Which of the opinions on the forum do you agree with? Compare in small groups.

Reading 3: practice with facts and opinions

A Skim read the passage below and on the next page and tick the sentence below that summarizes it.

☐ a. Stuckism is a movement that celebrates conceptual art and the writer agrees with their views.
☐ b. Stuckism is a movement that celebrates conceptual art, but the writer disagrees with their views.
☐ c. Stuckism is a movement that challenges conceptual art and the writer agrees with their views.
☐ d. Stuckism is a movement that challenges conceptual art, but the writer disagrees with their views.

Stuckists Advocate a Return to Common Sense

A   I have always held the belief that it is a mistake to try to define art and that phrases like *each to his own, beauty is in the eye of the beholder* and *one man's meat is another man's poison* relate perfectly to the billions of paintings and sculptures and the infinite number of other designs and artistic works that have been created over the centuries. I agree with the famous American artist, Ben Shahn, who once said that if it were left to artists to choose their own labels, most would choose none. Ultimately, each and every artist must be free to create as he or she wishes and I abhor the self-appointed judges of good taste and those who take it upon themselves to decide what is and what is not worthy.

B   However, I have to admit that when I first heard the term *Stuckism* and then read more about the Stuckist movement, I welcomed the common-sense views and found myself quickly drawn to the cause. Stuckism is an art movement that challenges the more ridiculous aspects of modern conceptual art and champions the basic skills of drawing and figurative painting. The movement was founded in 1999 by artist and musician Billy Childish and poet Charles Thomson. Apparently, the term *Stuckism* originates from an insult hurled at Childish during a conversation with his one-time partner and eminent British artist Tracey Emin. When confronting her about the artistic validity of a piece of her work, she told him that his views were outdated and that his own work was *stuck*. Since its humble beginnings, Stuckism has become an international art movement with over hundreds of members around the world.

C   The Stuckists, I should hasten to add, are not simply a bunch of judgemental reactionaries who wish to define, censor and control the art world. Their aim is to expand rather than suppress artistic licence and they look to the future as much as they look to the past. What they are in opposition to is the pervasiveness of post-modern conceptualism and the excesses which have seen the age-old skills of drawing and the basic disciplines of design and use of colour become redundant. It is this stance that I sympathize with. I am all for experimentation and pushing boundaries, but when Britain's most celebrated artistic honour – the Turner Prize – is frequently awarded to people who do not even paint, something has to be wrong. When the most celebrated works of recent years include an unmade bed strewn with daily clutter and a shark suspended in formaldehyde, it is time to ask questions.
A few years ago, not a single painter was among those considered for the £40,000 Turner Prize. The eventual winner was an artist who had filled a huge black tower with discarded computers. Another recent winner exhibited a wooden shed, which he then dismantled, rebuilt as a boat, sailed down the river Thames and rebuilt as shed at the other end of his journey! This, of course, is why it is called conceptual art – it is all about the concept. And it is this that has angered people to the point of founding a movement. As the Stuckists proclaim, 'If you do not paint, you are not an artist!'

D   I ask myself what the reaction would be if perceptions of normality and tradition in other areas were challenged so unreasonably. Would we accept that somebody walking up and down stairs in heavy boots were music? Would we be satisfied if we were served a plate of colourful plastic clothes pegs as a delicious meal in a fashionable restaurant? I think not.

E   I do not propose that it is solely artists who are responsible for any perceived lack of harmony in the art world. When the afore-mentioned shark suspended in formaldehyde, a Damien Hirst creation, can fetch £50,000, it is little wonder that aspiring Picassos throw away the paintbrush and look for new vehicles of expression. The art establishment itself must take a fair portion of the blame. The Stuckists complain that a tiny elite of collectors, critics and curators has a monopoly over what becomes known to the public and hence feels that it also have a monopoly over taste and wisdom. As I see it, this powerful minority surely has a duty to ensure that a work of art is more than simply an intellectual exercise conducted for a handful of so-called experts to pontificate over.

F   The Stuckists call for the reclamation of an artistic tradition that is centuries old and the reinstatement of beauty, spirituality and artistic skill. The ability to paint and draw is the very essence of art and it must be restored to its rightful place. I am certainly with them on this. When the vast majority of ordinary people see art as incomprehensible nonsense, there is a risk that society will lose its art. When a society loses its art, it is no longer a society.

B Read the passage again carefully and answer the questions.

The passage has six sections, A–F. Which paragraph contains the following information? Write the correct letter A–F into the space. You will not need to use all the letters.

1. a dramatic comparison   ___
2. a warning about possible consequences   ___
3. descriptions of creative ideas   ___
4. the reason for the movement's title   ___
5. criticism of people with power   ___

For questions 6–13, decide if the following statements reflect the opinions of the writer in the passage? Write:

- **(Y) YES** if the statement reflects the claims of the writer.

- **(N) NO** if the statement contradicts the claims of the writer.

- **(NG) NOT GIVEN** if it is impossible to say what the writer thinks about this.

6. Individuals should decide what they like and do not like.   ___
7. Artists generally like to be put into categories.   ___
8. It took a while to appreciate the Stuckists' views.   ___
9. The amount awarded for the Turner Prize is too generous.   ___
10. Transforming a shed into a boat is not art.   ___
11. Most people would question whether somebody walking up stairs was music.   ___
12. It is understandable that young artists opt to create conceptual works.   ___
13. Collectors, critics and curators have a healthy approach to art.   ___

C Check the key on page 267. How many questions did you answer correctly?

D Tick the sentences about the Reading task that are true for you and think about how you can answer more questions correctly next time.

- ☐ 1. I found it quite easy to identify what was fact and what was the writer's opinion.
- ☐ 2. I generally understood the point the writer was making and why he feels as he does.
- ☐ 3. I found the information I needed to answer questions quite quickly.
- ☐ 4. I am happy with how many questions I answered correctly.

E Do you agree with the Stuckists or do you think they are stuck?

Key vocabulary in context

A In pairs, discuss the exact meaning of the three idioms in the first paragraph. Do you have similar expressions in your own language?

B Discuss the meaning of the compound adjectives below. Use the context to help you. The section number is given brackets.

self-appointed (A)   *one-time* (B)   *age-old* (C)   *so-called* (E)

C Explain in your own words the verbs and adjectives from the passage below. The section number is given brackets.

1. worthy (A)   2. eminent (B)   3. humble (B)
4. censor (C)   5. suppress (C)   6. pontificate (E)

WB See *Vocabulary development* on Workbook page 242.

WB For focus on reading skills, go to Workbook page 243.

Writing 1: preparing to write

A In pairs, look at the pictures below and discuss what they show about how libraries have changed.

B In pairs, answer the questions below.

1. Do you think use of public libraries is increasing or decreasing? Why?
2. What can libraries do to be more in tune with the needs of people in the modern age?
3. Do you personally use public libraries? What for? / Why not?

C Read Extracts A–C. Do they mention any of the points you discussed in Exercises A and B?

A

Library usage is declining as students at colleges and universities switch from traditional research to Internet research. Undergraduates have become more used to retrieving information online than making a visit to a library. As each generation becomes familiar with the Internet, their desire to locate and source information as quickly and conveniently as possible has increased. A recent survey shows that 95% of undergraduate students state that finding information online is preferable to using a library. Seventy-five per cent claim that they do not have time to visit a library and that they take for granted the convenience of the Internet. While retrieving information from the Internet may be efficient and time-saving, research has shown that undergraduates are most generally sourcing only 0.3% of the entire web. Information might be more readily available and more easily retrievable, but it may not be as in depth as information from books available at a physical library.

B

The future of UK libraries appears to be somewhat gloomy as book borrowing continues to decline. In 2002, there were around 16,000 borrowers. By 2008, that figure had dropped by 20% to just over 12,000. The total number of full-time staff employed by libraries fell over the same period by 6.5%, with trained specialists most severely affected. The average number of books in stock at a typical library decreased by 12%. Over the last ten or so years, book borrowing has fallen by around a third and 40 libraries have closed across the country.

C

As libraries attempt to adapt to modern requirements, many have abandoned the bureaucracy surrounding membership, no longer asking for identification before lending books. Almost all now have computers with Internet access and many have introduced Wi-Fi. Interiors have been refurbished and modernized with well-known franchises being invited to set up coffee shops while opening hours have been extended to better suit changing work and study schedules. In several towns, the changes have led to a dramatic increase in visitor numbers with more books being borrowed.

D Close your books and, in pairs, compare the information you read.

E In pairs, describe a library in the town or city you live in. Is it a new building or has it been modernized recently?

Writing 2: describing change

A Look at the two plans. In pairs, discuss how the library has changed.

Poolsville Library 2005

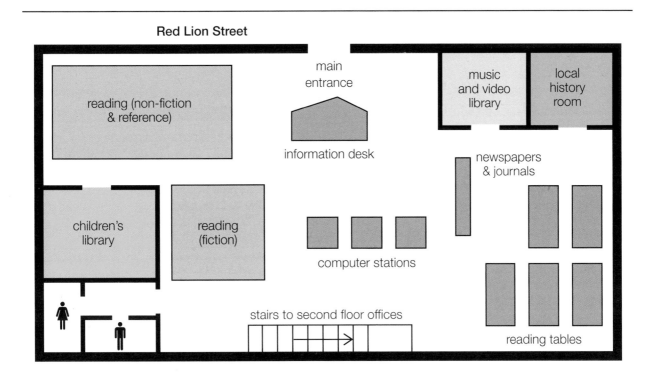

Poolsville Library today

Red Lion Street

main
entrance

DVD library

computer centre
(internet & WiFi access)

coffee
shop

reading (non-fiction
& reference)

information desk

reading
(fiction)

children's
library

newspapers & journals

stairs to second floor offices

reading tables
(with WiFi access)

B In pairs, look at the instructions for a typical IELTS Writing task below and then answer questions 1–3.

> *The diagrams show a public library now and the plans for changes to the library that will be completed by the end of next year.*
>
> *Summarize the information by selecting and reporting the main features, and make comparisons where relevant.*
>
> Write at least 150 words.

1. How are the tenses you need to use for the Writing task different from the tenses you needed in Exercise A?
2. Which planned changes do you want to include in your report?
3. How do you feel about writing a report like this compared with those you have practised previously?

Exam tip: When you are presented with a task like this, look carefully at the dates at the top of the diagram. If changes have already been made, you will need to use mainly the present perfect. If changes are planned in the future, you will need to use a range of future forms, including the future perfect. Vary the future forms you use – a report written using only active forms and *going to*, for example, will be dull and will not show what you are capable of.

C Complete the report on the next page by putting the verb in brackets into the correct form. In some cases there is more than one option.

The diagrams show that by next year, some radical changes (1) _____ (make) to Poolsville library.

There are plans (2) _____ (add) a whole new computer centre, part of which will be a coffee shop. This will mean (3) _____ (dispense) with the local history room and music and video library. A DVD library will be available in the computer room.

The children's library (4) _____ (expand), meaning that the cloakrooms (5) _____ (have to) be moved to the other side of the floor. There will be fewer reading tables, but Wi-Fi access will be available in that area.

(6) _____ (make) room for the new computer centre and the expansion of the non-fiction reading area, the information centre (7) _____ (move) to the centre of the floor. The newspapers and journals section (8) _____ (be) in the area where the old computer stations were.

D Check the completed model report on page 267 at the back of the Course Book.

Grammar check

The future perfect is used to look back at an event that has not yet taken place, from a fixed point in the future.
By the end of next year, the library will have undergone some major changes.

This can be expressed using the passive.
By the end of next year, some major changes will have been made to …

Note that other modal verbs can be used instead of will to form very similar perfect structures.
By then, we should have finished … / By 2050, we may have found …

In written language, an infinitive of purpose can be used at the beginning of a sentence, especially when it refers back to something that has previously been mentioned.
To make room for the new computer centre and the expansion of the non-fiction reading area, the information centre will be moved …

Watch out!
typical errors

By the end of the week, I'll finish my … ✗

By 2020, a cure will be found. ✗

For create space for the new centre, the old local history room will … ✗

E Look at the Exam Practice Module on page 147 for the Writing task.

Speaking

A Put the jumbled expressions below into the correct order.

1. it I adore absolutely.
2. see know I what don't it they in.
3. really not thing It's my.
4. off I've it gone.
5. very I'm on it keen.
6. put I it couldn't down.
7. doesn't much do me It for.
8. fan a his huge of I'm.

B Here are two typical task cards for Part 2 of the Speaking test. Work with a partner – one of you is A, the other is B. Think about the topic for a minute and make notes.

A

Talk about a writer that you especially like.
Say ...
• who the writer is.
• why you especially like him/her.
• which of his or her books you enjoyed most.
• how reading his or her books makes you feel.

B

Talk about an artist whose work you especially like.
Say ...
• who the artist is.
• why you especially like him/her.
• which piece of work you especially admire.
• what you feel when you look at his/her work.

C Take turns to speak about what's on your card for about two minutes.

Vocabulary

A Match adjectives in Box A with nouns in Box B to make common collocations.

A vivid traumatic household social self-appointed humble

B name beginnings experience imagination conventions judge

B Complete each sentence with a root word made from the word in brackets.

1. Her first novel may not be a classic, but it's a _____ piece of writing. (note)
2. She escaped a life of _____ and abuse. (cruel)
3. In the 19th century, his work was very _____. (influence)
4. When they were children, they spent their lives in an _____ world. (imagine)
5. She was furious that her _____ had been invaded. (private)
6. She was angry when he challenged the _____ of her work. (valid)

C Correct the spelling mistakes in each of the *difficult to spell* words below.

1. exibition
2. carismatic
3. seudonim
4. inseperable
5. eminant
6. beurocracy
7. surpress
8. critisism

Errors

A There are errors with grammar or punctuation in all of these sentences. Correct them.

1. Having took all my exams, I went on holiday.
2. Working a ten-hour day, I finally crawled into bed.
3. By 2025, books will become extinct.
4. By the time I'm old, they should had found a cure.
5. For improve my English, I read every night.
6. Studying in Madrid will mean move away from home.

Writing

A Work in pairs. Match the art galleries 1–8 with the cities a–h. See which pair has the most correct answers.

1. Le Louvre
2. El Prado
3. The National Gallery
4. The Metropolitan Museum of Art
5. The State Hermitage Museum
6. Galleria degli Uffizi
7. The Rijksmuseum
8. Musei Vaticani

a. Florence
b. St Petersburg
c. Amsterdam
d. Paris
e. Rome
f. New York
g. Madrid
h. London

B Which of the galleries would you most like to visit? Why? Compare thoughts with a partner.

C Do you think art galleries have had to adapt to changes in the same way that libraries have had to? Why? / Why not?

D Look at the instructions for the Writing task below. Choose five or six points that you want to make about the information shown and make notes. Then compare with a partner.

> *The diagrams show a small art gallery now and plans for changes that will be made to the gallery over the next three years.*
>
> *Summarize the information by selecting and reporting the main features, and make comparisons where relevant.*
>
> Write at least 150 words.

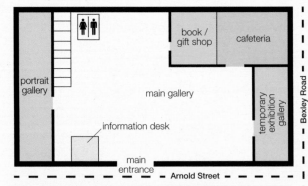

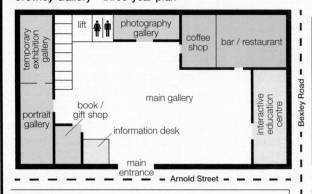

 Exam tip: To write this type of report well, you need to use range of verbs that typically express change. Note the following verbs from the Writing and Exam Practice Modules.
add / dispense with / expand / install / locate / move / relocate / transform

E Read the model report from the Writing Module and the Exam tip again. Then write your report. Check the model on page 268.

10 Rain or shine

'Weather is a great metaphor for life - sometimes it's good, sometimes it's bad, and there's nothing much you can do about it but carry an umbrella.'

Terri Guillemets

Vocabulary 1: the weather

A Check that you know the highlighted words and phrases in the sentences below. Then tick the sentences that describe the weather in your country.

☐ 1. During the rainy season, there can be torrential rain. It's common for villages to experience floods.

☐ 2. The weather can be very changeable, especially in spring – warm and sunny in the morning and then heavy showers all afternoon. That's when you might see a rainbow, and occasionally, there's hail.

☐ 3. Winters are mild rather than extreme. It's chilly in winter, but rarely very cold. We occasionally get sleet, but I've only seen proper snow when I've been abroad.

☐ 4. Last year, we had a heatwave in August. Temperatures hit 40 degrees most days.

☐ 5. I love wintry mornings when there's a clear blue sky and frost covering the ground.

☐ 6. The narrow streets of the old town are very atmospheric when there's a thick fog.

☐ 7. I get fed up when the sky's overcast for weeks and there's drizzle in the air half the time.

☐ 8. The summer heat can be too much for me. It's very muggy at night with no breeze at all.

☐ 9. Most people enjoy seeing a blanket of snow, but it's a bit depressing when it warms up and the snow all turns to yellow slush.

☐ 10. There are often violent storms with thunder and flashes of lightning.

☐ 11. I've never experienced a hurricane, but I've seen strong gales blow tiles off the roof.

☐ 12. A cloudless sky and the sun beating down. That's my idea of heaven!

Pronunciation check

Words like *lightning* are difficult for most students to pronounce properly. Native speakers produce a sound in the top of the nose, which does not appear on a typical phonetic chart.

🎧 Listen to these words that contain the sound. Then practise saying them.

1. lightning   2. frightening   3. frightened   4. certainly   5. important

---

B In pairs, compare your answers in Exercise A. Explain why you have ticked any sentences.

Exam tip: In the Speaking test, Part 1, when the examiner asks about everyday topics, you will sound more natural if you use informal, even slightly colourful, vocabulary. For example, you can say *it's a bit chilly* rather than *it's quite cold*.

C Adjectives are often formed by adding *y* to a noun. Many of these adjectives are quite informal. In pairs, discuss the meaning of the phrases in the box.

> wintry showers
> a stormy night
> icy conditions
> patchy cloud
> a summery dress

Speaking 1: talking about the weather

A 🎧 Listen to some interview exchanges. Make notes about what each student says.

B Compare your notes with a partner. Which new words or phrases do you want to learn?

C 🎧 Listen again and complete the sentences.

1. We can depend on the weather … and this allows us _____ an outdoor lifestyle.
2. The frequent bad weather stops people _____ a lot of outdoor activities.
3. It discourages them _____ to meet friends for a picnic or barbecue.

Grammar check

Effect (or causative) verbs link ideas. They are used to say what causes something to happen or not to happen. Effect verbs that tell us what makes something happen are followed by an object and an infinitive.
The warm weather allows us to enjoy an outdoor lifestyle. / The storm forced me to turn back.
Remember that the common verbs *make* and *let* are followed by a bare infinitive (an infinitive without *to*).
My parents made me do my homework. / They didn't let me watch TV all evening.
Help can be followed by either a full or bare infinitive.
The Internet has helped me (to) learn English.

Effect verbs that tell us what makes something not happen are followed by an object and an ~*ing* verb. The preposition *from* is sometimes necessary.
It discourages people from arranging to meet friends. / The rain stopped us enjoying the picnic.

Complete each sentence with the correct form of the verb in brackets and *from* if necessary.

1. Working part-time enables me _____ (enjoy) the summer months.
2. The severe weather prevented us _____ (take) the ferry.
3. Staying with Dave and Emma saved us _____ (have to) book a hotel.
4. The hurricane forced Liz _____ (cancel) her holiday.

Watch out!
typical errors

They encouraged me doing well. ✗

It saved me to get sunburnt. ✗

Speaking 2: discussing climate issues

⏳ **Exam tip:** Remember that in the Speaking test, Part 3, the examiner will develop a topic from earlier parts of the interview and talk about a more serious matter.

A In pairs, discuss some extreme weather events that have been in the news recently. Check that you know the words in the box.

hurricane	tornado	
typhoon	flood	avalanche
mudslide	drought	

B Look at the questions and think about points you want to make. Then, in pairs, ask and answer the questions below.

1. So, do you think the climate of your country is changing?
2. Is global warming a real threat or has it been exaggerated?
3. Are extreme weather events purely natural or does man have some influence?

C 🎧 Listen and match each student with a question in Exercise B.

Student A ___   Student B ___   Student C ___

D 🎧 Listen again as you read the tapescript. Notice that you do not need to be an expert to give a good extended answer.

Vocabulary 2: metaphors

A We often use the weather as a metaphor for people's feelings or how they behave. In pairs, discuss what you think the phrases below mean.

1. I'm feeling a bit under the weather.
2. They've had a stormy relationship.
3. I was given a very warm welcome.
4. He was given a frosty reception.

B Do you have a similar area of metaphor in your own language? Do you have the expressions in Exercise A in your own language? Compare in groups of three.

Listening 1: preparing to listen

A Check that you understand the words and phrases in the box. Then, in pairs, explain the connection between the two pictures below.

> rainforest   deforestation   logging   soil   erosion   mudslide

B 🎧 Listen to the first part of a lecture about how deforestation can cause mudslides. Check your ideas in Exercise A.

C 🎧 Listen again and note down some of the other effects of deforestation that were mentioned.

Listening 2: listening to complete a flow chart

A 🎧 Listen to the next part of the lecture and complete the first part of a flow chart.

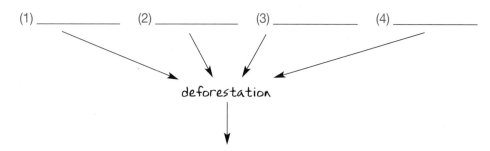

(1) _____   (2) _____   (3) _____   (4) _____

deforestation

B Talk in pairs. What have you previously learnt about completing a flow chart?

🖐 **Question-type tip:** A flow chart shows a series of events or actions and their possible results. In the Listening test, you will sometimes need to complete information shown on a flow chart. Having a chart like this helps you because you can predict how the talk will be organized and divided into parts. You know when the speaker is going to move on from one point to the next.

Listening 3: practise listening to complete a flow chart

A 🎧 Listen to the rest of the lecture and complete the flow chart below.

deforestation

Without tree (1) _____ soil cannot be held to the (2) _____.

No (3) _____ (leaves/branches) means water runoff cannot be stored.

The (4) _____ is carried away – the foundation is weaker.

An area of land breaks away and slides downwards.

A small landslide can destroy (5) _____ homes or small villages.

A landslide which begins higher on the hillside picks up soil and (6) _____.

At the bottom of the slope, (7) _____ can be buried in mud.

B Check the key on page 267. How many questions did you answer correctly?

C Tick the sentences about the Listening task that are true for you and think about how you can answer more questions correctly next time.

☐ 1. Looking at the flow chart helped me make predictions about what I would hear.
☐ 2. Looking at the flow chart as I listened helped me follow what the speaker said.
☐ 3. I could guess how to spell words and phrases specific to the topic.

D Can you remember why the following items were mentioned during the lecture?

| Panama   Venezuela   cars   the Philippines |

Key vocabulary in context

A Match words 1–4 with words a–d to form common compound nouns.

1. indigenous   a. metals
2. natural   b. tribes
3. precious   c. matter
4. solid   d. habitat

B Match verbs 1–6 with their definitions a–f.

1. deprive … of   a. go faster
2. weaken   b. collect
3. destabilize   c. make less secure
4. accelerate   d. disappear
5. gather   e. make less strong
6. vanish   f. take from

C 🎧 Listen and mark the main stress on the words from the lecture. Then, in pairs, practise saying them.

1. indigenous   2. precious   3. accelerate   4. catastrophe   5. catastrophic

WB▶ See *Vocabulary development* on Workbook page 246.

10

Reading 1: recognizing references

A Look only at the title of the passage below and the figure. In pairs, discuss what you think an *urban heat island* is.

B Match the adjectives 1–5 with their opposites a–e. Do you now have a better idea of what an *urban heat island* is?

1. urban
2. shaded
3. permeable
4. surface
5. moist

a. exposed
b. atmospheric
c. dry
d. impermeable
e. rural

C Read the first part of the passage and check your ideas. Don't worry about the highlighted words and phrases for now.

Urban Heat Islands

As urban areas develop, changes occur within their landscape. Buildings, roads, and other features of infrastructure replace open land and vegetation. Surfaces that were once permeable and moist become impermeable and dry. These changes cause urban regions to become warmer than their rural surroundings, forming an 'island' of higher temperatures within the landscape.

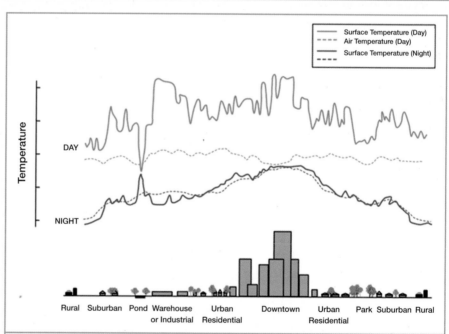

Surface and atmospheric temperatures vary over different land use areas. Surface temperatures vary more than air temperatures during the day, but are fairly similar at night. The dip and peak in surface temperatures over the pond show how water maintains a fairly constant temperature day and night, due to its high heat capacity.

Heat islands occur on the surface and in the atmosphere. On a hot, sunny summer day, the sun can heat dry, exposed urban surfaces, such as roofs and pavements, to temperatures up to 50°C hotter than the air, while shaded or moist surfaces, often within more rural surroundings, remain close to air temperatures. Surface urban heat islands are present day and night, but tend to be strongest during the day when the sun is shining.

In contrast, atmospheric urban heat islands are often weak during the late morning and throughout the day and become more pronounced after sunset due to the slow release of heat from urban infrastructure. The annual average air temperature of a city with a population of 1 million or more can be 1–3°C warmer than its surroundings. On a clear, calm night, however, the temperature difference can be as much as 12°C.

The heat island sketch shows how urban temperatures are typically lower at the urban–rural border than in dense downtown areas. The graphic also illustrates how parks, open land, and bodies of water, such as lakes, ponds and reservoirs, can create cooler areas within a city.

D In pairs, discuss how the highlighted words and phrases in the passage refer back to something previously mentioned or ahead to something not yet mentioned.

 Exam tip: When you read, it is important to understand how words and phrases refer back to something previously mentioned or ahead to something not yet mentioned in a passage. These might be pronouns or possessive adjectives, or general referencing nouns that avoid repetition or prepare you for examples.

E Close your books. In pairs, discuss what urban heat islands are in your own words.

Reading 2: practise recognizing references

A In pairs, answer the questions below.

1. What do you think some of the effects of urban heat islands are?
2. What measures do you think could be taken to address the issue of urban heat islands?

B Skim read the rest of the passage below and on the next page and check your answers in Exercise A.

C Read the passage again and put the reference devices in the box below into the correct space. Use capital letters when necessary.

health issues	it	its	they (x 2)	them	their (x 2)	ones	most
properties	materials	vegetation	this drawback	approach	term
those	these finance-related considerations

Effects of Heat Islands

Higher temperatures resulting from urban heat islands, particularly during the summer, can affect a community's environment and quality of life. While some impacts may seem positive, such as lengthening the plant-growing season, (1) _____ are negative and include:

- **Increased energy consumption:** Higher temperatures in summer increase energy demand for cooling and add pressure to the electricity grid during peak periods. One study estimates that the heat island effect is responsible for 5–10% of peak electricity demand for cooling buildings in cities.

- **Elevated emissions of air pollutants and greenhouse gases:** Increasing energy demand generally results in greater emissions of air pollutants and greenhouse gases from power plants. Higher air temperatures also promote the formation of ground-level ozone.

- **Compromised human health and comfort:** Warmer days and nights, along with higher air pollution levels, can contribute to general discomfort along with (2) _____, such as respiratory difficulties, exhaustion, heat stroke and heat-related mortality.

- **Impaired water quality:** Hot pavement and rooftop surfaces transfer their excess heat to storm water, which then drains into storm sewers and raises water temperatures as (3) _____ is released into rivers, streams, ponds and lakes. Rapid temperature changes can be stressful to aquatic ecosystems.

Reducing the Effects of Heat Islands

Trees and plants help cool the environment and utilizing (4) _____ is a simple and effective way of reducing urban heat islands. (5) _____ lowers surface and air temperatures by providing shade and through evapotranspiration. Shaded surfaces are likely to be between 11–25°C cooler than the peak temperatures of unshaded materials. Evapotranspiration, alone or in combination with shading, can help reduce peak summer temperatures by up to 5°C. This (6) _____ is especially beneficial when vegetation is planted in strategic positions around buildings or to shade pavements and parking lots. Researchers have found that planting deciduous trees or vines noticeably cools a building, especially if (7) _____ shade windows and part of the roof.

Although trees and plants are expensive initially and then to maintain, (8) _____ benefits outweigh the cost incurred. Vegetation that directly shades buildings decreases demand for air conditioning, improves air quality and lowers greenhouse gas emissions. By reducing energy demand, trees and plants decrease the production of associated air pollution and greenhouse gas emissions. They also remove air pollutants and store carbon dioxide. A sufficient quantity of vegetation reduces rainwater runoff and improves water quality by absorbing and filtering it. Apart from (9) _____, trees and plants have aesthetic value, can reduce noise and provide a habitat for wildlife.

A green roof or rooftop garden is a vegetative layer grown on a rooftop. Green roofs provide shade and remove heat from the air through evapotranspiration, reducing temperatures of the roof surface and the surrounding air. On hot summer days, the surface temperature of a green roof can be cooler than the air temperature, whereas the surface of a conventional rooftop can be up to 50°C warmer.

Green roofs can be installed on large industrial and business constructions to small private residences. (10) _____ can be as simple as a 6cm covering of grass or as complex as a fully accessible park complete with trees. Rooftop gardens are becoming popular in various large cities, where the costs and benefits are much the same as (11) _____ offered by ground-level vegetation. The reduction of heat transfer down through the building's roof is even more noticeable, however, hugely improving indoor comfort and lowering heat stress associated with extreme weather.

In 2006, a study compared the costs of conventional roofs with the cost of a 1,950 m² green roof and all its benefits. The green roof cost $464,000 to install, compared to $335,000 for the conventional roof. However, over (12) _____ lifetime, the green roof was estimated to save about $200,000 from reduced energy costs.

A cool roof relies on solar reflectance, the ability to reflect sunlight and heat away from a building, and high thermal emittance, the ability to both absorb and radiate the sun's heat, to reduce surface temperatures. Together, these (13) _____ help cool roofs to absorb less heat and remain up to 28–33°C cooler than conventional roofs during peak summer weather.

Cool roofing products have been widely used for more than 20 years on commercial, industrial and residential buildings and may be installed on low-sloped or steep-sloped roofs. Cool roofs bring many of the financial and ecological benefits of previously described solutions, but may deflect some desired heat gain during the winter. Despite (14) _____, however, cool roofs result in net energy savings, especially in areas where electricity prices are high.

A cool pavement includes a range of established and emerging technologies that communities are exploring as part of (15) _____ heat island reduction efforts. The (16) _____ refers to paving surfaces that reflect more solar energy, enhance water evaporation or have been otherwise modified to remain cooler than conventional pavements. Conventional paving surfaces can reach peak temperatures of 50–65°C, transferring excess heat to the air above and heating storm water as it runs off into local waterways.

Cool pavements can be constructed with existing paving (17) _____, like asphalt and concrete, as well as newer (18) _____, such as the use of coatings or grass paving. Cool pavement technologies are not as advanced as other heat island reduction strategies, but it is known that permeable surfaces allow storm water to soak in, reducing runoff and filtering pollutants. Both permeable and non-permeable cool pavements can help lower the temperature of runoff, resulting in less thermal shock to aquatic life in rivers and ponds. There is the added bonus of lower tyre noise and improved night-time visibility for motorists.

D Read the whole passage again and answer the questions.

For questions 1–5, complete the notes. Use NO MORE THAN THREE WORDS for each answer.

Positive effects of heat islands

(1) _____ may last longer

Negative effects of heat islands

(2) _____ buildings consumes more energy
(3) _____ emit pollutants / harmful gases
(4) _____ / health issues due to rising temperatures / air pollution
water quality reduced – warm (5) _____ raises temperature of rivers, etc.

For questions 6–12, look at the ideas A–D. Match each question with the correct feature A, B, C or D.

6. can protect wildlife from warm runoff
7. will have an apparent disadvantage in cold weather
8. may be less than half as hot as a conventional alternative
9. help some people to see better
10. can be costly to look after
11. can vary hugely in terms of sophistication
12. should be carefully located

A trees and plants at ground level
B green roofs / roof gardens
C cool roofs
D cool pavements

E Check the key on page 267. How many questions did you answer correctly?

F Tick the sentences about the Reading task that are true for you and think about how you can answer more questions correctly next time.

☐ 1. I could quickly see what reference words and phrases referred to.
☐ 2. Understanding reference devices helped me read the passage and to answer some questions.
☐ 3. I was happy with the number of questions I answered correctly.

Key vocabulary in context

A In pairs, discuss the meaning of these commonly used verbs from the passage.

1. lengthen 2. utilize 3. maintain 4. outweigh
5. absorb 6. filter 7. deflect 8. soak in

B Now discuss the meaning of these adjectives from the passage.

1. dense 2. strategic 3. aesthetic 4. emerging

WB See *Vocabulary development* on Workbook page 246.

WB For focus on reading skills, go to Workbook page 247.

Writing 1: preparing to write

A Look at the pictures and talk in pairs. Which of the 'natural' disasters below do you consider to be completely natural and which does man have some responsibility for?

B Read the extract below and decide if it agrees with what you discussed in Exercise A.

Some scientists are suggesting that man is moving into a whole new geological era – one that he has created himself, especially in terms of the environment. This age is being referred to as the *anthropocene*. The bottom line is that heat that would once have been radiated back into space is now trapped in our atmosphere. That energy has a range of effects – seas warm up and ice melts. The last few years have been the warmest on record and scientists and insurance companies alike are blaming global warming for a spate of recent catastrophes. Droughts, heatwaves and mega-floods felt across the planet, they claim, are undeniably linked to rising temperatures and referring to many of these disasters as 'natural' is no longer accurate.

Writing 2: having enough to say

A Look carefully at the instructions for a typical IELTS Writing task and then, in pairs, answer the questions on the next page.

Write about the following topic:

We are moving into an age in which many so-called natural disasters can at least be partly attributed to man.

To what extent do you agree with this claim?

Give reasons for your answer and include any relevant examples from your own knowledge or experience.

Write at least 250 words.

1. What is the minimum number of words you can write for this task?
2. Do you feel that you have enough to say?
3. Will you need to write a long introduction and conclusion in order to achieve the word limit?
4. Are you confident that you can write this composition well?

B In pairs, brainstorm points you could make that agree and disagree with the claim.

> Mudslides often occur as a direct result of deforestation.

> Huge disasters like earthquakes are not related to global warming in any way.

C Work in groups of five.
1. Each of you should read one of the newspaper reports below.
2. Check that you understand the report and look up any key words or phrases you don't know.
3. Exchange information with the other students in your group.

A week after the earthquake in El Salvador, worsening weather conditions are posing a fresh threat. Heavy rains may cause mudslides on hillsides loosened by the quake. Approximately 750,000 people have already been left homeless by the disaster, which saw over 1,000 people buried under a huge landslide. Now there is anger that man-made problems have aggravated the impact of the quake. Intensive farming and deforestation of the region's steep hillsides makes land unstable. Dense concentrations of people and poor construction methods mean the casualty toll is far higher than in less populated areas. Rescue workers claim that the huge landslide in El Salvador was due to the mountain overlooking Las Colinas being cut away by developers, despite protests. Some describe the event as 'a disaster waiting to happen'.

Research verifies that the arid landscape in the West of the United States is largely a direct result of man's interference. The study focused on what has happened since 1950 in the states of Colorado, Nevada and California. Computer simulations prove that changes are not simply down to a natural dry cycle, but can rather be blamed on human activity. The region is looking at severe water shortages in the very near future. The snow pack in the West has decreased steadily over the last 60 years and that is where the large urban areas, like Los Angeles and Las Vegas, get their fresh water from. Due to an increase in greenhouse gases, temperatures have risen and the snow melts earlier in the spring. Water levels in the summer have decreased severely and in the worst cases, rivers are running dry.

Environmentalists claim that the flash floods in West Papua that have claimed over 100 lives, were caused by damage in upstream areas, where the forests have been cleared for mining and plantation purposes. Illegal logging is at an all-time high and there are fresh calls for the government to reassess its policies on the exploitation of natural resources.

Sandstorms drifting from the Sahara Desert are ten times more likely than they were 50 years ago and they are now a threat to the global climate. The cause is what is being referred to as 'Toyota-ization' – the increasing number of four-wheel drive vehicles speeding over the sand dunes. These modern vehicles have replaced camels, and drivers hurtle around disturbing the surface sand.

An avalanche that killed two people and injured 30 more at a snowmobile rally may have been triggered by daredevil toboggan riders who apparently loosened a deadly wall of snow that fell on 200 people

below. It is believed the slide was triggered by high-marking, a stunt to see who can race up a slope and leave the highest mark. Those responsible have not yet been identified and may be among the injured.

D In your group, discuss which information from the reports you could use in your composition.

Writing 3: making sure you write enough

A Read a student's composition below and on the next page. What is the problem?

Not long ago, when people talked about natural disasters, they assumed that they really were all natural – 'acts of God' some might say. As the human race has developed and as we understand more about the consequences of our actions, we realize that some of these events are in fact caused by what we do to the planet.

Huge floods are often caused by deforestation. When whole forests of trees are cut down, there is nothing to hold the rainwater. Mudslides are another result of destroying the *rainforests. Droughts are increasing and becoming common in places where once they were unknown. Even disasters that are not actually caused by our interference with nature can have more serious consequences because of the way we live. Earthquakes hit hardest in areas where land has been destabilized. Hurricanes and tornadoes seem to affect the poorest people since they live in the least stable housing.*

Of course, not all disasters can be blamed directly on man, but I agree that we are moving into an age when more can be.

B In pairs, discuss:

1. where the writer could explain something in more depth or give examples.
2. where the writer could give an example from his own experience? (He is from Libya.)
3. how the writer could expand the final paragraph into a more appropriate conclusion.

C Read another version of the composition below and decide how each sentence could be expanded. Then check your ideas against the model on pages 267 and 268.

Not long ago, when people talked about natural disasters, they assumed that they really were all natural – 'acts of God' some might say. As the human race has developed and as we understand more about the consequences of our actions, we realize that some of these events are in fact caused by what we do to the planet.

The huge floods that we have seen recently in many parts of the world are often caused by deforestation. When whole forests of trees are cut down, there is nothing to hold the rainwater and _____, which _____. Mudslides are another result of destroying the rainforests. Areas of deforested land _____. Droughts are increasing and becoming common in places where once they were unknown. We produce _____, which we release into the atmosphere, _____. In my country, sandstorms _____. People drive too fast _____.

Even disasters that are not actually caused by our interference with nature can have more serious consequences because of the way we live. Earthquakes hit hardest in areas where land has been destabilized _____. Hurricanes and tornadoes seem to affect the poorest people since they live in the least stable housing.

Of course, not all disasters can be blamed directly on man. There have _____. However, I agree that we are moving into an age when man is at least partly to blame for more of these events.

 Exam tip: If your composition is too short, you may not need to make a whole new point. You will usually be able expand explanations and add examples that support a point you have already made. Always think about how you can add an example that is specific to your own life or where you live.

WB Go to Workbook page 250 for the Writing task.

Speaking

A In pairs, answer the questions using information that you have learnt in the unit.

1. How do you feel about the destruction of the world's rainforests?
2. What measures are being taken in urban areas to reduce urban heat islands?
3. Do you think humans are responsible for more of the planet's so-called natural disasters?
4. Why are the world's poorest people most directly affected by climate change?
5. What concerns you most about changes in weather patterns?

B In pairs, talk about an occasion when you experienced:

1. extremely hot weather.
2. extremely cold weather.
3. a violent storm.
4. weather conditions that made it difficult to drive.
5. weather conditions that made you change your plans for the day.

Vocabulary

A In pairs, answer the questions below. Write the answers in your notebook to check your spelling.

1. What do we call *very light rain*?
2. What might you see in the sky when it is sunny, but there has been rain?
3. What does snow turn to when the temperature rises?
4. Do you know three different words for winds of varying strength?
5. What might cover the ground on a wintry morning? (Not snow or ice!)
6. What do we call *light frozen rain*? What if it falls in larger stones?
7. Which informal word means *quite cold*?
8. What do we call *a long, unexpected period of very hot weather*?
9. Which informal word means *humid and airless*?
10. How many extreme weather events can you list?

B Match words from Box A with words from Box B to form common two-part phrases.

A

B

Errors

A There are errors with grammar or punctuation in all of these sentences. Correct them.

1. The rain stopped people to enjoy themselves.
2. The heat discouraged people leaving their homes.
3. The news forced us changing our plans.
4. The warm weather allows us spend time outside.
5. My dad made me to wear my raincoat.
6. The system's benefits outweigh it's drawbacks.

Listening

A In pairs, look at the pictures and answer the questions below.

1. What is the possible risk shown in the first picture?
2. What has been done to avert that risk in the second picture?

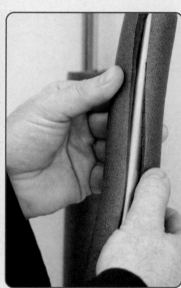

B You will hear a talk about water pipes freezing. In pairs, discuss why the items in the box below will be mentioned.

> a television cable   a can of soda
> foam   rubber / fibreglass
> a dripping tap

C 🎧 Listen to the talk and answer the questions.

For questions 1–4, complete the notes. Use NO MORE THAN TWO WORDS for each answer.

> Houses in north
> water pipes within (1) _____ – protected from freezing temperatures
>
> Houses in south
> at risk during (2) _____ in winter – (3) _____ less aware of risk
> water pipes in unprotected parts of house / exterior (4) _____

For questions 5–7, complete the sentences. Use NO MORE THAN THREE WORDS for each answer.

5. When people are warm indoors, they underestimate outside _____.
6. Homes that are temporarily _____ are more at risk.
7. A can or bottle of liquid forgotten _____ will explode.

For questions 8–11, complete the flow chart.

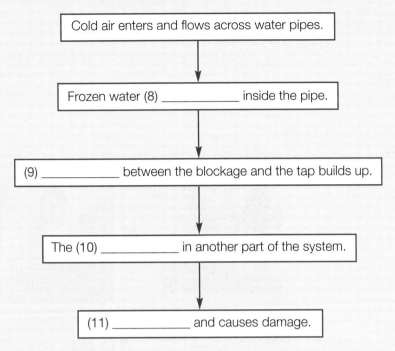

Cold air enters and flows across water pipes.

↓

Frozen water (8) _____ inside the pipe.

↓

(9) _____ between the blockage and the tap builds up.

↓

The (10) _____ in another part of the system.

↓

(11) _____ and causes damage.

For questions 12–15, choose the correct letter a, b or c.

12. In modern houses, water pipes are …
    a. placed in lofts, attics and basements.
    b. not placed in vulnerable areas.
    c. not an important consideration.

13. In existing houses …
    a. it is easy to move water pipes to a safer place.
    b. insulating water pipes is the usual option.
    c. owners must accept that cold air will sometimes enter.

14. Which of these statements about insulation is true?
    a. Materials can only be bought in specialist stores.
    b. Extra-thick pipe sleeves are over-priced.
    c. It will not be always be effective if a lot of cold enters the house.

15. Why is it sometimes a good idea to leave a tap dripping?
    a. It reduces water pressure.
    b. Running water cannot freeze.
    c. The homeowner knows that there is no blockage in any pipes.

11 Sink or swim

'It is not enough to succeed. Others must fail.'
Gore Vidal

Speaking 1: defining *success*

A Look at the list of definitions of success below.

1. Decide which you agree and disagree with.
2. Choose one that you particularly like.
3. Choose four that you would like to say something about.
4. Compare your thoughts with a partner.

Success is ...

completing what you planned.

doing what you said you would.

being known for what you have achieved.

making other people jealous.

making money and accumulating material possessions.

fulfilling your potential.

overcoming difficulties and setbacks.

being liked and respected by other people.

finding contentment.

B In pairs, discuss whether you have your own definition of *success*.

C In pairs, discuss whether it is possible to define *failure*.

D 🎧 Listen to somebody describing a situation and answer each of the questions she poses. Then discuss the situation in your pair.

Grammar check

Most auxiliary verbs can be used rather like pronouns. It is not necessary to repeat the main verb. This is sometimes referred to as ellipsis.
Success is doing what you said you would. NOT *... doing what you said you would do.*
Which auxiliary verb to use depends on what is understood from the context.
She said she would be famous and she is. / He said he would play for his country and he has.
They think I can't do it but I can. / I think she can do it but she won't.

Watch out!
typical errors

She said she would win and she would. ✗

Vocabulary 1: success and failure

A Mark the qualities below (S) if they relate to success or (F) if they relate to failure. Check any words you don't know in a dictionary.

ambition __   belief __   courage __   cowardice __   defeatism __   desire __   determination __
drive __   faith __   hesitation __   hunger __   indecision __   insecurity __   optimism __
persistence __   pessimism __   purpose __   resignation __   resilience __   self-confidence __
self-doubt __   self-pity __   strength of mind __   weakness __   willpower __

Note that many of the positive qualities do not have negative antonyms. We commonly say *a lack of* + positive noun: *a lack of purpose / a lack of self-confidence*, etc.

B Write the adjective that describes the person who shows the qualities listed below.

1. ambition   _____
2. courage   _____
3. cowardice   _____
4. determination   _____
5. drive   _____
6. hesitation   _____
7. indecision   _____
8. insecurity   _____
9. optimism   _____
10. persistence   _____
11. purpose   _____
12. resilience   _____

C In each list below, ONE option is wrong. Delete it.

1. set   goals / a target / an ambition / yourself a challenge / your heart on something
2. overcome   difficulties / an obstacle / a setback / a disability / a plan
3. fulfil   an ambition / a dream / your potential / your optimism / your promise

D In pairs, discuss what a person needs to be successful, using vocabulary from Exercises A, B and C.

> *Successful people need to be driven and set themselves goals.*

Pronunciation check

In natural rapid speech, assimilation occurs when the sound at the end of one syllable or word merges into the sound at the beginning of the next. Parts of the mouth and vocal cords start to form the sound at the beginning of the second syllable or word before the sound at the end of the first has been completed. *Setback*, for example is pronounced something like /ˈsepbæk/. The *t* is dropped as the mouth prepares to pronounce *b*.

🎧 Listen to the words and phrases carefully and then practise saying them in pairs.

1. my big break
2. set goals
3. last chance
4. make plans
5. don't hold back
6. take good care

Speaking 2: answering the question properly

A Look at the questions below and think about how you would answer them.

1. Does succeeding mean doing better than other people?
2. Why do you think some people succeed while others fail?
3. Is it easier for people from certain backgrounds to succeed?
4. Do you think success brings happiness or that happiness equals success?

B 🎧 Listen to some students answering the questions. In pairs, decide:

1. which student gives a perfectly good answer.
2. what the problem with each of the other three answers is.

Exam tip: During the Speaking test, remember that:
- if the examiner asks you a *yes/no* question, he or she is inviting you to speak.
- make sure you answer the examiner's question – a well-expressed, grammatically correct opinion is no good if it doesn't answer the original question.
- if you don't know a key word, find another way of saying what you want to say. Don't try to use words that you don't know how to use properly.

C 🎧 Look at the tapescript and listen again.

D In pairs, ask and answer the questions in Exercise A.

11

Listening 1: recognizing context and register

A In pairs, answer the questions about the IELTS Listening test.

1. How are the four sections of the Listening test different from each other?
2. How many speakers are there in each section?
3. In which section is the language likely to be most formal?
4. In which section(s) is the language more likely to be informal?

B 🎧 Listen to extracts from each section of the Listening test. Identify which section you think each extract comes from.

Extract A: Section ___   Extract B: Section ___   Extract C: Section ___   Extract D: Section ___

C In pairs:

1. compare your answers to Exercise B. What helped you decide which section of the Listening test each extract is from?
2. discuss the topic of each extract.

Exam tip: In the four sections of the IELTS Listening test, you'll hear both formal and informal English. You'll understand more if you recognize the register the speaker is using.
- Section 1 is a conversation between two speakers in a social situation. The language can be informal – a conversation between friends or somebody phoning for information about joining a club – or more formal – an interview or somebody complaining about a product or service.
- Section 2 is a non-academic talk given by one speaker. In most cases, the language is neutral – it is a talk, but the speaker will use friendly, relatively informal language.
- Section 3 is a conversation (up to four speakers) related to education or training. The language can be quite formal – a discussion between academic staff at a college or very informal – students discussing a college event or which university they want to apply to.
- Section 4 is a talk or short lecture on a topic of general academic interest. The language will be more formal than language you hear in the other sections.

D 🎧 Listen again and note examples of formal and informal use of language. Compare thoughts with a partner.

Listening 2: practise recognizing context and register

A 🎧 Listen to longer versions of each extract and answer the questions.

Section 1: For questions 1–6 complete the notes. Use NO MORE THAN TWO WORDS for each answer.

strengths: customer services – resolving problems / averting (1) _____

weaknesses: says he's a (2) _____ / personally takes on jobs that should be (3) _____

example of challenge met: stopped (4) _____ going to competitor

recommendations: brings (5) _____ to position / professional / can be trusted / regarded as a (6) _____

Section 2: For questions 7–9, choose THREE letters A–G. The order of your answers is not important. According to the speaker, which THREE statements are true of successful business owners?

7. _____   8. _____   9. _____

Section 3: For questions 10–15 complete the sentences. Use NO MORE THAN TWO WORDS for each answer.

A	They are good at identifying reasons for not attempting something.
B	They often look back at opportunities they missed.
C	They clearly outline their objectives.
D	They make sure they have the right machinery.
E	They take care of their staff.
F	They delegate everyday tasks to lower ranks within the organization.
G	They do not waste time worrying about small problems.

10. Lucas's parents are not happy with his college _____.

11. Lucas and his parents disagree about his level of _____.
12. It was not easy for Lucas to get into college because his _____ were poor.
13. Lucas's father is worried that his son's _____ is not his priority.
14. Lucas points out that he does not really want an _____ job.
15. Lucas's mother emphasizes that having _____ will make life difficult for her son.

Section 4: For questions 16–20 complete the summary. Use NO MORE THAN TWO WORDS for each answer.

The term *survival of the fittest* has been misused. It was not supposed to mean the same thing as (16) _____. Kropotkin understood the term to apply to a (17) _____ made up of individuals co-operating rather than individuals in competition. He called this *mutual aid*. Most species of (18) _____ endure unfavourable conditions and increase their number best by working together. Mutual aid has been central to man's (19) _____. If we go back to the very beginning we can see that the (20) _____ we hold are born of this co-operation.

B Check the key on page 268. How many questions did you answer correctly?

C Tick the sentences about the Listening task that are true for you and think about how you could answer more questions correctly next time.

☐ 1. I recognized the difference between the sections of the Listening test quite easily.
☐ 2. I recognized formal and informal language within the extracts.
☐ 3. Recognizing register helped me complete the tasks.

Key vocabulary in context

A Mark the sentences from the extracts below (F) if they are especially formal or (I) if they are especially informal. Then discuss what each means with a partner.

1. I especially pride myself on my customer service skills.   ___
2. I possess the skills outlined in the job description.   ___
3. It's that sense of a chance not seized – a fish that got away!   ___
4. … an organizational structure that functions as a well-oiled machine.   ___
5. We moved heaven and earth to get you onto this course.   ___
6. The bottom line is there's always something you'd rather be doing.   ___
7. In the progress of man, mutual support rather than mutual struggle has had the upper hand.   ___

B Read through the tapescript and highlight further examples of formal and informal language.

WB See *Vocabulary development* on Workbook page 251.

11

Reading 1: preparing to read

A In pairs, look at the well-known proverb and answer the questions below.

> If at first you don't succeed, try, try again.

1. Do you have a similar proverb in your own language?
2. Do you agree that it gives good advice?
3. Can you remember an occasion when you followed the advice?

B Look at the pictures and talk in pairs.

1. Do you know all the people pictured?
2. What did each of the people achieve?
3. How do you think the proverb in Exercise A applies to each person?

C Read the passage below and check your answers in Exercise B.

D In pairs, cover the passage and answer the questions below.

1. Why is each pictured person mentioned in the passage?
2. What sort of things do people often assume when a person is successful?
3. What actually brings success, according to the passage?

If at First, You Don't Succeed

In December 1903, a New York Times editorial questioned the intelligence of the Wright Brothers, who were trying to invent a machine that was heavier than air and would fly. 'It simply defies the laws of physics,' they stated. A week later, the Wright Brothers made their famous first flight.

If we study history, it is clear that all stories of great success are also stories of triumph over adversity. We overlook the setbacks and see only the end success. We think the person got lucky or simply benefited from being in the right place at the right time. We may assume the person was exceptionally smart or talented or that he or she had the right connections. While each of those notions may have been a contributory factor, what ultimately led to success was the person's refusal to allow setbacks and failures to define them.

Albert Einstein was unable to speak until he was four or read until he was seven, causing his parents and teachers to conclude that he was slow and anti-social. He was later expelled from school and refused entry to the Zurich Polytechnic School. He clearly had a slower start than many of his childhood peers, but most people would agree that he eventually caught up, his name now synonymous with genius.

As a young cartoonist, Walt Disney faced countless rejections from newspaper editors, who asserted that he lacked natural talent. A local church minister took pity on the young cartoonist and hired him to draw cartoons in a small mouse-infested shed behind the church. On seeing one of these tiny rodents, Disney became inspired and Mickey Mouse was born.

One day, a partially deaf four-year-old boy came home with a note from his teacher. It read 'Your Tommy is too stupid to learn and we cannot have him at our school.' His mother decided to educate her son herself. Partially deaf and with only three months of formal schooling, Tommy grew up to be Thomas. Thomas Edison went on to fail approximately 10,000 times before he succeeded in inventing the light bulb.

Oprah Winfrey had her fair share of struggles and setbacks early on. She did not become one of the most influential women in the world by allowing others to define her, giving in to her self-doubt or giving up when the going got tough. After enduring a rough and often abusive childhood, Oprah was fired from one of her first positions as a television reporter, being told she was 'unfit for TV.' She now has her own media network.

People may feel that they have little in common with any of these now famous characters, but they are wrong. They were not born with superhuman resilience that shielded them from disappointment or self-doubt. They each had to wage their own inner battle with fear of failure as they worked hard to overcome the obstacles that lined their path to success. What distinguishes these people is that they did not become a victim to their failures. When they fell down, they got back up and when people told them it couldn't be done, they refused to accept their lack of belief.

Reading 2: matching sentence endings

Question-type tip: You may have to do a task where you match sentence beginnings with sentence endings. There will always be more endings than beginnings, so you don't have to use all the endings. The endings will almost always begin with the same part of speech, so you can't just match grammatically.

A Read the passage again and complete each sentence 1–5 with the correct ending A–J. Highlight the part(s) of the passage that provides each answer.

1. The Wright Brothers ____
2. Albert Einstein ____
3. Walt Disney ____
4. Thomas Edison ____
5. Oprah Winfrey ____

A had help from a figure in the community.
B left school to study at polytechnic.
C achieved a great deal at a very early age.
D upset some people by contradicting accepted scientific beliefs.
E accepted what other people said.
F had an ambition to work with animals.
G lost a job.
H did not learn as quickly as classmates at school.
I made very few friends.
J had impaired hearing.

B In pairs, answer the questions below about the task you have just done.

1. How is this task similar to other tasks you have practised?
2. Was there anything about the task you found difficult?

Exam tip: In terms of the strategies you need to use, a task that requires you to match sentence beginnings to endings is similar to other matching and identifying tasks that you've practised. Don't guess answers that seem to make sense – read carefully and identify the specific part of the passage that provides the answer. If it's difficult to find the correct ending for a beginning, cross off the endings that you know are definitely wrong. It's easier to make a decision if you have fewer options.

A Look only at the book titles highlighted in the passage. In pairs, discuss which you know and which you have read.

B Read the title of the passage. What do you think all the books mentioned in the passage have in common?

C Skim read the passage and check your answer to Exercise B.

FAMOUS BOOK REJECTIONS

It may be the tired old advice that mothers have always given – *Don't be a quitter; If you fall off your bike, get straight back on; Always finish what you've started* and so on – but this short list of authors is surely proof that being rejected by a publisher or two (or even 27!) doesn't necessarily mean you haven't written a classic.

William Golding's **Lord of the Flies** is now studied in schools across the world. *Time* magazine ranked it as one of the top 100 English-language novels ever written. The book has sold more than 14.5 million copies since it was first published in 1954 and Golding won a Nobel Prize for Literature largely based on this particular work. The publisher who read the original manuscript for it and declared it, 'an absurd and uninteresting fantasy which was rubbish and dull' must have spent much of his career after that seriously regretting his words.

The same could be said about George Orwell's **Animal Farm**. It also made *Time's* list of best English-language books of all time and was ranked at number 31 on the Modern Library's List of Best 20th-Century Novels. However, Orwell's classic was written off and completely misunderstood by a publisher who stated, 'It is impossible to sell animal stories in the United States.' Orwell's peer and good friend T. S. Eliot was also unimpressed. When Orwell sent him a draft, he responded by saying that the writing was good, but the view was not convincing. He felt that publishers would only accept the work if they personally had sympathy for a Trotskyite viewpoint.

Gone With the Wind is one of the most enduring novels and movies of all time. The line 'Frankly, my dear, I don't give a damn' is known and used by English speakers everywhere. It was 38 publishers, however, who originally told author Margaret Mitchell that they didn't give a damn. When she finally found a publisher, the book sold in stores for $3 apiece – quite a sum in 1936. Even at this price, it sold more than one million copies by the end of the year and won the Pulitzer Prize a year later.

Moving on to a modern classic, **Harry Potter and the Philosopher's Stone**. The main character may be known as *the Chosen One* but plenty of publishers, including Penguin and HarperCollins, took one look and decided not to choose him. JK Rowling finally decided to try a small London firm called Bloomsbury, who accepted only after the Chief Executive's eight-year-old daughter read the book and declared it a winner. The subsequent accolades and commercial success hardly need describing.

'His frenetic and scrambled prose perfectly expresses the feverish travels of the Beat Generation. But is that enough? I don't think so,' is what one publisher said about Jack Kerouac's **On the Road**. After it came out in 1957, *The New York Times* wrote a review that expressed the exact opposite opinion, describing it as 'The most beautifully executed, the clearest and most important utterance of the generation.'

Creators of children's characters fare no better. It was actually thanks to a critic that Norman Bridwell was finally published. The author of **Clifford the Big Red Dog** had tried multiple publishers and was told repeatedly that his dog pictures were boring and unoriginal. One editor finally told him to create a story to go along with his illustrations in the hope that the story might spark more interest. So he did, and less than a month later, Scholastic Books sent Bridwell a contract to publish everyone's favourite house-sized dog.

These are just a selection of the many, now famous, authors who faced rejection, criticism and even humiliation before their masterpieces were unleashed on the world. In truth, anyone who has ever achieved success has at some time has also failed. Hopefully, this short list will reassure all those budding Shakespeares that literary success is rarely an easy ride and that persistence is the key.

Read the passage again and answer the questions.

For questions 1–6, complete each sentence with the correct ending A–J.

1. *Lord of the Flies* ___
2. *Animal Farm* ___
3. *Gone With the Wind* ___
4. *Harry Potter and the Philosopher's Stone* ___
5. *On the Road* ___
6. *Clifford the Big Red Dog* ___

A was considered too short.
B was considered suitable only for somebody with a particular political outlook.
C was sold fairly cheaply when first published.
D met with a hugely varied reaction.
E was published by a very large publishing company.
F was originally assessed by somebody who may wish he or she could read it again.
G met with a rather ironic total lack of interest.
H was improved when words were added to pictures.
I was successful due to a child's recommendation.
J was difficult to follow.

E Check the key on page 268. How many questions did you answer correctly?

F Tick the sentences about the Reading task that are true for you and think about how you can answer more questions correctly next time.

☐ 1. Skimming the passage first helped me get a general idea.
☐ 2. I read the sentences in the task carefully before I read the text again more carefully.
☐ 3. I knew what to look for when I read the text again.
☐ 4. It found it quite easy to choose the correct ending even though there are a lot of options.
☐ 5. I am happy with how many of the questions I answered correctly.

Key vocabulary in context

Check the key word or phrase in the passage and highlight the correct option.

1. If you **defy** something, you *challenge it / agree with it*.
2. If you **triumph over adversity**, you *overcome difficulties / give up*.
3. If you **take pity on** somebody, you show *disapproval / sympathy*.
4. If something is **shielded**, it is in *danger / protected*.
5. A **quitter** is somebody who *tries hard / gives up easily*.
6. If something is **written off**, it is *rejected or thrown away / becomes popular*.
7. An **accolade** is a very *positive / negative* assessment.
8. **Humiliation** is a feeling of *pride / shame and embarrassment*.

WB See *Vocabulary development* on Workbook page 251.

WB For focus on reading skills, go to Workbook page 253.

11

Writing 1: preparing to write

A In pairs, answer the questions below.

1. Is unemployment in your country currently rising or falling?
2. Is the unemployment rate among graduates an issue at the present time?
3. Are graduates in your country generally less affected by rates of unemployment than non-graduates?
4. Do graduates have to make any compromises in order to find their first job?

B Read the extract below and check whether it agrees with points you made in Exercise A.

Having a degree in the United States is still certainly an advantage. While the national unemployment rate has climbed to almost 10%, the rate for graduates over 25 is still under 5%. By contrast, non-graduates between 20 and 24 are contending with an unemployment rate of close to 20%. Though graduates generally cope with periods of economic decline far better than those without a degree, the last few years have been especially difficult. The jobless rate for younger workers with a college degree has more than doubled since the beginning of the recession, from 3.5% in 2007 to the current 6.5%. Finding stable work is particularly challenging for graduates under 25. Around half of this group are either unemployed or under-employed, meaning that they work part-time or do a job outside the conventional college labour market, such as waiting in restaurants or bartending.

C Cover the extract. In pairs, summarize it in a sentence or two.

D In pairs, discuss what sort of compromises graduates might make when they accept their first job.

E Look at the labels on the bar graph on the next page and check your ideas in Exercise D.

Writing 2: deciding what to say and how to say it

A Look at these instructions for a typical IELTS Writing task and start thinking about what you would say.

The bar chart shows the various compromises made by graduates in the United States in 2006–2007 and 2009–2010 in order to find their first job.

Summarize the information by selecting and reporting the main features, and make comparisons where relevant.

Write at least 150 words.

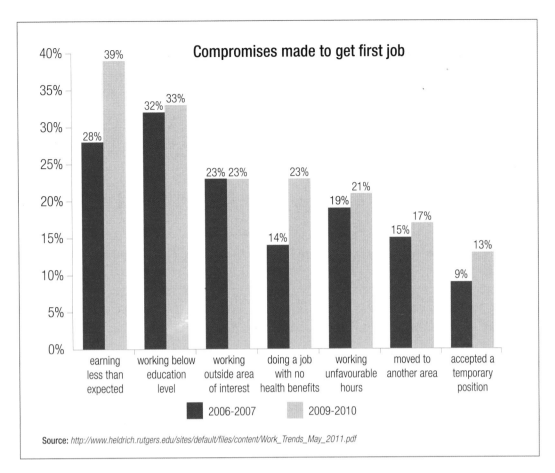

Compromises made to get first job

Source: http://www.heldrich.rutgers.edu/sites/default/files/content/Work_Trends_May_2011.pdf

B In pairs, discuss what information stands out and what will interest a reader.

C In your pair, write a report of the information.
- Spend five minutes planning and making notes.
- Spend 12 minutes writing the report.
- Spend three minutes checking that you are happy with the report and that there are no errors.

D Compare your report with those of other students in the class. Don't check the model report yet.

Writing 3: elements of a good written report

A Below and on the next page are possible sentences that make up a model report. Before you read them, look at the points below.
- Some sentences are more relevant than others.
- Some sentences more accurately describe information shown in the figure than others.
- Some sentences are more appropriately expressed than others.
- A small number of sentences contain errors with grammar or spelling

B In pairs, choose the sentences that you think make up the complete report and put them in order. Write the letters in the spaces below each paragraph. Discuss your choices.

ⓐ The bar chart shows what graduates in the United States have to do to get their first job.

ⓑ It shows that some of these compromises mean postgraduates are far less happy at work.

ⓒ It shows the percentage of graduates that made each of those compromises in the years 2006-2007 and 2009-2010.

ⓓ The bar chart shows the percentage of graduates what made various compromises in order to find their first job in the United States in two selected years.

ⓔ The bar chart shows the various compromises that graduates in the United States might make in order to find their first job.

ⓕ It shows that the number of graduates making certain compromises is changing a lot.

    1. ___   2. ___

ⓖ The biggest increase was in the percentage of graduates earning less than expected, but the smallest increase was in the percentage who worked below their education level.

ⓗ Those earning less than expected rose from 28% in 2006-2007 to 39% in 2009-2010, while the percentage working with no health benefits increased by over a third to 23%.

ⓘ The percentage accepting a temporary position was still quite low in 2009-2010, but had climbed by a third.

ⓙ Not many graduates accepted only a temporary position, but the percentage did increase a bit.

ⓚ The most noticeable increases were in the percentage of graduates earning less than they expected, the percentage working with no health benefits and the percentage accepting a temporary position.

ⓛ The percentage of graduates working in jobs with no health benefits really went up a lot between 2006-2007 and 2009-2010.

ⓜ The amount of graduates earning less than they expected soared up from 27% in 2006-2007 to just under 40% in 2009-2010.

    3. ___   4. ___   5. ___

ⓝ The percentage of graduates who moved to another part of the country rose by 2%, as did the percentage working unfavourable hours.

ⓞ It's surprising that the percentage of graduates working outside their area of interest did not rise, since all the other compromises did.

ⓟ The percentage working below their education level rose only slightly, but was high anyway at around 33%.

ⓠ Apart from 'working outside area of interest', all the compromises increased in frequency over the period.

ⓡ Over the time, it also became more regular for graduates to move in another area and work unfavourable hours.

ⓢ As well as the big percentage increases, there were some smaller increases too. The percentage of graduates that moved, the percentage of graduates that ended up working unfavourable hours and the percentage of graduates that worked below their education level all went up only a little.

    6. ___   7. ___   8. ___

C Look at the model report on page 269 and check your answers to Exercise B.
Is the model report similar to the one you wrote with your partner earlier?

WB Go to Workbook page 255 for the Writing task.

Speaking

A Look at some examiner's questions below and think about how you would answer them.

1. Give me an example of somebody who you think has been very successful.
2. What has been your biggest achievement so far?
3. Is it important to persevere or is it best to give up if you know that something is bound to fail?
4. What have you failed to achieve recently and how did that make you feel?

B 🎧 Listen to some students answering the questions. For each question, tick the student that you think gives the better answer.

1. Student A ☐   Student B ☐
2. Student A ☐   Student B ☐
3. Student A ☐   Student B ☐
4. Student A ☐   Student B ☐

C 🎧 Listen to the students' answers again. In pairs, discuss why you feel that one student's answer was better in Exercise B.

D Ask and answer the questions in Exercise A with a partner.

Vocabulary

A Delete the odd word in each list of near-synonyms below.

1. success / failure / triumph / achievement
2. goal / target / setback / objective
3. ambition / desire / hunger / cowardice
4. determination / willpower / self-pity / drive
5. courage / faith / belief / optimism
6. self-doubt / uncertainty / resilience / insecurity

B Fill each gap with a root word made from the word in brackets.

1. Many successful people have had to overcome _____. (adverse)
2. I don't see why you think the plan will fail. That's pure _____. (defeat)
3. Going back to college at nearly 60 was very _____. (courage)
4. It was _____ that meant the opportunity was lost. (hesitate)
5. His constant _____ discourages everyone else from putting in effort. (pessimist)
6. Nobody wants to be thought of as a _____. (quit)
7. Succeeding in such _____ conditions was totally unexpected. (favour)
8. Walt Disney had to accept _____ rejections before he found success. (count)
9. We need to deal with the situation before it becomes _____. (manage)

Errors

A There are errors with grammar or punctuation in all of these sentences. Correct them.

1. He thought he would win, but he wouldn't.
2. I want her to help, but she doesn't.
3. He prayed he would pass, but he didn't do.
4. He only succeeded to make things worse.
5. She prides herself in her appearance.
6. If you've put your heart on it, you must have it.

11

Reading

A In pairs, discuss again the meaning of the phrase *survival of the fittest*.

B Look at the pictures below and discuss how some animals have had to adapt to urban environments in order to survive.

C Read only the title of the article on pages 175 and 176 and the topic sentence at the beginning of each paragraph. Then tick what you think is the correct summary of the article.

☐ 1. Urbanization has had some benefits on the diversity of wildlife.

☐ 2. The impact of urbanization on wildlife has been only negative.

☐ 3. Most wild animals are suited to an urban environment once they have adapted.

D Check that you understand the key words and phrases in the box below, using a dictionary if necessary. Then, in pairs, discuss why you think each will be mentioned in the passage.

urban sprawl   laboratories   teeming habitats   nocturnal creatures   suburban culling

Human Impact on Biological Diversity

Without doubt, man has had a negative impact on biodiversity, particularly since the industrial revolution. Overfishing and hunting, the destruction of habitats through agriculture and urban sprawl, and the use of pesticides and herbicides have all taken their toll. The World Conservation Union names 16,000 entries in its Red List of Threatened Species – 5,624 vertebrates, 2,101 invertebrates and 8,390 plants. The number of documented extinctions since 1500 CE is 784 species and extinction rates are now estimated to be 50 to 500 times higher than previously calculated from fossil records.

It is not all bad news, though. Many animal and plant species have adapted to the new stresses, food sources, predators and threats in urban and suburban environments, where they thrive in close proximity to humans. Their success provides researchers with valuable insights into evolutionary and selective processes. Because these adaptations have had to be rapid, cities are ideal laboratories for studying natural selection.

The study of adaptation to human habitats yields vital information for conservation efforts and helps to soften the environmental impact of housing, roads, business parks and waterways. In fact, these types of construction can enhance biodiversity and encourage species to colonize urban areas. They create ecological corridors and networks to evade obstacles, providing access to favourable habitats. Small mammals, for example, can cross roads and railways by using dedicated pathways that are constructed within existing tunnels or bridges. Urbanization can also aid the development of teeming habitats. Rather than being confined to remote areas and wildlife parks, creatures that congregate can thrive in densely populated areas. In a recent study of 25 business parks in Holland, 90 bird species were identified, including 18 that are listed as endangered.

Indeed, business parks exemplify how urban environments help wildlife thrive and can even be exploited and enhanced by conservation initiatives. They tend to be located in the centre of or on the outskirts of cities and have three valuable properties. They are open spaces that can be cultivated for vegetation and wildlife, they consist of buildings with large flat roofs that can be turned into green areas and they have a tendency to be quiet at night, providing havens for nocturnal creatures.

Bird species are the most studied in an effort to gain insight into the abilities of wildlife to adapt to urban habitats. Urban settings have different selective pressures from those on wild habitats. They impose close proximity to humans as well as to rivals, predators and prey, but can also reduce threats and create favourable conditions, including ready access to food and shelter from seasonal variations and adverse weather conditions. The role of the city as a moderator of natural forces is reflected in the discovery that the abundance of birds in urban environments does not decrease as one moves northwards in Europe, as it does in wild environments.

However, city-dwelling animals still face a range of new challenges. For species that rely on sound to communicate or execute mating strategies, noise pollution presents a problem. Extensive studies on songbirds show that many species have adapted by adjusting various aspects of their song to overcome residual noise. Several successful city species are able to adjust their spectral frequency in response to traffic noise, for example. Species lacking the flexibility of post-dispersal learning and without a wide range of song use may be at a disadvantage in noisy neighbourhoods, however. Humans are not the only source of noise, and the species best able to adapt to city residence might be those that had to cope with competing sounds in their natural environments. This raises the question of how adaptation to an urban setting occurred. Did it require the selection of individuals with specific genotypes within the overall population or did it exploit existing phenotypic potential?

Until recently, there was no direct evidence of an evolutionary response to urbanization that involved genetic adaptation. One of the first widely cited examples is the dark-eyed junco, a common North American species of sparrow whose adaptation to San Diego in California has been accompanied by a significant decrease in the amount of white in its tail feathers. The precise selective mechanism is unclear, but it is likely that white tails evolved in the wild as a way of standing out among potential mates. The advantage of white tails for sexual signalling would be diminished in an urban environment, where there is less competition.

The question now is whether these environments have higher levels of biological diversity, at least locally. It seems dense urban environments tend to reduce overall diversity among smaller animals and plants, though those that do adapt, such as foxes and pigeons, can proliferate greatly. Suburban areas, on the other hand, combine open areas of parkland and woodland with the trappings of urbanization, such as food sources, and can increase diversity over a large area.

Even small human settlements in rural areas can have an ecological impact on a much larger area. The effect of rural homes on native species' population dynamics can be felt hundreds of kilometres away. A small village, for example, could provide a sheltered habitat during extreme conditions for a species of bird that would otherwise be forced to migrate elsewhere. In this way, the ecological make-up of a wider area is disrupted. This can affect conservation efforts within nearby protected areas. The killing of grizzly bears on private lands may threaten bear populations in Yellowstone National Park, for example. Bears are free to roam in and out of the park so any culling on private land reduces the numbers that enter the park.

The impact of mankind on biodiversity has clearly been detrimental to many animals and plants, but the story is more complex and subtle than has been appreciated. Urbanization provides ready-made laboratories for studying evolution and adaptive processes. It enables us to examine the influence of humans on wildlife and creates the potential to mitigate any negative effects. Perhaps we should be more positive about our relationship with the natural world. We need to celebrate the creative aspects of our impact in addition to concerning ourselves with all that is negative.

E Read the whole passage and answer the questions.

For questions 1–10, complete each sentence with the correct ending A–N on the next page. You will not need to use all the endings.

1. Extinction rates ___
2. Cities ___
3. Tunnels and bridges ___
4. Teeming habitats ___
5. Business parks ___
6. Birds in wild environments ___
7. Some songbirds ___
8. Dark-eyed juncos ___
9. Suburban areas ___
10. Grizzly bears ___

A   are more numerous in the south.
B   have the benefits of both rural and city landscapes.
C   flourish in highly populated areas.
D   are hunted illegally.
E   force wildlife to adapt quickly.
F   have slightly changed in appearance.
G   have evolved to deal with close human contact.
H   are ideal as wildlife habitats for a number of reasons.
I   are far more extreme than once believed.
J   are potentially threatening to some species.
K   do not always remain in areas where they are safe.
L   can house passages which may protect some small animals from danger.
M   are not as serious as once feared.
N   make different sounds to contend with fresh competition.

For questions 11–13, choose the correct answer a, b, c or d.

11. Which of the following is not mentioned as a benefit of typical urban constructions?
    a. The design offers safe routes for some animals to move around in.
    b. Many animals breed more successfully when living within them.
    c. Creatures which live in very large groups appear to flourish around them.
    d. There are periods of relative silence.

12. Many bird species adapt well to urban environments because …
    a. they have to contend with fewer predators.
    b. they find food more easily.
    c. they are comfortable around humans.
    d. weather conditions are more favourable.

13. Why is the dark-eyed junco losing some of the white in its tail feathers?
    a. It probably needs to impress other birds less.
    b. It is makes it less noticeable to potential predators.
    c. It has a less healthy diet.
    d. Most animals undergo some physical change when they adapt to a new environment.

For questions 14–18, complete the summary of part of the text below. Use ONE WORD ONLY from the text for each answer.

Most of the research into animal adaptation to urban environments has been conducted on birds. Although urban habitats present difficulties and dangers, they are frequently (14) _____, providing new sources of food and (15) _____ when there is rain and snow. Some songbirds have triumphed over (16) _____ by changing features of the sounds they make. The dark-eyed junco appears to be losing some of the white in its tail feathers – the only example of a (17) _____ change so far identified. A small human settlement might enable some birds to remain where there is protection rather than (18) _____. In this way, an adaptation in one small area can have a far-reaching impact.

12 Crime and punishment

'Society prepares the crime, the criminal commits it.'
Henry Thomas Buckle

Vocabulary 1: crime

A In pairs, answer the questions below. Use a dictionary to check the highlighted words as you go, if necessary.

1. What is the difference between a crime and an offence or a criminal and an offender?
2. We don't say *do* or *make* a crime, so which verb do we usually use?
3. Is committing a crime the same as breaking the law?
4. Is there any difference between illegal, unlawful and against the law?
5. Which of the collocations below is not possible? What do each of the others mean?
   serious crime / violent crime / offensive crime / petty crime
6. In American English, is a felony a crime or an offence?

B As a class, brainstorm as many different crimes as possible in ten minutes.

C In pairs, discuss the difference in meaning between the crimes below.

1. attempted murder / manslaughter
2. theft / robbery
3. shoplifting / burglary
4. fraud / forgery
5. blackmail / bribery
6. vandalism / arson

D Explain to your partner a crime that you don't know the word for in English. See if your partner knows the word.

> This is the crime of stealing money from the company you work for.

Speaking 1: talking about crime

A Here are two typical task cards for Part 2 of the Speaking test. Work with a partner – one of you is A, the other is B. Think about the topic for a minute and make notes.

A

Talk about a crime that is common in your hometown or city.
Say ...
- what the crime is.
- what sort of person commits the crime.
- what effect the crime has on victims/society.

B

Talk about a crime that you think is typical of the modern age.
Say ...
- what the crime is.
- who commits the crime and why.
- what effect it has on victims/society.

B 🎧 Listen to two students talking with an examiner.

1. Make notes about what each student says about each of the three points on his or her card.
2. Compare the notes you've made with a partner.

C Take turns to speak about what's on your card for about two minutes using your own ideas.

Vocabulary 2: the police, the courts and prison

A Mark each of the words and phrases (P) police work, (C) in court or (PR) in prison, depending on which area you think they most relate to. You may want to mark some with more than one letter.

suspect __	trial __	inmates __	verdict __	life sentence __	arrest __	jury __
investigation __	judge __	search __	cell __	an oath __	witness __	rehabilitation __
evidence __	the accused __	crime scene __	parole __	statement __	barrister __
plead guilty __	defence __	wardens __	enquiries __	prosecution __

B Discuss Exercise A with a partner.

1. Say why you have marked words and phrases in a certain way.
2. Discuss the meaning of any words and phrases you are not sure about.

C Match the verbs 1–8 with the nouns a–h to form common phrases.

1. launch   a. enquiries
2. pass   b. a verdict
3. question   c. an oath
4. take   d. a suspect
5. reach   e. a sentence
6. make   f. sentence
7. serve   g. evidence
8. give   h. an investigation

Speaking 2: discussing crime and punishment

A Look at the questions below and think about how you would answer them.

1. Should prisoners be released early if they show remorse or seem to be rehabilitated?
2. Would there be so much crime if people were more equal?
3. Is crime ever acceptable if driven by extreme poverty?
4. Is the main role of prison to punish or to rehabilitate offenders?

B 🎧 Listen to some students answering the questions. Do you agree with any of the points they make?

Grammar check
Discuss the form and use of the conditional structures in the examples below from the tapescripts in this module.

Watch out!
typical errors

If society would be fairer, there … ✗

If didn't steal that money, I wouldn't have ended up in prison. ✗

If he wouldn't have robbed that bank … ✗

If I'd have studied harder at school … ✗

1. If you feel there's no hope of getting out before 20 years, say, is up, there's no reason to improve yourself.
2. Would there be so much crime if people were more equal?
3. If I hadn't clicked the window with the offer, it wouldn't have happened.
4. There are prisoners everywhere who are thinking that if they'd had a few more opportunities when they were younger, they wouldn't be behind bars now.

Rather than think of conditionals as first, second and third, it often helps to think about whether they express real or unreal concepts and if they express the present, the future or the past. Look at the tapescripts and find more examples of conditional structures.

Pronunciation check
The contrast between stress and weak forms (there are a lot of contractions) and using appropriate intonation are an essential part of the message when conditionals are used.

🎧 Listen to some native speakers saying the sentences from the *Grammar check*. Then practise saying each sentence two or three times with a partner.

C In pairs, ask and answer the questions in Exercise A.

Listening 1: preparing to listen

A In pairs, look at the pictures and answer the questions below.

1. What is happening in each picture?
2. Are these crimes common where you live?
3. What are some ways that each crime can be avoided?
4. Have you ever been the victim of any of these crimes? What happened?

B 🎧 Listen and match the Extracts 1–3 with the pictures a–c.

Extract 1 ___   Extract 2 ___   Extract 3 ___

Listening 2: transferring answers to the answer sheet

A 🎧 Listen to the first extract again complete the police report. USE NO MORE THAN TWO WORDS OR A NUMBER for each answer.

Incident:	theft in High Street – perpetrator not seen
Time:	(1) _____ p.m.
Name of victim:	Joanna (2) _____
Item stolen:	(3) _____ – silver (checked design) with golden (4) _____
Contained:	(5) £_____ cash + debit and credit cards, I.D. and (6) _____.

B Check a student's answer sheet below. Which answers are correct? Which are not? What mistakes has the student made?

1. 2.20
2. More
3. perse
4. clasp
5. 17
6. student bus pass

Exam tip: More than half of the tasks that can occur in the Listening test involve writing words and phrases as answers. You MUST spell your answer correctly and you MUST NOT use more than the stated number of words. Use the ten minutes you have to transfer answers to the answer sheet slowly and carefully, and check all your answers two or three times.

Listening 3: practise transferring answers to the answer sheet

A 🎧 Listen to the second and third extracts again and answer the questions.

Extract 2: For questions 1–7, complete the summary with words from the text. Use NO MORE THAN TWO WORDS for each answer

> Many break-ins occur because the (1) _____ is left unlocked. People either forget to lock up or think it unnecessary when making a (2) _____ journey. A burglar seizes this opportunity and needs only (3) _____ to commit a successful crime. Burglars want to minimize the time a break-in takes and any (4) _____ they may arouse. Burglars choose an (5) _____ property or one that appears less protected. They will notice open windows and gates and take advantage when a (6) _____ of a house is blocked by fences or trees. Anyone who shares a block with other tenants should take care when using an (7) _____ to allow callers in.

Extract 3: For questions 8–11, complete the sentences. Use NO MORE THAN TWO WORDS for each answer.

8. A thief entered the victim's car by breaking the _____.
9. The thief stole a jacket and a _____ that contained some valuable items.
10. While he is on the phone, the victim remembers that some _____ were also taken.
11. The victim did not think it was unsafe to leave the items unattended while he went to leave _____.

For questions 12–14, complete the notes. Use NO MORE THAN TWO WORDS for each answer.

> Incident: theft from motor vehicle
> Location: in (12) _____ approx. 30 m north of (13) _____ restaurant.
> Name of victim: (14) _____

B Transfer your answers on to the answer sheet below.

1		8	
2		9	
3		10	
4		11	
5		12	
6		13	
7		14	

C Check the key on page 269. How many questions did you answer correctly?

D In pairs, answer the questions below and think about how you could answer more questions correctly next time.

1. Were most answers fairly easy to transfer?
2. Did you get any answers wrong because they were not spelt correctly, they were transferred wrongly or because you used too many words?
3. Are you happy with the number of questions you answered correctly?

Key vocabulary in context

Read the tapescript for Extract 2 and check how the phrases and expressions below are used in context. Discuss the meaning of each with partner.

1. make off with   2. arouse suspicion   3. asking for trouble   4. be mindful of   5. grant entry

WB See *Vocabulary development* on Workbook page 256.

12

Reading 1: timing yourself in the Reading test

A In pairs, answer the questions below about the Reading test.

1. How many sections are there to the Reading test?
2. Is there ever more than one passage in any of the sections?
3. Are the passages all of the same length and equally challenging?
4. Should you spend an equal amount of time (20 minutes) on each section? If not, why not?

 Exam tip: The Reading test consists of three sections, each of which is one passage. The 40 questions must all be answered in 60 minutes. The passages become more challenging and usually slightly longer. Most students plan to spend an equal amount of time on each section, but there are options. You may wish to devote more time to the third section as it's more challenging, and complete the first section slightly more quickly. Remember, though, that you will get into a rhythm and start working faster. This will compensate for the increasing challenge of the passages. Whatever you decide, don't spend longer than 20 minutes on either the first or second sections as you will then not have sufficient time for the third, and most challenging, section. It is essential that you watch the time carefully as you work and write your answers directly onto the answer sheet as you go – you will not have time at the end to transfer answers.

B Look at the various stages that apply to reading passages in the Reading test. Decide how long you want to spend on each stage and fill in the times. Then compare thoughts with a partner.

1. Read the heading and look at any supporting visuals. ___ minutes
2. Skim the text to get a general idea of what it's about. ___ minutes
3. Read the instructions and questions carefully and think about where in the text you will find answers. ___ minutes
4. Read the text again to more carefully to find answers to the questions. ___ minutes
5. Is there a reason that some people live to a very old age or is it just luck? ___ minutes

Reading 2: practise timing yourself in the Reading test

A Read the first passage from a Reading test below and answer the questions that follow. Write your answers directly onto the answer sheet on page 262.

BULLYING IN THE 21ST CENTURY

A Cyber bullying has become a disturbing trend that affects children and teens in an increasingly alarming way. Latest figures suggest that one in every six children has been the victim of this type of victimization. Its significance is particularly pertinent for youngsters using communication technology on a regular basis. Children in their final year of primary school report an especially high incidence of this form of persecution.

Cyber bullying manifests itself in a variety of ways. The definition encompasses the use of the Internet, instant messaging, texting, pagers, chat rooms, blogs, websites and e-mails for the purpose of intimidation. For many individuals from primary school age through to adolescents and young adults, these are resources used on a daily basis.

B Cyber bullying is frequently an extension of playground or classroom bullying and what is disturbing is that it means the intimidation continues outside school and becomes a constant and often overwhelming presence in the victim's life.

A tenth of year six pupils claim to have been targeted by bullies while alone. Cyber bullies can easily remain anonymous and the fear and emotional injury they inflict is very difficult to counteract. The use of defamatory and derogatory websites, blogs and photographic images are all commonly used to victimize and intimidate.

C The use of abusive and threatening text messages is a common form of cyber bullying. Harmful rumours can be spread in an instant to a large number of recipients. Texting can be particularly damaging as it extends the terrorization beyond the school grounds and into the victim's own home. Unlike computers, mobile phones are hard to monitor. Youngsters are inseparable from their phones and bullying can be unrelenting. Text messages have been directly responsible for cases of child suicide.

As well as spreading harmful gossip about an individual, bullies use e-mails to harass their victims directly. E-mails are difficult to track when fake user accounts can be set up so easily, and they are usually sent from a public computer. Computer-literature bullies have been known to add an even more sinister twist, hacking into e-mail accounts and sending false e-mails in the victim's name.

Chat rooms and social networking sites like Facebook are a breeding ground for cyber bullies. The instantaneous nature of the message allows them to threaten, abuse and belittle victims. These could be anonymous strangers or people known to the victim. Either way, this kind of bullying has dangerous consequences and can be extremely distressing.

D Cyber bullying adds another dimension to school bullying. Children who partake do not receive the same kind of feedback as they would in a physical face-to-face scenario. Since they do not see the affect their behaviour is having on the victim, they feel less sympathy and subsequently less remorse. Their actions appear to have no tangible consequences and they feel less responsible for what they do or for the person they are hurting.

Preventing bullying is all about education and monitoring. Any parent who has reason to believe that their child is a victim of bullying or might be inclined towards being a bully needs to take immediate action. Modern-day parents need to understand the Internet and other technologies their sons and daughters are using. They must be aware that bullying is starting at an earlier age and they should consider restricting a young child's access to an independent mobile phone. They should supervise Internet use and discuss the concept of cyber bullying as well as all the others dangers that exist online. Chat rooms, e-mails and websites can all be monitored with parental control software.

F Children with low self-esteem are most likely to become victims of all kinds of bullying. Parents and teachers need to be involved in a child's development and stay involved. Helping a child to develop confidence and a strong sense of self-worth will do a great deal to prevent them becoming a victim of bullying or a bully themselves. Adults should also remember that a bullied child will almost certainly not volunteer to share his or her experience and they need to look for any signs which suggest it may be happening. It is possible that a child's life could be saved by putting in place a few simple measures.

The passage has six sections labelled A–F. For questions 1–6, choose the correct heading for each from the list of headings in the box. You do not need to use all the headings.

i.	The effects are not so evident
ii.	How to get revenge
iii.	How avenues of attack are exploited
iv.	Technology is to blame
v.	24-hour intimidation
vi.	Those most at risk
vii.	Identifying those involved
viii.	A worrying development
ix.	Fewer prosecutions

1. Section A ___   2. Section B ___   3. Section C ___
4. Section D ___   5. Section E ___   6. Section F ___

For questions 7–12, decide if the information given below agrees with the information given in the text. Write (T) true, (F) false or (NG) not given, if there is no information on this.

7. Teenagers are the age group most likely to be targeted.   ___
8. Victims of cyber bullying are most likely to be targeted when at home.   ___
9. Cyber bullies often pretend to be somebody else when e-mailing.   ___
10. On social networking sites, bullies sometimes target people they do not know.   ___
11. Many cyber bullies later regret their actions.   ___
12. Many parents are not familiar with modern communication channels.   ___

CCTV – A Huge White Elephant?

A According to recent figures, less than 3% of street robberies are solved using CCTV. Only one crime for every 1,000 CCTV cameras is solved each year. Managers of large department stores are being told that camera surveillance is so ineffective that they would better benefit from training staff to be more aware of suspicious behaviour. Now, in a bizarre twist, it has come to light that a journalist, using powers enshrined in the Data Protection Act, wrote to his local council asking to see images that a CCTV had taken of him. The authorities could not oblige, the footage being of insufficient quality to identify him, even though he had revealed exactly where he had been, at what time and what he had been wearing.

B If CCTV cameras cannot identify someone in broad daylight who is deliberately trying to be spotted, what hope is there that they can identify a mugger stalking a dark street wearing a balaclava? As the Home Office has itself admitted, four out of every five images requested by the police are of such poor quality as to be of no use whatsoever in the fighting against crime. In many cases, the police do not even get as far as requesting the images. The head of the Metropolitan Police's Visual Images, Identifications and Detections Office, has complained that police officers are not accessing CCTV footage since searching through it is such a lengthy and dull process. Cameras originally installed to deter or detect crime have been repositioned to monitor bus lanes and record vehicle number plates. Despite expenditure running into billions, many commentators are now admitting that the entire history of the technology has been a fiasco.

C Based on the assumption that CCTV cameras help to cut crime, the British public has been remarkably tolerant of it. Around 75% of the population have a favourable attitude, ignoring warnings that their country is turning into a Big Brother-style surveillance society. However, it has been clear for some time that the technology is simply not doing the job it was installed to do. In fact, by giving authorities an excuse to cut police patrols, CCTVs have actually been hampering the fight against crime.

D Britain's 4.3 million CCTV cameras represent an estimated one in four of the cameras in the entire world. The average citizen in the UK is caught on film 300 times a day. In theory, the British should be living in the safest country on Earth, but that is not the case. Street robbery and violence, two offences that one might expect to be especially well-tackled by CCTV cameras, have soared at the same time that cameras have proliferated. Robberies are 50% higher than a decade ago and violence against a person has more than doubled. Police patrols have diminished under the assumption that cameras had taken over the role of protector.

E Naturally, there are well-known cases in which CCTV footage played a major role in an investigation. The image of the London bombers arriving at Luton railway station on their way to kill 52 victims on the London transport system will long be remembered, and it was shopping precinct cameras

that in 1993 captured two 10-year-olds leading away two-year-old James Bulger before they murdered him. However, a far greater number of serious crimes go unrecorded because cameras are poorly positioned, out of focus or simply broken. A recently documented case revealed that police accessed CCTV footage which they believed would provide vital evidence in an attempted murder incident, only to find that the videotape had run out.

F Recent research was conducted in Northampton, a town which boasts nearly 500 CCTV cameras. Ten of these have been fitted with loudspeakers in a £500,000 project designed to allow CCTV operators to address perpetrators from their control rooms. Over a two-hour period, researchers witnessed a mugging, a fight involving five men and the vandalizing of a car in the main shopping street. At no time did they hear an admonishment via CCTV. Nor, importantly, did they see a single police patrol. Interestingly, records show that for a period just before Christmas 2005, Northampton police deployed police horses to quell merrymakers on the town's streets. The result was an instant 27% fall in violent crime, suggesting that the cavalry succeeds where CCTV does not. Like a number of towns, Northampton is now policed largely by remote control. Paradoxically, it appears that the more cameras are deployed, the more street crime rises.

G Now the Home Office – the body that was responsible for the installation of all the cameras in the first place – has decided that it is time for a major and long-overdue rethink on where the crime prevention budget should be spent. However, rather than admit that the CCTV programme was a huge white elephant when it was installed, they now claim that change is necessary because it is an intrusion on privacy. This may be true, but the British public will surely be asking what alternative strategies are planned to reverse the increase in violent crime.

For questions 13–18, identify the paragraph which contains the following information. Write the correct letter A–G in the space.

13. a suggestion that traffic surveillance has replaced crime detection ___
14. reluctance to admit a mistake ___
15. a warning that shoplifting is not being tackled ___
16. examples of major police operations ___
17. a tendency to remain positive ___
18. failure to respond to a series of petty crimes ___

For questions 19–24, answer the questions. Use NO MORE THAN THREE WORDS from the text for each answer.

19. Who was told that his CCTV captured images were not good enough to identify him?
20. How do police officers describe watching CCTV footage?
21. What are CCTV cameras in bus lanes taking pictures of?
22. Which well-known literary character is Britain's surveillance society compared to?
23. What have declined in frequency as the number of CCTV cameras has increased?
24. Where were some infamous terrorists filmed on CCTV?

For questions 25–27, complete the summary using the list of words A–H below. Write the correct letter as your answer.

In Northampton, CCTV cameras were installed with a system that allowed operators to (25) _____ offenders publicly. However, the measure did little to (26) _____ order. In contrast, when police attempted to (27) _____ crowds of people around the Christmas period, a heavy physical presence proved successful.

A catch	B prevent
C control	D arrest
E warn	F return
G maintain	H direct

C Check the key on page 269. How many questions did you answer correctly?

D In pairs, answer the questions below about the task you have just done.

1. Did you spend an equal amount of time on both passages? If not, why not?
2. Did you have sufficient time to answer all the questions, write answers and then check answers?
3. Are you happy with the number of questions you answered correctly?

Key vocabulary in context

In pairs, discuss the slight difference in meaning between the words in each pair or list below.

1. harass / intimidate / victimize / terrorize
2. sympathy / remorse
3. rumours / gossip
4. disturbing / sinister
5. supervise / monitor / patrol
6. install / deploy

WB See *Vocabulary development* on Workbook page 256.

WB For focus on reading skills, go to Workbook page 258.

12

Writing 1: preparing to write

A In pairs, discuss whether imprisonment is a suitable punishment for each of the offences below.

| burglary | shoplifting | armed robbery | stealing a car | football hooliganism |
| tax evasion | attempted murder | violent assault | possession of drugs | drink-driving |

1. Say why you think imprisonment is suitable or unsuitable.
2. Discuss any considerations – if it's a first offence or one of a series of offences, for example.
3. Suggest an alternative if you think prison is unsuitable.

B What is the purpose of prison? In pairs, discuss how important you think each of the purposes below is. Check the meaning of the highlighted words.

1. It's a punishment – offenders deserve to be punished.
2. It's a deterrent – it deters potential offenders from committing crime because they are afraid of being locked up.
3. It protects society – people feel safer if they know that dangerous offenders are behind bars.
4. It offers rehabilitation – offenders are rehabilitated by engaging in activities and learning skills that they will be able to use when released.

Writing 2: deciding what to say and how to say it

A Look at these instructions for a typical IELTS Writing task and start thinking about what you would say.

Write about the following topic:

Imprisonment is nothing more than a punishment. At the end of their sentence, offenders are released only to reoffend almost immediately. Society needs an alternative way of dealing with crime.

To what extent do you agree with this claim?

Give reasons for your answer and include any relevant examples from your own knowledge or experience.

Write at least 250 words.

B A student has decided to write a balanced argument. Complete her notes below with one key word in each space. Compare ideas with a partner.

Yes – agree
More than half of prisoners released reoffend within a year. (I read this!)
Prisoners mix with other criminals in prison – often who have committed more _____ crimes.
When released – prisoners have no _____ / nowhere to _____ / have lost _____.

No – don't agree
Putting offenders in prison _____ society.
Prison life is hard – the fear of going to prison _____ offenders.
Nowadays, prisons have _____ programmes – inmates learn useful skills.
What is the alternative? Any alternative is _____ than prison.

C Check the actual notes on page 269. Were your ideas the same?

D In pairs, answer the questions below.

1. Which of the arguments from the notes in Exercise B would you use in your composition?
2. What additional points would you like to make?

Writing 3: elements of a good discursive composition

A Read the composition that the student wrote below and on the next page. In pairs, discuss what you like and what you don't like about it.

I agree with the claim partly but not completely. I read that over half of offenders released offend again within a year so of course some people question how useful is imprisonment and ask if another option can be more effective. I think these released prisoners go back to crime because in prison they make friends with other criminals somewhat are even more dangerous criminals than they are – they end up knowing more about crime than they did before they went in! I think as well many prisoners are released with no hope to find a job and often have nowhere to live. They lose their family during the time they are locked up too.

Apart from these arguments against prison there are strong cases for prison too. First people are afraid to be locked in prison and so this punishment stops them commit a crime in the first place. Second when dangerous people are locked away the public is safer. Third there is rehabilitation now in all the prisons – prisoners learn social abilities and new skills for get a job when they go out. Finally, I'm not sure what is the alternative the claim asks for – a fine? Or maybe community service? I don't think people like these soft punishments for dealing with real criminals.

To finish I want to say that criminals should not be put in prison for small offences if it means they lose everything and it makes a bigger problem for society. But I do believe that prison is the only place for dangerous criminals that do a lot of crimes.

B In your pair, discuss where:

- points could be expanded to make the composition up to 250 words.
- language could be expressed in a more appropriately formal style.
- different words could be used to avoid repetition.
- grammatical errors should have been checked.
- sentences need to be properly punctuated
- full forms could be used instead of contractions.

C Read another composition based on the original notes. Put the linking devices in the box into the correct space. Use capital letters when necessary.

because	of course	in any case	however	although	on the other hand
	since	still	despite	also	

Prisons have existed in all societies for thousands of years and most people do not stop to think about whether they are a suitable form of punishment. (1) _____, (2) _____ many offenders go straight back to a life of crime when released, many people question the benefits of imprisonment and ask whether there is a more effective alternative.

The main argument against the effectiveness of imprisonment is the high rate of reoffending. I read that over half of released offenders reoffend within a year. This may be (3) _____ in prison they socialize with other criminals – often criminals who have committed more serious offences. Prisoners who have committed petty offences are released knowing more about crime than they did before. Another reason could be that many prisoners are released with little hope of finding a job and often have nowhere to live. They may (4) _____ lose their family during the time they are locked up.

(5) _____ these reservations, I (6) _____ believe that prison is the only real option when dealing with serious offenders. The fear of being incarcerated deters potential offenders from committing crime and the public is safer when dangerous criminals are behind bars. (7) _____ rehabilitation may not work for all inmates, many do learn new skills and are given the chance to reintegrate into society. (8) _____, I am not sure what alternatives really exist. Fines or some sort of community service are not appropriate when tackling the majority of offences. The public are generally not satisfied with these soft options.

In conclusion, I would say that I can see why the claim is made, but do not fully agree with it. (9) _____, offenders should not be imprisoned for petty offences if it means they lose everything and then create an even bigger problem for society. (10) _____, prison really is the only place for those who are a danger or commit a number of offences.

D In pairs, discuss why the second composition is better than the first. Find examples of how weaknesses identified in Exercise B have been addressed.

E Look at the Exam Practice Module on page 191 for the Writing task.

Speaking

A Choose FIVE of the sentences below and plan how you want to complete them. Then compare ideas with other students in the class.

1. A crime that seems to be on the increase is …
2. A social issue that affects my hometown/city is …
3. A petty offence that makes me angry is …
4. In my country, there was recently a story about …
5. Fewer people would commit crime if …
6. Young people are drawn into criminal activity when …
7. The best way to deal with … is …
8. Prison is not a suitable punishment for …
9. The worst crime anyone can commit is …
10. The death penalty …

B Work in pairs – one of you is A, the other is B.

1. Student A: Tell your partner about cyber bullying.
2. Student B: Tell your partner about problems with CCTV cameras.

Vocabulary

A Write the crime that is defined in each case below

1. The offender kills somebody without intending to.   _____
2. The offender threatens to reveal information unless they are paid money.   _____
3. An official is offered money in return for a favour.   _____
4. A document is illegally copied.   _____
5. The offender sets fire to a building.   _____
6. The offender falsely claims insurance.   _____
7. Windows are smashed and graffiti sprayed on a door.   _____
8. A number of houses are broken into.   _____
9. Some items are stolen from a supermarket.   _____
10. A man's nose is broken during a fight.   _____

B Match words in Box A with words in Box B to form common noun phrases.

A

crime   police   life
petty   FIRST-TIME   suspicious

B

sentence   offender   patrol
crime   scene   behaviour

C Correct the spelling mistakes in each of the words below.

1. prosecuetion   2. deterant   3. rehabilatate   4. servelinece   5. disterbing   6. harasment

Errors

A Correct the sentences below that are grammatically incorrect.

1. I wouldn't walk home if I could afford a taxi.
2. If I wasn't walking in that street, I wouldn't have been attacked.
3. If he'd put the money on that horse, he'd be sitting on his new yacht right now.
4. If I'd known she would get so upset, I wouldn't tell her.

Writing

A In pairs, look at the pictures and answer the questions below.

1. In what ways do the prison conditions differ in the two pairs of images?
2. Which image in each pair do you think is a more accurate representation of prison in most countries now?
3. Which images do you think are a more accurate representation of prison in your country now?
4. Do you think prison life has become too comfortable for many inmates?

B Look carefully at the instructions for this IELTS Writing task.

1. Highlight key words and phrases and make sure you understand them.
2. Identify the issues that you need to address in the composition.
3. Start thinking about whether you want to agree, disagree or present both sides of the argument.

Write about the following topic:

These days, most prisons in the developed world provide inmates with a relative range of comforts and the opportunity to study and learn new skills. Some people believe that prison is now too soft and that taxpayers' money is being wasted.

To what extent do you agree with this view?

Give reasons for your answer and include any relevant examples from your own knowledge or experience.

Write at least 250 words.

C In pairs, discuss the task and make notes together about points you might include.

D Write your composition. Remember – you don't need to include all the points you discussed or listed.

 Exam tip: Remember that Writing Task 2 carries more marks than Writing Task 1. You are advised to spend 40 minutes planning and writing the discursive composition for Task 2, compared to 20 minutes planning and writing the report for Task 1. Then check the model on page 269.

Review 3

Speaking and Vocabulary

A Mark each of the following topics like this:

> (++) I can talk about this topic easily and have plenty to say.
>
> (+) I can talk about this topic quite well and have some things to say.
>
> (–) I don't enjoy talking about this topic and don't know what to say.

1. my taste in the arts and entertainment ___
2. literature ___
3. paintings and other works of art ___
4. climate and weather ___
5. extreme weather events ___
6. ecological issues ___
7. success and failure ___
8. crime and how it affects people ___
9. the purpose of prison ___

B Discuss your answers with a partner.

C Work in pairs. Take it in turns to ask and answer questions about the topics in Exercise A.

D Write important words and phrases that you have learnt in Units 9–12 under each heading.

literature

_____
_____
_____
_____

art

_____
_____
_____
_____

typical climate and weather

_____
_____
_____
_____

extreme weather / natural disasters

_____
_____
_____
_____

(**my words and phrases**)

qualities that determine success

_____
_____
_____
_____

crime

_____
_____
_____
_____

punishment

_____
_____
_____
_____

Listening

A Work in pairs. Take it in turns to ask and answer the following questions about the listening skills you practised in Units 9–12. The student asking the question can look back at the unit and check the exam or question-type tips.

1. If a recording is about a number of related but separate themes, what sort of matching task is often set? In what ways is that type of task challenging?
2. How does looking at a flow chart help you to know what to listen for?
3. In which sections of the Listening test is the language likely to be most formal?
4. In which sections of the Listening test is the language likely to be most informal?
5. Which section of the Listening test is always related to education?
6. What do you need to do at the end of the Listening test? How long do you have to do it?
7. What mistakes can you make when writing an answer, even if you understand perfectly what the speaker says?

B Mark each of these statements about your listening skills (Y) if they are true for you or (N) if they are not. Then compare answers with a partner.

1. My listening has improved considerably since I started this course. ___
2. I know what to listen for specifically in order to answer questions. ___
3. I am confident about writing answers in note form at the same time that I listen. ___
4. I am better at working out the meaning of unknown words and phrases from the context as I listen. ___
5. I am more confident about identifying unknown key words and guessing how to spell them if I have to use them as answers. ___
6. I feel confident about transferring answers to the answer sheet in ten minutes. ___

Reading

A Work in pairs. Take it in turns to ask and answer the following questions about the reading skills you practised in Units 9–12. The student asking the question can look back at the unit and check the exam or question-type tips.

1. When are Y/N/NG tasks set rather than T/F/NG tasks?
2. Do you find Y/N/NG tasks any more challenging than T/F/NG tasks?
3. What different referencing devices do you need to become familiar with when reading longer, more academic, texts?
4. What do you remember about matching beginnings and endings of sentences? How can you make it easier to choose from a number of options?
5. Why is it so important to time yourself as you work through the Reading test?
6. Why should you make fewer mistakes when writing answers during the Reading test than when writing answers during the Listening test?

B Mark each of these statements about your reading skills (Y) if they are true for you or (N) if they are not. Then compare answers with a partner.

1. My reading speed has improved noticeably since I began this course. ___
2. I feel far more confident about reading longer passages now. ___
3. I understand the general idea of almost any text I read now. ___
4. I know what to look for in order to answer specific questions. ___
5. I don't worry about words and phrases I don't know anymore. ___

Writing

A In pairs, answer these questions about Writing Task 1.

1. Do you prefer writing a report based on information shown in any particular figure type?
2. Do you find describing information shown in any particular figure type more challenging than any other? Why?
3. When writing your report, do you generally find it more difficult to find enough information to describe or more difficult to say everything you feel you need to in only 150 words?
4. Do you usually feel that 20 minutes is long enough to absorb information and write your report?
5. Which aspects of your report writing have most improved during this course? Think about:
   - answering the question/selecting relevant data.
   - cohesion and coherence.
   - organization and linking of ideas.
   - using appropriate style/register.
   - using appropriate grammatical structures.
   - using an appropriate range of typical vocabulary.
   - spelling and punctuation.

B Find a report that you wrote early in the course and one that you have written in the last couple of weeks. Show them both to a partner and ask him/her to identify the most obvious areas of improvement.

C In pairs, discuss each of the aspects of discursive composition writing below.

1. To what degree have you improved each aspect during the course?
2. Are there any aspects you feel you still need to work on?

   - knowing what to say and having enough ideas to write 250 words
   - giving reasons and examples that support opinions
   - planning and organizing ideas before writing
   - organizing points logically within the composition
   - writing suitable introductions and conclusions
   - using paragraphs appropriately and introducing them with topic sentences
   - using the appropriate style and register
   - using words and phrases that introduce ideas and link points together
   - using appropriate grammatical structures effectively and accurately
   - spelling words correctly and punctuating the text

D Find a discursive composition that you wrote early in the course and one that you have written in the last couple of weeks. Show them both to a partner and ask him/her to identify the most obvious areas of improvement.

What next?

Congratulations! You've finished the course. You've heard the different types of talk or conversation that you will hear in the Listening test and you've read the various types of passage that you will have to read in the Reading test. You've practised every task type for each test. Hopefully, you feel much more confident about taking the exam now.

A Look at these comments made by students about taking the IELTS exam. In pairs, discuss which you most agree with. Can you give your partner any advice about taking the IELTS test?

> *I get very nervous in exams. I can't concentrate on the tasks.*

> *Some people are good at doing exams and some people are not.*

> *If other students in the exam are writing a lot and seem to be doing well, it makes me anxious. I think I'm not as good as they are.*

> *My mind goes blank as soon as I sit down in an exam hall.*

> *I worry too much about getting the answers right and not enough about whether I understand.*

> *I can't sleep the night before an exam so I'm always really tired during the exam.*

> *Revising for exams is really boring.*

> *Revising just before an exam is a waste of time. You either know it or you don't.*

B Read the tips below about taking exams and revising.

✓ Revision doesn't have to be boring. It's boring if you do it for too long or try to do it all at once. It'll make you feel anxious if you try to revise too much. Don't wait until the night before the exam to do all your revision. Revise when you would otherwise be wasting time, like on the bus!

✓ Remember that revision means looking back at what you've learnt – not trying to learn things that you haven't learnt yet.

✓ Practise the Speaking test with other students who are taking the exam. Revise the typical vocabulary that you need to talk about the most common topics of conversation. Make sure you know the words and phrases you need to talk about your own life.

✓ Revise for the Listening test by borrowing CDs that practise typical IELTS listening tasks. Remember, though, that the important thing is to improve your all-round listening skills so continue to follow the advice from the previous Review section.

✓ Revise for the Reading test by doing Reading tests from past IELTS papers. Look back at the reading modules from earlier units in this book. Look at how the texts have become more challenging and how your reading skills have improved.

✓ Practise writing reports and compositions and ask your teacher or someone who reads English very well to check them. Continue to look at as many model answers to test questions as you can.

✓ Get a good night's sleep the night before the test. You don't want to feel tired. Make sure you arrive at the centre some time before the exam starts. You want to feel relaxed and confident – not in a terrible rush.

✓ Try not to be nervous. Remember that the important thing is to understand what you hear and what you read. If you can, you will answer questions correctly. Don't worry about how other people are doing – you are not in competition with them.

Good luck!

Key exam vocabulary

The key vocabulary is a list of words and phrases that occur in *IELTS Target 6.5* that you should learn to improve your performance, particularly in the IELTS Academic Reading and Writing tests. The most useful related words are also given, though these may not necessarily have occurred in the course. These words and phrases are those that frequently occur in the type of texts that you will read in the IELTS Academic exam, and which you will need to write effectively in both writing tasks. These words and phrases will also help you to better understand certain topics in the Listening test.

Some very common words and phrases are not included because you will already know what they mean and how to use them. Vocabulary that you will need for the Speaking test is not included as this will be more personal to you. Look back at the first module of each unit to check particular words and phrases that you need to improve your speaking.

Phrasal verbs and idiomatic expressions that occur in the course are not listed unless particularly likely in academic writing (*weigh up*, for example). It is not very helpful to list this type of lexis without a supporting context.

The part of speech is given for each item, except when it is a longer phrase or expression. When a verb or adjective is always or frequently used with a preposition, the preposition is given in brackets. When other combinations of words are listed, only the basic part of speech is given so, for example, verb + noun combinations are generally labelled as (v) and compound nouns as (n). Passive forms are occasionally included when a verb is frequently used passively. When collocations are very strong, the whole phrase is given – *stormy relationship*, for example.

Spend some time checking all the words and phrases in the list and check anything you are not sure about in a good dictionary.

A

abandon (v) / abandonment (n)
abroad (adv) / (go) abroad (v)
absorb (v) / absorption (n)
absence (n) / absent (adj) / absenteeism (n)
abstract (adj)
absurd (adj) / absurdity (n)
abundance (n) / abundant (adj)
abuse /əˈbjuːs/ (n) / abuse /əˈbjuːz/ (v) / abusive (adj)
accelerate (v) / acceleration (n)
access (n/v) / accessible (adj) / accessibility (n)
accolade (n)
accommodate (v) / accommodation (n)
accumulate (v) / accumulation (n)
accuracy (n) / accurate (adj)
accusation (n) / accuse (v) / the accused (n)
achievable (adj) / achieve (v) / achievement (n)
acquire (v) / acquisition (n)
action (n) / take action / put into action
activate (v) / active (adj) / activity (n)
adapt (to) (v) / adaptable (adj) / adaptation (n)
admonish (v)
adolescence (n) / adolescent (n)
adopt (v) / adoption (n) / adoptive (adj)

adoration (n) / adore (v)
adulthood (n)
advantage (n) / take advantage (v) / advantageous (adj)
advent (n)
adventure (n)
adverse (adj) / adversity (n)
aesthetic (adj)
affect (v)
affection (n)
affluence (n) / affluent (adj)
afford (v) / affordable (adj)
ageing (adj)
age-old (adj)
aggravate (v)
aggression (n) / aggressive (adj)
ahead of his/her/its time
allergic (to) (adj) / allergy (n)
alternative (adj/n)
ambiguous (adj) / ambiguity (n)
ambition (n) / (un)ambitious (adj)
amicable (adj) / amicably (adv)
anaesthetic (n)
anger (n/v)
anonymity (n) / anonymous (adj)

antidote (n)

anxiety (n) / anxious (adj)

apparent (adj) / apparently (adv)

application (n) / apply to (v)

appreciate (v) / appreciation (n)

apprehension (n) / apprehensive (adj)

approach (n/v)

appropriate (adj) / appropriateness (n)

architect (n) / architectural (adj) / architecture (n)

arrest (n/v) / be arrested (v)

arson (n)

articulate (v)

artistic (adj)

aspect (n)

aspirations (n) / aspire (to) (v) / aspiring (adj)

assemble (v) / assembly (n)

assess (v) / assessment (n)

assign (to) (v) / assignment (n)

associated (with) (adj) / association (n) / in association
    with / by association

assume (v) / assumption (n)

astonish (v) / astonishing (adj)

attend (v) / attention (n) / attentive (adj) / it needs
    attention

attitude (n)

atmosphere (n) / atmospheric (adj)

authoritative (adj) / authority (n)

avalanche (n)

average (adj)

aversion (n) / avert (v) / have an aversion to

award (n/v) / be awarded to / be awarded with

aware (of) (adj) / awareness (n)

B

background (n)

backlog (n)

balance (n/v) / balanced diet (n)

ban (n/v) / banned (adj)

barrier (n)

barrister (n)

bureaucracy (n)

behave (v) / behaviour (n) / behavioural (adj)

believe (in) (v) / belief (n)

belong (to) (v) / a sense of belonging

beneficial (adj) / benefit (n/v) / benefit (from) (v)

best-seller (n)

bias (n) / biased (adj)

biographical (adj) / biography (n)

biodiversity (n) / biological (adj) / biology (n)

birth (n) / birth rate (n)

blackmail (n/v)

blame (n/v) / (be) blamed (for) (v) / blame s/th on s/b /
    blame s/b for s/th / take the blame for s/th

block (v) / blockage (n)

blossom (v)

boast (n/v)

bond (n/v) / bonding (n)

the bottom line (n)

boundary (n)

break the law (v)

breed (n/v) / breeding ground (n)

breeze (n)

bribe (n/v) / bribery (n)

brief (adj) / briefly (adv)

bring up (v)

budget (n) / budget (for) (v)

build up (v) / build-up (n)

bully (n/v) / be bullied (v)

burden (n)

burglary (n) / burglar (n) / burgle (v)

burnout (n)

burst (n/v)

bury (v) / be buried (v)

C

captivate (v) / captivating (adj)

casualty (n)

catastrophe (n) / catastrophic (adj)

category (n) / categorize (v)

cause (n/v) / be the cause of

caution (n) / cautious (adj)

cell (n)

censor (v) / censorship (n)

(be) central (to) (adj)

challenge (n/v) / challenging (adj)

changeable (adj)

chapter (n)

character (n) / characteristics (n) / characterize (v)

charisma (n) / charismatic (adj)

childhood (n)

chill (n/v) / chilly (adj)

choice (n) / make a choice (n)

circumstances (n)

claim (n/v)

clarity (n)

classic (adj/n) / classical (adj)

clear (v) / clearance (n)

climate (n) / climate change (n)

cloud (n) / cloudless (adj) / cloudy (adj)

collaborate (v) / collaboration (n) / collaborative (adj)

combination (n) / combine (with) (v)

comfort (n) / comfortable (adj)

committed (to) (adj) / commitment (n)

common (adj)

community (n)

comparable (adj) / compare (to/with) (v) / comparison (n) / make a comparison (v)

compete (with) (v) / competition (n) / competitive (adj) / competitor (n)

complex (adj) / complexity (n)

components (n)

compress (v)

compromise (n/v) / make compromises

conceal (v)

concern (n/v) / concerned (with) (adj) / concerning (prep) / be concerned about / concern yourself with s/th

conclude (v) / conclusion (n) / draw a conclusion / conclusive (adj)

condition (n/v) / conditioning (n)

conduct /ˈkɒndʌkt/ (n) / conduct /kənˈdʌkt/ (v)

confirm (v) / confirmation (n)

conflict (n) / conflicting (adj) / in conflict with

confront (v) / confrontation (n)

congested (adj) / congestion (n)

(in) conjunction (with) (n)

conscious (adj)

consequence (n) / consequential (adj) / consequentially (adv)

considerate (adj) / consideration (n)

consist (of) (v) / consistency (n) / consistent (adj)

constant (adj) / constantly (adv)

constrain (v) / constraint (n)

consume (v) / consumption (n)

contemplate (v) / contemplation (n)

contemporary (adj)

contend (with) (v)

content (n/v) / contentment (n)

contradict (v) / contradiction (n) / contradictory (adj)

contrast (n/v) / contrasting (adj) / in contrast to

contribute (to) (v) / contribution (n) / make a contribution to / contributory (adj)

controversial (adj) / controversy (n)

convention (n) / conventional (adj)

conversion (n) / convert (v)

co-operate (v) / co-operation (n)

cope (with) (v)

correlation (n)

cost (n/v) / costly (adj)

counteract (v)

counterpart (n)

countless (adj)

courage (n) / courageous (adj)

coward (n) / cowardice (n) / cowardly (adj)

create (v) / creation (n) / creative (adj) / creativity (n)

crime (n) / criminal (adj/n) / commit a crime / crime scene (n)

criteria (n)

critical (adj) / criticism (n) / criticize (v)

crucial (adj) / crucially (adv)

cruel (adj) / cruelty (n)

cruise (n)

cull (v) / culling (n)

cultivate (v) / cultivation (n)

cultural (adj) / culture (n) / cultured (adj)

current (adj) / currently (adv)

cutbacks (n)

cutting-edge (adj)

cycle (n)

D

damage (n/v) / damaging (adj)

damp (adj)

data (n)

deal with (v)

dearth (n)

debt (n) / be in debt

decay (n/v)

decent (adj)

decide (v) / decision (n) / decisive (adj) / make a decision

declare (v) / declaration (n)

decline (n/v)

decrease (n/v)

defeat (n/v) / defeatism (n)

defence (n) / defend (v) / defensive (adj)

define (v) / definition (n)

deflect (v) / deflection (n)

deforestation (n)

defunct (adj)

defiance (n) / defiant (adj) / defy (v)

degree (n) / to a degree

delegate (v) / delegation (n)

demand (n/v) / demanding (adj) / be a demand for

demonstrate (v) / demonstration (n) / demonstrative (adj)

dense (adj) / density (n)

deploy (v) / deployment (n)

deprive (v) / be deprived of (v) / deprivation (n)

depth (n) / in-depth (adj)

derelict (adj)

derogatory (adj)

design (n/v)

desire (n/v) / desirable (adj)

destabilization (n) / destabilize (v)

destination (n)

destruction (n) / destructive (adj) / destroy (v)

detect (v) / detection (n)

deter (v) / deterrent (n)

deteriorate (v) / deterioration (n)

determination (n) / determine (v) / determined (adj)

develop (v) / development (n) / developed countries (n) /
    developing countries (n) / the developing world (n)

deviate (from) (v) / deviation (n)

differ (from) (v) / difference (n)

diminish (v)

disabled (adj) / disability (n)

disadvantage (n)

disapproval (n) / disapprove (of) (v)

discipline (n/v)

discomfort (n)

discover (v) /discovery (n)

dismantle (v)

disobedience (n) / disobey (v)

disparate (adj)

dispense (with) (v)

disperse (v)

displace (v) displacement (n)

disrupt (v) / disruption (n) / disruptive (adj)

distant past (n)

distinction (n) / distinguish (between) (v) /
    distinguishable (adj)

distress (n/v) / distressing (adj) / be in distress

distrust (n/v)

disturb (v) / disturbance (n) / disturbing (adj)

diverse (adj) / diversity (n)

diversion (n) / divert (v)

division (n)

divorce (n/v)

donate (v) / donation (n) / donor (n) / make a donation

dramatic (adj) / dramatically (adv)

draw (v) / be drawn to (v)

drawback (n)

drive (n) / driven (adj)

drizzle (n)

drop (n/v)

drought (n)

duration (n)

dutiful (adj) / duty (n) / a sense of duty

dwell (v) / dwellers (n) / dwelling (n) / dwelling place (n)

E

eccentric (adj) / eccentricity (n)

economic (adj) / economical (adj) / economic boom (n) /
    economic downturn (n) / economy (n)

effect (n) / effective (adj) / effectiveness (n) / have an
    effect on

efficiency (n) / efficient (adj)

effort (n) / make an effort

elderly (adj)

eligible (for) (adj) / eligibility (n)

eliminate (v) / elimination (n)

elite (adj/n)

elsewhere (adv)

eminent (adj) / eminence (n)

emerge (v) / emergence (n)

emergency (n)

emphasis (n) / emphasize (v) / emphatic (adj)

employ (v) / employee (n) / employment (n)

emulate (v) / emulation (n)

enable (v)

encompass (v)

encourage (v) / encouragement (n) / encouraging (adj)

endangered (adj) / endangered species (n)

endurance (n) / endure (v) / enduring (adj)

energetic (adj) / energy (n)

engage (in) (v) / engagement (n) / engaging (adj)

enhance (v) / enhancement (n)

enjoyable (adj) / enjoyment (n)

enquire (v) / enquiry (n) / make an enquiry

environment (n) / environmental (adj) /
    environmentalist (n) / environmentally friendly

equal (adj/n) / equally (adv) / the equal of (n) / equality (n)

erode (v) / erosion (n) / erosive (adj)

escape (n/v) / escape (from) (v) / escapism (n)

essence (n) / essential (adj)

establish (v) / establishment (n)

estimate /ˈestɪmət/ (n) / estimate /ˈestɪmeɪt/ (v) /
    estimation (n)

evaluate (v) / evaluation (n)

event (n) / eventful (adj)

evidence (n) / evident (adj) / evidently (adv) / give
    evidence

evoke (v)

evolution (n) / evolutionary (adj) / evolve (v)

exception (n) / exceptional (adj) / exceptionally (adv)

excess (n) / excessive (adj) / excessively (adv)

execute (v) / execution (n) /

executive (n)

exhibit (n/v) / exhibition (n)

exist (v) / existence (n) / existing (adj)

excite (v) / excitement (n)

exclude (v) / exclusive (adj) / exclusively (adv)

excursion (n)

exodus (n)

exotic (adj)

expand (v) / expansion (n)

expect (v) / expectations (n) / meet expectations

expedition (n)
expenditure (n)
expel (v) / expulsion (n)
experience (n/v) / experienced (adj)
expert (adj/n) / expertise (n)
exploitation (n) / exploit (v)
exploration (n) / explore (v)
expose (v) / be exposed to (v) / exposure (n)
extend (v) / extended (adj) / extended family (n) /
    extensive (adj) / extent (n)
external (adj)
extinct (adj) / (become) extinct (v) / extinction (n)
extract (n/v) / extraction (n)
extreme (ad) / extremely (adv) / extremity (n)
eyesore (n)

F

facet (n)
facilitate (v)
factor (n)
faith (n) / faithful (adj) / in good faith
fan (n) / fanatical (adj)
far-reaching (adj)
fascinate (v) / fascination (n) / fascinating (adj)
favour (n/v) / favourable (adj)
fear (n/v) / fearful (of) (adj)
feature (n/v)
feedback (n)
felony (n)
feminism (n) / feminist (n)
fertile (adj) / fertility (n)
festival (n)
fiasco (n)
fiction (n) / fictional (adj)
filter (n/v)
finance (n) / financial (adj)
findings (n)
flash (n/v) / flash of lightning (n)
flood (n/v) / flooding (n)
flow (n/v)
fluctuate (v) / fluctuation (n)
focus (n) / focus (on) (v) / focused (adj)
fog (n) / foggy (adj)
fond (adj) / fond memories (n)
forbid (v) / forbidden (adj)
force (n/v) / forceful (adj)
forgery (n)
fossil (n) / fossilize (v)
foster (v)
found (v) / founder (n)
franchise (n)

fraud (n)
freedom (n)
freeze (v) / freezing (adj) / frozen (adj)
frequency (n) / frequent (adj) / frequently (adv)
frost (n) / frosty (adj) / frosty reception (n)
fulfil (v) / fulfilment (n)
function (n/v) / functional (adj)
fundamental (adj)
funeral (n)

G

gale (n)
gallery (n)
gather (v)
gender (n)
gene (n) / gene pool (n) / genetic (adj) / genetically (adv)
genius (n)
geological (adj) / geology (n)
ghastly (adj)
glamorous (adj) / glamour (n)
global (adj) / global warming (n) / globe (n)
gradual (adj) / gradually (adv)
graduate /ˈgrædʒuːət/ (n) / graduate /ˈgrædʒuːeɪt/ (v) /
    graduation (n)
a great deal (n)
grand (adj)
grant (n/v)
greenhouse gases (n)
grey area (n)
grief (n)
grow up (v) / grown-up (adj/n)
growth (n)
guarantee (n/v) / guaranteed (adj)
guidance (n) / guide (n/v)
guilt (n) / guilty (adj) / plead guilty or not guilty

H

habitat (n)
hail (n) / hailstones (n) / hailstorm (n)
hamper (v)
harmony (n)
harass (v) / harassment (n)
health (n) / health care (n) / healthy (adj)
heat (n/v) / heatwave (n)
hectic (adj)
hereditary (adj) / heredity (n)
hesitant (adj) / hesitate (v) / hesitation (n)
hideous (adj)
highlight (v)
historic (adj) / historical (adj) / history (n)
homesick (adj) / homesickness (n)

honour (n)

household (adj) / household name (n)

huge (adj) / hugely (adv)

humble (adj)

humiliate (v) / humiliation (n)

hunger (n) / hungry (adj)

hurricane (n)

I

icy (adj) / icy conditions (n)

identical (adj) / identical twins (n) / identification (n) / identity (n)

ignorance (n) / ignorant (adj)

ignore (v)

ill effects (n)

illegal (adj) / illegality (n)

illiterate (adj) / illiteracy (n)

illustrate (v) / illustration (n) / illustrative (adj)

imaginary (adj) / imagination (n) / imagine (v) / use your imagination

immune (to) (adj) / immune system (n) / immunity (n)

impact (n) / have an impact on

impermeable (adj)

impetus (n)

implicate (v) / implication (n) / imply (v)

impose on (v) / imposing (adj) / imposition (n)

inability (n)

inadequacy (n) / inadequate (adj)

inappropriate (adj)

inborn (adj)

income (n)

incomprehensible (adj)

increase /ˈɪŋkriːs/ (n) / increase /ɪnˈkriːs/ (v)

indecision (n) / indecisive (adj)

independence (n) / independent (adj)

indicate (v) / indication (n)

indigenous (adj) / indigenous tribes (n)

individual (adj/n) / individuality (n)

ineffective (adj)

inefficient (adj)

inequality (n)

inevitable (adj) / inevitability (n)

inexperience (n)

infancy (n) / infant (n) / infant mortality (n) / in its infancy

infect (v) / infection (n)

inferior (adj) / inferiority (n)

inflict (v)

infrastructure (n)

influence (n/v) / influential (adj) / have an influence on

inhabit (v) / inhabitants (n)

inheritance (n) / inherit (v)

initiative (n)

inmate (n)

innate (adj) / innately (adv)

inquiry (n)

inseparable (adj)

inspiration (n) / inspirational (adj) / inspire (v) / inspired (adj) / inspiring (adj)

install (v) / installation (n)

insecure (adj) / insecurity (n)

instinct (n) / instinctive (adj) / instinctively (adv)

instrumental (adj)

insulate (v) / insulation (n)

insult (n/v) / insulting (adj)

intake (n)

intellect (n) / intellectual (adj)

interact (with) (v) / interaction (n)

interfere (with) (v) / interference (n)

internal (adj) / internally (adv) / internalize (v)

interrupt (v) / interruption (n)

intricate (adj)

intimidate (v) / intimidation (n) / intimidating (adj)

intrude (v) / intruder (n) / intrusion (n) / intrusive (adj)

investigate (v) / investigation (n) / launch an investigation

isolate (v) / isolated (adj) / isolation (n)

J

jobless (adj)

journey (n) / make a journey

joy (n) / joyful (adj)

judge (v) / judgement (n) / judgemental (adj)

jury (n)

K

keen (adj) / be keen on (adj)

L

labour (n/v) / labour market (n)

lack (v) / a lack of (n) / lacking (adj)

landscape (n)

law (n) / lawful (adj) / against the law

leadership (n) / leadership qualities

leisure (n) / leisure time (n)

length (n) / lengthen (v) / lengthy (adj)

level playing field (n)

life-changing (adj)

life expectancy (n)

life sentence (n)

lifespan (n)

lifestyle (n)

lightning (n)

likelihood (n) / likely (adj)

limit (n/v) / limited (adj) / limitless (adj)
link (n/v)
literacy (n)
loathe (v)
local (adj) / locality (n)
locate (v) / location (n)
logging (n)
logical (adj) / logically (adv)
longevity (n)
long-term (adj)
look forward to (v)
loose (adj) / loosen (v)
loss (n)
lower (v)
luxurious (adj) / luxury (n)

M

magnificent (adj) / magnificence (n)
maintain (v) / maintenance (n)
major (adj)
majority (n) / the majority of (n)
management (n) / manager (n) / managerial (adj)
manifest (v)
man-made (adj)
manslaughter (n)
maximize (v) / maximum (n)
marriage (n)
masterpiece (n)
mature (adj/v) / maturity (n)
meagre (adj)
measurable (adj) / measure (v)
memorable (adj) / memory (n) / memorize (v)
menial (adj)
mentor (n/v)
middle age (n) / middle-aged (adj)
migrate (v) / migration (n)
mild (adj)
mind (n/v) / mindful (adj) / mindless (adj)
minimal (adj) / minimize (v)
minority (n) / a minority of (n)
mirror (v)
misunderstand (v) / misunderstanding (n) / be
    misunderstood (v)
misuse /mɪsˈjuːs/ (n) / misuse /mɪsˈjuːz/ (v) /
    be misused (v)
mitigate (v) / mitigation (n)
moderate /ˈmɒdərət/ (adj) / moderate /ˈmɒdəreɪt/ (v) /
    moderation (n) / in moderation
modern (adj) / modernize (v)
modify (v)
moist (adj) / moisture (n)

monitor (v)
monopolize (v) / monopoly (n)
monstrosity (n) / monstrous (adj)
monument (n) / monumental (adj)
moral (adj/n) / morality (n)
motivate (v) / motivating (adj) / motivation (n)
mould (n/v)
movement (n)
mudslide (n)
mug (v) / mugging (n)
muggy (adj)
multiple (adj) / multiplication (n) / multiply (v)
mundane (adj)
mutual (adj)
mysterious (adj) / mystery (n)
myth (n)

N

natural (adj) / naturally (adv) / natural disaster (n) /
    nature (n)
nearby (adj/adv)
necessitate (v) / necessity (n) / basic necessities (n)
negative (adj) / negativity (n)
neglect (n/v) / negligence (n) / negligent (adj)
negotiate (v) / negotiation (n)
neighbourhood (n)
nocturnal (adj)
non-fiction (n)
nonsense (n)
non-stop (adj)
norm (n) / normal (adj) / normality (n)
nostalgia (n) / nostalgic (adj)
noticeable (adj) / noticeably (adv)
notion (n)
novel (n) / novelist (n)
number (v)
numerous (adj)
nurture (n/v)

O

oath (n) / take on oath (v)
obese (adj) / obesity (n)
obligation (n) / obligatory (adj) / oblige (v) / be obliged (v)
occasion (n) / occasional (adj) / occasionally (adv/adj) /
    on occasion
offence (n) / offender (n) / offensive (adj)
off the beaten track
old age (n)
one-time (adj)
ongoing (adj)
only child (n)

opportunism (n) / opportunist (n) / opportunistic (adj) /
   opportunity (n)

oppose (v) / opposed (to) (adj) / opposition (n) / be in
   opposition to

oppress (v) / oppression (n)

optimism (n) / optimist (n) / optimistic (adj)

organization (n) / organizational (adj) / organize (v) /
   organizer (n)

organism (n)

origin (n) / original (adj) / originality (n)

overhaul (n)

overload /'əʊvələʊd/ (n) / overload /əʊvə'ləʊhd/ (v)

overwhelm (v) / overwhelming (adj)

overwork (n/v) / overworked (adj)

otherwise (adv)

outbreak (n)

outline (n/v)

output (n)

outstanding (adj)

outweigh (v)

overcast (adj)

overcome (v)

overdue (adj)

P

package holiday (n)

paperback (n)

paradox (n) / paradoxically (adv)

parasite (n) / parasitical (adj)

parent (n/v) / parental (adj) / parental control (n)

part (n/v) / partly (adv) / be a part of s/th / in part / on
   the part of

partake (in) (v)

participate (v)

particular (adj) / particularly (adv)

partition (n/v)

pass (on) (v)

passion (n) / passionate (adj)

patrol (n/v)

peculiar (adj)

peers (n)

penetrate (v) / penetration (n)

percentage (of) (n)

perceive (v) / perception (n)

perfect (adj) / perfection (n) / perfectionist (n) /
   perfectly (adv)

perform (v) / performance (n)

permanence (n) / permanent (adj) / permanently (adv)

permeable (adj)

permission (n) / permit (v)

perpetrate (v) / perpetrator (n)

persecute (v) / persecution (n)

perseverance (n) / persevere (v)

persist (v) / persistence (n) / persistent (adj)

perspective (n)

persuade (v) / persuasion (n)

pertinence (n) / pertinent (adj)

pervasive (adj) / pervasiveness (n)

pessimism (n) / pessimist (n) / pessimistic (adj)

petty (adj) / petty crime (n)

phenomenal (adj) / phenomenon (n)

physical (adj) / physically (adv) / physical strength (n)

pioneer (n) / pioneering (adj)

pittance (n)

pity (n/v) / pitiful (adj)

plain (adj)

plea (n) / plead (v) / plead guilty or not guilty

pleasurable (adj) / pleasure (n)

plot (n)

poem (n) / poet (n) / poetry (n)

policy (n)

pollute (v) / polluted (adj) / pollutants (n) / pollution (n)

pontificate (v)

portrait (n)

pose (v) / pose a threat (v)

positive thinking (n)

possess (v) / possessions (n)

potential (n) / potentially (adv)

poverty (n)

power (n) / powerful (adj) / powerless (adj) /
   powerlessness (n)

precious (adj)

precise (adj) / precision (n)

predator (n) / predatory (adj)

predict (v) / prediction (n) / make a prediction

predominant (adj)

prefer (v) / preferable (adj) / preference (n)

pregnancy (n) / pregnant (adj)

prejudice (n)

prescribe (v) / prescription (n)

present /'preznt/ (n) / present /prɪ'zent/ (v) /
   presence (n) / presentation (n)

pressure (n/v) / pressurize (v) / under pressure

pretentious (adj) / pretentiousness (n)

prevent (v) / prevention (n)

pride (n) / take pride in / pride yourself on s/th

primary (adj)

primitive (adj)

principal (n)

principle (n)

prioritize (v) / priority (n)

privacy (n) / private (adj)

privilege (n) / privileged (adj)

proceed (v) / proceeds (n)

process (n/v)

profession (n) / professional (adj)

profit (n) / profit (from) (v) / profitable (adj)

progress /ˈprəʊgres/ (n) / progress /prəˈgres/ (v) / make progress / progression (n) / progressive (adj)

proliferate (v) / prolific (adj)

promise (n/v) / promising (adj)

prompt (adj/n/v)

prone (to) (adj)

property (n)

prosecute (v) / prosecution (n)

prosper (v) / prosperous (adj)

protect (v) / protection (n) / protective (adj)

proof (n) / prove (v) / proven (adj) / prove right / prove wrong

provoke (v)

proximity (n) / in close proximity to

pseudonym (n)

punish (v) / punishment (n)

purpose (n) / purposeful (adj) / a sense of purpose (n)

put forward (v)

Q

qualifications (n) / qualify (v)

quality (n)

quell (v)

question (v)

queue (n/v) / queue-jumping (n)

quirky (adj)

quit (v) / quitter (n)

R

radical (adj)

rainbow (n)

rainforest (n)

rainy season (n)

rank (n/v)

rare (adj) / rarely (adv) / rarity (n)

rational (adj) / think rationally (v)

reaction (n) / reactionary (adj/n)

realistic (adj) / realistically (adv) / reality (n)

reassess (v) / reassessment (n)

reassurance (n) / reassure (v) / reassuring (adj)

recall (v) / recollection (n)

recent past (n)

recipient (n)

reclaim (v) / reclamation (n)

recommend (v) / recommendation (n)

recreation (n) / recreational (adj)

redundant (adj)

refer (to) (v) / reference (n)

refrain (from) (v)

refusal (n) / refuse (v)

refurbish (v)

regard (v) / be regarded as (v) / regarding (adj) / regardless (adj)

region (n) / regional (adj)

regret (n/v) / have regrets / regrettable (adj) / regrettably (adv)

rehabilitate (v) / rehabilitation (n)

reinstate (v)

reject /ˈriːdʒekt/ (n) / reject /rɪˈdʒekt/ (v) / be rejected (v) / rejection (n)

release (n/v)

relevance (n) / relevant (adj)

relief (n) / relieve (v) / relieved (adj)

relocate (v)

reliable (adj) / reliance (n) / rely (on) (v)

remain (v) / remain steady (v)

reminisce (v)

remind (v) / it reminds me of

renounce (v)

replace (v) / replacement (n)

replenish (v)

represent (v) / representation (n) / representative (adj/n)

require (v) / requirements (n)

research (n/v) / (do) research (v) / researchers (n)

reside (v) / resident (n) / residential (adj)

resign (v) / resigned (to) (adj) / resignation (n)

resilience (n) / resilient (adj)

resist (v) / resistance (n)

resort (n) / holiday resort (n)

resolution (n) / resolve (v)

resource (n) / resourceful (adj) / resourcefulness (n)

respond (to) (v) / response (n) / responsive (adj)

responsible (for) (adj) / responsibility (n)

restrict (v) / restriction (n)

retire (v) / retired (adj) / retirement (n)

retrievable (adj) / retrieve (v)

reveal (v) / revelation (n)

reverse (v/adj)

reward (n/v) / rewarding (adj)

risk (n/v) / (take) risks (v) / risky (adj)

roam (v)

rob (v) / robber (n) / robbery (n)

role (n) / play a role (v) / role model (n)

romance (n) / romantic (adj)

routine (adj/n)

ruin (n/v)

rumour (n) / spread rumours

run-down (adj)
rural (adj)

S

sadness (n)
scale (n)
search (n/v)
secure (adj) / security (n)
sedentary (adj)
seize (v) / seize a chance / seize an opportunity
self-appointed (adj)
self-confidence (n) / self-confident (adj)
self-doubt (n)
self-esteem (n)
self-pity (n)
self-reliant (adj)
self-worth (n)
sense (n) / sensible (adj) / sensibilities (n) /
    sensitive (adj) / sensitivity (n)
sentiment (n) / sentimental (adj)
separate /ˈseprət/ (adj) / separate /ˈsepəreɪt/ (v) /
    separately (adv)
serve (as) (v)
set a goal (v) / set a target (v)
setback (n)
setting (n)
settle (v) / settlement (n)
severe (adj) / severity (n) / severely (adv)
shade (n) / shaded (adj) / in the shade
shame (n)
shape (v)
sheer (adj)
shield (n/v) / be shielded from
shelter (n/v) / sheltered (adj)
shoplift (v) / shoplifting (n)
shortage (n)
short-term (adj) / short-term solution (n)
shower (n)
shrink (v) / shrinking (adj)
sibling(s) (n)
sight (n) / lose sight of
sightseeing (n)
signal (n/v)
significance (n) / significant (adj) / significantly (adv) /
    signify (v)
similarity (n)
simplicity (n)
sinister (adj)
sketch (n/v)
sleet (n)
slight (adj) / slightly (adv)

slope (n)
soak (v) / soaked (adj)
so-called (adj)
social (adj) / social issue (n) / social problem (n) /
    society (n)
sole (adj) / solely (adv)
solution (n) / solve (v)
sophisticated (adj) / sophistication (n)
source (n/v) / be the source of
souvenir (n)
spark (n/v)
species (n)
specific (adj) / specifically (adv) / specify (v)
spectacular (adj)
speed (n) / speed (up) (v)
spell (n) / a spell of warm or cold weather
spirit (n) / spiritual (adj) / spirituality (n)
splendid (adj)
spontaneous (adj) / spontaneously (adv)
sprawl (n/v) / sprawling (adj)
squalor (n)
stable (adj) / stability (n) / stabilize (v)
stage (n)
stalk (v)
stance (n)
statement (n) / make a statement
status (n)
steady (adj) / steadily (adv)
steep (adj)
stereotype (n/v)
stern (adj)
stimulate (v) / stimulation (n)
stock (n) / be in stock
storm (n) / stormy (adj) / stormy relationship (n)
straightforward (adj)
strategic (adj) / strategy (n)
strength (n) / strength of mind (n) / strengthen (v)
stress (n) / stressful (adj) / stress levels (n)
structural (adj) / structure (n/v)
stubborn (adj)
struggle (n/v)
stunt (v)
substandard (adj)
suburb (n) / suburban (adj)
succeed (v) / succeed in doing (v) / success (n) /
    successful (adj) / successfully (adv)
suffer (from) (v) / suffering (n)
suicide (n)
suit (v) / suitable (adj) / suitability (n)
superior (to) (adj) / superiority (n)
supervise (v)

support (n/v) / supportive (adj)
suppress (v) / suppression (n)
surface (adj/n)
surgery (n)
surpass (v) / surpassable (adj)
surreal (adj) / surrealism (n)
surround (v) / be surrounded by / surroundings (n)
surveillance (n)
survey /'sɜːveɪ/ (n) / survey /sə'veɪ/ (v)
survive (v) / survival (n) / surviving (adj) / survivor (n)
susceptible (to) (adj) / susceptibility (n)
suspect (n)
suspicion (n) / suspicious (adj) / arouse suspicion
sustain (v) / sustainable (adj)
symbol (n) / symbolic (adj) / symbolize (v)
sympathy (n) / sympathetic (adj) / sympathize (with) (v)
syndrome (n)

T
tackle (v)
take after (v)
take s/th seriously (v)
tangible (adj) / tangibility (n)
target (n/v)
technique (n)
temperament (n) / temperamental (adj)
temperature (n)
temporarily (adv) / temporary (adj)
tempt (v) / temptation (n) / be tempted by (v)
tenant (n)
tend (v) / tendency (n)
tension (n)
terror (n) / terrorist (n) / terrorism (n) / terrorization (n) /
    terrorize (v)
thank (v) / thankful (adj) / thanks to
theft (n) / thief (n)
theorize (v) / theory (n)
thought (n) / thoughtful (adj)
threat (n) / threaten (v) / threatening (adj)
thrive (v) / thriving (adj)
thunder (n)
thwart (v)
timeless (adj)
tolerance (n) / tolerant (adj) / tolerate (v)
toll (n)
tornado (n)
torrential (adj)
tour (n/v) / tourism (n) / tourist (n)
tough (adj)
trace (n/v) / trace something back to
tradition (n) / traditional (adj) / traditionally (adv)

tragedy (n) / tragic (adj) / tragically (adv)
traffic (n) / traffic congestion (n)
trait (n)
transform (v) / transformation (n)
transmission (n) / transmit (v)
transplant /'trænsplɑːnt/ (n) / transplant /træns'plɑːnt/ (v)
trauma (n) / traumatic (adj)
treat (v) / treatment (n)
trial (n)
trigger (n/v)
trip (n)
triumph (n/v) / triumphant (adj)
trust (n/v) / be trusted with (v) / have trust in (v) /
    trustworthy (adj)
turning-point (n)
turnover (n)
typhoon (n)
typical (adj) / typically (adv)

U
uncertain (adj) / uncertainty (n)
uncommon (adj)
unconscious (adj)
underestimate (v)
undergo (v)
underpaid (adj)
understandable (adj)
unemployed (adj) / unemployment (n)
unfavourable (adj)
unfit (adj)
unfulfilled (adj) / unfulfilling (adj)
unique (adj) / uniquely (adv)
unlawful (adj)
unrealistic (adj)
unreasonable (adj)
unrelated (adj)
unrelenting (adj)
unsightly (adj)
unspoiled (adj)
unstable (adj)
unsuccessful (adj)
unstructured (adj)
unsuited (to) (adj)
unthinkable (adj)
unwind (v)
upbringing (n)
upmarket (adj)
uproot (v)
up to date (adj)
urban (adj) / urbanization (n)
utility (n) / utilization (n) / utilize (v)

V

vain (adj) / vanity (n)

valid (adj) / validity (n)

valuable (adj) / value (n/v)

vandal (n) / vandalism (n) / vandalize (v)

vanish (v)

variation (n) / variety (n) / various (adj) / vary (v)

vast (adj) / the vast majority of (n) / vastly (adv) / vastness (n)

vegetate (v) / vegetation (n)

vehicle (n)

verdict (n) / reach a verdict

victim (n) / be the victim of / victimization (n) / victimize (v)

voluntary (adj) / volunteer (n/v)

violate (v) / violation (n)

violence (n) / violent (adj)

virtue (n) / virtuous (adj)

viral (adj) / virus (n)

visible (adj) / visibility (n)

vital (adj) / vitality (n) / vitally (adv)

vivid (adj) / vivid imagination (n)

vulnerable (adj) / vulnerability (n)

W

warm (adj) / warm up (v) / warm welcome (n)

watercolour (n)

weak (adj) / weaken (v) / weakness (n)

wealth (n) / wealthy (adj)

weigh (v) / weight (n) / weigh up (v) / weigh down (v)

weird (adj) / weirdness (n)

welcome (n/v)

well-being (n)

well-oiled machine (n)

whole (adj) / the whole + *noun* / wholly (adv)

wield (v) / wield power

will (n/v) / have the will to / willing (adj) / willpower (n)

wintry (adj)

witness (n/v)

workload (n)

worldwide (adj)

worsen (v) / worsening (adj)

worship (n/v)

worth (adj) / worthwhile (adj) / worthy (adj)

Y

yield (v)

Z

zero tolerance

IELTS Target 6.5

Preparation for IELTS Academic

Workbook

Chris Gough

1 Life and death

Vocabulary development

A In the Course Book unit, you learnt the words and phrases *lifestyle, life expectancy, lifespan* and *life-changing*. Explain to a partner what they mean.

B There are many other words and phrases formed with *life* as a root. Discuss the meaning of these words and phrases with a partner. Use the context of each sentence to help.

1. Learning to fly a plane was Tim's *lifelong* ambition.
2. I don't mind commuting to London every day. I guess it's become *a way of life*.
3. Mary discovered what she really wanted quite *late in life*.
4. Most people believe that the punishment for murder should be *a life sentence*.
5. Having IT support 24 hours a day is a real *lifeline*. I don't know how we'd manage without it.
6. Not all forms of cancer are *life-threatening* these days.

C Complete the sentences and exchanges with the expressions in the box. Then decide if you have similar expressions in your own language.

life's too short   that's life   life goes on   not on your life   this is the life

1. We're all disappointed that James didn't get into university, but _____. You have to look to the future, don't you?
2. 'I can't believe they gave me a parking ticket. I was only there for five minutes.'
   'Well, _____, I'm afraid. It's happened to all of us.'
3. _____ to worry about what other people think. I'm just going to do it.
4. Mm, _____ – sun, sand and sea. Could you rub some suntan lotion on my back?
5. 'Are you going to invite Martin and Suzy to your wedding?'
   '_____! They drive me crazy and Mary can't stand them.'

D Below are very common phrases used to talk about various aspects of life. Complete each with the correct form of either *do, have* or *make*.

1. I don't know whether to take the job or not. I have to _____ **a decision** soon, though.
2. _____ **exercise** keeps people fit and relieves stress.
3. My grandfather _____ **a big influence** on my life. He lived with us after my grandmother died.
4. It's nice to _____ **a good impression** when you meet people for the first time.
5. The important thing is to always _____ **your best**. Nobody can criticize you if you try hard.
6. Losing my job two years ago _____ **a big impact** on my life.
7. I'm going to Bristol University in September. I hope I've _____ **the right choice**.

Listening

A Remember, understanding the gist of a talk or conversation will help you to understand detail and answer questions.

🎧 Listen to four extracts and write the number of each against the topic below. There are two topics you will not hear about.

a. Why get married? ___
b. Why have children? ___
c. Why live abroad? ___
d. Why retire early? ___
e. Why buy your own home? ___
f. Why change career? ___

B Write down some words, phrases or whole sentences that helped you decide what the topic of each extract was. Then compare with a partner.

1. _____
2. _____
_____
_____

3. _____
4. _____
_____
_____

C 🎧 Listen again as you read the tapescript.

Reading

A In pairs, answer the questions below.

1. Do you have the saying in your language *life begins at forty*?
2. Why do people say it?
3. Do you think it's true?

B Read the text below and on the next page quickly (for about two minutes) and tick the summary below that is most accurate.

☐ 1. Life improves noticeably when people reach 40 years of age.
☐ 2. After 40 years of age, life is very difficult for most people.
☐ 3. Reaching 40 years of age has some disadvantages, but it's not all bad news.

Does Life Really Begin at Forty?

A Everyone knows the saying *life begins at forty*. However, it's a myth. Research has found that the fourth decade heralds the beginning of the end. A study of more than 2,000 people aged 18 to nearly 90 found that hitting 40 was synonymous with forgetfulness, lack of concentration and poor focus. While general intelligence appeared to remain stable over time, psychologists concluded that everyday mental skills, such as remembering a telephone number or a person's name, showed a marked decline from the age of 40 onwards.

B Professor Keith Wesnes, from Cognitive Drug Research Ltd, a private research company in Reading, discovered that people aged between 40 and 50 were 15% slower at completing simple computerized tasks than those in their 20s. He told the British Psychological Society's conference in London, 'The decline is most strongly associated with speed rather than accuracy. People in their forties clearly get worse at remembering, recalling and recognizing things. This can be very embarrassing when someone walks into a busy room and can't remember people's names. At this age you can't concentrate as well, and you can't focus and ignore distractions to the same extent that you used to.'

C The computerized tasks performed by the volunteers included tests of their reaction time, their memory of words, pictures and digits, and their ability to maintain concentration. What causes the decline in memory remains uncertain. One theory is that the problem is linked to the deterioration of the messaging system in the brain. It is understood that as people age, their brain cells lose some of their ability to communicate with each other via chemicals called neurotransmitters.

D However, researchers insisted that there was no cause for alarm. Dr James Semple, a brain specialist at Addenbrooke's Hospital in Cambridge, said that with age came experience, and a series of defence mechanisms. He said, 'Old dogs have strategies that they can bring to mind and draw on to compensate for the loss of speed. Older people may be slowing down, but they have years of experience that they can rely on.'

E Clinical trials have showed that herbal remedies can help to improve memory among older people. A recent study found that the memory of people aged between 40 and 65 improved by 7.5% after taking supplements containing ginkgo and ginseng.

C Read the text again and match these headings with four of the paragraphs.

1. Nothing to panic about ____
2. Causes not clear ____
3. Help is at hand ____
4. Still able but not as quick ____

D Cover the text and match the words 1–6 with words a–f to form common two-part nouns related to thinking and learning. Then look at the text to check.

1. general	a. times
2. poor	b. skills
3. mental	c. intelligence
4. reaction	d. cells
5. brain	e. mechanisms
6. defence	f. focus

Writing task

A Work in pairs to collect data about your classmates, design a chart or graph, and write a report. Follow the steps below.

1. Decide what information you want your figure to show. It could be one of the following ideas or your own idea.
   a. your classmates' hobbies and interests
   b. the year your classmates first went abroad
   c. countries your classmates have visited
2. Write some questions that you need to ask in order to collect the data.
3. Decide on the best way to show and compare the data – is a bar chart, a line graph, a pie chart or a table the best option?
4. Design your figure and then compare it with other students in the class.
5. Write a report describing what your figure shows. Compare your report with the reports that classmates have written.

Nature or nurture

Vocabulary development

A The verbs below are from the texts and tapescripts in the Course Book unit. Divide them into two groups and write them in boxes A and B. Then, in pairs, explain what the verbs in each box have in common.

> make   show   affect   determine   demonstrate   influence
> illustrate   shape   prove   confirm

A
_____
_____
_____
_____

B
_____
_____
_____
_____

B Complete each sentence with a word formed from the root word in brackets.

1. My grandfather was a very _____ figure in my life. (influence)
2. Most children's books have _____ to bring the stories to life. (illustrate)
3. We need to see _____ of identity before you can enter. (prove)
4. Nobody knows exactly what _____ the new regulations will have. (affect)
5. You will be sent written _____ within a month. (confirm)
6. There will be a full _____ of the product at the conference. (demonstrate)

C In the Course Book unit, you learnt the following expressions. Explain what they mean to a partner.

1. It runs in the family.
2. You can't tell them apart.
3. They're chalk and cheese.
4. I'm going to follow in my father's footsteps.

D Here are some more common expressions used to talk about families and growing up. Try to complete each with one of the words below.

> peas   cat   black   eye   water

1. Debbie left school at 15 and then ran away from home. She's **the _____ sheep of the family**.
2. Martin's father gave him the job ahead of 20 other applicants. They say **blood is thicker than _____**.
3. You can see Catherine and Eve are sisters. They're **two _____ in a pod**.
4. My brother and I are chalk and cheese. We don't see **_____ to eye** on anything.
5. I wish my children would get on better. They **fight like _____ and dog** most of the time.

E Discuss the meanings of the expressions in Exercise D with a partner. Say whether you have similar expressions in your own language.

Listening

A 🎧 Listen and write the numbers you hear in the extracts.

1. _____   2. _____   3. _____
4. _____   5. _____   6. _____

B 🎧 Listen and write the dates you hear in the extracts. Write only the month and a figure.

1. _____   2. _____   3. _____
4. _____   5. _____   6. _____

C 🎧 Listen and write the names and addresses you hear in the extracts.

1. name: _____   2. name of hotel: _____
   address: _____   address: _____

   _____   _____

   _____   _____

   _____   _____

Reading

⏳ **Exam tip:** In the IELTS exam, the words and phrases used in the questions are not the same as those used in the text. You will not be able to simply lift answers from the text without understanding. Recognizing paraphrased language is an essential IELTS reading skill. You will practise recognizing paraphrased language frequently as you work through this course.

A Look at this sentence from the Reading Module in the Course Book.

In the 1930s, Dr B. F. Skinner and his pioneering studies of behaviour and conditioning had a huge impact. Building on the ideas of earlier behaviourists, he ...

Now look at the question you answered.

Whose ideas did Dr B. F. Skinner develop in the 1930s?

Notice how the order of some information is different and *develop* has been used to mean the same as *building on*.

B Fill the gaps in a–f with the bold words and phrases in 1–6. The sentences must have the same meaning.

1. The first impression can be that **the twins** are absolutely identical.
2. All sorts of **events** have a huge impact on an individual's future.
3. The significance of **trauma in early life** is not yet fully understood.
4. Research has revealed that human behaviour is more complex than **the behaviourist model** indicated.
5. It is now generally accepted that **certain aspects of our personalities** are innate.
6. **Female only children** are often burdened with the responsibility of being the sole carer of ageing parents.

a. What happens in one's later life is shaped by a multitude of _____.
b. It is now clear that what we do and why we do it is not quite as simple as _____ led us to believe.
c. Initially, it seems that there is no difference whatsoever between _____.

d. It is frequently left to _____ to look after older family members with little or no help.

e. Today, most people recognize that we are born with _____.

f. There is much we have still to learn about the importance of _____.

Writing

A Read the sentence below from the model composition in the Course Book Writing Module. Notice how the highlighted adverb clause is placed in the middle of the sentence to add information and clarify.

Research has shown that identical twins, even those that have grown up apart, can have very similar personalities and even lifestyles.

B Write the clauses a–d into the appropriate place in the middle of sentences 1–4. Use commas in each case.

1. Siblings frequently fight over small matters.
2. Everything we experience shapes who we later become.
3. Adopted children frequently have irregular sleeping habits.
4. Single parents need a support network of family and friends.

a. except those placed at a very young age
b. especially those of similar age
c. even what we completely forget
d. particularly those with more than one child

Writing task

A Look at the Writing task below and think about:

1. whether you tend to agree or disagree.
2. what points you could make agreeing with the statement.
3. what points you could make that disagree with the statement.

Write about the following topic:

People who grow up with siblings (brothers and sisters) have many advantages over people who grow up as only children. Only children lack the social skills that lead to success.

Do you believe this statement to be true?

Give reasons for your answer and include any relevant examples from your own knowledge or experience.

Write at least 250 words.

B Talk and compare your thoughts about the topic of the Writing task with other students.

Note that in this unit, it would be a good idea to complete the Exam Practice Module before attempting the Writing task. The text discusses the topic and introduces points that you might want to include in your composition.

C Write your composition. Then check the model on page 263.

Boys and girls 3

Vocabulary development

A Complete the sentences with words made from the root words in brackets.

1. It was very _____ of you to buy Liz those flowers. (thought)
2. Some people think that men think more _____ than women. (logic)
3. People that are _____ always want to win. (compete)
4. If people are _____, they don't like taking risks. (caution)
5. It's no good waiting until it's too late. You must be _____. (decide)
6. These days, women have the same _____ qualities as men. (lead)
7. Women understand what other people are thinking. I think they're more _____ than men. (sense)
8. Most people feel _____ towards children. (protect)

B Read the descriptions below carefully. Then complete each gap with *he*, *she*, *him*, *his* or *her* depending on what you think is more likely.

1. ____ likes ____ partner to show ____ feminine side sometimes.
2. People think that ____ pierced nose and all those tattoos make ____ look a bit scary.
3. ____ father told ____ to stop crying in front of the other children.
4. ____ just loves driving down the street in ____ sports car with music blaring from the radio.
5. ____ kicked off ____ sandals. ____ loved the feel of the soft carpet on ____ bare feet.
6. ____ had arranged to meet ____ mates in the pub before going to the football match.

C Compare Exercise B with a partner. Explain your answers.

D Check the similarities and differences between the words in the two boxes below in a dictionary.

masculine manly macho boyish	feminine womanly ladylike girly

E Use the word from Exercise D you think is most appropriate to complete each sentence below. There is sometimes more than one possible answer.

1. I don't like it when girls use bad language. It just isn't very _____.
2. Brad Pitt and Tom Cruise are popular because they have _____ good looks even in middle age.
3. I think men drive fast because they think it's _____.
4. Some parents worry if their sons like _____ games like playing with dolls or skipping.
5. Sue is happy doing _____ things like dressmaking and arranging flowers.

F Look at how the highlighted expressions are used in context below. Discuss what they mean with a partner and decide if you have similar expressions in your own language.

1. I know it's cold, but will you stop complaining. Come on, **be a man**.
2. I think it's a good thing that Steve is leaving home to study. **It'll make a man of him**.
3. 'Did you hear that Dave crashed the car he's just bought? Apparently, he was racing with a friend.'
   'Well, **boys will be boys**.'
4. Jessica's **a bit of a tomboy**. She loves playing with guns and toy soldiers.
5. Gavin's always worrying about something. If it's not money, it's his health. He's **a bit of an old woman** to tell you the truth.

Listening

A 🎧 Listen to a talk about women in horse racing and choose the correct answer a, b or c.

1. The speaker says that …
   a. most owners of racehorses are women.
   b. the biggest races are usually won by horses owned by women.
   c. women racehorse owners have had their share of success.

2. The speaker says that racehorse owners …
   a. do not think for very long about where they want their horses trained.
   b. are happy for women to train their horses
   c. do not always want to place horses with female trainers.

3. Which of these does the speaker NOT say about women jockeys at the end of the 1960s?
   a. They started to ride in important races.
   b. They were successful when they rode in races.
   c. They won some of the best-known races.

4. Colonial Affair was the name …
   a. of a race course in the United States.
   b. of the horse that Julie Krone rode in a major race.
   c. of a major race in the United States.

5. Which of these does the speaker NOT say about grooms, exercise riders and pony girls?
   a. They enjoy the attention they get from being in horse racing.
   b. They have a very important part to play in horse racing.
   c. They work hard but are not paid much.

B Check the answers and then look at the tapescript on page 283. Highlight the lines in the talk that provide the answers. Notice how the language used in the questions paraphrases the language used in the talk.

Reading

 Exam tip: Remember that, in certain parts of the Reading test, you need to look quickly for paraphrased language – parts of the text that mean the same as the words and phrases in the question. You won't find the exact words and phrases from the question in the text.

A Read a summary of the text from pages 43 and 44 of the Course Book and use the underlined parts to answer the questions that follow.

A In the world of medicine, surgeons are <u>the highly trained elite</u>. <u>Feared as much as revered</u>, they occupy a male stronghold in the traditionally masculine medical field. What, then, if the surgeon is a woman?

B Recent researchers have gained entry into the closely guarded world of surgeons to examine how women fulfil their dreams of practising <u>a profession in which 95% of their colleagues are men</u>. It reveals that being a woman does not guarantee a traditionally feminine approach to patient care. <u>Some female surgeons are caring and nurturing, while others are cold and slightly aggressive.</u>

C Moreover, female surgeons are treated differently from their male counterparts on virtually every level by superiors, colleagues, nurses, and patients. In fact, <u>women surgeons face a sort of daily Catch-22</u>. They are expected to behave in a womanly, maternal and loving manner. <u>When they do not, they are punished by their co-workers</u>. On the other hand, if women surgeons do behave in a conventionally feminine way, sustaining leadership roles becomes difficult. It seems that male surgeons are seen as surgeons, period. Female surgeons are seen as women first, then surgeons. Being treated as professional equals is a daily struggle.

D <u>Examples of mistreatment are numerous and varied</u>, but the underlying tone is the same; a mix of disrespect and fear. One witness talks of a male senior surgeon who so hated having women assist him that when a female junior surgeon was assigned to the task, <u>he stood outside the operating room and shouted, 'Anybody but the girl. Give me a trained monkey. I'd rather have anybody but the girl.'</u>

For questions 1–4, identify the paragraph which contains the following information. Write the letter of the paragraph in the space.

1. The vast majority of surgeons are male.   ___
2. People respect surgeons but are also afraid of them.   ___
3. However female surgeons behave, they seem to lose.   ___
4. There are many cases of female surgeons being treated unfairly.   ___

For questions 5–8, decide if the information given below agrees with the information given in the text. Write (T) true, (F) false or (NG) not given, if there is no information on this.

5. Surgeons belong to a very small minority within the medical profession.   ___
6. Female surgeons generally relate to their patients in the same way.   ___
7. Female surgeons that do not behave like typical women have been physically attacked by co-workers.   ___
8. One male surgeon refused to carry out an operation with a female assistant.   ___

Writing

Exam tip: When you write a report based on information in a graph or chart, there are a lot of typical verbs and fixed verb phrases that you need to learn how to use.

A Match the phrases below with the line graphs 1–7 below and on the next page.

> increased slightly   increased gradually   increased steadily
> increased dramatically / soared   remained constant
> fluctuated   reached a peak

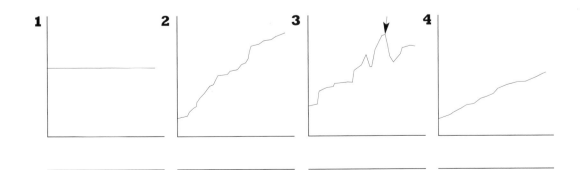

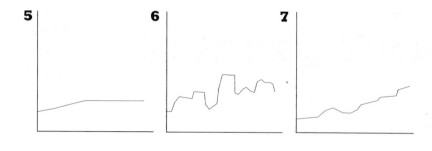

5   6   7

_____   _____   _____

 B Draw simple line graphs that illustrate these verbs and fixed and phrases.

1. fell slightly
2. fell gradually
3. fell steadily
4. fell dramatically / plummeted
5. reached a low

Exam tip: When you see graphs and charts, the information will often be about a period in the past so you will use the past simple. Sometimes the information will be about a situation now, so you will use the present simple or present continuous. You might need to use the present perfect if the information links the past with now.

 C Complete the table with the correct form of these two very common, but very irregular verbs.

present simple	past simple	present perfect
_____	rose	have / has _____
fall / falls	_____	have / has _____

Exam tip: When you are describing graphs and charts, write what you know how to write confidently. Don't try to use fixed phrases that you have seen, but don't really understand.

Past and present

Vocabulary development

A These sentences include words made from the key words you learnt in the Course Book unit. Read them and answer the questions a–e that follow.

1. It was certainly a **memorable** occasion.
2. My grandfather's becoming very **forgetful** as he gets older.
3. The only way to learn irregular verbs is to **memorize** them.
4. It was an **unforgettable** experience. I was so lucky to get the opportunity.
5. The photograph was a constant **reminder** of what he had lost.
6. It was a **regrettable** incident and nobody talked about it.

a. Which two words mean more or less the same thing and mean impressive, exciting or magical?
b. Which word is a verb that means learn something so that you never forget it?
c. Which adjective describes something everyone wishes hadn't happened?
d. Which adjective describes a person who can't remember things?
e. Which noun is something that helps you remember or stops you forgetting something or somebody?

B In pairs, answer the questions below.

1. When did you last have a memorable or unforgettable experience?
2. Are you good at memorizing names and numbers?
3. Do you have anything that you keep as a reminder of something that happened in the past?

C In the talk about the history of the bicycle, the speaker says ...

Bicycles now number around one billion worldwide.

Exam tip: You know the word *number*, but you probably haven't seen it used as a verb like this. As your level advances, you will notice how words that you know are used in new ways, especially when you read longer text.

Use the common words in the box as verbs in the sentences below. Check the form.

1. Many families are still waiting to be _____ a year after the earthquake.
2. Children _____ privately are generally more successful in higher education.
3. Some films may be violent, but I think that only _____ society.
4. Many people are unhappy that waste is _____ from Europe to other parts of the world.
5. A number of small businesses have been _____ the property.

| school |
| ship |
| house |
| eye |
| mirror |

D Look at this sentence from the text in the Course Book unit. Notice the highlighted verb/adverb collocations.

Nostalgia is one of those words which everyone understands and uses quite freely, but which is almost impossible to clearly define.

Use the adverbs in the box to complete these sentences.

1. I _____ **remember** seeing Tina there, but I can't be sure.
2. I understand instructions when they are **explained** _____.
3. Hitchcock is _____ **regarded** as the greatest director of suspense.
4. We _____ **regret** any offence we may have caused.
5. David _____ **admits** that he stole the money.

> freely
> clearly
> widely
> deeply
> vaguely

E Look at how the bold expressions are used in context below. In pairs, discuss what they mean and decide if you have similar expressions in your own language.

1. I'm looking for a new apartment. I'm staying with my brother **for the time being**.
2. I wouldn't say Mark is a good friend, but I still see him **from time to time**.
3. The project must be finished by next week. It's **a race against time**.
4. I loathe train journeys. I play games on my computer **to pass the time / kill time**.
5. Everyone will live in a smart house soon. It's just **a question of time / a matter of time**.
6. I haven't started revising yet, but **when the time comes**, I'll be prepared.

Listening

A 🎧 Listen and match each extract to a type of diagram below. Write the number of the extract in the space.

a map	___	a graph	___	a process	___
an appliance	___	a building	___	the human body	___

Reading

A Tick the advice below that you think is good.

☐ 1. It is easy to say that information in a text is not given. If there is nothing in the text that relates to the statement, it is obviously not given.

☐ 2. It is sometimes difficult to decide whether information is given or not. What the statement says is often similar to what the text says, but not exactly the same.

⏳ **Exam tip:** You may think that it is easy to say that information is not given in the text, but be careful. There is usually something in the text that relates to the statement.

B Look at this example from the Reading Module in the Course Book. Why is the correct answer NG?

> A new arrival in a big city will think about friends back home, while a college student struggling with an assignment will bolster his confidence by reliving high school glories. Nostalgia can motivate people and make them feel they are rooted, rather than being blown around by the vagaries of everyday life.

People who do not think about the past much have little direction in life.   **NG**

C Read the two short extracts on the next page. Decide which of the statements that follow is (T) true, which is (F) false and which is (NG) not given.

A

Infantile, or childhood amnesia is characterized by the relative absence of memory before four years of age. It is not the complete absence of memories, but the relative lack of memories from infancy. This lack cannot be accounted for by the normal tendency to forget a percentage of what is experienced.

1. Small children only remember the most significant events.   ___
2. Most children remember very little from the first four years of their lives.   ___
3. Small children forget early experiences like adults forget unimportant events.   ___

B

The incomplete development of language in young children may be a cause of childhood amnesia in that infants do not have the language capacity to encode and interpret memories in the same way that adults do. The typical schedule of language development seems to support this theory. Babies of one year old tend to be limited to one word utterances, and childhood amnesia predicts that adults have very few, if any, memories of this time.

1. Children and adults generally retain memories in a similar way.   ___
2. Small children that learn to talk earlier are more likely to retain memories.   ___
3. It is suggested that small children cannot remember events because they cannot apply words to them.   ___

Writing

A   Below is a version of the first half of the model composition from the Course Book unit with various errors. Work in pairs. One of you is A and the other is B.

Student A: Find five incorrect prepositions.

Student B: Find five words that are spelt incorrectly.

Computers are everywhere nowdays. Everyone uses a computer at work and children are using them increasingly at school. Computers are used in shops and hospitals and to drive trains. Most familys have a computer in home and perhaps a laptop too. So, do we rely for computers too much and is that having a negitive effect in how we live? Many people think the answer is 'yes'.

At the workplace, computers do everything quickly and effisiently. It is difficult to imagine going back to pen and paper. E-mailing is more convenient than making phone calls. In schools, children can learn with interesting interactive programmes about the world and its history. However, all this could mean that people comunicate less. In offices, people stare to a screen instead of talking to each other and, at school, children work less in groups to solve problems.

B   Work together to correct the errors you have identified. Then check the model again in the Course Book on page 62.

C   Look at the second part of the composition on the next page and work in the same way.

Student A: Find six grammatical errors.

Student B: Find five words (not grammar words) that are used incorrectly.

People love having a computer at home. They can find the information online immediately and use the Internet for shop and order holidays. Young people enjoy to play computer games and making friends in chat rooms. However, there are disadvantages here too. Families communicate less and perhaps do not go out so often. Some Internet sites are uncomfortable for children and parents have to check that they are safe.

Individually, I think the advantages far overbalance the disadvantages. Computers are making life more convenient and enjoyable. Information is at our fingertips instead of having search through books. Of course, people should not sit at a computer all day every day, whether at work, at school or at home, but as long as they are used sensitively, computers should be seeing as a great benefit.

Writing task

A Look again at Writing Tasks A and C on pages 60 and 61 of the Course Book. Choose the one that you want to answer. Follow these steps before you start writing.

1. Make a list of points that you want to include. You can use the points that you discussed in Writing 2A if you want to.
2. Organize your points in a table like the one in Writing 3A. Try to plan a balanced approach, rather than simply express your own opinion throughout the entire composition.
3. Look again at the stages in Writing 3C and plan the organization of your composition.
4. Write a rough draft of each paragraph. Think about introducing the topic in a way that shows you understand the question and plan your conclusion in advance.

B When you have written your composition, check the two model compositions on pages 264 and 265.

Work and play

Vocabulary development

A Add the correct prefix from the box below to the root word in brackets at the end of each sentence to fill the spaces.

| non under re de over anti |

1. With so many people on holiday, there's just too much work. Frankly, we're _____. (staff)
2. I think they've just _____ me in that shop. This was supposed to be £10, not £20. (charge)
3. Companies often _____ to countries where labour is less expensive. (locate)
4. Most people have an _____ programme that protects their computer. (virus)
5. The schedule was a little _____. I didn't think we could finish the job that quickly. (ambitious)
6. My background has been working for charities and _____ organizations. (profit-making)
7. Considering the education he's had, he could have done much better in life. Personally, I think he's _____. (achieve)
8. I think we should _____ our objectives. I think we've forgotten why we started this. (examine)
9. Doing the same thing day after day in a factory _____ people. I don't know how they stand the routine. (human)

B Complete the expressions from the Course Book unit below with one key word.

1. I've been **on the** _____ all day.
2. You have to **let your** _____ **down** every now and then.
3. I was busy in the restaurant last night. I was **rushed off my** _____.
4. I play rugby to **let off** _____.
5. Getting away to Ireland for a week really **recharged my** _____.

C Now look at how the bold expressions are used in context below. Discuss what each expression means with a partner and decide if you have a similar expression in your own language.

1. I'm going to have to work at the weekend. **I've got a lot on my plate** at the moment.
2. I haven't had a break all day. We're absolutely **snowed under** this week.
3. My new job's really difficult. I'm just about **keeping my head above water**.
4. I **work my socks off** all week and nobody even says 'thank you'!
5. I've done most of what I have to do this week. I can **take it easy** on Friday.

D Look again at the compound nouns from the Reading Module below. In pairs, try to remember what each one means.

| turnover burnout cutbacks lay-offs |

E These compounds are the noun forms of the phrasal verbs *turn over*, *burn out*, *cut back on* and *lay off*. Look at the compounds in the sentences below in context and then match each with a definition a–e from the box on the next page.

1. The plan is in place. I'm just waiting to get the **go-ahead** from management.
2. There's been a bit of a **shake-up** at the office. Several people will probably lose their jobs.
3. We like doing business with Emrod. They've got a very good **set-up**.

4. We haven't discovered much yet, but we're expecting **a breakthrough** soon.
5. I'm sure Tom and Susan will do everything as usual. I won't get a **look-in**.

> a. a development
> b. a big change
> c. an opportunity to participate
> d. permission to proceed
> e. an organization

Listening

A 🎧 **Listen to a talk about the Romans and how they liked to enjoy their free time. Complete the summary below using NO MORE THAN TWO WORDS for each answer.**

Pleasure was very important to the Romans and they had various ways of enjoying their (1) _____. The Romans loved the theatre and there were many (2) _____ when plays could be staged. Spectators knew if the (3) _____ were good or bad from the masks they wore. People also went to huge amphitheatres to be entertained by violent games. Gladiators fought, and often met their death, in combat with one another or with large (4) _____.

Chariot racing was also popular and the riders, like the gladiators, became well-known (5) _____ just like sportsmen nowadays. (6) _____ was popular and the Romans took animals like deer to various parts of their empire. The Romans would spend all day at bathhouses, exercising and swimming. Some people used the baths to do (7) _____.

B **Check the answers and then look at the tapescript on page 292. Notice how the language used around the words you need to write paraphrases the language used in the talk.**

Reading

A **Put the topic sentences 1–5 into the correct place at the beginning of each paragraph.**

1. So where does all the free time go?
2. When people claim that they do not have enough time, it usually demonstrates more about how they spend their time, rather than the actual quantity of it.
3. Recent research conducted in the United States examines use of time.
4. The key to people feeling that they have time is ensuring that enough time is spent doing what is important.
5. Advertising could be partly to blame for the misconception.

A ___ According to the findings, the common perception that people do not have enough time is simply not true. Statistics from a study using time-diaries show that work time and leisure time is pretty much evenly split. The average American works around 35 hours per week and enjoys the same number of hours of free time.

B ____ These days, a vast array of companies are in the business of making people feel that they have too little time. Products from convenience food to self-help books depend on consumers believing they are too busy.

C _____ According to the research, over half of it is spent watching television or browsing online. A surprisingly small percentage is spent socializing and engaging in recreational activities. Reading and listening to music seem to now be minority pastimes.

D _____ Of course, no single individual actually has any more time than any other individual. People simply spend time in different ways. When people perceive that their time is being spent in an enjoyable or valuable way, they feel that they have more of it. There is a higher level of fulfilment.

E _____ This means establishing priorities and deciding what is valuable in advance. Spending free time doing what is enjoyable will not actually result in having more time, but it will increase the degree of satisfaction with how that time is spent.

B Match the headings in the box below with the paragraphs A–E. Write the letter of the heading i–vi as your answer. You do not need to use all the headings.

> i. Various free time activities
> ii. Plan activities ahead of time
> iii. It's good to keep a diary
> iv. Not the real picture
> v. Selling people time
> vi. We all have the same amount of time

1. Paragraph A ___   2. Paragraph B ___   3. Paragraph C ___
4. Paragraph D ___   5. Paragraph E ___

Writing

A Below is a version of the model report for Writing 3D in the Course Book. This version has not been organized into paragraphs and contains several errors. Work in pairs.

1. Find eight errors. There are both grammatical errors and wrong words used.
2. Divide the report into four short paragraphs so that it is easier to follow.

> The bar chart shows the differences of the percentage of time that men and women in various age groups take off work in the United Kingdom because they are sick. The first thing for saying is that women take much time off work than men in every age group. Women between 25 and 34 are more likely to take time off work than anyone else. They take 3.1% of time off, when men in this age group take only 2.2%. Younger employees take more time off than older employees. In effect, workers over 60 take less time off than someone else. In this age group, however, there is the biggest difference between the time took off by men and women. Men over 60 take only 1.5% of work time off sick, while women take 2.1%. All in all, it seems that the older are employees, the less time they take off sick.

B In your pair, compare ideas and write the correct version of the report.

C Check the model report again on page 265. Make a note of any errors you didn't identify.

Writing task

A Look at the bar chart below and make sure you understand what it shows.

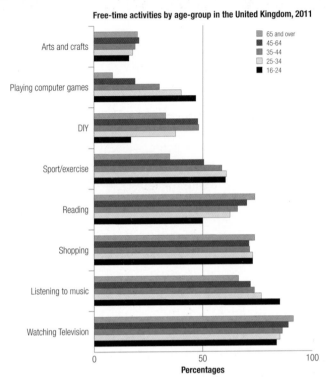

Free-time activities by age-group in the United Kingdom, 2011

Legend:
- 65 and over
- 45-64
- 35-44
- 25-34
- 16-24

Categories (top to bottom): Arts and crafts, Playing computer games, DIY, Sport/exercise, Reading, Shopping, Listening to music, Watching Television

X-axis: Percentages (0, 50, 100)

Source: *http://www.ons.gov.uk/ons/dcp171766_258996.pdf*

B Look at the typical IELTS Writing task and follow the steps below.

1. Identify information that stands out and will interest the reader.
2. Make notes about what you want to include in your report.
3. Write a suitable opening line that shows that you understand the information shown.
4. Organize your points to write the rest of the report.
5. Write a concluding line if you feel it is appropriate.

> *The bar chart shows selected free-time activities enjoyed by different age groups in the United Kingdom in 2011.*
>
> *Summarize the information by selecting and reporting the main features, and make comparisons where relevant.*
>
> Write at least 150 words.

C When you have written your report, check the model on page 265.

_____

_____

_____

_____

_____

_____

_____

_____

_____

_____

Home and away

Vocabulary development

A Find ten travel-related words in the grid. The words can go across or down.

S	I	G	H	T	S	E	E	I	N	G
A	U	A	M	R	G	C	T	N	I	I
F	T	E	X	C	U	R	S	I	O	N
A	D	V	E	N	T	U	R	E	J	L
R	N	R	A	S	T	I	R	E	O	E
I	R	E	L	E	L	S	N	E	U	K
J	Y	S	O	U	V	E	N	I	R	A
P	E	O	M	C	A	M	P	I	N	G
Q	O	R	U	R	D	E	R	I	E	N
A	P	T	R	I	P	H	A	C	Y	R

B Match the adjectives 1–8 with the nouns a–h to make common phrases that appeared in the Course Book unit.

1. sustainable
2. traditional
3. memorable
4. financial
5. unspoiled
6. privileged
7. menial
8. managerial

a. education
b. work
c. burden
d. culture
e. tourism
f. experience
g. position
h. beauty

C Complete the phrasal verbs in the sentences below with the correct particle.

1. Everyone needs to **get** _____ from their 9–5 routine from time to time.
2. Some travellers seem to **look** _____ **on** people who go on package holidays.
3. When tourism grows, traditional industries, like fishing, sometimes **die** _____.
4. Once tourism begins to develop in an area, all manner of businesses **grow** _____ around it.

D The expressions below all appear in the two texts in the Reading Module of the Course Book. Look at them again in context and then, in pairs, discuss the meaning of each.

Weighing Up the Benefits of Tourism
1. the lion's share (Paragraph 2)
2. fall victim to (Paragraph 3)

The Problem with Package Holidays
1. it struck me (Paragraph A)
2. on a shoe-string budget (Paragraph E)

Listening

A 🎧 Look at the map. Listen to a conversation between a hotel receptionist and a guest and write the correct letter A–G next to the four places below.

1. Rosario's ___   2. The Lotus Flower ___   3. cash-point ___   4. taxi rank ___

Reading

A Cover the text opposite. Below are the topic sentences from five paragraphs in a text about holidays. Read them and then in pairs:

1. discuss what the whole text will be about.
2. discuss what information you expect each paragraph to contain.

Paragraph A: Tourists are starting to get fed up with the same old sun and sea and city break holidays.

Paragraph B: Many travellers hanker for sunshine, but want something more than lying around on the beach for a week.

Paragraph C: Another option increasing in popularity is an educational break.

Paragraph D: For many would-be adventurers, bizarre and exotic accommodation is enough to get their adrenaline flowing.

Paragraph E: Perhaps the most unusual of recent holiday developments is the paranormal adventure.

B Decide in which paragraph you expect to find each of these supporting ideas.

going back to the classroom   ___
wanting to be frightened   ___
travellers not doing what everyone else is doing ___
enjoying extreme sports in the desert   ___
staying in unusual surroundings   ___

C Read the text and check your ideas.

Looking for Something New

A Tourists are starting to get fed up with the same old sun and sea and city break holidays. Travellers are seeking ever more adventurous destinations and experiences that will stay in their memory for a lifetime. The trend seems to be to ignore the herd and follow an individual path towards holiday heaven. The planet is a big place and there is still plenty for even the most frequent of holidaymakers to discover.

B Many travellers hanker for sunshine, but want something more than lying around on the beach for a week. There are all sorts of ways in which sun can be combined with a dash of adventure. In Australia, people are opting for a camel safari across the outback, while sand dune surfing is all the rage in Dubai. Sporty types who were once content with a week skiing in the Alps are now taking a glacier tour in Iceland via snowmobile or playing a midnight round of golf in Lapland.

C Another option increasing in popularity is an educational break. Being a student again might not be everyone's idea of a relaxing break, but large numbers are combining a trip abroad with a chance to brush up on skills and knowledge or learning something completely new. Breaks involving painting, writing or cooking are the most common escapes of this type. More extreme options include the ins and outs of space science in Alabama and caring for sick animals in Zimbabwe.

D For many would-be adventurers, bizarre and exotic accommodation is enough to get their adrenaline flowing. Hotels built from planes, trains and boats are now commonplace. Climbing 30 m to a room in a tree house is the preference in India, while, in Florida, guests opt for a few nights watching the fish swim by in an underwater capsule. In Scandinavia, sleeping under a reindeer skin in a room constructed of ice is the latest craze.

E Perhaps the most unusual of recent holiday developments is the paranormal adventure. Guests are queuing up to spend a night in a location supposedly home to ghosts and scary spirits. The Hilton Hotel in Honolulu is said to be haunted by a woman who has been seen wandering around the hotel only to vanish before witnesses' eyes. The Buffalo Holiday Inn in New York has been the subject of numerous ghost stories over the years. The ultimate spooky destination is a castle in Transylvania, birthplace and home of Count Dracula.

D Talk in groups of three about the holiday option from the text that most appeals to you.

Writing

A On the next page is the model composition for the Writing task in the Course Book. Put the words and phrases below back into the correct space. You will need to use capital letters at the beginning of some options.

in order to	since	however	the most important thing		as	not long ago
		as soon as	in the worst cases	even		

(1) _____ the tourist industry continues to develop, travellers are taken to ever more remote corners of the globe. (2) _____, holidaymakers were happy with a week in Spain, but now they want to experience exotic locations like Nepal and Madagascar. Unfortunately, (3) _____ even a modest number of tourists begin to visit a place, they have an impact which changes that place and makes it less appealing.

There are various ways in which the impact of tourism has a negative effect. Firstly, (4) _____ support tourism, there needs to be construction and infrastructure. This might mean hotels, bars and shops built where they would never have been for local people. It might mean roads and railway links that spoil an area's natural beauty. Airports may not be built in remote places, instead they will be built somewhere nearby and planes will fly over areas that were previously peaceful.

Deserted beaches might become crowded and less clean. Hundreds of people start visiting sites that are not suitable as tourist attractions. (5) _____, tourists damage countryside or coral reefs. (6) _____ a small amount of tourism probably means local people opening shops, bars and other businesses that are not typical of the culture. All this begins to make the destination less attractive.

It is difficult to suggest clear solutions (7) _____ once development begins, it is impossible to reverse. (8) _____, some measures could be taken. The authorities could limit the number of large hotels and encourage small guest houses. They could limit the number of foreign-owned bars and restaurants and not allow fast-food chains to open.

(9) _____, in my opinion, is for the tourists to become more aware of the impact they have. They must be prepared to fly to an airport some way from their final destination and understand why they should support local businesses and buy local products.

B Check your answers by reading the model composition on page 266 again. Make a note of the linking words and phrases that you want to use in your own compositions.

_____
_____
_____
_____
_____
_____
_____
_____
_____
_____
_____

Kill or cure

7

Vocabulary development

A In pairs, explain the difference between the words in each pair below.

1. condition / allergy
2. out of condition / under the weather
3. injury / wound
4. bitten / stung
5. transplant / graft
6. virus / parasite
7. outbreak / epidemic
8. moisture / precipitation
9. cure / treatment
10. operation / surgery

B Complete the expressions from the Course Book unit below with ONE key word.

1. Playing squash is what helps me to **stay in** _____.
2. I'm not going into work today. I feel a bit **under the** _____.
3. I need to sit down for a minute. **My back's** _____ me.
4. I got over the operation very quickly. I'm **fighting** _____ again.
5. Once you start smoking, it's very hard stop. It's **a slippery** _____.

C Now look at how the bold expressions are used in context below. Discuss what each expression means with a partner and decide if you have a similar expression in your own language.

1. I feel really tied and achy. I'm sure I'm **coming down with something**.
2. Everybody wishes you a **speedy recovery**.
3. Retiring early has given my dad **a new lease of life**.
4. Sadly, my grandmother **passed away** a few years ago.
5. Is old Stan still alive? I thought he'd **gone to meet his maker** ages ago.

D Complete the sentences with words made from the root words in brackets.

1. The _____ rejected the organ and died six months later. (receive)
2. Most transplants are very complicated _____ procedures. (surgery)
3. Global warming could trigger an increase in all sorts of _____ diseases. (dead)
4. There is likely to be a higher _____ of floods and droughts. (incident)
5. Everyone was impressed by the medical team's _____. (expert)
6. A _____ of the company discussed every aspect of the treatment with us. (represent)
7. Anyone who drinks needs to know what is a safe level of _____. (consume)
8. It is known that smoking can affect a woman's _____. (fertile)
9. Being drunk often causes people to behave _____. (responsible)
10. The college adopts a zero _____ policy. (tolerant)

Listening

A 🎧 Listen to a receptionist at a dental surgery talking to a patient and complete the form below. Use NO MORE THAN TWO WORDS OR A NUMBER for each answer.

Name: (1) _____

Address: (2) _____ Montreal (3) _____, Maidstone, Kent MD2 (4) _____

Tel. no.: 07984 650396

Mobile: (5) _____

Day and time of appointment: (6) _____

Last appointment: (7) _____

B 🎧 Listen to the patient making an appointment for his daughter and complete the form below. Use NO MORE THAN TWO WORDS OR A NUMBER for each answer.

Name: (8) _____

Age: (9) _____

Day and time of appointment: (10) _____

Reading

A Read about the Black Death and decide if the information given below agrees with information given in the text. Write (T) true, (F) false or (NG) not given, if there is no information on this.

1. In London, there were special places where dead bodies were buried. _____
2. The Bubonic was new to England when it arrived in 1665. _____
3. The symptoms of the disease were very painful. _____
4. The plague had killed many people in China. _____
5. In Europe, dead bodies were often left unburied. _____
6. St. Giles-in-the-Field was the most badly affected London parish. _____
7. In London, immediate help was offered to families affected by the disease. _____
8. Oxford was unaffected by the Black Death. _____

The Black Death

In the spring and summer of 1665, an outbreak of Bubonic Plague swept across London, spreading from parish to parish until thousands had died, and the huge pits dug to receive the bodies were full. Bubonic Plague was also called the Black Death and had been known in England for centuries. It was a ghastly disease, producing patches of black on the victim's skin and inflamed glands in the groin. This combined with compulsive vomiting and splitting headaches made it a slow, agonizing killer.

The plague originated in the East, possibly China, and quickly spread through Europe. Whole communities were wiped out and, in many towns and cities, corpses were simply left in the streets as there was no one left to bury them.

In England, the outbreak began in London, in the poor, overcrowded parish of St. Giles-in-the-Field. It started slowly, but by May 1665, 43 had died. In June, 6,137 people died, in July 17,036, and at its peak, in August, 31,159 people died. In total, 15% of the population perished during that terrible summer.

Incubation took just four to six days and when the plague appeared in a household, the house was sealed, condemning the whole family to death! These houses were distinguished by a painted red cross on the door and the words, 'Lord have mercy on us'. At night the corpses were brought out in answer to the cry, 'Bring out your dead', put in a cart and taken away to the plague pits.

King Charles II and his Court left London and fled to Oxford. The rich sent their families away from London, but the poor had no such means of escape. Samuel Pepys gives a vivid account in his Diary of the empty streets in London, those who could afford to having left in an attempt to flee the pestilence.

B In pairs, discuss the meaning of the highlighted words and phrases. Think again about:

- the general context – the other words around the highlighted word or phrase.
- the part of speech – if the highlighted word or phrase is a noun, verb, adjective, etc.
- parts of the highlighted word or phrase that you already know.
- if you know another (probably more basic) meaning of the word or phrase.

Writing

A Below is a version of the student's report from the Writing Module of the Course Book. There are full stops in the report, but no commas.

1. Put eight commas into the correct place in the report.
2. Check your answers against the report in the Course Book on page 110.

The diagram shows the stages in the process of medical tourism arranged by a private company. It shows what happens from when an initial request for information is received to when the patient enjoys a post-care holiday.

First of all when there is a request, information about specific services is sent back. When a specific request is received it is sent to the hospital that the company thinks appropriate. At this point the patient's medical records are checked at the hospital and a recommendation of what treatment is appropriate is provided. This is sent to the patient together with an estimate of the duration of their stay and what the treatment will cost. A suitable package is arranged and the bill paid.

The patient travels to Thailand where he or she is met by a company representative. The patient can tour the hospital and meet the medical team that will provide the treatment or perform the operation.

If the patient chooses a pre-care holiday he or she can now enjoy that before the treatment. If not the patient undergoes the medical treatment directly. Finally the patient can enjoy a post-care holiday before returning home.

Writing task

A Look at the flow chart and the instructions for the Writing task below and decide if each stage of the process is clear.

> *The flow chart shows the typical stages of a liver transplant.*
>
> *Summarize the information by selecting and reporting the main features.*
>
> Write at least 150 words.

Liver Transplantation Process

patient with liver disease referred to hospital

↓

patient attends interview at liver transplant unit

↓

patient undergoes exploratory surgery

↓

case submitted for discussion at weekly meeting

↙　　　　　　　　　↘

case accepted　　　　　　　　　case rejected

↓　　　　　　　　　↓

case placed on waiting list　　　　further evaluation agreed
　　　　　　　　　　　　　　　　or alternative treatment discussed

↓

suitable donor organ selected and
medical checks undertaken

↓

final consultation with patient

↓

transplant performed

B Write the report. Make sure you think about:

1. introducing the report without simply copying the instructions.
2. using the appropriate grammatical structures.
3. using the appropriate linking words and phrases.
4. punctuating appropriately.

Then check the model on page 266.

_____

_____

_____

_____

_____

_____

_____

_____

_____

Bricks and mortar

8

Vocabulary development

A Complete each phrase below with an adjective from the box.

rusty	plush	flimsy	derelict	macabre	hideous
	damp	cramped	meagre	affluent	

1. a _____ old bicycle left out in the rain
2. _____ families with detached houses and two cars
3. _____ housing waiting to be pulled down
4. _____ supplies of food that leave people feeling hungry
5. a _____ story about a series of murders
6. _____ new offices in the city centre
7. a _____ patch on the wall where rainwater has penetrated
8. a _____ old witch that casts evil spells
9. a _____ living space with little room to move
10. a _____ chair that can hardly bear the weight of a person

B Match the verbs 1–8 with their meanings a–h.

1. deteriorate   a. make stronger
2. disperse   b. leave without care
3. accumulate   c. divide into small units
4. neglect   d. spread out
5. ventilate   e. take in
6. partition   f. get worse
7. reinforce   g. provide fresh air
8. absorb   h. grow in quantity

C Match the words 1–8 with words a–h to form common compound nouns.

1. living   a. disaster
2. basic   b. line
3. natural   c. necessities
4. health   d. care
5. drug   e. materials
6. raw   f. conditions
7. poverty   g. downturn
8. economic   h. dealing

D Sentences 1–6 are spoken expressions from the conversations in the Listening Module of the Course Book. Complete each with a word from the box.

out	down	day	in	steep	place

1. It wouldn't look out of _____ as a green on a top golf course.
2. It'd certainly be worth you checking it _____.
3. The central heating system's had its _____.

4. You can fill me _____ on anything else when I get back.
5. It's on for 420,000, but I'm pretty sure they'd come _____.
6. Yeah, 420's a bit _____.

E Think about how each expression is used in context. Discuss what each means with a partner and decide if you have a similar expression in your own language.

Listening

A 🎧 Listen and match each social exchange with a situation. Write the number of the situation as your answer.

1. Two tourists are looking around part of a historical building.
2. The owner of a company talks about ecological construction on a TV show.
3. Somebody wants to rent a house.
4. An architect is being interviewed on the radio.

Exchange A ___   Exchange B ___   Exchange C ___   Exchange D ___

B 🎧 Listen again, and, in each case, complete the notes. Use NO MORE THAN THREE WORDS OR A NUMBER for each answer. You will need to identify key words and phrases and sometimes guess the spelling.

Exchange A:

house with (1) _____ bedrooms

(2) _____ part of living room (so can't be bedroom!)

one bathroom + downstairs (3) _____

small (4) _____ with potted shrubs - not really garden

meet landlady at (5) _____ p.m. - (6) _____ Lorna Road.

Exchange B:

Fountain of the Lions
(1) _____ lions around fountain representing (2) _____ and (3) _____

materials: (4) _____ of fountain - alabaster, lions - (5) _____

Exchange C:

early years: abilities related to (1) _____ and art
                (2) _____ was drawing plans

role of architect: helping (3) _____ to imagine end product bringing
                (4) _____ and (5) _____ together

benefits of job: making a real (6) _____ - not just art

Exchange D:

Green Building

(1) _____ and (2) _____ essential – not aesthetic appeal

infrastructure maximized – (3) _____ exploited for efficiency (e.g., one

(4) _____ for water & fewer branch lines / better insulation of (5) _____

materials recycled (e.g., leftover (6) _____)

Reading

A Read this summary of part of the text about the cage dwellings in the Course Book. Decide what type of word or phrase goes into each space. Write the letter in the space.

A an adjective
B a noun or noun phrase
C a past participle with a dependent preposition
D a verb in its full infinitive form
E an adverb

Hong Kong is full of huge (1) ___ and fashionable retail outlets, but the (2) ___ has not benefited the city's poorest inhabitants. Many people live in poverty, the situation having deteriorated since the (3) ___ came to an end. An extreme manifestation of all this is a (4) ___ slum block that has been home to the city's so-called cage dwellers for more than half a century. These people, many of whom arrived in the city after (5) ___ unrest at home, are crammed into accommodation that has been (6) ___ increasingly tiny units. The fact that so many vulnerable people live in such a dreadful environment is something that Hong Kong's more (7) ___ inhabitants seem unwilling to accept.

B Read the passage again on pages 120 and 121 of the Course Book and fill the spaces with the correct words. USE NO MORE THAN TWO WORDS for each answer.

1. _____ 2. _____ 3. _____ 4. _____

5. _____ 6. _____ 7. _____ 8. _____

C Read the extract below and on the next page from a webpage about caring for a thatched roof. In pairs, discuss the meaning of the highlighted words and phrases. Use the context to work out meaning. In some cases, you may need to guess.

Caring for your thatched roof

Whether your thatched home is a period cottage or a new property, if you give it the attention it requires, it will never lose its charm.

However, …

Just like any other part of a building, a thatched roof needs periodical maintenance and repair. You can prevent problems such as vermin damage or rot from shortening the lifespan of the roof.

Even small repairs should be carried out by a professional thatcher. Take time to stand and look at your roof – it is obvious if a thatched roof is in a poor condition.

If fixings are exposed all over the roof, it indicates that the thatch is either nearing, or has reached the end of its life. Excess wear around the chimney stack can indicate heat escaping through the chimney. If so, contact your local thatcher for advice on the possible need to conduct repairs to the chimney.

If gullies (deep vertical area of rot) are appearing, they will need the attention of a professional thatcher.

Dark wet patches on the eaves close to the wall indicate the thatch is leaking. Heavy moss could mean that the thatch is unable to breathe and is therefore unable to dry out properly.

If contractors have to work on your roof (to repair a chimney or fix an aerial), make sure they speak with your thatcher first to ensure any roof ladders or equipment they use do not damage your thatch.

D Match the definitions 1–9 below with the highlighted items in the extract.

1. a person who makes thatched roofs
2. how long something lasts
3. the part of the chimney that is visible above the roof
4. piece of equipment that receives television signals
5. where the thatch is fixed to the frame of the roof
6. small animals or insects that cause damage
7. soft green or brown plant that grows where it is wet
8. parts of the roof that continue out over the wall
9. the process of decay / decaying material

Writing

A Mark each opinion a, b and c in the sets below ✓ if it is expressed appropriately for a formal composition, ✗ if it is expressed a little too forcefully and ✗✗ if it expressed far too aggressively.

1. ☐ a) I can't imagine why people choose to live in dull suburban towns.
   ☐ b) Personally, I do not see the appeal of sleepy suburban towns.
   ☐ c) I couldn't bear the thought of living in a boring little suburban town.

2. ☐ a) I reckon it's absolutely brilliant that they're doing up so many old buildings.
   ☐ b) I think it's great that so many old buildings are being renovated.
   ☐ c) The renovation of so many old buildings is a very welcome development.

3. ☐ a) To my mind, traditional building methods were not necessarily superior than those used today.
   ☐ b) I don't think it's true that traditional building methods were better than building methods used now.
   ☐ c) People say old building methods were better – that's a load of rubbish!

B Rewrite the strongly-expressed opinions below so that they are more appropriate.

1. I can't stand the new museum they've built in my city. It looks really stupid.
2. It drives me crazy when ugly modern buildings suddenly go up in the middle of a pretty town.

3. In lots of cities, there are fantastic modern sculptures that are far more interesting than boring old statues.

1. _____

   _____

2. _____

   _____

3. _____

   _____

C The paragraph below is from the student's composition in the Course Book. The punctuation has been taken out.

1. Put in four full stops and use capital letters to begin a new sentence.
2. Put in two commas.
3. Check your answers against the report in the Course Book on page 123.

> Personally I find it sad when an interesting old building is destroyed and I think it should always be the last option preserving historical buildings and monuments is one way of passing our history on to the next generation children learn from visiting these buildings and develop an interest in and respect for the past perhaps when we pull down a magnificent old building we show a lack of respect for the architect and his work

Writing task

A Look at the Writing task below and think about:

1. whether you tend to agree or disagree.
2. what points you could make agreeing with the statement.
3. what points you could make that disagree with the statement.
4. how you can express your opinions appropriately.
5. vocabulary from the unit that you want to use.

Write about the following topic:

Most modern buildings in today's cities are ugly and far less appealing than the historical buildings they have replaced. Historical city centres are being ruined by modern architecture.

Do you believe this statement to be true?

Give reasons for your answer and include any relevant examples from your own or experience.

Write at least 250 words.

B Talk and compare your thoughts about the topic of the Writing task with other students.

C Write your composition. Then check the model on pages 266 and 267.

_____

_____

_____

_____

9

Words and pictures

Vocabulary development

A Delete the odd word out in each list below.

1. landscape / portrait / paperback / watercolour
2. novel / biography / play / chapter
3. abstract / classic / conceptual / surreal
4. inspired / compelled / driven / thwarted
5. affection / imagination / creativity / originality
6. astonishing / controversial / phenomenal / extraordinary
7. appealing / charismatic / stern / captivating
8. reactionary / modern / contemporary / fashionable
9. well-known / celebrated / eminent / humble
10. viewpoint / position / opposition / stance

B Complete each sentence with the correct preposition.

1. I can't relate _____ her work at all.
2. I don't know what people see _____ it.
3. I'm a very big fan _____ his work.
4. They wrote _____ assumed names.
5. Her contribution _____ literature is notable.
6. I was quickly drawn _____ their cause.
7. I sympathize _____ their views on this matter.
8. They are _____ opposition _____ the more excessive aspects of conceptualism.
9. She was the victim _____ slander.
10. Students have switched _____ traditional research _____ Internet research.
11. The Internet may not provide the _____ -depth information I need.
12. Libraries have had to adapt _____ change.

C There are various verbs in the Course Book unit that mean *like very much* or *do not like at all*. Those verbs are below, together with some new ones. Mark each verb (L) if it means like or (D) if it means dislike.

admire	__
loathe	__
detest	__
adore	__
idolize	__
worship	__
abhor	__
despise	__
revere	__

Listening

A You will hear a radio interview about three contemporary art movements of the last two decades. Before you listen, look at the pictures below. Can you guess what any of the movements are called?

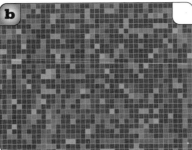

B 🎧 Listen and label each picture with the name of the movement it is an example of.

C 🎧 Look at the statements 1–8. Listen and match each statement with the correct movement A, B or C.

1. It may not be allowed in some places.
2. It frequently combines two of the senses
3. Some of the work is three dimensional.
4. It is one of several very similar art movements.
5. There may be nothing to actually look at all.
6. Its name is often abbreviated.
7. Its acceptance as an art form was helped by an award.
8. Not all artists welcome its mainstream popularity.

| A sound art |
| B Internet art |
| C street art |

D 🎧 Read the tapescript as you listen again. Make a note of any new words and phrases that you think are useful.

E Which of the three art forms appeals to you? Why? Compare ideas with a partner.

Reading

 Exam tip: When a passage is largely the writer's opinion, there will almost certainly be introductory phrases and expressions that help you appreciate that an opinion is being expressed. Learning some of these will help you read more quickly and efficiently.

A Mark the phrases below from the passage about Stuckism in the Course Book as follows:

- **(I)** if it is neutral and simply introduces an opinion.
- **(P)** if it is more likely to be used to express a positive view or agree with something.
- **(N)** if it is more likely to be used to express a negative view or disagree with something.

1. I have always held the belief that … ___
2. I have to admit … ___
3. I welcomed … ___
4. I found myself drawn to … ___
5. … that I sympathize with. ___
6. I am all for … ___

7. ... it is time to ask questions   ___
8. I ask myself ...   ___
9. I think not.   ___
10. I do not propose ...   ___
11. As I see it ...   ___
12. I am certainly with them on this.   ___

B Read the short article below and highlight the phrases that introduce an opinion or make clear that an opinion is being expressed.

C Answer the questions 1–6 that follow the article.

What Happened to the Classics?

My 16-year-old daughter recently asked me if I had read one of the novels she was reading for her GCSE English literature exam. The book was *Of Mice and Men*, John Steinbeck's sad tale of migrant workers during America's Great Depression. I told her I had, and we started comparing our thoughts. I was impressed by her understanding of it since she claimed to have read it in three days and I wondered why perhaps she hadn't been challenged to read one of Steinbeck's more substantial epics. *Of Mice and Men* is a minor classic, of course – it won the Nobel Prize – but it hardly has the depth of *The Grapes of Wrath*.

The discussion developed and I soon realized that six out of the seven books she was reading for the exam were what I would call modern literature – that is, written in the 20th century. Now, these are all perfectly fine books in their own right and books that I would certainly welcome her reading at some point in time, but I ask myself whether there could be far more balance in terms of specific course material.

I looked into the matter more deeply and discovered that very few of the teenagers who sat the most popular English literature exam last year based their answers on novels published before 1900. Of around 300,000 literature students, only just over 1,000 had studied *Pride and Prejudice* and a minuscule 185 studied *Wuthering Heights* as part of the test. These, of course, are two classics that most parents would like their children to have read before they are 18. Almost 90% of students, on the other hand, studied either *Of Mice and Men*, *Lord of the Flies* or *To Kill a Mockingbird*.

I also learnt that a major international study has reported that reading standards among British teenagers had slumped from 7th to 25th on a world league table in just over ten years. I ask myself whether this may in part be the result of the rather limited range of reading matter I have described. It seems that the education system in this country fails to encourage the young to appreciate the classics and is not widening their horizons. In short, I suggest we are not guiding our children to read enough of the right kind of thing.

For questions 1–6 decide if the following statements reflect the opinions of the writer in the passage? Write:

- **(Y) YES** if the statement reflects the claims of the writer.
- **(N) NO** if the statement contradicts the claims of the writer.
- **(NG) NOT GIVEN** if it is impossible to say what the writer thinks about this.

1. *Of Mice and Men* is not a particularily good book.   ___
2. *Of Mice and Men* is easier to read than *The Grapes of Wrath*.   ___
3. Passing the literature exam should mean reading more than seven books.   ___
4. More students should have read *Pride and Prejudice* and *Wuthering Heights*.   ___
5. *Lord of the Flies* and *To Kill a Mockingbird* are not suitable for a literature exam course.   ___
6. An emphasis on reading modern novels may be to blame for falling standards of reading.   ___

Writing

A Replace the highlighted verbs in the two model reports below from the Course Book with the correct form of verbs from the box below.

install	sacrifice	make room for	situate	relocate	fit	enlarge

The diagrams show that by next year, some radical changes will have been made to Poolsville library.

There are plans to add a whole new computer centre, part of which will be a coffee shop. This will mean dispensing with the local history room and music and video library. A DVD library will be available in the computer room.

The children's library will be expanded, meaning that the cloakrooms will have to be moved to the other side of the floor. There will be fewer reading tables, but Wi-Fi access will be available in that area.

To make room for the new computer centre and the expansion of the non-fiction reading area, the information centre will be moved to the centre of the floor. The newspapers and journals section is going to be in the area where the old computer stations were.

The diagrams show that within three years, some fairly major changes will have been made to the Crowley Gallery.

There are plans to provide a new interactive education centre, which means the existing temporary exhibition gallery will have to be moved. That will be located within the area that was the portrait gallery, meaning that the portrait gallery be will be smaller. A photography gallery will be a brand new feature.

The cafeteria will be transformed into a bar and restaurant and a separate coffee shop will open next door. To make that possible, the book and gift shop will move to the other side of the floor next to the information desk.

The stairs to the second floor will remain in place, but a lift will be installed too. To accommodate this, the toilets will be relocated.

B Complete the sentences below with the correct form of the verbs from the box.

introduce	restore	adapt	divide	enhance	reduce

1. Recently, a number of new features have been _____.
2. It may be necessary to _____ the size of the reception area.
3. There are plans to _____ the entrance so that disabled students are better accommodated.
4. The overall appearance has been _____ by the renovation work.
5. The gymnasium will be _____ into two separate smaller buildings.
6. The hope is that the chapel will be _____ to its former glory.

10 Rain or shine

Vocabulary development

A Match the beginnings and endings of the sentences below from the Course Book unit.

1. It carries away topsoil, weakening
2. Some impacts may seem positive, such as lengthening
3. Toboggan riders who apparently loosened

a. a deadly wall of snow.
b. the foundation that lies below.
c. the plant-growing season.

B In pairs, answer the questions below about the highlighted verbs in Exercise A.

1. What do the verbs have in common?
2. How is one verb formed in a slightly different way from the other two?

C Complete the sentences below with the correct form of verbs from the box.

threaten   strengthen   harden   lighten   soften   sharpen

1. The cement will _____ in approximately three hours in normal temperatures.
2. Severe weather is _____ to disrupt this weekend's sporting events.
3. Many people now filter tap water to _____ it.
4. You'll need to _____ that pencil before you use it.
5. This particular exercise helps to _____ muscles in the lower back.
6. The conversation was getting too serious, so Greg told a joke to _____ the mood.

D Mark each sentence in Exercise C (A) if the verb is formed from an adjective and (N) if it is formed from a noun.

E Read the sentence from the Course Book unit below. Then answer the two questions that follow with a partner.

Although trees and plants are expensive initially and then to maintain, their benefits outweigh the cost incurred.

1. Do you remember what the highlighted verb means?
2. What does the prefix *out~* mean in verbs like this?

F Use the context of each situation below to work out what the bold verbs mean. Then discuss the meaning of each verb with a partner.

1. She completely **outclassed** her opponent, winning the match 6-1, 6-2, 6-1.
2. It is not uncommon for women to **outlive** their husbands by 10 or 12 years.
3. These batteries **outlast** most other brands on the market.
4. If you are in a fast vehicle, you may be able to **outrun** a tornado.
5. There is a danger that cyber-criminals are **outsmarting** the antivirus programmes that protect computers from attack.
6. Jenny is a clever little girl who **outshines** most children of her age.

G Delete the adjective in the list below that means the opposite of all the others.

major / slight / severe / extreme / intense / acute

Listening

A 🎧 Listen to a news report about an unusual weather event and answer the questions.

1. Which parts of the world are mentioned? Why?
2. Why was the weather event unusual?

B 🎧 Listen again and answer the questions.

For questions 1–7, answer the questions using NO MORE THAN THREE WORDS from the recording for each answer.

1. Where had the dust been carried in from?
2. Which adjective did meteorologists use to say the sand was not a risk to health?
3. Where were most people when showers of rain dropped the sand?
4. When did something similar last happen in the UK?
5. Where does wind that affects the UK usually come from?
6. What did drivers in France say caused problems?
7. In which country were journeys by air affected?

For questions 8–11, complete the flow chart below.

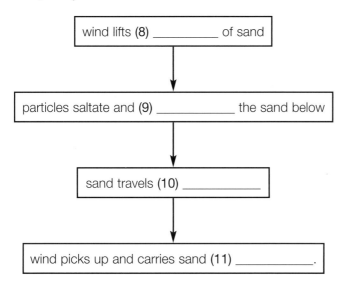

wind lifts (8) _____ of sand

↓

particles saltate and (9) _____ the sand below

↓

sand travels (10) _____

↓

wind picks up and carries sand (11) _____.

For questions 12–14, complete the notes using NO MORE THAN THREE WORDS OR A NUMBER from the recording for each answer.

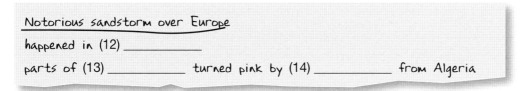

Notorious sandstorm over Europe

happened in (12) _____

parts of (13) _____ turned pink by (14) _____ from Algeria

Reading

A The extract on the next page is from the Writing Module of the Course Book, but reference words have been removed. In pairs:

1. write the appropriate reference word into each space.
2. check your answers by reading the extract on page 156 of the Course Book again.

Some scientists are suggesting that man is moving into a whole new geological era – (1) _____ that he has created himself, especially in terms of the environment. (2) _____ age is being referred to as the *anthropocene*. The bottom line is that heat that would once have been radiated back into space is now trapped in our atmosphere. (3) _____ energy has a range of effects – seas warm up and ice melts. The last few years have been the warmest on record and scientists and insurance companies alike are blaming global warming for a spate of recent catastrophes. Droughts, heatwaves and mega-floods felt across the planet, (4) _____ claim, are undeniably linked to rising temperatures and referring to many of (5) _____ disasters as 'natural' is no longer accurate.

B Read the extracts below and, in each case, write what the highlighted general referencing noun refers back to.

1. In the future, there will be huge changes in temperature and average annual rainfall. These are important factors in determining whether or not a new territory becomes hospitable to an arbovirus.
   Factors refers back to <u>changes in temperature and average annual rainfall</u>.

2. A team of researchers claims to have new evidence that global warming is melting Antarctic ice more rapidly than had previously been believed. They claim that the resulting rise in sea levels is being underestimated. It is thought that around 15,000 sq km of Antarctic sea ice has been lost in the last 50 years. The findings were announced at a Climate Change Conference in New York last week.
   Findings refers back to _____.

3. Floods and mudslides have claimed more than 100 lives on several Indonesian islands since the rainy season began in November. Many of the incidents have been blamed on deforestation caused by unbridled illegal logging.
   Incidents refers back to _____.

4. This agreement requires wealthy nations to reduce their own emissions while providing assistance to developing countries in pursuing a cleaner energy future. While these measures may not have a drastic immediate effect, it is hoped that they are a step in the right direction.
   Measures refers back to _____.

5. Local farmers clear forest to plant crops or provide grazing for livestock. Each year, one farmer may cut down and burn several acres of vegetation. This process is often referred to as *slash and burn* agriculture.
   Process refers to _____.

C Highlight the correct general referencing noun in each sentence below.

1. Diseases like malaria and typhoid could spread into parts of the world where they are so far unknown. This is an *aspect / issue / matter* of global warming that many people do not consider.

2. Green roofs and cool pavements are becoming ever more common *characteristics / features / qualities* of many city landscapes.

3. Local farmers slash and burn forest to plant crops or provide grazing land. When the sheer number of farmers is taken into account, it is clear why this *practice / exercise / event* is so damaging.

4. The government so far appears to have punished individual farmers harshly, while allowing logging companies to carry on clearing forest unchecked. This is *an action / a movement / a policy* that many see as both unfair and unlikely to address the real issue of deforestation.

5. Planting trees and shrubs in strategic positions around buildings or to shade pavements is common. This *notion / approach / development* is especially beneficial if vegetation shades windows or part of the roof.

Writing

A Below is a version of the model composition from the Writing Module of the Course Book with all the cohesive devices removed.

1. Write the appropriate word or phrase from the box into each space, using capital letters when necessary.
2. Check your answers by reading the model on page 158 of the Course Book again.

| which (x 2) | even | because | since | not long ago | however | and |
| when (x 2) | of course | in fact | where | in my country | as | because of |

_____, when people talked about natural disasters, they assumed that they really were all natural – 'acts of God' some might say. _____ the human race has developed and as we understand more about the consequences of our actions, we realize that some of these events are _____ caused by what we do to the planet.

The huge floods that we have seen recently in many parts of the world are often caused by deforestation. _____ whole forests of trees are cut down, there is nothing to hold the rainwater and it washes down into rivers, _____ then overflow. Mudslides are another result of destroying the rainforests. Areas of deforested land break away from a hillside and can cause tremendous damage. Droughts are increasing and becoming common in places _____ once they were unknown. We produce far higher levels of greenhouse gases, _____ we release into the atmosphere, causing temperatures to rise. _____, sandstorms have become more frequent _____ so many people now drive large vehicles in the desert. People drive too fast _____ disturb the top layer of sand.

_____ disasters that are not actually caused by our interference with nature can have more serious consequences _____ the way we live. Earthquakes hit hardest in areas where land has been destabilized by overuse and can easily come away from a hillside. Hurricanes and tornadoes seem to affect the poorest people _____ they live in the least stable housing.

_____, not all disasters can be blamed directly on man. There have always been earthquakes, volcanoes and hurricanes and there always will be. _____, I agree that we are moving into an age _____ man is at least partly to blame for more of these events.

Writing task

A Look at the Writing task below and think about:

1. whether there is anything in the statement that you want to disagree with.
2. what points you could make to support the statement.
3. what points you could make that disagree with the statement.
4. how you can express your opinions appropriately.
5. information that you learnt in the Course Book unit about the topic that you can use.
6. vocabulary from the unit that you want to use.

Write about the following topic:

It is easy to assume that everyone is affected equally by climate change, but it is the very poorest who are frequently the hardest hit.

To what extent do you agree with this statement?

Give reasons for your answer and include any relevant examples from your own knowledge or experience.

Write at least 250 words.

B Talk and compare your thoughts about the topic of the Writing task with other students.

C Write your composition. Then check the model on page 268.

Sink or swim

Vocabulary development

A Complete the common verb phrases in the sentences below with the correct verb.

1. I think we're _____ progress.
2. I've never _____ a deadline **yet**.
3. You'll just have to _____ **more** effort.
4. You should _____ every opportunity.
5. A kind benefactor _____ **pity** on him.
6. She's _____ a **huge** contribution.

B Write the noun that corresponds to each of the adjectives below. Be careful with spelling!

1. insecure _____
2. cowardly _____
3. indecisive _____
4. resilient _____
5. hesitant _____
6. optimistic _____
7. persistent _____
8. adverse _____

C Look at the compound nouns below and, in pairs, revise the meaning of each.

> self-doubt   self-confidence   self-pity

Now match the compound adjectives 1–5 with the definitions a–e.

1. self-centred
2. self-conscious
3. self-righteous
4. self-sufficient
5. self-made

a. over-aware of other people's judgements
b. having achieved success through your own hard work
c. only interested in your own concerns
d. assuming that your own beliefs (especially moral) and values are superior
e. not relying on other people

D Look at the how some bold expressions from the Course Book unit are used below in context.

1. Discuss the meaning of each with a partner.
2. Decide whether you have the same or similar expressions in your own language.

a. Great achievers have drive and endless determination. That's what **sets them apart from** the rest of us.
b. I'm especially impressed when somebody who's had no advantages in life succeeds **against all the odds**.
c. Some people simply won't give up once they've **set their heart on** something.
d. Most parents will **move heaven and earth** to help their children succeed in life.
e. **The bottom line** is that if this year is as bad as the last, we'll be out of business.
f. Successful people don't give up when the **going gets tough**.
g. I'll always think back to that job as **a fish that got away**.

E Below are some more commonly used expressions related to success and failure. Complete each with the correct form of a verb from the box. Then, in pairs, answer questions 1 and 2 from Exercise D about each expression.

| make fall pull go set stop |

1. You'll need to _____ **your socks up** if you expect to get the grades you're hoping for.
2. Jim's very ambitious. He'd _____ **at nothing** to get what he wants.
3. Jenny's clearly _____ **her sights on** the director's job. She's determined to get right to the top.
4. To be honest, I thought Tom was a much nicer person before he _____ **it big**.
5. The new coach is building an excellent team. They're _____ **from strength to strength**.
6. Mark told everyone that he was going to succeed, but when he really came up against some stiff competition, he _____ **flat on his face**.

Listening

A 🎧 Listen to two extracts from a Listening test, one from Section 2 and the other from Section 3. What is the common theme of both extracts?

B 🎧 Listen again. Can you identify any examples where the same idea is expressed formally in one extract and informally in the other?

C 🎧 Listen to the Section 2 extract and, for each question, choose a, b or c as your answer.

1. Which of the following is not mentioned as a tactic to address the recession?
   a. selling products or services that were not previously sold
   b. doing business six or seven days a week
   c. aiming at a more select market

2. One potential disadvantage of diversification is …
   a. not knowing enough about a new area of business.
   b. additional competition.
   c. having to restate original objectives.

3. What is mentioned as a more drastic solution to fighting the recession?
   a. taking on more staff
   b. employing fewer people
   c. paying people less money

D 🎧 Listen to the Section 3 extract and complete the notes. Use NO MORE THAN THREE WORDS for each answer.

small businesses - hit harder - are more (1) _____
bigger businesses can weather the storm - have (2) _____ customers

smaller businesses must (3) _____ - find new products / services
must target (4) _____
need to adapt, but not abandon (5) _____
may need to (6) _____ workers as last resort

E Match examples of formal language 1–6 with examples of informal language a–f.

1. affected more dramatically
2. survive
3. diversify
4. target
5. versatile
6. make staff redundant

a. stay afloat
b. lay people off
c. aim at
d. hit harder
e. branch out
f. be an all-rounder

F Read the tapescript. Highlight any other words, phrases or expressions that you think will be useful to remember.

Reading

A Read the passage and then decide which definition of *rags to riches* below is correct. Don't worry about the highlighted part for now.

1. becoming famous and then losing everything
2. working your way to the top from nothing
3. having the advantage of being born into a wealthy family

Rags to Riches – Celebrities

Here are a few things you may not associate with the rich and famous: working as a janitor. Being part of an impoverished family of 14. Living on welfare. Getting shot. Serious family issues.

And yet, early experiences like these have shaped and driven some of the most powerful and important celebrities in the world, from Jim Carrey, Tom Cruise and Sean "Diddy" Combs to Celine Dion and Oprah Winfrey. Is there a tie between a tough upbringing and fame? Social scientists, who are just beginning to study the phenomenon, say yes.

"We all have a basic need for acceptance and approval by social groups," says Orville Gilbert Brim, author of *The Fame Motive: A Treatise on its Origin and Life Course*. "If it's not satisfied, if a person is excluded either in infancy, childhood or, in many cases, adolescence, this frustration becomes the source of a motive or a desire to become famous." Put another way, fame "offers the possibility to transcend what you have been given as your lot in life," says P. David Marshall, author of *Celebrity and Power: Fame in Contemporary Culture*.

Consider Marilyn Monroe. In her unfinished autobiography, the foster child turned cultural icon wrote of her fame, "I knew I belonged to the public and to the world, not because I was talented or even beautiful, but because I had never belonged to anyone or anything else." For Monroe, and those who share her background, fame offered a sense, real or not, of belonging and mass acceptance. And while anyone can be driven toward celebrity, people from poor upbringings can find fame to be an alluring way to fulfil some otherwise unfulfilled need.

A survey conducted by Syracuse University professor Carol M. Liebler and Jake Halpern, author of *Fame Junkies: The Hidden Truth Behind America's Favorite Addiction*, found that teenagers who described themselves as often or always depressed were more likely to believe that becoming a celebrity would make them happier. And what's more, teens who described themselves as feeling lonely were also more likely to believe that fame would have a positive impact on their lives.

According to Halpern, money once filled this void or at least, it appeared to fill the void. Consider the classic Horatio Alger rags to riches story: redemption was found through financial gain. Today, Halpern says, it is fame rather than fortune that offers the most dramatic and resounding form of redemption. "In the past, it may have been difficult to become rich, but theoretically anyone could do it, whereas it seemed more unrealistic to even think about fame," he says. But in today's YouTube culture, where everything from reality TV to a MySpace page can launch a career, it is no longer entirely impractical to think that fame and celebrity is attainable. James Houran, a clinical psychologist who researches celebrity worship, also argues that growing up with limited means not only motivates, but actually fosters the imagination and ultimately fuels one's drive for fame. "Because you don't have a lot of action figures or princess dresses to play with, you tend to get very creative," he says. "You have to make do with what you have, and that kind of feeds the resourcefulness part of that ambitious personality."

But exactly how those stars who have elevated themselves from rags to riches handle their fame depends on several things, including how quickly they attain it and what kind of support system they surround themselves with once they have it. There are those who achieve fame and become overly generous, explains Houran. The way he sees it, these folks came from nothing and are, therefore, driven to do their part. Among his examples: queen of all media Oprah Winfrey. Having spent her early years poverty-stricken in rural Mississippi, Winfrey later faced serious family issues including the death of her child as she aged. Today, the chat-show host is as well known for her generosity as she is for her fame. Funding a $40 million school for girls in Africa is just one of Winfrey's many do-gooder acts. And then there are those who achieve fame and become very indulgent – quick to meet not just their every need, but their every desire. "In many ways, they announce their success with the items that they buy," explains Ellis Cashmore, author of *Celebrity Culture*. This may explain the behaviour of New York City-born rapper Sean "Diddy" Combs, who moved upstate as a child after the murder

of his father. Today, the hip-hop impresario has evolved into a celebrity, in the truest sense of the word. And while he does his part for charity, Combs has never shied away from the luxuries that fame affords. Let his numerous houses and million-dollar soirées serve as evidence.

But the irony in all of this, according to Brim, is that fame doesn't provide the sense of belonging that its seekers long for. Quite the opposite – it leaves many who attain it feeling empty. "You think it will make you feel loved, approved of and accepted," he explains, "but in fact, the desire for fame is insatiable."

B Look at the sentence beginnings 1–6 below. In pairs, discuss what you remember about how each sentence could continue.

1. Living on state benefit
2. Being excluded
3. A desire to be rich
4. Becoming famous
5. Having a limited number of toys
6. Extreme generosity or indulgence

C Look at the sentence endings A–I in the box below. Compare your ideas in Exercise B with the endings here.

Exam tip: The sentence endings will all fit grammatically with the sentence beginnings. More than one sentence ending will appear to make sense with a sentence beginning. You MUST read carefully to check that the whole sentence – beginning and end – reflects what is stated in the passage.

D Look at the part of the passage that a student has highlighted to help answer the first question.

1. Find words in the sentence endings below that paraphrase *associate with* and *rich and famous*.
2. Decide which sentence ending A–I paraphrases both phrases.

A is associated with a sudden rise to celebrity.
B has been replaced with a desire to be famous.
C inspires invention.
D brings happiness to those who achieve it.
E can drive people to seek fame.
F helps people to form relationships.
G is not typically equated with celebrities.
H is now a more realistically achieved desire.
I prevents people from achieving their goals.

E Complete each sentence 1–6 in Exercise B with the correct ending A–I.

Writing

A Below and on the next page is another version of a model answer to the Writing task presented in the Course Book. Complete it using the correct form of the verbs in the box below.

accept (x 2)   make   find   rise   take   remain   become   work (x 2)

The bar chart shows how various compromises (1) _____ by graduates in the United States in order to find their first job increased in frequency between the years 2006-2007 and 2009-2010.

The percentage of graduates (2) _____ with no health benefits increased dramatically from around 14% in 2006-2007 to around 23% in 2009-2010. Though the actual percentage (3) _____ a temporary position was still quite low in 2009-2010, the number of graduates (4) _____ this option rose by around a third.

In 2006-2007, the most common compromise was for graduates (5) _____ below their education level. Around 32% (6) _____ this. Between then and 2009-2010, the percentage taking this option (7) _____ only slightly to around 33%. In contrast, the percentage working for less money than expected increased from around 28% in 2006-2007 to just under 40% in 2009-2010 and it (8) _____ the most typical compromise.

The only compromise which did not increase in frequency over the period was 'working outside area of interest'. The percentage of graduates that (9) _____ themselves in this situation (10) _____ at around 23%.

Writing task

A In pairs, answer the questions below.

1. How many gold medals do you think the USA won at the 1984 Olympics? 50, 60, 70 or 80?
2. How many gold medals do you think China won at the 1984 Olympics? 15, 35, 55 or 75?
3. How many gold medals do you think the USA won at the 2008 Olympics? 30, 40, 50 or 60?
4. How many gold medals do you think China won at the 2008 Olympics? 20, 30, 40 or 50?

B Look at the Writing task below.

1. Make a note of information that stands out and will interest a reader.
2. Plan how you will organize your ideas and link them together.

The bar chart shows the number of gold medals won by the United States and China at each of the Olympic Games from 1984 to 2008.

Summarize the information by selecting and reporting the main features, and make comparisons where relevant.

Write at least 150 words.

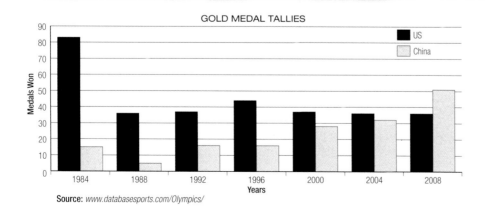

GOLD MEDAL TALLIES

Source: www.databasesports.com/Olympics/

C Write your report. Then check the model on pages 268 and 269.

12 Crime and punishment

Vocabulary development

A Delete the wrong verb in each sentence below.

1. Police have *fired / launched* a full-scale investigation after the discovery of a body.
2. The perpetrator has *given / shown* little remorse for the crime he committed.
3. Police have been *making / asking* enquiries in the local area.
4. Her lawyer persuaded her to *plead / claim* guilty.
5. After ten hours, the jury finally *reached / found* a unanimous verdict.
6. Most offenders do not actually *fulfil / serve* their whole sentence.
7. The hope is that a witness is less likely to lie having *made / taken* an oath.
8. A number of witnesses were called to *say / give* evidence.
9. Communication technology allows people to *spread / stretch* harmful rumours more easily.

B Match the verbs 1–9 with their meanings a–i.

1. proliferate	a.	deliberately try to frighten somebody
2. deploy	b.	be too much for somebody to cope with
3. intimidate	c.	move around an area in order to prevent trouble
4. soar	d.	be in charge of and check that something is functioning
5. overwhelm	e.	offer freely
6. inflict	f.	quickly increase in number
7. supervise	g.	cause something harmful to happen
8. patrol	h.	use (members of a team) for a specific purpose
9. volunteer	i.	quickly increase to a very high level

C Now match the adjectives 1–6 with their meanings a–f.

1. derogatory	a.	non-stop
2. unrelenting	b.	very upsetting
3. sinister	c.	clear and noticeable
4. tangible	d.	from an unknown source
5. anonymous	e.	showing a negative opinion / insulting
6. distressing	f.	threatening evil

D Look again at the title of the second passage in the Reading Module in the Course Book on page 184. Tick the correct meaning of *white elephant* below.

- [ ] a. a clever idea that exceeds expectations
- [ ] b. an important and expensive project that fails
- [ ] c. an unfair decision that people protest about

E Look at how the animal images are used in context below. In pairs, discuss what they mean and whether you have similar expressions in your own language.

1. Having left school at 16 and run away from home to join a gang, Tony was considered the **black sheep** of the family.
2. Lucy's immature and very insecure. She's a **sitting duck** for the school bullies.
3. Jim's very shy and not much of a dancer. He clearly feels like a **fish out of water** when he has to go to college parties.

4. I don't think Graham has the people skills to be a good manager. He's like a **bull in a china shop** at times.

5. Sally's certainly **a dark horse**. She was the last person any of us expected to get the manager's job.

F Match each expression in Exercise E with its correct definition below.

a. an obvious and easy target
b. somebody in a situation they are not comfortable in
c. somebody who surprises others with their success
d. one of a group that is disapproved of
e. clumsy and lacking diplomacy

Listening

A Look at the questions below before you listen to the recording. Make predictions about what you will hear.

For questions 1–6, complete the sentences. Use NO MORE THAN TWO WORDS OR A NUMBER for each answer.

1. Many prisoners lack basic qualifications and have no _____ history.
2. Few prisoners form close _____ in the way that other people do.
3. Practical difficulties are complicated by drinking, drug taking and issues related to _____.
4. People who grew up _____ are more likely to go to prison.
5. A prisoner is ten times more likely to have been a child who was frequently absent _____.
6. Around half of prisoners have _____ no better than a 12-year-old.

For questions 7–10, complete the notes. Use ONE WORD ONLY for each answer.

Prison can make situation worse

1 in 3 have no (7) _____ when released

2 in 3 have no (8) _____ when released

half do not have (9) _____ to rely on

health can deteriorate and (10) _____ are a temptation

For questions 11–12, complete the flow chart below. Use NO MORE THAN TWO WORDS for each answer.

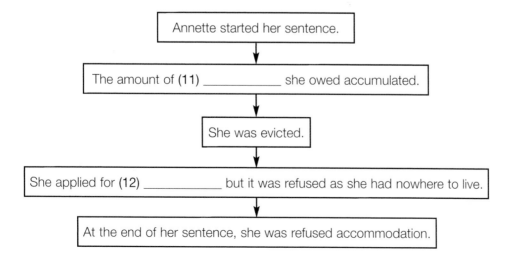

Annette started her sentence.

↓

The amount of (11) _____ she owed accumulated.

↓

She was evicted.

↓

She applied for (12) _____ but it was refused as she had nowhere to live.

↓

At the end of her sentence, she was refused accommodation.

🎧 Listen and answer the questions.

Take ten minutes to transfer your answers to the answer sheet provided below.

1		7	
2		8	
3		9	
4		10	
5		11	
6		12	

Reading

A Look at the title of the passage and the exercises that follow the passage. Make predictions about what the passage will say. Note that the visual support that is provided for some of the questions helps you to do this.

The history of fingerprinting

A A great many books and scientific papers have been published on the subject of fingerprints. In fact, mention of 'the prints from man's hand' can be found even in the Bible. The study of the application of fingerprints for useful purposes appears to have started in the latter part of the 17th century when, in 1684, the anatomist Doctor Nehemiah Grew published a paper on the subject, illustrated with drawings of various fingerprint patterns. In about the same period, in Italy, Professor Malpighi was investigating the function of the skin.

B The use of fingerprints as a reliable means of individual identification dates back to 1860. Sir William Herschel, an administrator in India, appreciated the unique nature of fingerprints and established the principle of their persistence. Fingerprints are formed in full detail before birth and remain unchanged throughout life, unless affected by serious injury. A method of classifying fingerprints and research in this field was initiated by Sir Francis Galton and Henry Faulds independently at the end of the 19th century.

In 1900, a committee was appointed by the Home Secretary to enquire into methods of the Identification of Criminals by Measurement and Fingerprints. About this time, Mr E. R. Henry – later to become Sir Edward Henry, Commissioner of the Metropolitan Police – published his book, *The Classification and Use of Fingerprints*. This proposed a method of fingerprint classification and comparison to supersede the inaccurate Bertillon Anthropometric Measurement System, in use at the time. Henry was one of 16 witnesses invited to appear before this committee to explain the system he had devised. Following the recommendations made by this committee, the Fingerprint Branch at New Scotland Yard was created in July 1901, using the Henry System of Classification.

C The Fingerprint Branch at New Scotland Yard, which initially employed just three people, has expanded over the years, with the present Identification Service now provided by a staff of 600 technical and administrative officers. Today, a pair of Fingerprint Bureaux at New Scotland Yard work in tandem; the National Fingerprint Office, which together with the National Criminal Record Office forms the National Identification Bureau; and the Metropolitan Police Scenes of Crime Branch, which incorporates the Fingerprint, Photographic and Scenes of Crime Examination Services.

The importance of having a National Fingerprint Collection has been recognized by all police forces in the United Kingdom, even though they have their own local fingerprint bureaux. Each day, the fingerprints of those sentenced to a term of imprisonment and those arrested and charged with anything other than the most minor offences, are sent to New Scotland Yard for processing. The prints of those who are not subsequently convicted are destroyed. One of the primary functions of the National Fingerprint Office is to establish whether the person has a previous record. After a name check has been made, the enquiry fingerprints are compared with the master set of any suggested match. If this proves negative, the fingerprints are coded and the coding transmitted to the Police National Computer at Hendon.

D The coding of the enquiry prints is analyzed by the computer, and only criminals whose prints could possibly match are listed as respondents on a computer printout. Until recently, Identification Officers would make a comparison of the enquiry with the paper fingerprint forms of the respondents, which are all filed in the National Fingerprint Collection, in order to establish whether any computer suggestion was positive. However, after some years of research and planning, an automatic retrieval system known as the 'Videofile System' was installed and fingerprint comparisons are now made by Identification Officers at Visual Display Units. These processes, which have eliminated the need for much laborious searching, often result in a rapid reply from the computer, indicating that there is no inclusion which matches the coding enquiry fingerprints.

E Finger and palm marks are sent to the Metropolitan Police Scenes of Crime Branch at New Scotland Yard where, after various elimination and checking procedures, the finger marks are coded for search on either the Police National Computer or the Automatic Fingerprint Recognition System. The suggested possible fingerprint matches may be compared using the Videofile System or by browsing through the actual fingerprint collections. The Automatic Fingerprint Recognition System is a computerized method of matching fingerprints found at scenes of crime with recorded fingerprints of known offenders. The computer lists, in order of probability, any possible fingerprint matches, but does not itself make any 'identical or not identical' decisions. Final comparisons between crime scene marks and offenders' prints, and decisions as to the identity, are carried out by Identification Officers.

F One of the earliest cases involving the use of fingerprint evidence was in 1905, when a greasy thumbprint, left on a cash box at the scene of a murder in Deptford, was identified as belonging to Alfred Stratton, one of two brothers. As a result of this identification, they were jointly charged with the crime and subsequently hanged. Since then, fingerprint identification has played an important role in many major investigations, including the Great Train Robbery in 1963, the sad case of Lesley Whittle, who was kidnapped and found brutally murdered in a reservoir drainage shaft in 1975, and the intriguing case of the 'Stockwell Strangler', who was responsible for several crimes, including, most notoriously, the macabre deaths of a number of pensioners in 1986.

Like any other major organization, the Identification Services are always seeking ways of improving the service provided. Although computerization leads to greater efficiency, it cannot replace the individual expertise of trained Identification Officers and the final decision as to identity, which is always made by a qualified Fingerprint Expert.

B Read the passage and answer the questions. Time yourself as you work. You should spend no more than 20 minutes on the task.

The passage has six sections, A–F. Which section contains the following information? For questions 1–8, write the correct letter A–F on your answer sheet. You will need to use some letters more than once.

1. an explanation of how one process replaced another ___
2. a comparison of computer and human roles in a process ___
3. an account of specific examples of fingerprint application ___
4. a description of the growth of an organization ___
5. an assertion that fingerprint patterns are permanent ___
6. a comparison of older and newer fingerprinting techniques ___
7. reference to an ancient suggestion of fingerprinting ___
8. an acknowledgment of the benefit of a centralized system ___

For questions 9–13, decide if the information given below agrees with the information given in the text. Write (T) true, (F) false or (NG) not given, if there is no information on this.

9. In Italy, Professor Malpighi studied fingerprinting. ___
10. Sir Edward Henry's investigations received little support. ___
11. Two departments at New Scotland Yard are dedicated to fingerprinting. ___
12. The police keep the fingerprints of everybody they charge with a crime. ___
13. Most people whose prints are taken have previously committed crime. ___

For question 14, choose the correct answer a, b or c.

14. Which image shows the National Fingerprint Collection?   ___

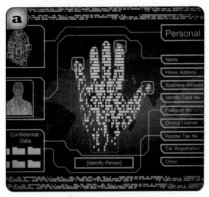 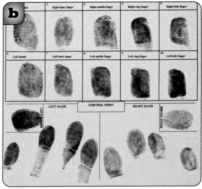 

For questions 15–18, complete the table below. Use NO MORE THAN TWO WORDS
for each answer.

case	details
Alfred Stratton case	police found (15) _____ at crime scene
	(16) _____ charged and hanged for murder
(17) _____ case	discovery of body underground
'Stockwell Strangler' case	(18) _____ murdered

c Take 10 minutes to transfer your answers to the answer sheet provided below.

1		10	
2		11	
3		12	
4		13	
5		14	
6		15	
7		16	
8		17	
9		18	

Writing

Exam tip: Remember that while many tasks in Writing Task 2 require you to say whether you agree or disagree with a statement, others will require you to give reasons as to why a problem exists and to suggest some possible solutions.

A Look at an alternative to the task that you completed in the Exam Practice Module of the Course Book. In pairs, discuss whether you would prefer to attempt this task or if you would find it more challenging than the one you did.

Write about the following topic:

Many offenders are released from prison only to reoffend within the first year. Suggest some reason for this situation and suggest some possible solutions.

Give reasons for your answer and include any relevant examples from your own knowledge or experience.

Write at least 250 words.

B Make notes and plan your composition. Look back at information that you could use in your composition. Check the:

- model composition for the Exam Practice Module in the Course Book on page 269.
- tapescript for the Listening task from this unit on page 320.

C Write your composition. Then check it against the model on pages 269 and 270.

Answer Sheet for Unit 12 Reading 2A and B

1		15	
2		16	
3		17	
4		18	
5		19	
6		20	
7		21	
8		22	
9		23	
10		24	
11		25	
12		26	
13		27	
14			

Answer key

Answers for selected Course Book and Workbook listening and reading tasks and model compositions and reports for writing tasks.

Unit 1, Listening 2B and C

Exercise B:
   1. a   2. b   3. b   4. c

Exercise c:
   1. a garden   2. long hours
   3. Manchester / London 4. 50 years

Unit 1, Reading 2E

   1. T   2. F   3. T   4. NG
   5. C   6. E   7. B
   8. A   9. F   10. D

Unit 2, Listening 2C

   1. into two   2. two eggs
   3. ⅓ / a third   4. human genetics
   5. blood group   6. (about) 50%
   7. 35 (years old)   8. height and weight
   9. personalities 10. identity
  11. cancer   12. cakes
  13. a face / your face

Unit 2, Reading 2C

   1. a pendulum
   2. earlier behaviourists
   3. a reward
   4. 133
   5. temperament / temperamental style
   6. T   7. NG   8. F
   9. F 10. T 11. NG 12. F

Workbook Unit 2, Writing task C

In many parts of the world the number of families with only one child is increasing. I read that, in China, it is the norm for families to have only one child due to government policies. In the USA and Europe, couples are choosing to have one child more for economic and financial reasons. Now, more than ever, it is essential that there is debate about whether children with brothers and sisters have advantages over those who do not.

Many people assume that children with brothers and sisters are happier because they see them playing together and interacting. They feel that they naturally learn important social skills that are essential to succeeding in life. On the other hand, people assume that an only child spends a lot of time playing alone and will fail to develop in a way that will help them achieve success. It is argued that parents are either busy, so leave only children to entertain themselves, or devote too much time to only children making them self-centered and spoilt.

Personally, I think that there are some practical disadvantages to being an only child, but not the huge social disadvantages suggested. Teenagers often need a sibling to talk to about personal issues that they do not want to share with parents. However, it could be that only children develop closer relationships with school friends or cousins to compensate. I do think that, later in life, an only child will have an additional burden in terms of looking after ageing parents.

In conclusion, I would say that despite the practical considerations, I do not think that children with siblings have huge advantages, especially since it is becoming so much more common to be an only child. I have three close friends without siblings and although they sometimes say that they would like a brother or sister, they are perfectly well-adjusted and not spoilt. I also have friends with siblings who they do not get on well with. They do not feel that they have any advantages.

Unit 3, Listening 2A

   1. b (the male-dominated world of sport / women face enormous chauvinism and prejudice)
   2. a (girls are used as exercise riders before the races)
   3. a (women are not as robust as men and will get injured)
   4. c (Football … isn't only about strength and speed … smaller players who rely on skill and positional awareness)
   5. hit the ball 6. male 7. successful 8. promise
   9. big events 10. prize money 11. seriously

Unit 3, Reading 2B

   1. D   2. F   3. E
   4. I   5. A   6. C
   7. T   8. F   9. NG 10. T
  11. T 12. F 13. NG 14. F

Unit 3, Writing 4C

The line graph shows that the percentage of women of working age in employment in the United States increased between 1948 and 1998, but fell slightly between 1998 and 2009. The percentage of women over 65 working changed very little.

In 1948, there were more women aged 16–24 working than women of any other age. However, the percentage of young women working did not increase for 20 years. In contrast, the percentage of women aged 25–54 in work rose sharply in that period. The percentage of women aged 16–24 in work rose dramatically between 1966 and 1978, but fluctuated between 1978 and 2009.

Between 1998 and 2009, the percentage of women under 54 working fell slightly. However, the percentage of women aged 55-65 working rose once again. In the last two or three years shown, there was a slight rise in the percentage of women over 65 in work. The percentage of older women working continues to rise while the percentage of younger women falls.

Unit 3, Exam Practice Writing E

The graph shows that between 1979 and 2008 the number of deaths from heart disease in the United States decreased for men but not for women.

In 1979 more men died from heart disease than women. Over the next few years numbers of deaths fluctuated slightly for both genders, but by 1986 the number for women was higher.

Between 1986 and 2008 the number of deaths for men decreased fairly steadily, though the fall was sharper between 1988 and 1991 and there was a slight increase between 1991 and 1995. Since 1995, numbers for men have been steadily declining. Over the same period the number of deaths for women fluctuated, but ultimately rose slightly.

Between 1985 and 1990, there was a sharp fall in the number of deaths for women, but in 1991 the number began to rise once more and did so until 200, when numbers reached a peak. Since 2000, numbers for women fell noticeably, but in 2008 were still 24,000 higher than for men.

Unit 4, Listening 2A

1. B (They are the principal means of transportation in many regions.)
2. C (… have been adapted for such uses as children's toys, adult fitness, military and police applications …, etc.)
3. E (… been improved, especially since the advent of modern materials and computer-aided design.)
4. hub   5. steel   6. rubber
7. mounting step   8. moustache
9. c   10. d   11. b   12. a

Unit 4, Reading 2B

1. D (All of the second half of Paragraph D.)
2. H (The idea that things were 'better in the good old days' is generally a myth + explanation in rest of paragraph)
3. B (… feeling nostalgic about generally painful schooldays, a job they loathed or even a spell in hospital or prison.)
4. G (All of Paragraph G.)
5. F (Most of our days are filled with routine activities with no significance, like travelling to and from work or shopping for groceries.)
6. T (There is not yet a great deal of scientific literature on nostalgia.)
7. NG (Smell and touch are the senses that tend to most readily prompt nostalgia, perhaps …)
8. NG (Research suggests that a negative memory can evoke feelings of nostalgia as long as the period or situation to which the feeling relates was eventually overcome.)
9. T (… record collections … are full of songs … listened to more for old times' sake than for their timeless quality.)
10. b (The brain is an incredibly energy-intensive organ, …)
11. c (… that incapacitated sufferers through intense homesickness)

Note that 12–14 can be in any order.

12. A (… improves mood, increases self-esteem, …)
13. B (… strengthens social bonds)
14. D (… gives meaning to life)
15. c (… those recollections have always been viewed through rose-coloured spectacles.)
16. b (Because we tend to focus on fond memories, we edit out what we do not want to remember.)

Workbook Unit 4, Writing task B

Task A   There are stories in the media these days about the number of people who are overweight or even obese. This applies not only to adults – children too are less healthy and are putting on weight. The blame for this is usually attached to the amount of fast food that young people eat and the fact that families eat pre-cooked food that has a lot of fat and little goodness.

I have to say that I can't really say how much of a problem this is. I don't know how healthily people ate 20 years ago and my own diet now is a healthy balance. My friends and I go to fast-food restaurants occasionally, but no more than my parents did.

I must admit that I see more and more fast-food places in my town and they are very popular. I suppose, in some families, the diet is less healthy too. Women work more now and perhaps don't have time to cook meals with fresh ingredients every day. It is convenient to eat frozen food. Nevertheless, I can't say that I see more overweight people, and young people I know play sports and stay fit.

There is a lot that could be done if this really is a problem. Fast-food restaurants are now encouraged to have healthier options like vegetarian burgers and salad and this is a good start. Supermarkets could have campaigns to convince people to buy fresh products and they could make fresh meat and fish less expensive. Most importantly, parents must show their children how to eat well.

Task C   If you go to any big city and even most towns now, the first thing you notice is the amount of traffic.

At certain times, there is terrible congestion and people are sitting in cars going nowhere. Apart from the number of cars on the road and the ridiculous number parked along every street, the pollution caused by all this traffic is a huge concern.

It is clear that governments must discuss the issue and then take action that will reduce the number of cars. At the moment, it seems they are putting the interests of the car manufacturers first. If the situation is allowed to continue, cities will simply be car parks and nobody will be able to breathe the air. Already, people wear masks.

The first step is to improve public transport. Underground systems need to be modern and safe, and buses should be more comfortable and less crowded. This could be achieved by having more buses and more bus routes. There should be a ban on cars in the city centre or high parking charges that could pay for public transport. In some cities, there is a charge to drive in the centre now. People could be encouraged to use bicycles more too. There are cycle lanes in all cities, but roads can still be dangerous.

All in all, I think people will only stop using cars when it is not convenient anymore or they cannot afford to do it. Personally, I think the only way to reduce the number of cars is to offer some tax deduction or other financial incentive to people who do not use them.

Unit 5, Listening 1E

1. stories (spelling mistake)
2. lectures (too many words used)
3. sitting around (too many words / words not used in recording)
4. to sell (answer grammatically wrong / words not used in recording)
5. true (word (truth) not used in recording)

Unit 5, Listening 2B

1. grants   2. in debt   3. public   4. parties
5. bands   6. politics   7. paying back   8. reduced

Unit 5, Reading 2B

1. ii   2. vii   3. i   4. vi   5. ix   6. iv
Note that 7–10 can be in any order.
   7. A   8. B   9. E   10. F
11. T   12. NG   13. T   14. F

Unit 5, Writing 3D

The bar chart shows the differences in the percentage of time that men and women in various age groups take off work in the United Kingdom because they are sick.

The first thing to say is that women take more time off work than men in every age group. Women between 25 and 34 are more likely to take time off work than anyone else. They take

3.1% of time off, while men in this age group take only 2.2%.

Younger employees take off more time than older employees. In fact, workers over 60 take less time off than anyone else. In this age group, however, there is the biggest difference between the time taken off by men and women. Men over 60 take only 1.5% of work time off sick, while women take 2.1%.

All in all, it seems that the older employees are, the less time they take off sick.

Unit 5, Writing 3G

The pie charts show the various reasons why men and women take time off work as percentages. Although there are similarities, there are some noticeable differences too.

The most common reason for absence for both men and women is a short period of sickness. Nearly two thirds of time taken off by men is due to this, while for women it is just over half. Time taken off for more serious illness is about the same for men and women.

Women are more likely to take time off to care for a child or older relative. At 17%, this is the second most common reason for women to be absent. Caring for another person accounts for only 5% of time taken off by men.
Absence due to long-term disability or stress is similarly likely for both men and women as is a visit to the doctor or dentist. Men, however, are more than twice as likely to take time off due to accidental injury.

Workbook Unit 5, Writing task C

The bar chart shows how different percentages of people in different age groups enjoyed a number of selected free-time activities in the United Kingdom in 2011.

The most common activity – watching TV – and the least common activity – arts and crafts – were more or less equally popular with all age groups, though a slightly higher percentage of older people enjoyed watching TV. Shopping was another activity equally popular with all age groups.

There were noticeable differences in the popularity of most other activities. Sport/exercise was significantly less common among the over 65s, while reading was slightly more popular. Fewer people in the youngest age group read frequently. DIY was mainly enjoyed by people in the middle age groups, but very little by younger people.

The biggest variation was in playing computer games. While only 10% of over 65s enjoyed playing computer games, almost half of all 16–24s participated.

Unit 6, Listening 3B

1. E   2. G   3. J   4. C
5. H   6. I   7. A   8. B

Unit 6, Reading 3D

1. E 2. B 3. D 4. A 5. C
6. Y 7. NG 8. Y 9. N
10. NG 11. N 12. NG

Unit 6, Exam Practice, Writing D

As the tourist industry continues to develop, travellers are taken to ever more remote corners of the globe. Not long ago, holidaymakers were happy with a week in Spain, but now they want to experience exotic locations like Nepal and Madagascar. Unfortunately, as soon as even a modest number of tourists begin to visit a place, they have an impact which changes that place and makes it less appealing.

There are various ways in which the impact of tourism has a negative effect. Firstly, in order to support tourism, there needs to be construction and infrastructure. This might mean hotels, bars and shops built where they would never have been for local people. It might mean roads and railway links that spoil an area's natural beauty. Airports may not be built in remote places, instead they will be built somewhere nearby and planes will fly over areas that were previously peaceful.

Deserted beaches might become crowded and less clean. Hundreds of people start visiting sites that are not suitable as tourist attractions. In the worst cases, tourists damage countryside or coral reefs. Even a small amount of tourism probably means local people opening shops, bars and other businesses that are not typical of the culture. All this begins to make the destination less attractive.

It is difficult to suggest clear solutions since once development begins, it is impossible to reverse. However, some measures could be taken. The authorities could limit the number of large hotels and encourage small guest houses. They could limit the number of foreign-owned bars and restaurants and not allow fast-food chains to open.

The most important thing, in my opinion, is for the tourists to become more aware of the impact they have. They must be prepared to fly to an airport some way from their final destination and understand why they should support local businesses and buy local products.

Unit 7, Listening 3A

1. liver 2. heart 3. one year
4. 3,500 5. 1981 6. 18 days / eighteen days
7. patient recovery 8. hand 9. 1944
10. programme 11. partial 12. France
13. her dog / a dog 14. nose 15. mouth

Unit 7, Reading 3C

1. Outbreaks 2. active
3. prevention measures (*treatment* is uncountable, so not correct)

4. 15 degrees 5. 40 degrees 6. 10 degrees
7. parasites and viruses 8. geographic range
9. high-risk areas 10. malaria-free
11. food resources 12. fleas 13. contact
Note that 14–15 can be in any order.
14. B 15. C

Workbook Unit 7, Writing task B

The flow chart shows the stages in the process of a liver transplant. It shows what happens from the moment a patient is first referred to a hospital to the point where the operation is performed in the liver transplant unit.

First of all, when a patient is referred to the hospital, he or she attends an initial interview and then undergoes exploratory surgery at the specialist unit. Each patient's case is then submitted for discussion at a weekly meeting, where it will either be accepted or rejected. If the case is accepted, it is placed on the waiting list and the next part of the process begins. If the case is rejected, further evaluation might be agreed or alternative treatment could be suggested.

When a case is accepted, a suitable donor organ is selected. At this point, all medical checks are undertaken before there is a final consultation with the patient. Finally, the transplant is performed.

Unit 8, Listening 2C

1. D
2. Detached 3. balcony 4. loft
5. cellar 6. central heating 7. rewiring
8. Plaster 9. floorboards 10. chimney
11. guttering 12. kitchen 13. 420 14. asking price

Unit 8, Reading 2A

1. characteristics 2. shacks
3. natural disasters 4. social problems
5. disease 6. trash

Unit 8, Reading 2C

1. C 2. D 3. I 4. F 5. H

Unit 8, Reading 3C

1. Chinese rule 2. economic boom
3. refugees 4. units
5. Most affluent/Affluent 6. new tenants
7. J 8. E 9. N
10. L 11. B 12. F

Workbook Unit 8, Writing task C

These days, it is common to hear people, especially older people perhaps, complaining that modern buildings are ruining the appeal of town and city centres. They claim that modern architecture is ugly and that buildings are out of place in historical centres close to magnificent old buildings and beautiful squares. Though I understand this view and appreciate that there is some truth in it, I tend to disagree. First of all, it is important to remember that when many of these magnificent old buildings were built, they were probably seen as modern and unsuitable for the existing city landscape. People flock to Barcelona to see *La Sagrada Familia*, but many people would say that it is an ugly building. When the Eiffel Tower was built, there was uproar that such a hideous construction would ruin the beauty of Paris.

It is probably true that less time and money is spent on the construction of buildings nowadays. Centuries ago, it took years to build and furnish a cathedral and that is simply not possible now. However, that does not mean that modern buildings are ugly. In cities from London to Shanghai, there are wonderful examples of architecture that generations of people will grow to love. Modern buildings like airports will be viewed as works of art in the same way that medieval town halls and churches are today.

Certainly, I agree that some modern constructions like tower blocks and leisure centres do little to add to the appeal of the urban landscape, but generally speaking, I feel that it is unfair to claim that modern architecture is ruining cities.

Unit 9, Listening 3A and B

Exercise A:
1. C	2. D	3. B	4. A
5. C	6. A	7. C	8. D

Exercise B:
9. strong female character
10. rites of passage
11. background

Unit 9, Reading 3B

1. D	2. F	3. C	4. B	5. E
6. Y	7. N	8. N	9. NG	
10. NG	11. Y	12. Y	13. N	

Unit 9, Writing 2C

The diagrams show that by the end of next year, some radical changes will have been made to Poolsville library.

There are plans to add a whole new computer centre, part of which will be a coffee shop. This will mean dispensing with the local history room and music and video library. A DVD library will be available in the computer room.

The children's library will be expanded, meaning that the cloakrooms will have to be moved to the other side of the floor. There will be fewer reading tables, but Wi-Fi access will be available in that area.

To make room for the new computer centre and the expansion of the non-fiction reading area, the information centre will be moved to the centre of the floor. The newspapers and journals section is going to be in the area where the old computer stations were.

Unit 9 Exam Practice, Writing E

The diagrams show that within three years, some fairly major changes will have been made to the Crowley Gallery.

There are plans to provide a new interactive education centre, which means the existing temporary exhibition gallery will have to be moved. That will be located within the area that was the portrait gallery, meaning that the portrait gallery be will be smaller. A photography gallery will be a brand new feature.

The cafeteria will be transformed into a bar and restaurant and a separate coffee shop will open next door. To make that possible, the book and gift shop will move to the other side of the floor next to the information desk.

The stairs to the second floor will remain in place, but a lift will be installed too. To accommodate this, the toilets will be relocated.

Unit 10, Listening 3A

1. root systems
2. bedrock
3. tree litter
4. topsoil / top soil
5. isolated
6. (other) debris / solid matter
7. whole villages

Unit 10, Reading 2D

1. plant-growing season
2. cooling
3. power plants
4. discomfort
5. storm water

6. D	7. C
8. B	9. D
10. A	11. B 12. A

Unit 10, Writing 3C

Not long ago, when people talked about natural disasters, they assumed that they really were all natural – 'acts of God' some might say. As the human race has developed and as we understand more about the consequences of our actions, we realize that some of these events are in fact caused by what we do to the planet.

The huge floods that we have seen recently in many parts of the world are often caused by deforestation. When whole forests of trees are cut down, there is nothing to hold the rainwater and it washes down into rivers, which then overflow. Mudslides are another result of destroying the rainforests. Areas of deforested land break away from a hillside and can cause tremendous damage. Droughts are increasing and becoming common in places where once they were unknown. We produce far higher levels of greenhouse gases, which we release into the atmosphere, causing *temperatures to rise. In my country, sandstorms have become more frequent because so many people now drive large vehicles in the desert. People drive too fast and disturb the top layer of sand.*

Even disasters that are not actually caused by our interference with nature can have more serious consequences because of the way we live. Earthquakes hit hardest in areas where land has been destabilized by overuse and can easily come away from a hillside. Hurricanes and tornadoes seem to affect the poorest people since they live in the least stable housing.

Of course, not all disasters can be blamed directly on man. There have always been earthquakes, volcanoes and hurricanes and there always will be. However, I agree that we are moving into an age when man is at least partly to blame for more of these events.

Workbook Unit 10, Writing task C

When people think about climate change or global warming, as it is now frequently called, they tend to think of it as an issue that we are all affected by equally, whether we are man, woman or child, and regardless of whether we are wealthy or poor. Perhaps we should remember too that it is not only humans who own this planet – climate change is having a terrible impact on animals too!

If people stop to think more deeply, however, they will soon realize that climate change is bound to affect the world's poorest people more than anyone else. They rely more directly on natural resources, are more vulnerable to disaster and are less protected.

We have seen for many years how droughts in parts of Africa result in crop failure and lead to famine. Now, with temperatures rising, those parts of the world are becoming even hotter and drier and the desert is spreading. There is little hope for the world's poorest farmers. In many parts of Asia and South America, floods and landslides are caused by deforestation. You can be sure that it is the poor who live in rural areas at the foot of the hillside and who are hit hardest by any catastrophe. It seems that some countries, usually very poor countries, are especially unlucky – Haiti and Honduras seem to just be recovering from one disaster when they are hit by another.

Of course, there are natural disasters that hit large cities in the first world and climate change is having an effect on all of us. We must look at this situation as one that we are all in together if we have any hope of addressing the problem. However, we must also remember that educated people with skills can escape from areas that become unbearably hot, dry or cold and that it is the poorest who are left behind to suffer.

Unit 11, Listening 2A

Section 1:
1. difficult situations
2. perfectionist
3. delegated
4. client
5. expertise
6. team player

Section 2:
7. B
8. C
9. F

Section 3:
10. report
11. commitment
12. exam results
13. future
14. office
15. no qualifications

Section 4:
16. natural selection
17. community
18. animal
19. evolution
20. ethical values

Unit 11, Reading 3D

1. F (… publisher who read the original manuscript … must have spent much of his career … regretting his words.)
2. B (…publishers would only accept the work if they personally had sympathy for a Trotskyite viewpoint.)
3. G (… 38 publishers … told author … that they didn't give a damn – *ironic because that is a line from the story*).
4. I (… the Chief Executive's eight-year-old daughter read the book and declared it a winner.)
5. D (*All of relevant paragraph, especially* … expressed the exact opposite opinion
6. H (… create a story to go along with his illustrations in hope that the story might spark more interest.)

Unit 11, Writing 3C

The bar chart shows the various compromises that graduates in the United States might make in order to find their first job. It shows the percentage of graduates that made each of those compromises in the years 2006-2007 and 2009-2010.

The most noticeable increases were in the percentage of graduates earning less than they expected, the percentage working with no health benefits and the percentage accepting a temporary position. Those earning less than expected rose from 28% in 2006-2007 to 39% in 2009-2010, while the percentage working with no health benefits increased by over a third to 23%. The percentage accepting a temporary position was still quite low in 2009-2010, but had climbed by a third.

Apart from 'working outside area of interest', all the compromises increased in frequency over the period. The percentage of graduates who moved to another part of the country rose by 2%, as did the percentage working unfavourable hours. The percentage working below their education level rose only slightly, but was high anyway at around 33%.

Workbook Unit 11, Writing task C

The bar chart shows the number of gold medals that the United States and China won at each of the Olympics Games between 1984 and 2008. It reveals that over that period, China gradually caught up with the United States and finally overtook them.

In 1984, the United States won over 80 gold medals, by far their biggest tally over the period shown, and at least double what they won at any other Games. By contrast, China won around only 15 medals that year.

At the next Games in 1988, The United States' tally was halved to fewer than 40, while China's tally dropped to only three or four. This was the lowest number of gold medals they won within the period shown.

Over the next 20 years, the number of gold medals won by the United States remained fairly constant at around 40, while the number won by China rose steadily. In 2004, China won almost as many gold medals as the United States. Four years later, in the 2008 Games, China won more gold medals than the United States for the first time.

Unit 12, Listening 3A

Extract 2:
1. front door
2. local
3. 5 minutes / five minutes
4. suspicion
5. unoccupied
6. natural view
7. intercom system

Extract 3:
8. (back) windscreen
9. briefcase
10. flight tickets
11. a message
12. Upper Street
13. La Fourchette
14. Brian Rafferty

Unit 12, Reading 2A and B

Exercise A:
1. viii   2. v   3. iii
4. i   5. vii   6. vi
7. F   8. NG   9. T
10. T   11. F   12. NG

Exercise B:
13. B   14. G   15. A
16. E   17. C   18. F
19. a journalist
20. lengthy and dull
21. vehicle number plates
22. Big Brother
23. police patrols
24. Luton (railway station)
25. E   26. G   27. C

Unit 12, Writing 2C

Yes – agree
More than half of prisoners released reoffend with a year.
(I read this!)

Prisoners mix with other criminals in prison – often who have committed more serious crimes.
When released – prisoners have no job / nowhere to live / have lost family.

No – don't agree
Putting offenders in prison protects society.
Prison life is hard – the fear of going to prison deters offenders.
Nowadays, prisons have rehabilitation programmes – inmates learn useful skills.
What is the alternative? Any alternative is softer than prison.

Unit 12, Exam Practice, Writing D

Whereas at one time prisons were dark and dirty with poor sanitation and no facilities, today many in the developed world are modern, and provide inmates with comfort and a range of recreation and educational facilities. While some people believe that a degree of comfort is humane and increases the likelihood of successful rehabilitation, others feel that institutions are now little more than holiday camps, suggesting even that some criminals may have a better life inside them than they do outside.

For many people, the principal purpose of prison is to punish. Therefore, they believe that imprisonment should be a dreadful experience that makes offenders constantly regret their crimes. They also believe that the fear of imprisonment should deter crime and that if prisons are dark, miserable places, both first-time offending and reoffending will be reduced. They are angry that taxpayers' money is used to make life comfortable for criminals who may have ruined somebody else's life.

Though I do appreciate these concerns, I do not really agree that prison is too easy. The important thing is that offenders lose their freedom and that society is protected. Making prisoners endure terrible conditions does not make the streets safer. Rehabilitation in prison and facilities that enable offenders to learn and improve themselves are vital. Prisoners are far more likely to reoffend if they have no hope of finding work and cannot socialize. While the fear of prison may deter the vast majority of law-abiding people from committing crime, most crime is committed through desperation. Those most likely to commit crime do not think about the consequences.

In conclusion, I would say that I am not convinced anyway that prisons, even in the developed world, are so luxurious. I am from France, which is certainly a developed country. However, there are frequently stories about the poor conditions in prisons. A few years ago, there were protests about the lack of facilities. Newspaper articles about prisoners enjoying themselves all day are hugely exaggerated.

Workbook Unit 12, Writing C

There is a lot of evidence that shows that rehabilitating offenders in prison is a huge challenge. Despite improved facilities and programmes in prisons that mean inmates can learn to socialize better and acquire new skills, over half reoffend within a year of being released from prison.

There are various reasons for this depressing statistic. Firstly, most people that are sent to prison in the first place are hugely disadvantaged. Many have grown up in care and lack real friendships. Many have had a very poor education and lack appropriate reading, writing and numeracy skills, and most have never been in employment. A high percentage of prisoners come from families where there is a history of criminal activity. All this means that even if opportunities to learn do exist in prison, many prisoners do not know how to access them.

Many prisoners reoffend because of their experience in prison. They socialize with other criminals who have sometimes committed more serious offences than they have and they are likely to be exposed to drugs. While they serve their sentence, they may lose their accommodation or a job, if they have one. Some may lose contact with their family. In short, they are released knowing more about crime and with more reasons to commit crime.

It is very difficult to offer concrete suggestions but, for me, it is clear that the problem must be addressed. Even if it is expensive to help released prisoners pay their rent and find a job, it must be more cost-effective than dealing with more crime. Perhaps programmes could be put in place where accommodation and a job in the community is arranged shortly before the release date.

Tapescript

Note that in some Course Book and Workbook listening extracts the speakers are foreign students. In these extracts there are occasional grammatical errors or words used wrongly. These errors are reproduced in the tapescripts.

Track 1

Unit 1 Speaking 1

C Listen to the complete exchanges and check your answers.

1
Speaker 1: What's your name?
Speaker 2: Orlaith.
Speaker 1: That's pretty. It's Irish isn't it?

2
Speaker 1: Where are you from?
Speaker 2: Well, originally from Bangor.
Speaker 1: Sorry, is that in Wales or Ireland?

3
Speaker 1: What are you studying?
Speaker 2: Psychology.
Speaker 1: Oh how interesting? What do you want to do in the future?

4
Speaker 1: What do you do for a living?
Speaker 2: I'm in film production.
Speaker 1: Oh, how glamorous. I wish I could do something like that.

5
Speaker 1: Have you got brothers and sisters?
Speaker 2: No, I'm an only child.
Speaker 1: Are you? My family's huge. There are eight of us!

6
Speaker 1: Are you married?
Speaker 2: Not yet, but I am engaged.
Speaker 1: How lovely. Have you set a date?

7
Speaker 1: Have you got any children?
Speaker 2: Yes two, one of each.
Speaker 1: That's nice. What are their names?

8
Speaker 1: What do you do in your free time?
Speaker 2: I play golf most of the time.
Speaker 1: Do you? I play a bit myself now and again.

Track 2

Unit 1 Speaking 2

C Listen to some students answering the questions in Exercise B. For each question tick the student that gives the better answer.

Question 1 – Student A
Examiner: Where did you grow up?
Student: Grow up? Oh yes, in my country. Belgium.

Question 1 – Student B
Examiner: Where did you grow up?
Student: Well, I was born in a small town called Myshkin, but my family moved to St Petersburg when I was nine, so really I grew up there – in St Petersburg.

Question 2 – Student A
Examiner: What important decisions have you made recently?
Student: Mm, well I had to decide if I wanted to go to a university near my home city and stay living at home or apply to a university in Rome and move there. I chose Rome.

Question 2 – Student B
Examiner: What important decisions have you made recently?
Student: Err, I don't know. Maybe to take my exams.

Question 3 – Student A
Examiner: Who influenced you as a child?
Student: Mm, my teachers.

Question 3 – Student B
Examiner: Who influenced you as a child?
Student: Sorry, influence? You mean like parents or teachers, or do you mean like people in sport or pop stars?
Examiner: You decide. Who had a big influence on your life when you were young?
Student: Well, lots of people - my parents and my older sister and some of my teachers. I guess my dance tutor influenced me a lot because I still dance and I might do it professionally one day.

Question 4 – Student A
Examiner: Do you have regrets about any choices you've made?
Student: What is 'regrets'?
Examiner: I mean, do you feel you would like to change something in the past – make a different decision.
Student: No, everything is good. I'm happy.

Question 4 – Student B
Examiner: Do you have regrets about any choices you've made?
Student: Mm, that's a difficult question. I think everyone has some regrets, but I don't think you should look back. You must look forward in life and think about how you can be happy in the future.

Question 5 – Student A

Examiner: Tell me about a turning point in your life?

Student: *Turning point*? Do you mean an event that changed my life – made things different?

Examiner: Yes, exactly.

Student: Well, two years I finished a relationship. I was going to get married, but really I was young – only 20. It was a very difficult decision to make, but I'm glad I made it. My life is very different and I feel freer.

Question 5 – Student B

Examiner: Tell me about a turning-point in your life?

Student: *Turning point* is big thing in your life I guess. For me it was get my first job.

Question 6 – Student A

Examiner: Do you ever worry about growing old?

Student: No, I'm young – too young to worry about being old.

Question 6 – Student B

Examiner: Do you ever worry about growing old?

Student: Mm, I don't really worry about it, but I don't look forward to it. I'm healthy and very active, and I see a lot of old people who don't have good health. I don't want to be an old person that can't do things.

Track 3
Unit 1 Listening 1

B Listen to four extracts and match them with the pictures. Write the number of the extract in the box.

Extract 1

Woman 1: So, does it really change your life as much as everybody warns you?

Woman 2: Nobody can warn you – it turns your life upside down! You go from thinking about and looking after yourself, to thinking permanently about and looking after another little person. Life will never be the same again.

Woman 1: Oh dear. Don't you get any time to yourself?

Woman 2: Well, yes – at about 11 o'clock after the last feed – but then you're too tired to do anything.

Woman 1: Mm – but once they're at school it must get easier, surely.

Woman 2: Yes, I'm sure it does, but that seems a long way off at the moment.

Extract 2

Voice: … it's an activity that unites the mind, body and spirit. The mind and the body become one and that's therapeutic. People become aware of body posture, alignment and how they move. The body becomes more flexible and it's possible to maintain relaxation even in a stressful atmosphere. People have more energy and are happier all-round with life.

Extract 3

Boy 1: So, have you thought about this 'People of the World' presentation we have to do yet?

Boy 2: Mm, I've thought about it. I can't say I've got any real ideas, though. I was thinking about doing something about the Egyptians – you know, I think their lives were very interesting.

Girl: No, you're supposed to talk about people that live now. As far as I know, Egyptians now live just like we do! It has to be a presentation about people whose lives are totally different from ours now.

Boy 2: Oh, I didn't realize that. So, something like the lives of Eskimos, you mean?

Boy 1: Or Aborigines, maybe.

Girl: Well, maybe …, but neither of those is very imaginative, is it? I'm not sure there are many Eskimos now, anyway.

Boy 2: Oh right – so what are you going to talk about then?

Girl: Well, I was thinking about Bedouins in the Sahara Desert. I can show some really good …

Extract 4

Male voice: Okinawa is something of a phenomenon. It has a population of around a million people, but 900 of those are centenarians – that means they are 100 years old or more. That is four times the number of centenarians in most other parts of the world. What is perhaps even more remarkable is that this seems to be the only place in the world where both men and women are equally likely to reach a hundred. Now, much of this is to do with Japanese lifestyle, but there's much more to it …

Track 4
Unit 1 Listening 1

F Listen to the four extracts and match them with the images in Exercise E.

Extract 1

Voice: … generally, it's agreed that ultimately there are four main areas of life in which people look to find fulfilment. What is difficult – some might say impossible – is to find fulfilment in all of those areas at the same time. Now, let's start by …

Extract 2

Tutor: David, how's the project going? I … I sort of got the impression you weren't making much progress.

Student: Oh … it's fine, really. I was a bit stuck, but now I know which writer I want to write about, it's all going quite well.

Tutor: Oh, good. So, which writer have you chosen after all?

Student: Noel Coward. I'm going to write my project on Noel Coward.

Extract 3

Woman 1: Uh huh, yeah, but haven't you got the directions on the invitation?

Woman 2: Well, yes, but ... but Steve threw it out. Once we'd told you we were coming ... you know Steve.

Woman 1: Well, the church is in Argyll Road. It's really easy to find. Look, Sue and Tim are coming too. Why don't you give them a call and come up together? You can all share a taxi when you get off the train – then you won't get lost, will you?

Extract 4

Voice: ... and they were very important. They were far more than places simply to wash. They were central to the community – places where people from all walks of life could meet to talk and relax, exercise or conduct business. The ruins of these magnificent ...

Track 5
Unit 1 Listening 2

B Listen to Extracts 1–4 and choose the correct summary a, b or c, for each extract.

Extract 1

Man: Frankly, we just need somewhere bigger. We're bursting out at the seams here.

Woman: Well, yes, I agree. You know I do, but it's not that easy, is it? We'd have to pay a fortune for somewhere bigger round here.

Man: So, let's start looking further afield, then.

Woman: Haven't we already discussed that? I really don't want to uproot the kids. They're happy at school, and they've got so many good friends. We've got so many good friends. I don't want to start all over again.

Man: We won't have to. People would come and see us. The kids would get used to it pretty quickly. I grew up with a big garden – running around outside all the time. I want them to have that. I just think ...

Extract 2

Voice: ... you must also try to ensure a goal doesn't directly interfere with other aspects of life. If business travel is a frequent part of your schedule or you're inclined to work 70 or 80 hours a week, it'll have a drastic effect on your personal relationships. The travel and long hours might result in poor health or family breakdown. In a nutshell, certain goals are mutually exclusive and are not compatible with other goals.

Extract 3

Female 1: So, have you decided yet?

Female 2: No, not yet. It's so difficult – too many choices. It's such a big decision too. It's going to affect the rest of our lives.

Male: Well, certainly the next four or five years.

Female 2: So, what about you Keith, I bet you know exactly what to do, don't you?

Male: No, not really. I'd love to go to Manchester, but that's only because I think it'll be such a great place to live. The course isn't supposed to be especially good. Then there's London. The courses are supposed to be the best, but I really don't want to live somewhere quite so huge.

Female 1: I think you should base your decision on what's best for your future. Not on where's a great place to live.

Female 2: No, I don't completely agree. I definitely don't want to study too close to home. I'd have to stay living at home with mum and dad – I don't really want that. But if I do move away, it's got to be to somewhere exciting. I'm not going to spend four years in some dull place just so I can say I've got a 2:1.

Extract 4

Voice: Almost all the world's shortest life expectancies occur in Africa where the AIDS epidemic, malnutrition, curable diseases and civil unrest continue to take a dreadful toll on human life. Of 29 countries where life expectancy at birth is 50 years or lower, 28 are in Africa. Afghanistan, a country ravaged by war, is the only other country in that list of 29. There life expectancy is 42 years. Of the 40 countries with the shortest life expectancy, 38 are in Africa.

Track 6
C Unit 1 Listening 2
Listen again and complete the sentences.
[Play Track 5 again]

Track 7
Unit 1 Exam Practice – Listening

C Listen and answer the questions.

Tina: ... you know how it is. I don't really feel unhappy about any particular thing, just generally a bit fed up. You know, everything's always the same – not much to look forward to.

Susan: Oh Tina, you've got so much to look forward to. It's the school holidays soon. You'll have a great time with the children – days out, down to the seaside, camping. You're off to Italy soon too, aren't you?

Tina: Yes, I know there are big things like that. I mean things every week – every day. I think I just feel older ... and a lot less healthy than I did. I never get any exercise and I'm eating far more than I ever did.

Susan: Well, I've told you to join the gym, haven't I?

Tina: Mm, I don't know if I'm really a gym kind of person. I haven't got the discipline to keep going – you know me – start things but never finish them.

And it's all a bit isolated. I mean, it's not a very social thing to do, is it? Just going from one machine to the next for two or three hours.

Susan: Tina, that's absolute nonsense, and I think you know it is. Most people go to the gym because it is social. Everyone has a good chat before they exercise, and then they usually have a coffee afterwards. I've made some really good friends there. There are some women that spend more time nattering than they do on the machines.

Tina: Really? I thought gyms were full of really serious health fanatics. You know, women like stick insects that get all anxious if they even see a bar of chocolate and men with bulging muscles.

Susan: No. No. First of all, most women go on days when it's women only. The more serious ones go on the days when it's mixed. I think they like showing they're as fit as the men! Most of the women that go on the days I go just want to stay in shape. They're not really even trying to lose weight. They just don't want put to any more on!

Tina: Mm, isn't it very expensive? I heard it's about £300 a month or something.

Susan: £300!? Where did you hear that?

Tina: Well, how much is it then?

Susan: It depends. If you find it difficult to go regularly and you pay for each visit, then it works out a bit more. I'm not really sure because I've got a membership card and I pay a monthly rate. I think it's £8 if you pay on the door – you still have to be a member though and that's £100 a year. You have to pay another £2 if you want to use the swimming pool and another £3 for the sauna.

Tina: Mm, it adds up then. That's £13 and if you go every week that's a lot.

Susan: That's why people pay a monthly rate. It's £40 a month and for that you can use whatever you like. I think you have to pay to use the squash courts, but I never do, so I don't worry about that. I go at least once a week and sometimes twice a week so I make quite a big saving. You just pay the bill online too, so you don't have to mess around with cash at all.

Tina: Mm, I'm still not sure if it's me. I think going for a run or even playing tennis would be more up my street.

Susan: You just said that going to the gym wasn't very social. I can't see that you're going to make a huge number of friends running round the park by yourself. And, tennis – who are you going to play with? I bet you haven't picked up a racket for 15 years.

Tina: Yeah, OK, OK. I suppose I could think about it. What days do you …

Track 8
Unit 1 Exam Practice – Listening

F   Listen and answer the questions.

Voice: Now, let me start by asking a question. If you could just choose one or two habits to create and develop over the next few months – habits that would have the biggest impact on your life – what would they be? I'm often asked this question, because people are overwhelmed when it comes to positive life changes.

Now, over the years I've given advice to many people for many different reasons. I've helped people with career changes, I've helped people with relationships, I've helped people sort out their finances and I've helped people to stop smoking. All these people ask me what they should do to change their lives – how they should start seeing things and doing things differently. It's not an easy question to answer because everyone is different and everyone wants different things, but I'm going to talk about seven areas of behaviour – habits, if you like – that I think everyone needs to think about. These are habits that, if implemented, will change your life. The idea is to choose one or two of these habits and try to practise and develop them over a few months. Remember that the choices must be yours – no one should follow my advice as a set of rules. As Confucius said 'Men's natures are alike; it is their habits that separate them.'

So, first of all develop positive thinking. I mention this first as it's the keystone habit that will help you form the other habits. Of course, positive thinking by itself won't lead to success, but it certainly helps to motivate you to do the other things required. I learnt this when I gave up smoking – when I allowed myself to think negative thoughts, I would end up failing. When I learned how to squash negative thoughts and think positively instead, I succeeded.

The second habit is exercise. This may seem obvious and not especially life-changing, but it makes you feel better about yourself and more confident. That leads to success with other positive changes. It reinforces the positive thinking, as you need to think positively to sustain exercise. It relieves stress and gives you time to think. This leads to better mental well-being in your life overall.

Now, single-tasking – that's the opposite of multi-tasking. Why is it life-changing? Here are a couple of very good reasons. You'll be more effective with your tasks and you'll get more done. It's hard to achieve anything if you're constantly distracted by other things. You'll be less stressed and happier throughout your day.

Similarly, you should focus on one goal. Just as focusing on one task is more effective, so is focusing on one goal. While it might seem difficult, focusing on one goal at a time is the most efficient way of achieving it. When you try to take on many goals at once, you're spreading thin your focus and energy and that means you're more likely to fail.

Habit five – eliminate the non-essential. First, identify the essential – the things in your life that are most important to you, that you love the most. Then eliminate everything else. This simplifies things and leaves you with the space to focus on what matters. This process works with anything – with your life in general, with work projects and with relationships. This will change your life because it will help you to simplify.

Now, the next habit may sound strange. It's kindness. Yes, kindness is a habit and it can be cultivated. Focus on it every day for a month and you'll see profound changes in your life. You'll feel better about yourself as a person. You'll see a change in the way people react to you. How do you develop a habit like this? First, make it a goal to do something kind each day. At the beginning of the day, figure out what your kind act will be and then do it. Then, each time you interact with someone, try to be friendly and compassionate. Finally, try to go beyond small kindnesses to bigger acts of compassion – volunteering to help those in need and taking the initiative to relieve suffering.

And finally, daily routine. It's so simple, but creating a daily routine for yourself can make a big difference in your life. The best routines, I've found, come at the start and end of the day – both your workday and your day in general. That means, develop a routine for when you wake up, when you start work, when you finish your work and at the end of your evening. How will that change your life? It will help you have a great start to your day and finish your day by preparing for the next. It'll help you focus on what's important, not just what comes up. It'll help you make sure you get done all the things you want to get done. And that can mean a lot. Now, I'm going to go on to talk about how each habit can be …

Track 9

Workbook Unit 1 Listening

A   Listen to four extracts and write the number of each against the topic. There are two topics you will not hear about.

Extract 1

Voice: It could be that your life has changed and that when you first went into the line you're in, your situation was very different from what it is today. You may, for example, have been single then and now have a family. The crazy schedule or the frequent travel may not suit your new lifestyle. In this case, you should look for something more 'family friendly'.

Extract 2

Voice: Some people would say it's so they can live together, but many couples already do this without tying the knot. Having children might be a good reason, but again it can happen outside wedlock. Many couples claim that it's all about commitment and making things official, but that doesn't sound very romantic. Are these people just trying make it harder to walk away when the going gets tough? No – I think

there's only one reason and that it's all about divinity. Couples must feel that something bigger than the two of them is bringing them together.

Extract 3

Voice: Most importantly it allows you to get your priorities right. Nobody on his or her deathbed ever said, 'I wish I could have spent more time in the office.' Life goes whizzing by, and we are usually so busy worrying about what's ahead that we have no time to enjoy what's here now. Wouldn't you love to have the time to do what you want to do, when you want to do it and say goodbye to the tyrannical boss that says you can't?

Extract 4

Voice: My husband and I decided long ago that we were perfectly happy with our lives, and that we just didn't need the burden of parenthood. I remember watching a documentary about a couple in the southern states of the US or somewhere – they had 16 children. We just looked at each other and didn't need to say a word.

Track 10

Workbook Unit 1 Listening

C   Listen again as you read the tapescript.
    [Play Track 9 again]

Track 11

Unit 2 Vocabulary 1

Pronunciation check
Listen and mark where the stress falls in these related word pairs.
1   biology / biological
2   character / characteristics
3   parent / parental
Listen again and notice how the syllables that are not stressed are often produced as weak forms.

Track 12

Unit 2 Speaking 2

C   Before you start talking, listen to two students talking to the examiner. Which student do you think performs better? Why?

Speaker 1
Student: Can I just check something?
Examiner: Yes, of course.
Student: I know *look like* is about physical characteristics. Is *take after* more about personality and habits?
Examiner: Yes, that's right.
Student: OK – and your *upbringing* is how you are educated?
Examiner: Mm, not really educated – more about how your parents treat you and show you how to live.
Student: Yes, I understand.

Examiner: OK, are you ready, then?

Student: Yes, I want to talk about my friend Ivana. She looks like her mother – she has her eyes and her smile. They are both very pretty. I think so anyway. She takes after her father more, though. She's very ambitious and determined to do well – she always was like that. She's quite a serious person, like him, but also very friendly and kind. This is also what I want to say about how her upbringing affected her. She was brought up to be very confident and always had her parents' support. They wanted her to do well, but also to be happy. I remember she was always 'star of the week' even in primary school, and she did very well in all her exams. She was very cross if she didn't get a good grade for any school work. Now she's working as a journalist. Sometimes I see her on TV doing some reports. It's no surprise that she's successful.

Examiner: So, do you still see her?

Student: Yes, but not so much like I did. She lives now in Moscow and that's …

Speaker 2

Student: OK, I want talk about Jay-Z. You know the rap guy?

Examiner: Yes, I think so – there are so many.

Student: He's married to Beyoncé.

Examiner: Oh, yes I know who you mean.

Student: He's from a poor background. I mean, he had a tough start in life …

Examiner: … in what way?

Student: Mm, I think his family was poor. Maybe his father was in prison.

Examiner: But Jay-Z's very successful now?

Student: Yes, very successful. He's musician and an actor. He's a kind of businessman. I think he's very clever.

Examiner: So, tell me how you feel about him.

Student: I feel good. I mean, I admire him. He worked very hard for everything what he has now.

Examiner: OK, so tell me a bit more about …

Track 13
Unit 2 Listening 1

C   Listen and fill in the missing information.

Mother: Oh, hello, is it OK to come in?

Manager: Yes, of course. Hi.

Mother: I'm only round the corner. I thought it would be easier to pop round than speak on the phone … It's bigger in here than I expected. It looks quite small from outside.

Manager: Yes, lots of people say that.

Mother: Anyway, I wanted some information. I'm hoping to go back to work very soon and I need to get some childcare sorted out. I think it'll only be three

days a week, but we'll talk about that in a minute … I'm Anne, anyway.

Manager: Hi Anne, so how old is your … mm … do you have a boy or a girl?

Mother: Both actually – twins. So, it's two spaces I'm hoping for.

Manager: Goodness, I bet that's hard work. Mind you we've got 30 here so we know what's it like. Let's go through to the office. It's always terribly noisy out here.

Manager: Right, that's better. Now, first of all, let me say that we don't actually have any spaces at the moment, but spaces do come up pretty frequently. We've only got one other child on the waiting list, so it's worth taking your details.

Mother: And then you contact us as soon as there's a space?

Manager: Exactly. So, when would you want them to start?

Mother: At the beginning of July – that's about six weeks away.

Manager: Well, that might be a good time. Lots of parents take children out over the summer. You know, brothers and sisters off school, family holidays and so on. Shall I put July the first?

Mother: Yes.

Manager: OK, and what are their names? Are they identical twins, by the way, will we be able to tell them apart?

Mother: No, don't worry, they're not. Actually, identical twins are always the same sex.

Manager: Oh yes, I did know that.

Mother: Noah's my little boy and Katie's my little girl.

Manager: Noah, that's unusual. It's N-O-A-H, isn't it?

Mother: Yes, that's right. It's not as unusual as it was actually. We know a couple of other Noahs now.

Manager: And the family name?

Mother: Oh yes, that's Yeats – Y-E-A-T-S.

Manager: And how old are they?

Mother: They're two years and ten months – so coming up for three very soon. Are most of the children around that age?

Manager: Mm, they'll be a bit younger than most of the others, but we've got a few of that age. And you said you live round the corner.

Mother: Yes, Southampton Street, number 49.

Manager: Oh, I know Southampton Street. My auntie lives there. It's one of the nicest streets round here.

Mother: Yes, we like it anyway.

Manager: Mm, oh yes, phone numbers.

Mother: I'll just give you the mobile number. Then you can call any time. It's 07795 673453.

Manager: 07795 673453.

Mother: That's it.

Manager: OK, so why I don't I show you round and you can ask questions as we go.

Mother: Yes, OK. Can I just check prices first, though? I'm told it's £32 a day. Is there any reduction if they do three days?

Manager: No, I'm afraid there's only a reduction if they do a full week – all five days. However, there is a slight reduction if you have two children in the nursery. It'd be £26 a day each. I know it's not much but it all helps. Anyway, shall we take a little tour and then we'll go over any details once you've decided what you think. I'll make us a cup of …

Track 14
Unit 2 Listening 2

C Listen and complete the notes a student made.

Voice: Well, we've been looking at various aspects of genetics, and this morning I want to talk specifically about twins. Some of you were asking about twins last week and particularly about how environment or nurture affected their development.

First of all, I want establish the fact that there are two and possibly even three types of twins. I'm sure everyone has heard the term *identical twins*. The scientific term is actually *monozygotic twins*. Now, people assume that with identical twins it's all about appearance – that they look exactly the same. Now, that might be the case, but the important thing is actually how they form. Identical twins form when a single fertilized egg splits into two. *Non-identical twins* form when two eggs are fertilized separately. Twins that are not identical are usually called *fraternal twins*, though the scientific term here is actually *dizygotic*.

Around a third of twins are identical – two-thirds are fraternal. So, fraternal, or non-identical twins, are quite a lot more common than identical twins. Now, I mentioned a possible third category, but not very much is known about this yet. Some twins might be hybrid or half-identical. This may happen when an unfertilized egg splits into two and the two parts are then fertilized separately. I'm not going to say much about this today – I don't know much! – but there's a very good website where you can find out more. That's www.humangenetics.com. Human genetics is all one word. Take a look.

OK, some facts about the two types of twins. Firstly, identical twins are always the same gender – two boys or two girls, and they have the same blood group. Fraternal twins can be the same gender or a boy and a girl. They often have the same blood group, but not necessarily. Now, perhaps most importantly, identical twins share 100% of their genetic markers – fraternal twins share around 50%. So, it's clear that identical twins are more likely to be the same in many ways – not simply the way they look.

Now, before I talk about how twins can be very similar or what might cause them to be different, I'm going to mention another difference between the two types of twins – the reason that they are born as twins in the first place. We know that fraternal twins are more common when women have babies later in life – perhaps after 35 years of age. We also know that fertility treatment can increase the likelihood of twins. With identical twins, this doesn't seem to be the case at all. There are no known causes for identical twinning.

So, are identical twins the same in every way? No, they're not. They're probably very similar, but it's a question of nature and nurture. There are all sorts of factors and influences that determine how a person grows up and it's no different for twins. Even before birth, in the womb, twins can develop differently. It is common that one twin has a better connection to the placenta and this will mean he or she will grow bigger. Identical twins can often be slightly different heights and weights. Recent research suggests that although identical twins are born with many identical genetic characteristics, as they age and spend more time apart, these similarities diverge. Twins develop their own personalities and follow different interests. It is likely that identical twins even deliberately try to establish individual identities as they grow up. It is not known yet whether certain identical genes actually disappear as twins age, or whether external influences play a bigger part in determining individuality.

Now, this research has been carried out at a cancer research centre and this is important. It might be that the genetic make-up which makes identical twins so similar is also related to the development of disease like cancer and conditions such as autism.

But, to get back to similarities and differences – I like one comparison I've seen that compares twins to cakes cooked from the same or different recipes. Two cakes cooked from the same recipe are more likely to be very similar than two cakes cooked from two different recipes. The two cakes from the same recipe will be very similar, but not exactly the same. Various external influences will mean that each cake has something slightly different about it. Another way to look at this is to think about your own face. Both sides of your face come from the same DNA, but they are not exactly the same – they're not a mirror image of each other. All sorts of factors and experiences in life mean that one side of your face is almost certainly a little different, and in some cases very different, from the other side.

Track 15
Unit 2 Writing 2

C Listen to some British students discussing the Writing task and answer the questions below.

Male: What do you think about this composition then, Denise?

Female: Mm, I think it's easier to do because we've been discussing the topic this week. There's quite a lot to say about it.

Male: Really? I think it's quite difficult. I'm not a scientist, so I don't know whether nature or life experience is the bigger influence.

Female: But you don't have to be an expert on the topic. You need to show that you understand what the debate is about and then make some relevant points. You can balance your argument if you don't have a strong opinion.

Male: So, I guess we should write about the history of the debate. You know, when the debate started and what different scientists have believed at various times in the past.

Female: Mm, I'm not sure about that. It doesn't really answer the question. You could write pages about that too. First of all, we need to look at the statement and think about whether it's obviously true or whether it's there to be challenged. You know, whether the statement invites us to say that we don't really agree.

Male: So, what do you think of the statement?

Female: Well, it says that recent research shows that the characteristics we inherit are more important than what we experience as we go through life. I don't think that's true. What we've read this week does suggest that more may be passed on through our genes than was previously believed, but nobody's saying that we inherit everything. I mean, what we experience is still a hugely important factor.

Male: So, you think disagree with the statement – say that life experience is more important?

Female: Not necessarily. I would say that environment and nurture is very important, but that the really important thing is the interaction between what's inherited and what's then learnt or experienced.

Male: OK, but we have to give reasons and say something about our personal experience. Shall we mention something about studies with twins?

Female: Yes, good idea. Mentioning twins is a good argument to support the idea that genetics is important.

Male: And also that nurture's important. Twins are not exactly the same. Should we compare what's definitely inherited, like eye colour, with what is probably influenced by environment, like our tastes and interests?

Female: Mm, maybe – let me check the instructions again. Mm, the instructions say characteristics that have an influence on our personality. I don't think we need to mention physical characteristics at all. We could say something about why it's worrying to accept that our personalities are determined only by our genes. I mean, if that's the case, surely the children of aggressive or violent people will also be aggressive and violent. The nature only theory suggests that we are prisoners – we have no control over who we become.

Male: OK, but we have to write 250 words. We won't be able to say everything. I don't know what I can

say that's related to my own experience. I mean, I don't know any twins.

Female: I don't think that matters. You can say that you and your brother are very similar or very different, or that you're different from your father because you had a different education – something like that, anyway. I suppose I'm lucky because my cousins are twins.

Male: That's OK for you then. I must say I still find this part of the task a bit difficult.

Female: So, how do you think the composition should be concluded?

Male: Well, from what we've discussed that part should be easy now. We have to say that nature and nurture interact and that one is not more important than the other.

Female: OK, are you ready to start writing a rough plan then?

Track 16
Unit 2 Writing 2

E Listen to the students in Exercise C again. Highlight the points in the composition as you hear them.
[Play Track 15 again]

Track 17
Unit 2 Consolidation – Speaking

B Look at the cards and then listen to two students doing the exam. Which words do they check?
Speaker 1

Student: I just need to check a few words on the card before I make my notes? Is that OK?

Examiner: Yes, please do.

Student: This word *siblings* – I guess it means brothers and sisters. Is that right?

Examiner: Yes, that's what it means.

Student: So, when it says *a large family*, it means with lots of brothers and sisters?

Examiner: Yes. Now are you ready? You have a minute to plan what you want to say and make notes.

Speaker 2

Student: I want to make sure I understand a couple of words before I begin making my notes.

Examiner: Yes, OK, what do you need to check?

Student: Well, I guess it's clear from the context – *an only child* is a child with no brothers and sisters.

Examiner: Yes, exactly.

Student: OK, and *siblings* are brothers or sisters, then? I don't know this word.

Examiner: Yes, it's not a very common word. It's used in academic language more. But, yes, it means brothers or sisters.

Student: Thank you. I'll start making my notes.

Track 18
Unit 2 Consolidation – Vocabulary

B **Mark the main stress on these words. Then listen and check.**

biological
behaviour
parental
significance
likelihood
maturity
complexity
individuality

Track 19
Workbook Unit 2 Listening

A **Listen and write the numbers you hear in the extracts.**

Extract 1
Man: So, how old did you say you were?
Woman: I don't think I did.
Man: Oh, didn't you? Is it a secret, then?
Woman: No, of course not.
Man: Well?
Woman: I'm 42.

Extract 2
Client: Right, so how much do I owe in total?
Salesperson: Mm, let me see – altogether that's £273.
Client: Oh, I didn't think it was quite that much.

Extract 3
Receptionist: You'll need to give me your phone number – a mobile number ideally.
Man: OK, I never remember my mobile number. Just let me check. Yes, here we are. It's 07783 961224.
Receptionist: Sorry, I got the first part. Can you say the last three numbers again?
Man: Um, I'll say it all again a bit more slowly. 07783 961224.

Extract 4
Guide: … the town looks quite small – I think that's because the centre's very compact – but, in fact, the population is close to 11,000. Of course, numbers are swelled in the summer when …

Extract 5
Teacher: So, you've had the time I set. Who has the answer?
Boy: Mm, I think I've got it. Is it 7,845?
Teacher: What do the rest of you think? Anyone else got that answer? No? Well, it's the right answer. Well done, Geoffrey Clarke.

Extract 6
Voice: … and now house prices. For the third month running, prices have risen. The average price of a house in the UK is now £210,000. That's the highest figure since March last year. Economists say it's too early to say whether this looks like a continuing trend.

Track 20
Workbook Unit 2 Listening

B **Listen and write the dates you hear in the extracts. Write only the month and a figure.**

Extract 1
Man: There's a bank holiday soon, isn't there?
Woman: Yeah, at the end of August. The 27th, I think.

Extract 2
Woman: Greg, when do these documents need to be back by? I don't need to do them today, do I?
Man: Oh, no, not at all. The ones you're working on are due back by Thursday next week. That's the 3rd of February.
Woman: Oh, that's a relief.

Extract 3
Woman 1: Are you free next Saturday?
Woman 2: Um, I think so, why?
Woman 1: Well, I was thinking about making dinner for a few people. I'd love you and Mark to come along.
Woman 2: Let me check. Oh no, I'm not free. That's the 16th of October. It's my cousin's wedding. Goodness, I'd completely forgotten. Sorry.

Extract 4
Man 1: I've just been checking the football fixtures.
Man 2: Oh, yeah?
Man 1: United play Liverpool on December the 10th. That's Justin's birthday. Do you think I'd get tickets?
Man 2: Mm, difficult. You know how quickly tickets go for that game. Let me know if you do get some, though. I'd fancy going to that one with you.

Extract 5
Woman: Hey, come and check this out. Look, if we go on the twelfth, it's cheaper. We can fly into Prague for £95 each.
Man: Wow, that's good. Do you definitely want to go in May, though? People say it's really amazing in April.
Woman: No, I'm too busy in April.
Man: OK, May the 12th, then, book them up.

Extract 6
Voice: … now that brings us to a very important date. January the 22nd 2005. That was the day that the gallery first opened to the public after several years as a …

Track 21

C Listen and write the names and addresses you hear in the extracts.

Extract 1

Travel agent: … so would you like to go ahead and make a booking.

Woman: Yes, I think so.

Travel agent: OK, I'll need some details. First, can you give me your name?

Woman: Yes. It's Christine Howell.

Travel agent: Is that Christine with an *h*?

Woman: Yes, C-H-R-I-S-tine. Howell is H-O-W-E-double L.

Travel agent: OK, and your address with a postcode.

Woman: It's 57 Belle View Gardens. That's B-E-double L, E and then view as a separate word. Belle View Gardens, Maidstone, Kent.

Travel agent: Sorry, Maidstone? Is that M-A-I-D-stone?

Woman: Yes, that's right.

Travel agent: And Kent is K-E-N-T?

Woman: Yep.

Travel agent: OK, and a postcode?

Woman: MD6 8QP

Travel agent: OK, thanks and now, could you tell me …

Extract 2

Jim: Hello?

Craig: Hi, Jim. It's Craig.

Jim: Oh, hi Craig.

Craig: I'm just phoning to check the address of the guest house again before we set off. I'm not sure if I've got it quite right.

Jim: Wait a moment. I'll go and get it … OK, ready? It's called Rose Hill. That's two words – *rose* and then *hill* and it's 72 Elm Lane – that's E-L-M like the tree – Winchester.

Craig: And Winchester's in Hampshire, right?

Jim: Yes, it's Hampshire. I thought you'd know at least which county we're going to!

Craig: OK, OK, just checking.

Jim: I guess you don't need a postcode.

Craig: No, don't worry. I'm not going to write to them.

Track 22

Unit 3 Speaking 2

C Listen to some native speakers and decide which statement they are discussing. Write the number of the statement for each answer.

Conversation 1

Male: So, what do you think of this statement?

Female: Mm, it's difficult. Of course, it's ridiculous to say simply that this is true, but perhaps there's some truth in it. Some women obviously want to win and beat an opponent – there wouldn't be female sporting heroes if not. But I think generally men are more obsessed with outdoing each other. Women want to succeed and do well, but don't worry so much about beating other people. I mean, if you said to most women would you rather score 80% and be top of the class or score 90% but finish third, they would choose the latter – you know they want to do as well as possible. I think most men would choose the former. It's being better than someone else that matters. You know, they just can't bear the thought of other people scoring higher than they do.

Male: Oh, come on! You don't really think …

Conversation 2

Female: This is the statement that I disagree with most strongly. It's just nonsense.

Male: Yes, I thought you might not like this one. You must admit that there are still more men in positions of power, though.

Female: Yes, of course – that's because they don't give women a chance. When women are in positions of power they do just as well, if not better, than men. Women can manage other people without being competitive and overbearing. Frankly, I didn't really like Margaret Thatcher, but surely she proved that a woman can be a figurehead.

Male: Mm, I'm not sure she was a typical woman, though.

Female: Why not? What makes me really angry is attitudes like this in the workplace. There are still men who say they don't feel comfortable with a female boss or supervisor. There are women everywhere that could be much higher up the career ladder if only they were given the opportunity.

Conversation 3

Female: So, my guess is that you think this is true.

Male: Yes, absolutely true. The thing that drives me crazy about my wife is her inability to make choices – or at least her inability to stick to the choices she makes.

Female: That's because men just act on the first thought that comes into their head. Women need to consider all the pros and cons.

Male: Pros and cons! How can it take an hour to decide if a pair of shoes is the right pair of shoes? I mean, if I see a pair of shoes I like, I buy them. If I don't like them, I don't buy them. Why should it be more complicated than that?

Female: Yes, but then a week later you regret having spent so much on a pair of shoes you didn't really need.

Track 23

Unit 3 Speaking 2

D Listen and complete these sentences from the conversations.

1 It's being better than someone else that matters.

2 What makes me really angry is attitudes like this in the workplace.

3 The thing that drives me crazy about my wife is her inability to make choices.

Track 24
Unit 3 Speaking 2

Grammar check
Listen and check your answers.

1
It's men who think they are more intelligent than women that make me furious.
What makes me furious is men who think they are more intelligent than women.
The thing that makes me furious is men who think they are more intelligent than women.

2
It's the time women need to get ready that drives me crazy.
What drives me crazy is the amount of time women need to get ready.
The thing that drives me crazy is the amount of time women need to get ready.

Track 25
Unit 3 Speaking 2

Pronunciation check
Listen to all the emphatic sentences from Exercise D and the *Grammar check*.

1 It's being better than someone else that matters.
2 What makes me really angry is attitudes like this in the workplace.
3 The thing that drives me crazy about my wife is her inability to make choices.
4 It's men who think they are more intelligent than women that make me furious.
5 What makes me furious is men who think they are more intelligent than women.
6 The thing that makes me furious is men who think they are more intelligent than women.
7 It's the time women need to get ready that drives me crazy.
8 What drives me crazy is the amount of time women need to get ready.
9 The thing that drives me crazy is the amount of time women need to get ready.

Track 26
Unit 3 Listening 1

C Listen to four extracts and match them with the pictures.
Extract 1
Voice: There has not previously been a female jockey quite like Hayley Turner. In 2005, she became only the fourth woman in history to ride out her claim. This meant she could compete equally with male jockeys. In that year, she also became the first female

Champion Apprentice. She is the first female jockey to have ridden a 100 winners in a season and is now considered to be one of the best jockeys in the country. Her determination and self-discipline have made her not just an exceptional female jockey, but an exceptional jockey. She is as strong and tactically aware as any male and is respected in the profession as the equal of any of her peers.

Extract 2
Voice: The idea that men and women should compete on a level playing field has been discussed in relation to many sports. In major sports like football and tennis, the physical difference between male and female competitors is usually put forward as a reason for this not being possible. Here, however, no such physical difference is in any way relevant and surely there is nothing that should prevent women competing alongside men. It seems strange that most male players are against equality and believe that women should continue to play in their own competitions.

Extract 3
Voice: In 2009, Danica Patrick raced at the Indianapolis 500, where she finished third behind winner Helio Castroneves and second-place Dan Wheldon. This was her best finish in five attempts in the race, one place better than her 2005 finish, and a new record high finish for a female driver. Despite all her success, however, there are many who feel that she will not be suited to racing Formula 1, and there is still much prejudice that she will have to overcome.

Extract 4
Voice: The main argument against women succeeding in men's events has always been physical strength. Women simply can't hit the ball as far. When the ladies world number one, Annika Sorenstam, was invited to play in a major men's event in 2003, she missed the cut by five shots and was stunned by the experience. She later admitted that it had been much tougher than she had expected and that she was looking forward to going back to play where she belonged. Michelle Wie might be the woman to challenge the theory. At six foot and one inch, she can hit the ball as far as almost any male, and commentators all over the world have agreed that she has the potential to be as good as any male player.

Track 27
Unit 3 Listening 1

D Listen again and complete the sentences. There are two sentences for each extract.
[Play Track 26 again]

Track 28
Unit 3 Listening 1

F Listen again as you read the tapescript. Notice examples of paraphrased language as you read.
   [Play Track 26 again]

Track 29
Unit 3 Listening 2

A You will hear a talk given to students studying gender studies about women in sport. Listen and answer the questions.

Voice: … so I think we can say that despite some marvellous progress, it is still very difficult for women to succeed in the male-dominated world of sport. To actually compete against men in the same competitions is even more difficult, and women face an enormous amount of chauvinism and prejudice. Let me use horse racing as an example. For over 100 years women have been involved in horse racing as very successful owners and trainers, and for nearly 50 years as jockeys. It is still the case, though, that girls are used as exercise riders before the races and then snubbed when it comes to the racing. Even top female jockeys, who have done everything to prove that they are the equals of men, are not given the best rides and at meetings will regularly have two or three fewer rides than their male peers. The older generation of men who wield power still believe that a woman jockey will never win the very biggest races, like the Derby or the Grand National. Personally, I believe that they will soon be proved totally wrong.

Now, of course, it is true that men are generally physically bigger and stronger than women, and it's understandable that people feel that women will never compete with men at the highest level in contact sports, like football or basketball. People are afraid that women are not as robust as men and will get injured, or that men will refrain from playing as aggressively as they might against other men and that that would compromise the game. There are others who feel that it is inappropriate for males and females to be in such close physical contact. My feeling is that at younger ages, girls should play against boys if they are good enough. Football, for example, isn't only about strength and speed. There are many smaller players who rely on skill and positional awareness. If girls prove they are the equal of boys, they should continue playing as long as they are able to compete. I don't think there should be archaic rules that prevent girls from competing with boys once they reach a particular age.

Now, games like tennis and golf are interesting. These are not contact sports and there are fewer arguments to support the theory that men and women should not compete together. As women's tennis progresses, the difference between how hard players hit the ball becomes smaller and smaller. As long ago as the 1970s Billie Jean King, a former ladies Wimbledon champion, proved that women could beat men when she triumphed over a former male Wimbledon champion, Bobby Riggs, in a special showdown match. Not only did she win, but she won in straight sets. Riggs may have been past his best at the time, but it was a moment that women all over the world enjoyed. The world's best lady golfer, Annika Sorenstam, had a less successful time when she was invited to play in a major men's event in 2003. She found it all far more challenging than she had expected and failed to make it through to the main competition when she missed the cut by five strokes. When Michelle Wie burst onto the scene a few years ago, everyone believed that we had found a woman who was tall and powerful enough to be the equal of any male golfer. Professional male golfers claimed that she was as good as any young male player that they had ever seen. Unfortunately, it doesn't seem to have worked out, and Wie is still to fulfil that promise. Who knows how long we will have to wait for a true female champion in a male-dominated sport.

One important thing we have to consider is whether it would always be an advantage for women to compete against men at the very highest level anyway. In tennis, for example, it is generally accepted that Serena Williams, the women's world number one, would be rated at around 50th or 60th in the world if she were competing constantly against men. She would probably qualify through the earlier stages of the big events, beating male opponents as she did so, but she would find it very difficult to reach the semi-finals or even the quarter-finals. Now, we have to ask, would the best women players rather be big fish in a smaller pond or small fish in a very big pond? Williams certainly would be nowhere near as famous and would have accumulated a tiny percentage of her prize money had she been playing with men all these years. Perhaps we should be fighting for all women's sport to be taken as seriously as men's sport, rather than driving towards actually competing with men. Women's tennis is probably now as popular as men's tennis – I know I'd rather watch women play any day. We need other sports to be viewed in the same way.

So anyway, to conclude, I think it's fair to say there's still a long way to go, and if schools continue to allow girls to play basketball with the net a little lower or score two points instead of one each time they make a run in baseball, girls will still be seen as somehow inferior. What I think is important is …

Track 30
Unit 3 Consolidation – Speaking

C Listen to some students answering the question. Mark each speaker (✓) for a good answer or (✗) not a good answer.

Speaker 1

Examiner: How have traditional male and female roles changed in your country in the last 20 years?

Student: Um, you mean the roles of the men and the women? Well, I was only born 21 years ago so I don't know much about 20 years ago. I think maybe the women work more nowadays – I mean they have jobs.

Speaker 2

Examiner: How have traditional male and female roles changed in your country in the last 20 years?

Student: Um, yes, I think they change a lot. Twenty years is a long time and I think life for everyone, life changes very much. I think Italy maybe changes more than other countries in 20 years. Can you ask me again, what did you ask about the males and females?

Speaker 3

Examiner: How have traditional male and female roles changed in your country in the last 20 years?

Student: Mm, it's a big question. Some people think in my country it is still the womans in kitchen, but it is not so true – at least not for younger generation. Womans now, they work so hard like the men – sometimes they earn more money than the men. Also, now it is usual to see more girls out in town together – you know, before the girls go out in the night only with boys.

Speaker 4

Examiner: How have traditional male and female roles changed in your country in the last 20 years?

Student: Well, I think in France not so much has changed in 20 years – maybe in 50 years. I think women have gone to work, even when they have children, for a long time now, but I guess it's the kind of jobs they do that has changed. I know a friend whose mother is the big breadwinner – you know, she makes the money. She works in advertising or PR or something like that. Her father does most of the work around the house. I think maybe 20 years ago men in this situation would feel quite threatened.

Track 31
Unit 3 Consolidation – Speaking

D Listen again and make notes about each speaker's answer.

[Play Track 30 again]

Track 32
Unit 3 Listening

A Listen to a talk about women in horse racing and choose the correct answer a, b or c.

Voice: Though it is traditionally considered a male dominated sport, women have always played an important role in horse racing at every level.

Many of the most successful and influential owners have been women and, at some time or another, almost all of the biggest races in the United States have been won by a horse owned by a woman. There have also been many exceptional women trainers. At one time, a female trainer was something of a rarity. These days they are commonplace and the top owners do not think twice about placing their best horses in a yard under a woman's charge.

Female jockeys really appeared on the scene in the late 60s when Diane Crump became the first woman jockey to ride in one of the bigger races in America. Around that time, Barbara Jo Rubin was the first female jockey to win a race, and then Tuesdee Testa was the first woman rider to win a race at a major American race course.

The most successful woman jockey of all, certainly in the States, is surely Julie Krone. She is the all-time leading female jockey and was the first to win a classic when she took the 1991 Belmont on Colonial Affair. In 2002, after coming out of retirement, she was successful once again, becoming the first woman to win a Grade 1 race in California.

Apart from the women in racing who make history, we must also take a moment to say something about the girls who don't get the limelight. Horse racing couldn't survive without the grooms, the exercise riders and the pony girls that do the hard work every day for little financial reward.

Track 33
Unit 4 Speaking 1

C Listen to people talking about the pictures. Match each speaker with a picture.

Speaker 1

Voice: Pictures like this make me feel really nostalgic. I always loved this time of year when I was a kid. You know, freezing outside, but lovely and warm indoors. We had an open fire, so it was really cosy. I remember looking out my bedroom window and seeing a white carpet outside. There was something wonderful about being the first person to walk on it.

Speaker 2

Voice: Mm, this picture doesn't bring back very fond memories, I'm afraid. I wasn't happy around this time. You know, when all the other kids were cool and had boyfriends or girlfriends and I didn't. My dad wouldn't let me wear what my friends were wearing. I felt like a bit of an outsider.

Speaker 3

Voice: I like to think I can remember the first few years at primary school, but I'm not sure I can. I think I might have just heard my mum talking about it. I remember I had a teacher called Mrs Craig. She was lovely, but I can't really recall which year it was or exactly how old I was.

Speaker 4

Voice: Actually, this picture really takes me back. I'll never forget lying there trying to get to sleep. I used to have bad dreams and I remember waking up in the night. I hated the shadows that the moon made and the faces of some of my toys in the dark. My mum tucked me into bed every night, but she wouldn't lie with me.

Track 34
Unit 4 Vocabulary 1

Pronunciation check
Listen and write the sentences you hear. Underline the syllables that are most heavily stressed.
Example: I wish I wasn't so busy all the time.
1. I wish I was a bit taller.
2. If only I lived a bit closer to the school.
3. I wish I hadn't told you now.
4. If only I'd listened to what she said.

Listen again as you check the tapescript. Practise saying all the sentences with a partner. Then talk about your own life using I wish and If only.

Track 35
Unit 4 Listening 1

B **Listen to some people talking about some of the objects. Match each speaker with an object.**
Speaker 1
Voice: I guess this looks pretty old-fashioned to you, but back in the 80s everyone wanted one of these. Before they came along, the only way you could listen to music when you were out was to carry a huge tape recorder around. I can't believe people used to do that. Anyway, these were kind of like an iPod, but you could only play tapes and wear a very silly looking pair of headphones.

Speaker 2

Voice: These were all the rage when I was a kid. I remember getting told off at school for playing with one instead of listening to the teacher. When they first came out, the kids who could solve the puzzle –

I mean get all the colours in the right place – were thought of as really smart. Then, once they'd been around for a while, everyone learnt the trick. You know, there was a technique and when you knew that, you could do it. I guess that took away the fun really. You never see them nowadays – I guess everyone plays computer games instead.

Speaker 3

Voice: Oh yes, this takes me back a bit. I guess this was like the first really popular computer game. First, the game was on machines in amusement arcades and bars. People used to spend hours sitting there shooting these little aliens instead of talking to their friends – the shape of things to come, I guess. Then you could buy hand-held versions of the game you could play at home. It looks so dated now, but I think it still looks fun.

Speaker 4

Voice: You know, I think kids still have these now, but they're not so popular. I guess now there are fun centres and kids parks everywhere – who wants to bounce around on a big bag of air? I had one just like this one in the picture – I don't know if they were all orange, but I seem to remember most of them were.

Speaker 5

Voice: I remember I had one of these when I was … oh, about seven or eight. I think they were the first hand-held computer games that everyone had. They were the first time any of us had heard of *Nintendo* too – probably the first time we realized all our technology would come from Japan in the future! I remember the huge START and SELECT buttons – it all seems so dated so soon.

Track 36
Unit 4 Listening 1

C **Listen to a father talking to his daughter about two more of the objects in the pictures. Match the words 1–6 below with the letters a–f on the diagrams.**
Father: Hey, look at this. I haven't seen this for ages. I'd forgotten it was up here.
Daughter: Is that a record player? Goodness, it looks ancient.
Father: It is ancient. This was my first one – I had this when I was about 12 years old. I bet you don't even know how it works, do you?
Daughter: Well, I know DJs have pretty much the same thing now – a bit more modern, of course. I've never actually looked at one properly, though.
Father: Well, it's pretty simple really. Here, let me find a record and show you. Ah, here we are – they're a bit dusty. You know, we only had records when I was a kid – no iPods or MP3s.
Daughter: Not even CDs?

Father: Not even CDs. Anyway, this is the turntable. You put the record on here – see how the hole in the middle of the record fits over this little knob in the middle of the turntable? Then you moved the arm across.

Daughter: The arm?

Father: Yeah, the arm. This long bit here. You move it across until it's over the part of the record you want to listen to – usually the beginning, I mean the first track. You could play any part of the record you wanted, though – that's why I always preferred records to tapes. This little sharp bit on the end of the arm is the stylus – it's like a little needle point that goes into the grooves in the record and plays the music – don't ask me how.

Daughter: It looks very sharp. Didn't it scratch the records?

Father: No, not if you were … well, actually yes it did. If you didn't position the arm properly, the stylus slipped and scratched your records to bits. In fact, all my records were scratched. Ah, here. Now, this is mum's old typewriter. It's a bit dusty too.

Daughter: Aren't these old typewriters valuable now? You should sell it instead of leaving it up here.

Father: Actually, I was going to give it to you to do your homework on.

Daughter: Oh, ha ha. It's quite a lovely thing, though, isn't it? I can't imagine actually using it though.

Father: Well, if you look at it properly, you'll see it's not much different to a PC. I mean, the basics are in the same place – certainly the keyboard part anyway. We used to call it the keytop. Look – all the letters and numbers are in more or less the same place as they are on a PC now – see the space bar down here too?

Daughter: Oh yes. What about all this up at the top, though?

Father: This whole top part is the carriage. There's a roller here, look, and that's where you feed the paper in. These clips hold the paper in place. The carriage moves along as you type and when you're at the end of a line, it shifts back to the beginning again.

Daughter: So the keys actually physically jumped up and hit the paper – amazing. Did you have to keep putting ink on the keys, then?

Father: What? No, of course not. Look, just below the carriage here, there's a ribbon. The ribbon was full of ink and the keys hit the ribbon against the paper. You had to replace the ribbon every so often – just like you replace the cartridge now if you've got a printer. I wish I could show you it working properly. Shall we take it down and see if we can get it working?

Track 37
Unit 4 Listening 1

D Now listen to the father and daughter talking about an old telephone. Fill in the missing information on the diagram.

Daughter: Hey, I like this phone. Can't we have an old-style one like this?

Father: Mm, they're not very practical – you can't walk around with them, you know. I guess you've never used a phone with a conventional handset like this, have you?

Daughter: What do you mean?

Father: I mean the phone downstairs doesn't have a handset and most of the time you use your mobile anyway. Grandma's got a phone a bit like this, but I doubt you've ever answered it.

Daughter: No, I haven't. So, when you say the handset, you mean this part that you pick up?

Father: Yeah, we always used to call it the receiver, but in fact that's not correct. The receiver is actually the part of the handset that you listen to – the part that the other person's voice comes out of. It receives the message.

Daughter: So, what's the other end called? I mean the part you speak into?

Father: That's the microphone.

Daughter: Oh, I guess that makes sense.

Father: So, what do you think of the dial then? Can you imagine dialling numbers instead of just touching the keypad?

Daughter: The dial's this round bit on the front, right? I guess you put your fingers in the number you want and turn the dial?

Father: Exactly, the trouble was, though, that if you didn't turn the dial right round far enough, the phone didn't read that number. You were always getting wrong numbers.

Daughter: Mm, but that's no different from not touching the number on the keypad hard enough.

Father: True.

Track 38
Unit 4 Listening 2

A You will hear three parts of a talk about the history of the bicycle. Listen and answer the questions.

Voice: Bicycles were introduced in the 19th century and now number around one billion worldwide. Amazingly, that is twice as many as motor cars. They're the principal means of transportation in many regions. Bicycles also provide a popular form of recreation for many, if not most, people and have been adapted for such uses as children's toys, adult fitness, military and police applications, courier services and bicycle racing as a sport. The basic shape and configuration of a typical upright bicycle has changed little since the first chain-driven model was developed around 1885. However, many details have been improved, especially since the advent of modern materials and computer-aided design. The invention of the bicycle has had an enormous impact on society, both in terms of culture and of advancing modern industrial methods. Several components that played a key role in the development of motor vehicles were originally invented for the bicycle.

(Pause between parts)

Now, these bicycles, which I'm sure you have all seen before, were known by a number of names – *high wheeler* and *high wheel roller* were commonly used, but you'll probably recognize them as *penny-farthings*. They were, of course, noted for the huge front wheel and much smaller back wheel. The name penny-farthing actually wasn't used until they were almost defunct. The term originated when people noticed that the design resembled two coins of the day, a penny and a much smaller farthing, laid side by side.

Now, let me say something about the design and features of this type of bicycle. Let me find the slide – here we are. Now, the obvious feature is the much larger front wheel and that was there, of course, to enable much higher speeds. There were no gears back then and the pedals were welded directly to the hub in the centre of the front wheel. You see here how the relatively small pedals are attached to the hub. Each turn of the pedals took the rider further than the same turn would with a conventionally-sized front wheel. The larger wheel also made for a more comfortable ride as the rider was high above the cobbled stones that were typical of the day.

Another important feature of the penny-farthing was the steel frame. Most bicycles had previously had a wooden frame. Steel was much stronger and meant more support and comfort for the rider. Around the same time, rubber tyres were introduced. It seems unthinkable now, but before rubber tyres, bicycles simply had wooden or metal wheels and were often known as *bone-shakers* because they literally shook the rider's bones.

OK, so we know the penny-farthing had two wheels of very different sizes and from the picture, you can see that the rider was seated in the saddle pretty much over the front wheel – we've already said that pedals were fixed to the front wheel hub. This meant that it was often difficult for the rider to mount the bicycle – I mean get on the bicycle to ride it. You can see here that later designs had what is called a mounting step – a step that the rider could use to mount the bicycle.

Now, one final thing about the design. You see here the shape of the handlebars? Because the front wheel was so big, the rider's knees came up and were very close to the handlebars. Often riders' knees would hit the handlebars, especially if they were riding fast. This led to the design of what was called moustache handlebars – handlebars shaped like a moustache. The rider's knees could pass comfortably below the bars as he, or she for that matter, rode along.

Now, accidents. The height of the saddle and the …

(Pause between parts)

So, to bring us up to date. You'll probably all know about modern bicycles so I'm not going to go into great detail – it wouldn't be very interesting. What I would like to point out is some of the improvements that have been made and some of the details that have been made possible by technology.

As we said, the basic design has changed very little. I know the penny-farthing looked very different, but it was still ultimately two wheels attached to a frame and, in fact, the period of the high wheeler was rather unique. The bicycles that came before that were actually shaped more like modern bicycles of today.

The first thing I want to point out is the cogset, which on a typical mountain or racing bicycle is now amazingly advanced. For years, bicycles had just one gear. The rider often had to push the bicycle up a steep hill. When gears were first introduced, there were usually three and later five gears. You can see here, that the whole chain assembly, with the larger front derailleur by the pedals and the smaller back derailleur attached to the hub of the back wheel, looks very much like a bicycle of 50 years ago. But the cogset might now be made up of anything between 10 and 30 cogs, allowing the rider to choose that number of gears. Even the average cyclist can now take on the steepest hill! Another feature that makes pedalling so much easier now is the fact that the saddle height can be adjusted. Under the saddle here is the seat post. This is the part of the frame that can be adjusted, so that the rider is at exactly the right height – this feature is on every bicycle now, from a child's first bike to an expensive racing bike.

Now, safety. We said that there were frequent accidents on the high wheelers we looked at earlier. Modern bicycles are so much safer – safer all the time in fact – and, of course, serious riders wear plenty of protection anyway. On the diagram here, you can see there is a shock absorber. This is at the top of the fork above the front wheel. If there is impact, the shock absorber compresses and literally takes the shock. These are featured on all motor vehicles as well as bicycles.

Finally, I want to mention spokes. Some people ask why bicycle wheels have spokes and you probably wonder why I mention them now, since bicycle wheels have had spokes since their conception. Well, the wheels have spokes because a solid wheel would be so heavy that the bicycle would be impossible to ride. With advanced materials, some racing bicycles do now have solid wheels, but certainly not the majority. What has changed over the years is the shape of the spokes. At one time spokes were made of wood, so had no tension or compression. For many years, spokes were designed to be …

Track 39

Unit 4 Reading 1

E Before you check the answers to Exercise D, listen to some students talking about them. Which student gives the correct answer to each question? Write (M) male or (F) female.

Male: OK, I've got my answers. Shall we compare?

Female: Hang on a moment. I'm still thinking about number three and number seven.

Male: Yes, I thought number three was quite tricky – but also number eight – I'm not sure about number eight.

Female: OK, well, let's compare, then. Number one, I think the answer is c. The text mentions children's bricks and catapults and I think that activities like these always make you feel nostalgic.

Male: Mm, I don't think so. Those are just examples of nostalgia. The text says, 'the tiniest trigger'. I'm not sure about trigger, but tiniest means smallest. My guess is that trigger means make something happen – like the trigger on a gun. I think a is the right answer.

Female: Mm, OK. What about number 2, then?

Male: Well, it's definitely not c. The text says nothing about the future. I think it's a – the extract is all about memories.

Female: No. The extract is about memories, but this part says we are frequently told to live for the moment. That means that people are led to believe they should think about now. The answer is b. I'm quite confident about this one.

Male: OK, I see what you mean – perhaps you're right.

Female: OK, number three – we both thought this one was difficult. There are a couple of words I don't know. I think the answer is c. I think 'reliving high school glories' means thinking about proud moments – you know, what he succeeded in. I don't really know glories, though, so I'm working it out from the context.

Male: No, I don't think so. The student is struggling, so he finds something difficult. He thinks back to something that was also difficult at school. I'm not sure, but my answer is b.

Female: Well, we'll just have to disagree. We're not agreeing on many answers!

Male: No. Well, what about number four, then? I prefer these true, false, not given exercises.

Female: My answer is true. Everyone does feel nostalgic about school lunches. Now, there are even restaurants that serve food which people liked at school.

Male: Maybe, but that doesn't mean it's the right answer. The extract just gives thinking about school lunches as an example of nostalgia – I mean, what makes one person feel nostalgic. It certainly doesn't say that everyone reminisces about school lunches. No, I think the answer is NG.

Female: Mm, yes – you might be right. Let's go on to number five.

Male: I think the answer here is NG. The extract doesn't say anything about this.

Female: I disagree. The extract says, 'even for the least sentimental of us'. That line provides the answer. It's saying that people who are not especially sentimental – that is not especially sensitive or emotional – are also affected by nostalgia. My answer is false.

Male: OK, and number six? I think this one's true.

Female: Mm, I'm not sure that the information is actually given. I've put NG.

Male: No, the information is definitely given. It says that thinking about the past for half an hour can make you feel better about your current situation. That means how you live now.

Female: So, you think that 'contemplating' means thinking about?

Male: Well, yes I think so – anyway, I'm pretty sure the answer is true.

Female: Well, for number seven. I don't know the answer. I've put not given because I can't say that it definitely is given.

Male: I've put true. I think 'an antidote' is something that relieves or cures an illness – you know, a kind of opposite to something. Having nice memories is a kind of cure to sadness.

Female: OK, maybe you're right.

Male: So, what about the last one? This one is difficult. I've put true. I think that the extract is saying that people who don't think about the past are like leaves blown in the wind. They have no roots.

Female: Mm, I think that's the idea, but it doesn't actually state that these people are all directionless. It says that, 'nostalgia can motivate people'. It's one of those statements that are a bit misleading. I think when there are modal verbs like can or might the answer is often NG.

Male: OK, let's check the answers.

Track 40

Unit 4 Writing 2

C Listen to some people talking about the topics in the three tasks. Match each speaker with one of the tasks A, B or C.

Speaker 1

Voice: Well, I don't really see how anyone can complain about using them at work. They do everything in a tenth of the time it used to take. I can't imagine people going back to typewriters and waiting three days for a letter to arrive.

Speaker 2

Voice: Actually, I think this has a lot to do with women going out to work. I know I won't be popular saying this, but it's obvious. If women are out all day, they don't have time to cook proper meals. The kids come in from school and get a meal out of the freezer or grab something from a takeaway.

Speaker 3

Voice: They've just got to improve public transport. People use their cars because they're so much more comfortable than buses and the underground. They can listen to music or the news on the radio and they travel door to door. Even if the journey takes a bit longer, people feel it's more convenient and often safer too.

Speaker 4

Voice: I'm not sure it really is that big a problem. There might be some kids who only eat burgers and pizzas, but not the ones I know. Mine eat as much in the way of fruit and vegetables as I did. I'm pretty sure most of their friends do too. I think the media just make up these issues to scare people.

Speaker 5

Voice: Mm, I do think that a lot of people spend too long online these days. What with the gossip pages, chat rooms and shopping sites, they're never away from the screen. I'm sure it's affecting the way people relate to one another. Nobody actually talks anymore and what they look at has no real cultural value.

Speaker 6

Voice: I think there should be some sort of incentive to share journeys and pick up passengers. It doesn't make sense for so many individuals to sit there in their metal box. When we come in on the motorway, we can't believe the number of vehicles coming past us the other way with just the driver.

Speaker 7

Voice: Well, like all things, there are pros and cons, but surely the pros outweigh the cons. I mean, they're just sophisticated machines and, frankly, we've always lived with machines. I guess we rely on them a bit too much – if anything suddenly made them all crash, we'd be in trouble, but that's unlikely. I do worry about what my kids look at on the Internet, but that's my only real concern.

Speaker 8

Voice: When I was a lad, we used to nag our parents to take us to McDonald's or Burger King, but it wasn't all the time. Nowadays, there are so many different chains all selling more or less the same thing – they're everywhere and I'm sure a lot of teenagers live on that junk.

Speaker 9

Voice: I think they have to have some kind of city centre ban – you know, stop people driving into the centre or at least charge them if they do. They have to make it so that people don't want to drive – so that driving actually becomes inconvenient. Only then will people walk or take the bus.

Speaker 10

Voice: It does worry me a bit when I think about how far things could go. Would we ever need to leave the house? I mean, we could all end up sitting there all day and all night tuned into some fantasy world where we can be whoever we want and be doing whatever we want. Who wants real life if that's possible?

Track 41
Unit 4 Consolidation – Speaking

B Listen and check your answers.

Voice: When you are speaking with the examiner, he or she will listen and make a note of the vocabulary you use. However, you shouldn't worry about this. You can only use words and phrases you know and you shouldn't try to impress the examiner. If you try too hard to use the words and phrases that you don't really know, you'll use them incorrectly or inappropriately and you won't sound natural. At the same time, you don't want your language to be too simple. After the interview, you might regret that you didn't use a word or phrase that you know was right for the situation. Listen to what the examiner says and think for a moment before you speak.

Track 42
Unit 4 Consolidation – Speaking

D Listen to the same students using the more appropriate words and phrases. Check your ideas.

1

Examiner: Would you say that you were happy at school?

Student: Yes, I have some very good memories of school.

2

Examiner: What was your favourite time of year as a child?

Student: Winter. When it's winter now, I always feel nostalgic. I mean, it takes me back to my childhood.

3

Examiner: Is there a danger that people end up living in the past?

Student: Mm, I don't think so. Everyone likes to sit and reminisce occasionally.

4

Examiner: Do you have regrets about leaving university so early?

Student: Oh yes. Now, I wish I had my degree. If only I could turn back the clock.

Track 43
Unit 4 Consolidation – Vocabulary

B Mark the main stress on these words. Then listen and check. Practising saying the words.

recollection

reminisce

associate
association
fundamental
spontaneously

Track 44
Unit 4 Exam Practice – Listening

B **You will hear two parts of a talk about houses. Listen and answer the questions.**

Voice: OK, so, here we are. Can you see the image on the screen clearly enough at the back? … Oh good, OK then. Now, it's difficult to say exactly when houses like these were built because it probably happened at different times in different places. We talk about the Stone Age, but that lasted much longer in some parts of the world than in others. Houses like these may not have existed until what we call the Iron Age in many parts.

Anyway, the important thing is that during the Neolithic – or modern Stone Age – era, the way people lived changed dramatically. Before that, during the Palaeolithic era, people were nomadic. They moved from place to place and didn't really have houses at all – at least not permanent ones. They may have slept in caves or built very primitive shelters, but they didn't build houses. During the Neolithic era, people started to build houses. The growth of agriculture meant that people grew crops and kept their own animals. They no longer moved around hunting and gathering. For the first time, people wanted to settle and have a base.

Some houses from this period were rectangular, but the better preserved houses, those probably dating from a slightly later time, were usually round – like this one. These houses were made from stones or mud bricks, depending on where they were. In this picture, you can see that the walls were built with flint, a hard stone that was also used at the time for making tools. The stone or flint walls were then coated with plaster. At that time, plaster would have been little more than mud or clay, but it would have kept the rain out. The roofs were made from mud or sticks and grass. Doorways were sometimes at ground level as is usual now, but here you can see that sometimes they were actually cut into the roof and that there were ladders on either side of the roof for access. This would have been practised presumably to protect the inhabitants from large wild animals that couldn't climb. Inside the homes, strong wooden beams that were driven into the ground supported the roof. In the centre of most houses like this was a hearth. This was to keep people warm at night mainly, but may have been used for cooking too. Usually, these were little more than a fire made within a circle of stones, but later they were more like a primitive oven.

Some houses form this period had two separate rooms within. One of these would have been …

… I'm going to bring us right up to date now and talk about *smart houses*. I'm sure most of you will have heard the term smart house, but you might not know that much about what that means – unless you already live in one, of course. A smart house is a house that has a highly advanced automatic system. This can operate lighting, temperature control, security devices, window and door operations, multimedia and communication and potentially a host of other functions. *Smart* here means *intelligent* – the house is intelligent because it can monitor daily life within its walls and appears to make decisions. Not long ago, this would have sounded like something from a sci-fi movie, but now it's all very much reality.

In a smart house, the systems within the house are connected and can pass information to each other. So, for example, the security alarm can turn the lights on or off. You can also operate the systems from outside the house. You can turn on the heating so that the house is warm when you return. You can open and close curtains and turn on lights so that people think you are at home. The system can call your mobile to tell you that you've had a visitor or received mail and you can let visitors into your house if you want to. What's more, the systems could be connected to other buildings. The security system could be connected to the police station, so that it alerts the police if you have an intruder. The fridge could be linked to the local supermarket, so that it can order products, which will be waiting for you when you get home.

So, let's look at this house in the diagram. First of all, as the family arrives home, they activate the systems inside the house from inside the car – if they haven't already done so previously, of course. Above the garage here, there's a motion detector. This will detect any movement outside the house, whether it's an approaching vehicle or a person. When you are inside the house, you will know that you have a visitor well before they arrive. Outside the house, you can see that there are various external systems. External systems can check and maintain the temperature and cleanliness of a swimming pool or irrigate the garden, for example. Now, as you come round the front door here, there are security panels in the entrance area. These would be more sophisticated than conventional alarms – panels like these have an alarm, but also digital cameras and mechanisms for activating locks.

Now, inside the house, there would be various areas where parts of the system would function from. In this house, the master control is downstairs on the ground floor – the master control is the central part of the system – rather like a server to a system of computers. Upstairs, at the top of the house is the multimedia connection. This connects all the other systems to television screens and smaller computer screens around the house. In this house, the telephone connection is in a different location, but, of course, that could also be part of the multimedia apparatus in another house.

OK, now, down in the kitchen – personally, I think some of the kitchen features are the most interesting to talk about. Take the fridge, for example …

Track 45
Workbook Unit 4 Listening

A **Listen and match each extract to a type of diagram below. Write the number of the extract in the space.**
Extract 1
Voice: The glass is cut into what we call gobs, which are individual pieces fired down into the forming machine. In a matter of seconds, the glass is pressed and blown into shape inside a mould. It emerges as a brand new glass bottle or jar. Each container is rigorously checked in a series of quality controls.

Extract 2
Voice: The thermostat takes all the guesswork out of ironing. The user can preset the exact required temperature on the dial depending on the fabric being ironed. He or she can be confident that the correct heat is being maintained and that there is no risk of burning. A heat-sensitive contact cuts the supply as soon as a selected temperature is reached. When the iron cools, the current is resumed.

Extract 3
Voice: Brighton is a city on the south coast. It has many attractions that young visitors can enjoy. It's more or less directly south of London and is about an hour by train. Eastbourne and Hastings are smaller seaside resorts to the east of Brighton. Hastings is the larger of the two and has more in the way of leisure facilities. Another seaside town – this time further west in Dorset – is Bournemouth. Bournemouth is a large town popular with holidaymakers …

Extract 4
Voice: Early dwellings in Pompeii were built around an atrium, a large open main hall. There was usually a small opening in the ceiling, the compluvium, through which light and air were filtered. The impluvium was a hole in the floor which collected rainwater when it entered through the compluvium.

Extract 5
Voice: There are four chambers, two superior atria and two inferior ventricles. The atria are the receiving chambers and the ventricles are the discharging

chambers. The right ventricle discharges into the lungs to oxygenate the blood. The left ventricle discharges blood that circulates around the rest of the body via the aorta.

Extract 6
Voice: The biggest leap in the number of female smokers was between 1992 and 1993 when 30,000 more women smoked. By 1993, there were more female than male smokers. For three years, the number of women smoking remained fairly constant, but then between 1996 and 1997, there was another increase.

Track 46
Unit 5 Vocabulary 2

Pronunciation check
Listen to these examples.
1 outdoor activities
2 on the go all day
3 crazy about

Decide which sound intrudes in the following phrases and where. Then listen and check.
1 stay indoors
2 better option
3 two others

Track 47
Unit 5 Speaking 2

A **Guess the missing word in each of these examiners' questions. Then listen and check.**
1 Examiner: So, how do you spend your free time?
2 Examiner: Tell me about the free-time activities you enjoy.
3 Examiner: Have you taken up any hobbies in the last few years?
4 Examiner: Do you have a very active social life?

Track 48
Unit 5 Speaking 2

B **Listen to some students answering the questions. Complete the sentences below with ONE word in each space.**
1
Examiner: So, how do you spend your free time?
Student: Mm, in different ways. I'm really into painting, so I spend a lot of my time in my studio or out painting in the countryside. Sometimes I just like spending time with friends – you know, having a drink or a meal out together.
2
Examiner: Tell me about the free-time activities you enjoy.
Student: Well, I like to keep fit. I go running and I go to the gym two or three times a week. I guess my

passion is martial arts. I do karate and judo. I'm pretty good at that – I have a black belt in karate. It's not all exercise and sport, though. I go to the cinema a lot and I like other things that most people like, you know.

3

Examiner: Have you taken up any hobbies in the last few years?

Student: Um, yes, I have. I started doing yoga about nine months ago. I like to look after myself and yoga's very healthy. I stopped eating meat at that time too. I suppose I'm a bit of a health fanatic really. Apart from that, I'm very keen on music. I play violin and I'm in an orchestra – just an amateur one – but I really love it.

4

Examiner: Do you have a very active social life?

Student: Oh, I wouldn't say that. To tell the truth, I quite like staying in these days. I never was a party animal. I enjoy getting some takeaway food and watching a good movie on TV.

Track 49
Unit 5 Listening 1

B Listen to some students talking and tick each picture as you hear it mentioned.

Female 1: Have you read the stories in the newspapers recently about how hard, or should I say how little, students work?

Male 1: Mm, I saw something about it. I didn't really pay much attention.

Male 2: I haven't heard anything. What have they been saying?

Female 1: Oh, you know, the usual thing about students going to one or two lectures a week and then spending the rest of their time sitting around drinking coffee and smoking or going out to wild parties.

Female 2: It makes me really cross when I hear stories like that. They just say these things to sell their rags. I don't think they even believe any of it's true themselves.

Male 2: Yeah, but you do sit around drinking coffee all day. You never go to your lectures.

Female 2: Oh, ha ha! Seriously, I think I work as hard as most people that have a full-time job. I have eight lectures a week and then at least two assignments. The lectures take up 12 hours and then the assignments anything from another six to ten hours, once I've done all the research.

Male 1: Yeah, I think in the past students had things a bit easier. You know, they had bigger grants and they didn't have to worry about being in debt at the end of their course. Most students I know have to do a part-time job now on top of all the study.

Female 1: That's right. I mean, I do around 20 hours of study and then work another 15. That's pretty much a full-time job. I usually work Saturday lunchtime too. I have to say, I'm exhausted most of the time.

Male 2: Ah yes, but the average person doesn't see studying as real work. You'd have a job to convince Joe Public that you're doing a full-time job.

Female 1: I didn't say I was doing a full-time job. I just said that I work a lot of hours in the week.

Male 2: No, you said that …

Male 1: OK guys, calm down.

Female 2: So, do you really think we do more work than students did in the past?

Male 1: Well, like I said, I think they had it a bit easier. My dad talks about when he was a student and it's all about how many bands he went to see and how many parties there were. I wish I had enough money to go and see some bands!

Female 1: Yeah, I get the impression that my mum spent most of her time at university discussing politics or going on protest marches. I'm amazed she actually finished her degree!

Male 1: I have to say that I do worry about the amount of debt I'll accumulate. I worked out that I might owe around 10 or 12 thousand pounds by the time I've finished. I'll spend the first ten years of my working life paying it back.

Male 2: Yeah, but you're going to be a lawyer, aren't you? You'll be able to pay that much back in a couple of months.

Male 1: Oh, very funny. I wish you'd take a conversation seriously for once. I don't know why they've reduced the grants we get. I mean, it's not like families are all suddenly richer. My parents can't afford to give me lots of extra spending money. It's just not fair.

Female 2: No, that's true, but hey, look at the time. We're sitting round here chatting and we should be getting ready. It's Tina's party tonight, isn't it?

Track 50
Unit 5 Listening 1

D Listen to the first part of the conversation again and complete the summary.

Female 1: Have you read the stories in the newspapers recently about how hard, or should I say how little, students work?

Male 1: Mm, I saw something about it. I didn't really pay much attention.

Male 2: I haven't heard anything. What have they been saying?

Female 1: Oh, you know, the usual thing about students going to one or two lectures a week and then spending the rest of the their time sitting around drinking coffee and smoking or going out to wild parties.

Female 2: It makes me really cross when I hear stories like that. They just say these things to sell their rags. I don't think they even believe any of it's true themselves.

Male 2: Yeah, but you do sit around drinking coffee all day. You never go to your lectures.

Track 51
Unit 5 Listening 2

B Listen to the complete conversation again and complete the summary.
[Play Track 49 again]

Track 52
Unit 5 Consolidation – Speaking

B Listen and check your answers.
1 I get a lot of pleasure from cycling. It helps me think.
2 I probably work harder than I should. I'm on the go all day.
3 I usually go dancing somewhere at the weekend. I really need to let my hair down.
4 To tell you the truth, I like staying in more than going out these days. I've never really been a party animal.
5 Frankly, I'm thinking about looking for a new job. I'm overworked and underpaid where I am.

Track 53
Workbook Unit 5 Listening

A Listen to a talk about the Romans and how they liked to enjoy their free time. Complete the summary below using NO MORE THAN TWO WORDS for each answer.
Voice: Now, the Romans knew all about work and play, especially play! One of the things we associate with Ancient Rome now is the fact that they loved their free time and that they invented all sorts of ways of filling it. The poet Juvenal was famous for saying that the people of Rome only demanded two things from their rulers – bread and circuses. Both were needed for life – people needed to eat to sustain the body and to visit the circus for pleasure.

To start with, the Romans were frequent visitors to the theatre and, for them, the theatre encompassed everything from traditional plays to chariot racing. The Romans only staged plays on days that were public holidays – but since there were something like 200 days of public holiday in Ancient Rome, there were plenty of opportunities to stage productions! Plays were noisy and people would shout and join in with the story. As in Greek theatre, the actors often wore masks to show that they were good or bad characters, and the whole atmosphere was more like a pantomime than the civilized notion of theatre we have today.

The amphitheatres were huge and here, of course, the Romans staged their games. I'm sure everyone's seen the film *Gladiator* and knows how sensational and sometimes terrifying these games could be. Thousands of spectators came to see specially trained slaves and prisoners – gladiators – fight each other to the death. Sometimes they fought wild animals like lions and bears. At the end of the

shows, the crowd decided if the combatants should live or die. Some gladiators became famous and could demand huge sums of money – rather like boxers or footballers today. Chariot racing was another popular form of entertainment and the men who drove the chariots were also celebrities.

Societies, of course, had previously hunted for food, but wealthy Romans hunted for sport. They even tried to make hunting more enjoyable by introducing new species of animal, like deer, into the countries they occupied.

For total relaxation, the Romans went to bath houses. The ruins of Roman baths can still be found in many parts of the world that were once in the Roman Empire. The Romans would spend all day at the baths, exercising before bathing and then swimming afterwards. The baths were important meeting places and were where wealthy Romans conducted business as they bathed.

Track 54
Unit 6 Vocabulary 1

B Listen to two students speaking in the exam and write answers to the questions.
1
Examiner: So, what do you especially like about being on holiday?
Student: Actually, I like shopping more than anything else. Wherever I go, there's always something to buy and I love buying … mm … you know, little presents that remind you of the place.
2
Examiner: Wow, Egypt. Did you stay in Cairo?
Student: Yes, we were in Cairo for three nights and then we had a … erm … to Luxor, I mean we moved down to Luxor. They took a group of us from Cairo to Luxor in a coach.

Track 55
Unit 6 Speaking 2

A Listen to some more students talking with an examiner. Complete the sentences below with ONE WORD ONLY in each space.
1
Examiner: So, was New York all you hoped it would be?
Student: Oh, it was even better than I hoped it would be. There's something new around every corner. Have you been there yourself?
2
Examiner: So, tell me about Paris, then.
Student: Well, Paris wasn't quite as nice as I thought it would be. I mean, it is nice, but I was expecting more. Maybe I heard too much before I went. Barcelona, on the other hand …

3

Examiner: So, what was the highlight of your tour?

Student: I think the highlight was Prague. I didn't know very much about Prague before I came to Europe and I wasn't very interested to see it. However, it was far more beautiful than I imagined. I want to go back there again one day.

4

Examiner: Did you like Hong Kong? I never know if it really appeals to me.

Student: Oh yes, it was very exciting and not nearly as polluted as I expected. I heard it was impossible to breathe there, but actually …

Track 56
Unit 6 Speaking 2

Pronunciation check
Listen again to the exchanges in Exercise A. Notice how the modifying verbs are stressed to make the message clear.
[Play Track 55 again]

Track 57
Unit 6 Listening 1

B   Listen and match the extracts with the maps and plans.
   Extract 1

Customer 1: We've looked at the brochure and frankly all the hotels look quite nice. We've picked out a few that we'd like to know a bit more about. Do you have a map or a plan of the area so you can show where exactly each hotel is? They all say 'walking distance' to the beach and so on, but then they would, wouldn't they?

Travel agent: Yes, I've got a map and a more detailed plan of the harbour area. Let me see … OK, here it is. Now, which hotels are you looking at?

Customer 2: Can you tell us about this one first – *Las Gaviotas*. It looks really nice.

Travel agent: Yes, I like that one. *Las Gaviotas* means *The Seagulls*. I've stayed there myself and it's lovely. It's here … not right on the beach, but very close. Frankly, the hotels right on the beach can be a bit noisy. I mean, the noise from the beach bars and restaurants at night. *Las Gaviotas* is between the beach and the old village.

Customer 1: So, how far is that to walk to the beach?

Travel agent: Oh, less than five minutes. Really – maybe three or four minutes.

Customer 2: And about the same into the old village?

Travel agent: Less – about two minutes. You really do have the best of both worlds with this hotel. Now, which is the second one you wanted to know …

Extract 2

Voice: Right, so here we are in the main square. You can look round by yourselves in a moment, but first let me tell you something about the buildings and monuments around us – you'll enjoy looking round far more if you know what you're looking at. There's plenty more information in the guide book too. Right, first of all, this statue right beside us is Thomas Mendelssohn. He was the founder of the children's hospital, which we will visit later. He was responsible for many other projects and developments in the town and he's a very important figure. The statue was erected in 1954.

OK, to our left, at the end of the square, is the museum. I'll show you round the museum a little bit later, but you can have a quick look now if you like. Incidentally, just behind the museum is Thomas Mendelssohn's office. He worked there for almost all of the time he was resident in the town. You can get to it through a little lane by the side of the museum. At the other end of the square – to our right, that is – is the library. It's fairly modern compared with some of the buildings in the square, but worth having a look at. The old library was badly damaged by fire in the 1960s and it was decided that building a new one was better than trying to rebuild the old one. Next to the library is the town's oldest pub. Luckily, that wasn't damaged in the fire. I don't know if you can read it from here, but it's called Den Glade. Perhaps that would be a good place to meet again after you've had a look round.

Extract 3

Voice: There are a number of sites and features in the northern tip of the country and they can all be visited in a day – certainly if you're driving, anyway. I wouldn't want to rely on the buses up there! There are four islands off the coast of the northern tip and all of them are interesting. You can get to three of them by boat and the biggest is connected to the mainland by a road bridge. The island just to the north of that one – so the island off the west coast to the north – is the home of an important bird sanctuary. The island is called Mowbray and there are boats every two hours that will take you there in about ten minutes. It's a very peaceful place. Now, on the other side of the tip – so off the east coast – are two more islands. You can't get to the smaller island, but you can admire it from the mainland. The larger island is home to Old Finkley. That's the last surviving lighthouse in the country. There are ruins of others, but Old Finkley is in good shape and well worth a visit. You can climb to the top and get a wonderful view of the whole northern tip. Now, in the centre of the northern tip – so pretty much between the two sites I've talked about – is Breedly Castle. There's not much left of it I'm afraid, but it was an important building in its day. It's a nice place to stop for a picnic. There are better preserved castles in other parts of the country. About a 20-minute drive south going back towards the west coast will take you down to the Kneads Estate. There's a lovely old manor house and some beautiful gardens. You can look around the manor house on Wednesdays and Saturdays. So, finally, heading back east and slightly to the south – and you might prefer to come here first as you drive up – is the Fowley Wildlife Park. It's more like a big farm than a wildlife park really, but the kids love it. There are all the usual farm animals and some llamas and deer too. They've got some go-karts too, if I remember rightly. So, I hope that's helped you and that …

Track 58
Unit 6 Listening 1

C Listen to the first extract and circle *Las Gaviotas* (A, B, C, D or E) on the map.
[Play **Extract 1** of Track 57 again]

Track 59
Unit 6 Listening 1

D Listen to the second extract and label the plan with ONE WORD in each space.
[Play **Extract 2** of Track 57 again]

Track 60
Unit 6 Listening 1

E Listen to the third extract and label the map. Choose from the box below and write five letters A–I next to the labels 1–5.
[Play **Extract 3** of Track 57 again]

Track 61
Unit 6 Listening 2

A Listen again. Notice examples of a speaker repeating information.
[Play Track 57 again]

Track 62
Unit 6 Listening 3

B Listen and answer the questions.
Voice: OK, are you all in now? Don't worry, the staff will bring your cases in from the coach. While they're doing that and while the reception get ready to check all your passports, I'll take you for a very quick mini-tour just so you get a feel for the hotel and know where everything is when you've unpacked and had a shower.

As you can see, this is the entrance area, or foyer, and the reception desk is here on your right. There's somebody at reception at all times – so if you have any problems this is where to come. You can change

traveller's cheques or exchange currency here at any time. Now, I'll show you outside in a moment. It's beautiful and sunny and I'm sure you all want to get out there, but let me just point out a couple of things in here first. The bigger room over to the left is the restaurant. There's the entrance you can see from the foyer and another entrance out on to the outside dining area. There are always tables outside when the weather's like it is now. The restaurant's mainly self-service, but there are chefs serving speciality dishes too. Next to the restaurant, just here to the left, is the main bar. You can buy drinks in the restaurant with your meals and from the bar that is set up outside in the evenings, but for an aperitif before you eat or a late drink after your meal, this is the best place to come. It's open from 11:30 right through to 1 a.m. Now, over to the right, next to the reception, is the shop. It's not huge, but you can buy guidebooks and maps and all sorts of gifts and souvenirs. There are newspapers and magazines from around the world too. OK, now if we walk through the foyer to the doors out to the back of the hotel, we'll see how lovely it is. When the weather's like this, you probably won't want be in the hotel much at all.

So, immediately outside is this dining area. The outside bar is here on the left – it's not open now, but it'll be set up around 8 o'clock before dinner. On the right here, there's a little stage. We have performances two or three nights a week at this time of year and there'll be information about what's on in advance. Ahead of you is the beach and the sea – doesn't it look beautiful? You can see that the pool is close to the sea, so you can hop back and forth from the pool to the beach, if you want to. As you might be able to see, there's a separate children's pool at one end. OK, the rooms are spread around the garden area. To the right, running up to the beach are rooms 8–14 and round the corner to the right are rooms 1–7. Rooms 15–21 are over to the left. Now, just round to the left at the end of the dining area is the towel collection and return. It's a sort of office I suppose – more like a hut really. You can collect a towel for the beach or pool and drop it off when you come back in the evening. I'm sure I don't need to say, but that means no towels from the rooms taken down to the beach. Now, I said you can hop from the beach to the pool all day, but we do ask people to shower quickly as they come off the beach so that the pool area doesn't get too sandy. If you look across to the little pathway that takes you onto the beach, you'll see that just to the left are a couple of showers. They're warm, so there's no excuse for not quickly cleaning off before you jump back into the pool. OK, what haven't I mentioned? Ah, yes – the sauna. At the end of the row of rooms over there – that's rooms 15–21 – is the sauna and jacuzzi area. Some of you will have paid for that as part of your package and some of you will have to pay a small charge for using it. It's very popular so you do need to book. Go to reception the evening before you plan to use it.

OK, I think they're ready in reception to check all the passports now, but let me quickly mention horse riding. We have two horses in the stable, which is at the end of the path that runs along the beach from the back of the swimming pool. You need to book a ride at reception and then go to the stable about 15 minutes before your booking. Somebody will be there then to make sure you have the gear and run through a few things with you.

Anyway, I'm sure you all want to get to your rooms as quickly as possible – your cases will be in the rooms when you go in. There are plenty of other things to do and there's information about excursions and so on in reception. So, if you'd like to just come back into the foyer and have your passports ready, we'll …

Track 63
Workbook Unit 6 Listening

A Listen to a conversation between a hotel receptionist and a guest and write the correct letter A–G next to the four places.

Guest: … mm, that's right … thank you. Can you tell me if the restaurant is still open? I know it's late, but I hardly had anything to eat on the plane – the meal was dreadful, actually.

Receptionist: I'm sorry, the restaurant's closed now, but there are two or three very nice places to eat within a few minutes of the hotel.

Guest: Oh, good. I'll have a quick shower and then get something. Which restaurant do you recommend?

Receptionist: Well, it depends what you fancy. Rosario's does pretty much everything, from steak to pizza, and it's very reasonable.

Guest: Where's that, then?

Receptionist: When you come out of the hotel, go left and then right. You'll come into a square and there are a few bars and restaurants around it. Rosario's is on the opposite side. You'll see it as you enter the square.

Guest: What are the other places in the square like?

Receptionist: They're all very nice, but a bit more expensive than Rosario's. Personally, I like the Chinese restaurant down by the harbour. That's only a few minutes walk too.

Guest: What's it called?

Receptionist: The Lotus Flower. Again, you go left out of the hotel and then walk straight down. Turn left when you get down to the harbour and you'll see it there, close to the corner.

Guest: Thanks. Oh, is there a cash-point nearby? I didn't have time to get any money at the airport.

Receptionist: Yes, there's a bank virtually next door. The cash-point's inside the entrance area. You'll pass it on your way if you go down to the harbour.

Guest: Great. Oh, one more thing. I'll need to get a taxi quite early tomorrow to get to the conference. The taxi that brought me in dropped me right outside the hotel, so I didn't see if there was a place to catch one. Shall I order a taxi from here or is there a rank nearby?

Receptionist: I can certainly order you a taxi from here but, frankly, it's better to just walk down to the rank. They charge a little more for picking you up here. You go right when you come out and walk straight down for three or four minutes. Then you take a right and the taxi rank is round the corner. I'll explain it again tomorrow morning, if you like. I'll be here when you leave.

Guest: Oh, that's good. I'm a bit tired to take it in now. Anyway, thanks again. I'll go and get changed now.

Receptionist: OK, I'll see you when you come back down. Enjoy your stay with us.

Track 64
Unit 7 Vocabulary 1

Pronunciation check
Mark the words below /θ/ or /ð/ depending on how *th* is pronounced. Listen and check.
bath
bathe
breath
breathe
truth
clothes
teeth
teething

Track 65
Unit 7 Speaking 2

B Listen to some students answering the questions. How do they give themselves time to think?
1
Examiner: Do you think your generation has a healthier lifestyle than your parents' generation?
Student: Mm, I haven't really thought about it before. I guess there are certainly more fast-food restaurants …
2
Examiner: What do you think about alternative approaches to health care, like acupuncture or aromatherapy?
Student: Mm, alternative approaches. It's not a topic I've thought about very much, but I suppose …
3
Examiner: Does the government of a country have a responsibility to promote healthy lifestyle options?
Student: That's a very good question. I don't really think the government should interfere too much in …
4
Examiner: Is an ageing population placing too much of a health care burden on taxpayers?
Student: Goodness. I don't know if I can answer that in a few words. It's a very big question. Personally, I think …

Track 66

Unit 7 Speaking 2

C Listen again and fill in the gaps.
   [Play Track 65 again]

Track 67

Unit 7 Listening 1

C Listen to the introductory part of the talk. Answer the questions below in pairs.

   Voice: Is everyone here? Could you come inside the room at the back there and close the door, please? You won't be able to hear me properly if you're standing out in the corridor. Thank you. I'm sorry there aren't enough seats for everyone. I'm afraid some of you will just have to make your notes leaning on a book or something. There are a few clipboards at the back of the room there if anyone wants one. Anyway, I'm not going to say a huge amount and you won't need to make copious notes. The idea is that the brief outline I give you now will help you decide what you want to find out more about for yourselves. I've got a few images to show you on PowerPoint too, so make sure you can see the screen.

   Right, I'm going to talk about transplants. I'm going to give you an overview, hopefully whet your appetite, and motivate you to go away and find more information. I want you to choose one of the transplants I talk about and do some detailed research. That means that when we then go into each transplant type in more depth over the next week or so, each of you feels that you're experts on at least one particular area of the topic. Clear?

   OK, so – what is a transplant? No, I don't want you to shout out. I'll tell you. A transplant – at least in medical terms – is the moving of an organ from one body to another for the purpose of replacing a damaged or absent organ. So, how long have doctors been able to perform transplants? The answer is 'not very long', especially if we're talking about transplants of the major organs that we associate with this type of surgery. Of course, there are numerous accounts of transplants taking place long ago, but these were not successful and in many cases were simply notions. The Chinese physician Pien Chi'ao, for example, is reported to have exchanged the heart of a man of strong spirit but weak will, with the heart of a man of weak spirit but strong will in an attempt to achieve balance in each man! I think we can safely say that the physical operation never actually took place.

Track 68

Unit 7 Listening 2

B Listen to the first part of the talk and complete the table.

   Voice: The first properly successful transplant was actually carried out in a small town in Czechoslovakia,

now actually in the Czech Republic, in 1905. This was a corneal transplant, a surgical procedure where the damaged cornea is replaced by donated corneal tissue. Look at the screen here and you can see some images of eyes that have been operated on in this way. OK, let's move along. Now, it was a while – just over 50 years in fact – before the next major breakthrough occurred. In 1954, in Boston, in the United States, a successful kidney transplant was undertaken. The donor and recipient were identical twins and this minimized complications. Previously, a kidney transplant had been concluded in Illinois, but the recipient's body rejected the organ ten months later.

   Now, we jump on another decade to the end of the 1960s, when there were some major advances in transplant surgery. The first pancreas transplantation was performed in 1966, in Minnesota, in the United States. A pancreas, along with a kidney and a duodenum, were transplanted into a 28-year-old woman. The patient was, as is the case in most instances of pancreatic transplant, a sufferer of diabetes. Her blood sugar levels decreased immediately after transplantation. Anyway, I'll let you discover more there, if that's the area you opt for.

Track 69

Unit 7 Listening 3

A Listen to the rest of the talk and answer the questions.

   Voice: Right, in 1967, the first liver and heart transplants were performed. The liver transplant was performed by a surgical team in Colorado. It should be stressed here that success is defined as one-year post-transplantation survival – a number of transplants that ultimately failed to sustain life had previously been attempted. The world's first human heart transplant was performed in Cape Town, South Africa, in the same year on a man called Louis Washkansky – this is him on the screen. Less than 50 years later, 3,500 heart transplants are undertaken worldwide every year.

   OK – lung transplants. This is complicated as, for so long, attempts failed due to bodily rejection of the donated organ. As early as the 1940s, doctors showed that the procedure was possible, but the first operation didn't take place until 1963 and then the patient lived for only 18 days. For the next 15 years, multiple attempts at lung transplantation failed because of rejection and problems with bronchial healing. It was only after the invention of the heart–lung machine, coupled with the development of immunosuppressive drugs, that a lung could be transplanted with a reasonable chance of patient recovery. The first properly successful operation involved a heart and lung transplant, performed at Stanford University, in the United States, in 1981.

Over the next 15 years or so, developments revolved around further successes with the organs we've already mentioned. It was in 1998 – not long ago at all – that we move into what some might think of as futuristic territory, when the first hand transplant was carried out. Again, there had previously been many failed attempts at the surgery over a long period – the first serious attempt was as long ago as 1944. Even this success in 1998 was only partial. The recipient failed to follow the prescribed post-operative drug and physiotherapy programme and in 2001 the transplanted hand was removed at his request. A year later, a fully successful operation was concluded – the recipient has almost normal use of his transplanted hand today. Look at the image here – I'm not sure if this illustrates either of the cases I've mentioned, but it shows you just how mammoth an operation this is.

In 2005, the first partial face transplant was a success in France. Previously, a patient's own face had been reattached and you can find out more about that if you want to. I warn you, the details are a bit grizzly! Two thousand and five saw the first case of a donor transplant. Isabelle Dinoire – this is her – underwent surgery to replace her original face that had been ravaged by her dog. A triangle of face tissue from a brain-dead human's nose and mouth was grafted onto the patient. In 2007, a report 18 months after the transplant stated that the patient was happy with the results, but that the journey had been difficult, especially with respect to the response of her immune system. In 2010, the surgery moved on to a new level. A team of 30 Spanish doctors carried out the first full face transplant on a man injured in a shooting accident.

So, there we have it. I'll finish there and you decide what you want to know more about. As I say, we'll be looking at each type of transplant in more detail, but if you have done some research yourself in preparation, you'll …

Track 70
Unit 7 Writing 1

C Listen to a doctor talking. Compare what she says with your ideas in Exercise B.

Interviewer: Now, the terms *medical tourism*, *medical travel* and *health tourism* were initially coined by the media. Of course the concept existed, but the labelling made far more people aware, and those terms have become quite pejorative. So, would you say this development in tourism is all negative?

Doctor: Oh, no. I certainly wouldn't say it's all negative. I think there are concerns, but not all negative … no.

Interviewer: Before we go into that, can you tell me what medical care really means? Are we talking about cosmetic surgery, for example, that doctors in the patient's own country wouldn't perform?

Doctor: No, … well, sometimes yes …, but generally no. People are travelling abroad to get operations done more quickly. There are long waiting lists in many countries and this is a way to queue-jump. Let's say that someone wants a hip replacement. They could be waiting up to a year in their own country. They look round and see that they can have the operation wherever they like. What makes it even more attractive is that it can be combined with a holiday. People choose places where the operation costs very little and then spend two or three weeks on the beach convalescing.

Interviewer: Can patients have any kind of surgery?

Doctor: Pretty much. Joint replacement – hips, knees and so on, is very common, but heart surgery is also popular and dental surgery is now taking off too.

Interviewer: So, why should all this be frowned on? Is it jealousy?

Doctor: No, I don't think it's just that. Perhaps people are sceptical about the idea of combining relaxation with something as serious as potentially life-saving surgery. Perhaps they do feel there's an element of wealthy people queue-jumping. But I think also, there's a concern about the standard of care. I mean concerns about the expertise of the people performing operations. In many of the countries in which medical tourism is popular, the people actually doing the operations may not be nearly as qualified as surgeons in the patient's own country. There are many stories of surgeons performing operations outside their immediate area of expertise and of trainee surgeons undertaking the most critical surgery.

Interviewer: So, are you saying that people are putting their lives at risk by seeking medical care – even serious operations – in places that they fancy going for a holiday?

Doctor: Mm … you put it in very stark terms. I'm not sure I'd put it quite like that, but then again I can't really say that it isn't the case.

Track 71
Unit 7 Writing 1

D Listen again and make notes.
   [Play Track 70 again]

Track 72
Unit 7 Consolidation – Speaking

B Listen to a student talking and answer the questions.

Examiner: OK, so are you ready?

Student: Yes, I think so. OK, … I was on holiday … on holiday in Egypt. I was swimming or more … um … you know, with a snorkel. There were lots of very coloured fishes and it was so beautiful. Suddenly….

um ... I felt a pain. Not a big big pain, but quite ... err ... well, it hurt. Then I couldn't feel one arm. I was afraid and I swam back to beach. It wasn't easy to swim when I couldn't feel one arm. I lay on the beach and I couldn't feel at all one arm and all the side of my body. I went to the lifeguard and told him. I was surprised because he laughed. He said it was a ... err ... a medusa ... no ... I mean ... err ... a jellyfish. He said it happened every day for someone. He put some fresh water on my arm and said I must lie and wait for it go away. It was about 20 minutes and then it went away. I didn't go back in the sea that day.

Track 73
Unit 7 Consolidation – Speaking

B Listen to the same student speaking again. What does she do better the second time?

Examiner: OK, so are you ready?

Student: Yes. Well, this was about six months ago. I was on holiday in Egypt and I was snorkelling. There were hundreds of colourful fish that were swimming right round me. It was absolutely beautiful. Suddenly, I felt a pain, a sharp pain and I didn't know what it was. Then one of my arms went completely numb. I couldn't feel it at all. I was scared and I swam back to the beach, which wasn't easy not being able to feel one arm. By the time I got to the beach, I was numb all down one side of my body. There were lifeguards all along the beach and I told one of them what had happened. I couldn't believe it when he started laughing. He said it was a jellyfish and this happened every day, at least once. He poured some fresh water from a bottle on my arm and told me I had to lie down and wait for the numbness to go away. It was about 20 minutes before my side started to feel normal. I didn't go back in the sea that day, I can tell you.

Track 74
Unit 7 Exam Practice – Listening

C Listen and complete the tasks.

Female student: So, the summer break's coming up soon. I take it you're both off somewhere exciting.

Male student: Mm, well, it'd be nice, but I'm going to have to work for the first few weeks to save enough to go anywhere worthwhile.

Female student: What about you, Tim?

Tim: Oh, I've already saved enough. There's no way I'm studying all year and then sitting around here all summer. I'm off to Asia – India, Nepal and then on to Thailand and Vietnam.

Male student: Wow, that sounds amazing.

Tim: Yeah, except one thing.

Male student: What's that?

Tim: I've got to have my jabs this afternoon – malaria, tetanus, typhoid and hep B.

Female student: Ouch! I hate jabs. So, is it supposed to be dangerous where you're going?

Tim: I'm not sure dangerous is the right word, but it's best to be safe.

Male student: Here look – I'm checking on my laptop. There's a site with loads of advice for students travelling to far-off places. Actually, it looks like you might be safer staying here.

Tim: What does it say?

Male student: Well, apart from the jabs you're having, there are several other diseases you might go down with – yellow fever, rabies and dengue fever are apparently quite common, as well as those you've mentioned.

Tim: Well, I'll just have to deal with those when I get them.

Female student: Are you sure you need jabs for all of those? I thought most people took malaria tablets these days.

Male student: Yes, they say here that that's an option. Mm, I didn't know you had to pay for precautionary treatment before travelling. None of this is on the NHS, then?

Tim: No, I'm going to have to cough up a small fortune on top of all the physical pain.

Male student: Well, speaking of small fortunes, they also insist on extensive travel insurance.

Female student: Oh yes – that's good advice ... especially if you've got an existing medical condition of any kind. You have to tell them about anything like that, or you're not covered.

Male student: I trust that's all in order.

Tim: Erm ... I wouldn't say it was extensive. I've got insurance, though.

Female student: So, come on then ... what else should we be careful of if we go travelling?

Male student: Well, they divide it up into a number of categories. The first category is all related to what you eat and drink. The most common complaint among travellers – students or otherwise – is a simple stomach bug.

Female student: You mean sickness and diarrhoea?

Male student: Yes – and there's nothing you can do about it.

Tim: Well, nothing once you've got it, but plenty to stop you getting it in the first place. Most people just take silly risks like drinking water straight from the tap, or eating meat that hasn't been cooked properly.

Female student: Yes, bottled water is the only sensible choice. I think everyone knows that.

Male student: Yes, that's more or less the advice they give, but it's easier said than done when you run out of money. Something they say here, that you might not have thought about, is to stay away from ice.

Female student: Oh yes, they'll put ice in your juice in cafes and so on, won't they?

Male student: They also say – well in some countries anyway – that you should stay away from fruit and salad – certainly unpeeled fruit anyway.

Female student: Oh dear, you like eating fruit with the skin on, don't you?

Tim: I'm sure I can peel it for a few weeks. I'll just have to eat lots of bananas.

Male student: The second category is about insect bites – oh, and bites from other animals.

Tim: Other animals? What like tigers?

Male student: No, like dogs, but I'll tell you about that in minute.

Female student: What do they say about insects, then?

Male student: Well, you can probably guess that mosquitoes are the biggest concern.

Female student: Will they have mosquito nets in the countries you're going to?

Tim: I think they have nets in the nicer hotels. I'm not so sure about hostels. They only protect you at night though. I'll make sure I take plenty of insect repellent – cream and sprays. I think you can get little devices that you plug in into the wall too.

Female student: And don't let insects come into rooms during the day. They'll probably have shutters everywhere you stay, so you can open the windows. Even if you haven't got air con, don't leave the doors open, and don't be tempted to open up the shutters. They let enough cool air in, but keep the mosquitoes out.

Male student: The most important thing really is covering up. I know it's hot in the places you're visiting, but baggy trousers instead of shorts is advisable, and socks are a really good idea, especially in the evening, apparently. However much cream you put on, your ankles are exposed under tables and so on.

Female student: So, what was it they said about dogs, then?

Male student: Oh, yes – there might be lots of stray dogs around. Don't approach or try to pet stray dogs. They're not friendly, and a bite will mean ending up in hospital … even if you've had all the right jabs.

Female student: They probably say something about staying out of the sun too, don't they?

Tim: Well, that's something I'm usually careful about – ever since I got burnt in Mexico.

Male student: Apparently, there's no such thing as a safe suntan. The bottom line is that exposure to sunshine increases the risk of skin cancer – even if you think you're tanning gradually. Young travellers spend more time at the beach and are more at risk, especially in places where they're not used to the temperatures.

Tim: Like Mexico. Don't worry, I've learnt my lesson.

Male student: It's not just about sunbathing, though. Very high temperatures that you're not used to can cause sunstroke. They say, gradually increase exposure to daytime sunlight. Don't go out and spend your first day walking round temples in extreme heat.

Tim: So, is that it? Can I start thinking about enjoying my trip yet?

Male student: Erm, no, we haven't mentioned accidents yet. Accidents are especially common …

Track 75
Workbook Unit 7 Listening

A Listen to a receptionist at a dental surgery talking to a patient and complete the form below.

Receptionist: Good morning, Albion Hill Dental Practice.

Man: Oh, good morning. I'd like to make an appointment. I haven't been in for some time now.

Receptionist: But you are a patient at the practice?

Man: Yes.

Receptionist: And the name is?

Man: Martin Thompson.

Receptionist: Hmm … ah, yes … Is that Thompson with a P or without?

Man: With a P … T-H-O-M-P-S-O-N.

Receptionist: Yes, I've got you here. You're at 63 Montreal Place, aren't you?

Man: Yes, that's right.

Receptionist: Now, since you haven't been in for a while, can you just update the postcode. Some of them have changed recently. Is it still MD2 4RQ?

Man: No, it's now 5RQ. They've decided we live further out of town.

Receptionist: Yes, mine changed too. Now, I've got a phone number, but not a mobile number – have you got a mobile?

Man: Yes, but I don't know the number from memory. Hang on … it's just on the side here … It's 0 double 7 89 4356496.

Receptionist: 07789 4356496.

Man: Uh huh.

Receptionist: Right, so do you want an appointment for this week?

Man: If possible.

Receptionist: Well, Thursday's not too full up. How about 11.15 on Thursday morning?

Man: Yes, that's fine. After I've seen the dentist, I usually see the hygienist. Can I book that now too?

Receptionist: Actually, you can't. See your last appointment was such a long time ago, the dentist will want to check and then refer you.

Man: Was it really so long ago?

Receptionist: It was February 2011.

Man: Was it really? OK, I'll sort out the hygienist when I'm in.

Receptionist: Yes, that's best. Is that all, then? We'll see you on Thursday.

Man: Oh, actually, there's something else … I nearly forgot. I want to book an appointment for my daughter.

Track 76

B Listen to the patient making an appointment for his daughter and complete the form below.

Man: I nearly forgot. I want to book an appointment for my daughter.

Receptionist: Is she on our books too?

Man: Yes, her name's Naomi.

Receptionist: Naomi Thompson. Ah, yes, I've got her here. She's seven now, then. That's a lovely age. My daughter's eight.

Man: Well, she's lovely some of the time. Can I make the appointment for her straight after mine?

Receptionist: Let me see. No, sorry, I can't. It'd have to be a couple of hours later.

Man: No, that's not very convenient. What about another day?

Receptionist: Erm … next Monday. What time?

Man: Well, after school's best. I don't want her to miss class time if she doesn't have to.

Receptionist: OK, I can slot her in at 3.45. Can you make it here by then?

Man: Yes, that should be OK. Thanks.

Receptionist: OK, We'll see you on Thursday and then again next Monday.

Man: OK, bye bye.

Track 77
Unit 8 Speaking 2

C Listen to three students answering the question and make notes for each exchange.

Speaker 1

Examiner: Do you think there should be restrictions on the level of construction in certain places?

Student: Definitely. Some of the biggest cities in the world are enormous – ridiculously big in my opinion. I think the authorities must have some kind of green belt around the city where construction is not permitted.

Speaker 2

Examiner: Do you think there should be restrictions on the level of construction in certain places?

Student: Yes, I do. In many parts of my country, the coastline is ruined by overbuilding. Now, everyone knows it was a mistake to allow such levels of construction and some of it has stopped. In some places, buildings are not allowed to be over a certain height – two or three storeys, for example.

Speaker 3

Examiner: Do you think there should be restrictions on the level of construction in certain places?

Student: Well, I think authorities and town planners have a duty to make use of brownfield sites rather than greenfield sites. I mean, they must build in the city centre where there's empty land or where buildings are derelict. In some towns in my country, building on greenfield sites is forbidden. There's a kind of green belt around the town to protect it from expanding anymore.

Track 78
Unit 8 Speaking 2

D Listen again, and then, in pairs, discuss the meaning of the words and phrases.
[Play Track 77 again]

Track 79
Unit 8 Speaking 2

E Listen one more time as you read the tapescript and check your answers in Exercise D below.
[Play Track 77 again]

Track 80
Unit 8 Listening 1

B Listen to three extracts. Match each with a picture from Exercise A. Write the letter in the space.

Extract 1

Estate agent: Well, this is it – The Cedars.

Client 1: Oh, it does look nice, doesn't it?

Estate agent: People's first impressions of this property are always really good, and I have shown it to a few people already, I warn you. We'll go inside in a moment, but just take a closer look at some of these shrubs and bushes. Mm, I can smell that jasmine from here.

Client 2: Those shrubs growing around by the gate, they're magnolia, aren't they?

Estate agent: Yes, they certainly are. The lawn is absolutely beautiful, look. Frankly, it wouldn't look out of place as the green on a top golf course. Can you see the fish pond over in the corner, there, too? I certainly wish I could get my lawn looking like this! When we've seen the house, I'll show you the back garden – believe me, it's …

Extract 2

Inspector: Oh, hello … hello.

Workman: Hi. Can I help?

Inspector: Yes, I'm here from health and safety. I'm a little bit later than I planned, I'm afraid.

Workman: Oh, right.

Inspector: Can I just ask straightaway about that scaffolding there? I mean, has it been up long?

Workman: Mm, I'm not sure – about a week I think.

Inspector: Really? Well, it doesn't look as stable as it could. I noticed it as soon as I arrived. Anyway, I guess I'd better tell the right person.

Workman: Yes, the state of the scaffolding's not really my business – you'll need to speak to the foreman.

Inspector: Yes, of course. Where I can find the foreman?

Workman: He's probably in his office now. That's over there, look. See the portable cabin with the blue car by it? He'll be in there. I'd take you over, but I've got to get on with …

Extract 3

Salesman: There are a number of advantages.

Customer: Yes, but I think I've heard them all before.

Salesman: In a house like this, having double glazing saves you money in the long term. It may cost you money now, but I can guarantee you won't be sorry you've had it put in.

Customer: But we've recently had the roof insulated and that was supposed to save us money. It won't save us money if we then have to have double glazing as well.

Salesman: Well, it will. Having insulation is always a good idea. It stops heat escaping through the roof, which is the main source of heat loss. However, draughts come in through doors and windows too, and if that's still happening, you don't get the full benefit of the insulation. Good insulation and double glazing complement each other.

Customer: Mm.

Salesman: What's more, you're pretty near the road here. I bet you can hear the traffic most of the time you're in the house. You'd be amazed at the reduction in noise levels once you've had …

Track 81
Unit 8 Listening 1

C   Listen again and choose the correct letter a, b or c.
[Play Track 80 again]

Track 82
Unit 8 Listening 1

E   Listen again and write key words and phrases in the spaces. You may need to guess the spelling.
[Play Track 80 again]

Track 83
Unit 8 Listening 2

B   Listen to a couple talking about buying an old house and check your ideas in Exercise A.

Jenny: Hello.

Dan: Hi, Jenny.

Jenny: Oh, hi, Dan.

Dan: So, did you go and see the house?

Jenny: Uh huh.

Dan: And?

Jenny: Pretty good. Well, as good as most of what we've seen so far. It'd certainly be worth you checking it out. I've put it on the 'to see again' list.

Dan: So, where is it exactly? I wasn't really sure where Abbey Road was.

Jenny: It's where we went to that party a few months ago. You know, that friend of Steve's.

Dan: Mm, I vaguely remember the party, not the place though.

Jenny: You know when you come out of London Road station … onto London Road? Abbey Road's kind of opposite, but just to the right. You walk up about 30 yards and then it's opposite.

Dan: Oh yeah … I remember … it runs directly off London Road. So, where's the house?

Jenny: It's a little way up on the left … not far from the house with the party.

Dan: So, what's good about it then?

Jenny: Well, there's quite a lot really. It needs work, but work we could definitely do … or that wouldn't cost too much to get done. The price reflects the condition.

Dan: So, are they all semis around there?

Jenny: No, no … it's detached. There's quite a decent-sized garden. It isn't huge, but it's definitely a possibility.

Dan: Four bedrooms?

Jenny: Yeah, but the loft could easily be converted into a fifth. I looked up there. It's big enough for a bedroom with a shower room. One of the two bigger bedrooms has a nice balcony overlooking the garden too, big enough to walk out onto and maybe put a couple of chairs.

Dan: That sounds nice.

Jenny: It's got a good-size cellar too. It's been left unloved and it's a bit dark and damp, but I reckon we could dry it out and make a really useful space out of it.

Dan: That's good too. What about the state of the plumbing and the heating and so on?

Jenny: Not good. That would need a complete overhaul. The central heating system's had its day. The radiators are old and I'd say the water tank needs replacing too.

Dan: That'd be quite a big expense then.

Jenny: It would … but we'll talk about it. The whole place needs rewiring too. The electrics look quite dodgy, frankly. Plumbing and electrics would be the biggest jobs.

Dan: OK, I guess anywhere we buy will need rewiring. What about the walls and so on … you know, general upkeep?

Jenny: Not too bad. There's plaster coming away from the walls in places. It's worst in the hall. I'd say some rooms need replastering, but not necessarily from scratch.

Dan: Mm … you know what's it's like. It's often easier to just take it all off and start again.

Jenny: Yeah, I guess so. Some floorboards need replacing too. There are a few gaps. The floors will all need to be stripped and treated, but a few boards will definitely need replacing.

Dan: OK, what about …?

Jenny: Oh … sorry, I interrupted … but the roof'll need a bit of work too.

Dan: Tiles coming off?

Jenny: No, not that so much …, though I didn't really check. It's more the chimney and guttering. The estate agent warned me that the chimney had been a bit damaged and since there's an open fire in the living room, we'd have to look at it carefully. The guttering's coming away from the roof all along the front elevation … the drainpipe down is pretty rickety too. I think that'll all need to go.

Dan: Well, that's not a huge job. Anything we go for will probably need that sort of thing doing. I'm guessing the kitchen's pretty old too.

Jenny: Oh yeah … well, that goes without saying. We'll need to fit a new kitchen and probably replaster it first. There are some really gross grey tiles all over the kitchen. They'll have to come off and I doubt what's underneath is very pleasant!

Dan: OK … well, you can fill me in on anything else when I get back this evening. I guess I'd better get back and do some work now. Remind me of the price again.

Jenny: It's on for 420,000, but I'm pretty sure they'd come down. The estate agent wouldn't say it directly, but I think he knows they won't get the asking price.

Dan: Yeah, 420's a bit steep. Anyway, thanks for going and seeing it. Would it be a good idea for you to get back onto the agent again to arrange for both of us to go …

Track 84
Unit 8 Listening 2

C Listen again and answer the questions.
   [Play Track 83 again]

Track 85
Unit 8 Consolidation – Speaking

A Look at the exchanges between an examiner and some students. Listen to the students answering the questions. What do you think about the students' answers?

1

Examiner: So, tell me about a part of your city that you like.

Student: I don't like any part of my city. It's a horrible city.

2

Examiner: So, Paris must be a lovely to place to study. You're very lucky.

Student: No, it's overrated. Everything's too expensive for a student like me.

3

Examiner: What do you think of that amazing new museum they've just built?

Student: I hate it. It's a blot on the landscape.

Track 86
Unit 8 Consolidation – Speaking

B Listen to the students answering the questions again. How are their answers better?

1

Examiner: So, tell me about a part of your city that you like.

Student: Actually, there are not many parts of my city that I really like. To tell you the truth, I'm getting bored of it and I'll be glad to move away next year.

2

Examiner: So, Paris must be a lovely to place to study. You're very lucky.

Student: Mm, yes and no. Of course, there are some amazing buildings and the tourists love it. For a poor student like me, though, everything's a bit too expensive.

3

Examiner: What do you think of that amazing new museum they've just built?

Student: Mm, if I'm honest with you, I'm not very keen on it. Some people say it's a blot on the landscape.

Track 87
Unit 8 Consolidation – Speaking

C Look at the tapescript and listen again.
   [Play Track 86 again]

Track 88
Workbook Unit 8 Listening

A Listen and match each social exchange with a situation. Write the number of the situation as your answer.

Exchange A

Woman: Hello.

Student: Hello, I'm phoning about the place advertised in the Gazette. Is it still available?

Woman: Yes … well, I think so, anyway. Some people saw it yesterday, but they haven't got back to me.

Student: Oh that's good. I expected it to be gone. Places are going so quickly now term's started. I know there are four bedrooms, but there are actually five of us looking. Are any of the bedrooms big enough to share or could the dining room be another bedroom?

Woman: Mm, there isn't really a separate dining room – it's part of the living room. The biggest bedroom is quite big, but there's only one bed. You'd have to get another bed yourselves and it'd be a bit of a squash with five in the house. I think we'd have to talk about that.

Student: OK, well we can decide on that if we come over and take a look. It might depend on the number of bathrooms – five of us trying to share one – especially when we're all getting ready in the morning – might be impractical.

Woman: There's only one bathroom, but there's a cloakroom downstairs. I'm afraid you would all be fighting over the bathroom.

Student: And is there any outside space – I mean some kind of garden?

Woman: There's a small yard. It's been paved over and there are a few shrubs in pots. It's not really a garden, though.

Student: That's fine – as long as there's somewhere to sit out when it's nice. Anyway, I think the best thing is to come over and see it. Would this evening be OK?

Woman: Mm, let me think. I'm busy till six, but I could get over there by about half past. Does that suit you?

Student: That'd be fine. Lorna Road's near the church on West Hill, isn't it?

Woman: Yes, that's right. It's number 35. If you wait outside, I'll see you there. Will you all be coming?

Student: I'm not sure. Probably not – but three or four of us perhaps.

Woman: OK, I look forward to meeting you all. Bye.

Exchange B

Male: So, this is the Court of the Lions. I've heard about this part.

Female: Yes, I've been reading a bit about it – it's one of the most important parts of the whole palace.

Male: So, tell me about these lions then.

Female: This is the Fountain of the Lions. There are 12 of them and, apparently, they represent strength and courage.

Male: They're not very big, though, are they? I mean, you'd expect them to be a bit more imposing.

Female: I don't know about that.

Male: So, what are they made of … marble?

Female: Yes, they're made of marble. The basin of the fountain's alabaster, but the lions are marble.

Male: Well, you certainly did do a bit of reading up. I wouldn't have expected you to know what the basin of a fountain was made of. Perhaps I should've made a bit more effort …

Exchange C

Interviewer: So, how did you decide to go into this particular line?

Architect: It was all very natural. Teachers and family friends recognized from an early age that I had talents that seemed to combine both science and art. I was drawing plans of buildings and town layouts as a hobby – rather a strange one, I guess – from the age of ten.

Interviewer: So, tell us what you really do. I mean, it's not just about drawing a plan is it?

Architect: No, there's far more responsibility than that and the role changes as the project develops. To start with, it's all about making sure that the plan allows the client to envisage the finished building. They want to know exactly what it's going to be like –

not wait until it's finished and then be horribly disappointed. It's the architect's job to organize and manage the engineers and the various designers involved in the project right through the process.

Interviewer: What is it you enjoy most about what you do?

Architect: There's huge satisfaction as a project comes to fruition and you realize that what you've achieved will have an impact on people's lives. I wouldn't enjoy doing this nearly so much if it were just an art form – I mean, if people simply looked at and admired my work. For me, the joy is creating something that'll be used by people.

Interviewer: Tell us about some of your favourite buildings.

Architect: Mm, that's difficult. There are so many …

Exchange D

Interviewer: What exactly is the difference between green building and conventional building?

Owner: I think it's all about using common sense. Too much construction focuses on the finish – I mean the aesthetic appeal – what the building looks like both inside and out. For us, the central issue is always the structure and systems – how the building is built. Green building means optimizing the infrastructure – the power, the heat and the water systems – and making the most of natural daylight to ensure efficient use of resources.

Interviewer: What are a couple of concrete examples?

Owner: Well, take water. Hot and cold water should be provided from a single trunk line. Branch lines should be minimized. Hot water pipes should be insulated to the point of use. That's not usually the case with most construction.

Interviewer: And is recycling and reusing an important aspect of this?

Owner: Absolutely. We reuse materials whenever we can. Timber off-cuts are used for smaller jobs – many builders throw so much away. If we can't make use of materials on a current site, we'll store it for …

Track 89

Workbook Unit 8 Listening

B Listen again, and, in each case, complete the notes.
[Play Track 88 again]

Track 90

Review 2 – Writing

A Look at the interviewer's first question and then listen to the first part of the interview. Mark the statements below (T) true, (F) false or (NG) not given.

Interviewer: Do students tend to do better in Writing Task 1 or 2?

Examiner: Mm, that's difficult to say because, of course, the second task carries more marks and students have more time to write it. There are students who practise writing reports and know how to do them very well. Their reports are well-organized and easy to read. In contrast, they find the composition more of a challenge. Perhaps they don't know quite what to say and they don't organize ideas well. However, they actually score slightly better for the second task because the whole idea is that it's more challenging.

Interviewer: So, it's a question of balance?

Examiner: Yes, it is. Students must time themselves and not write too much for the first task even if they feel this is where their strength lies. They have to leave enough time to do the second task properly as they gain more from that.

Interviewer: So, would you say the first task is easier?

Examiner: Well, it depends. I wouldn't say it's easier – even though it carries fewer marks. It's a much shorter piece of writing and students don't need to use complex grammatical forms like conditionals and so on, but for some students it's actually more difficult. They clearly find it quite hard to read the information properly and decide what's relevant. It's a very stylized piece of writing and that suits some people more than others. Some students clearly feel more comfortable debating an issue and expressing an opinion.

Track 91
Review 2 – Writing

B Listen to the second part of the interview about Writing Task 1 and complete the notes.

Interviewer: So, what are some things you notice about the first task in particular?

Examiner: Well, certainly the students who do best are the ones that keep things fairly simple. By that, I don't mean they use very basic English – that depends on their level – but that they say what needs to be said and no more. They pick out what's relevant and what will interest the reader and then they express that using the most appropriate language. I think they understand that report writing is formulaic. They don't try to be creative or explain why they think something is a trend, for example.

Interviewer: Is practice important?

Examiner: Oh, very much so – for both writing tasks, in fact – but I think I notice it more for the first task. An advanced learner – perhaps even a native speaker – would find writing a report, based on two pie charts say, challenging if they'd never practised it. It's like somebody who's been driving for years might not pass a driving test if they suddenly had to take one again.

Interviewer: What are the most typical problems with the first task?

Examiner: The most typical problem is trying to report too much of the information. Students who can

probably write very well make the mistake of trying to comment on almost everything shown by the figure. They write far too much or try to cram too much information into a sentence. It's very important to spend some time looking at the figure before starting to write. In theory, it's the language used that's important and not what information the student has chosen to report. However, if a very obvious piece of stand-out information has been ignored while something fairly irrelevant is the focus of a paragraph, it suggests that the student hasn't really understood the figure. Another common mistake is for students – usually lower-level students – to try to use complex language they don't really know how to use well. Of course, there are marks for well-expressed sentences that express comparison and contrast, but students must stick to language they can use confidently.

Interviewer: Do many students make the mistake of trying to explain the reason for information?

Examiner: It's not a common mistake, but it does happen. Some students seem to think that all writing is creative and they just can't resist suggesting why a trend might have occurred at a certain time, for example.

Track 92
Review 2 – Writing

C Put the points into the order in which you hear them.

Interviewer: What about Writing Task 2 – the discursive composition? What do you look for?

Examiner: Well, there are various things to look for and it depends on the level of the student. I can see straightaway if the composition is written by a lower-level student or by a more advanced learner. There are certain aspects of a composition that are essential – and that's the same for any student taking the exam. Firstly, what the student writes must be relevant to the question – it doesn't matter how well-written the composition is, it's no good if it doesn't answer the question. It's quite common that a student can clearly write English well, but he or she just didn't really know what to say about a particular issue. I think they panic and then start inventing things that are off the point. Again, practice is vital. Many of the composition topics come up quite frequently. If students practise writing discursive compositions, there's a reasonable chance that an issue they've written about before will come up in the exam and then it's much easier to have plenty to say.

Interviewer: So, is it important to plan and make notes?

Examiner: It's absolutely essential! IELTS Writing tasks are quite sophisticated, but they're not designed to trip students up. I mean the issues are always issues that an educated person would have something to say about. The idea is not to resolve the issue or even to say anything especially intelligent, but what is said must be relevant, and a bit of time spent thinking and jotting down some ideas is invaluable. Trying to think of what to say as you write is almost impossible.

Interviewer: How important is the word count?

Examiner: It's also vital. The second composition must be at least 250 words and a very short composition will lose marks. Again, planning is so important. Students can easily ensure a composition is the right length by giving an example from their own experience or an extra reason to support an opinion they've expressed.

Interviewer: And does planning mean better organization?

Examiner: Definitely. In a discursive composition, points must be made in a logical order and ideas should be introduced and concluded. You can't do that if you make it all up as you go. Apart from a general logical flow of ideas, students should understand the purpose of paragraphs and introduce each with a topic sentence that helps the reader follow the train of thought. Students with a higher level of English should be able to use a range of reference words – that is words that refer back to an earlier idea or forward to something that has not yet been introduced – and suitable linking devices.

Interviewer: What about vocabulary, spelling and accurate grammar?

Examiner: It's all about a sensible balance. Lower-level students should stick to saying what they know how to say, but more capable students need to show they can use a range of language. I'm not saying they should try to use really complex structures for the sake of it or show off with advanced vocabulary that isn't totally appropriate, but they do need to show the examiner what they can do. I get the impression that some very capable students don't really stretch themselves by using vocabulary they probably know. They should make a list of suitable words and phrases that relate to the issue while they're planning. Stronger students should be able to use the appropriate grammatical structures without having to try too hard – I mean they should come naturally. Finally, the student needs to use language that is appropriate in style and register. I see too many compositions that contain inappropriately informal expressions and are full of contractions. Even though I'm impressed that the student knows an expression, I can't give extra marks if it's used inappropriately.

Track 93
Review 2 – Writing

D Listen again as you read the tapescript.
[Play Track 92 again]

Track 94
Unit 9 Speaking 2

B Listen and check your answers. Then mark each expression (L) like or (D) dislike.

1

Examiner: So, since you're studying art, tell me which artists you like and why.

Student: Well, I absolutely adore Picasso. I know he's not to everyone's taste, but I think he was brilliant. His work is so powerful. Some people would call some paintings weird, but they're actually very accessible. I saw …

2

Examiner: And what about poetry? Do you ever read poetry?

Student: Mm, it's not really my thing. Of course, I've read some poetry as part of the course and there are poems I like, but really I prefer a good story.

3

Examiner: Which period are you especially interested in?

Student: I like modern art and I'm very keen on pop art, especially from America. I like Andy Warhol and Jasper Johns … I really like that they exploit mass media and the fact that there was music at the time that complemented their work.

4

Examiner: And do you like contemporary art as well?

Student: I'm afraid most of it doesn't do much for me. I guess it depends what you call contemporary, but there's nothing much from the last 50 years that I'm very impressed by. Like I said before, I really like …

5

Examiner: And what about a novelist from your own country? I mean, Kafka is one of the greats, isn't he?

Student: Mm, not for me I'm afraid. I just don't know what people see in him. I mean, of course, I appreciate the quality of the writing, but I find the content very dull and the plots are so complicated.

6

Examiner: Well, having studied so much Shakespeare, I guess he's one of your favourites?

Student: Actually, I've gone off him. Maybe I studied him too much. Now I prefer something a bit more up to date.

7

Examiner: So, what's the best book you've read recently?

Student: That's interesting. Normally, I'm not so keen on biographies – you know, I prefer fiction. But I've just read a biography of Elizabeth Taylor – I liked her very much as an actress. Really, I couldn't put it down. It was really fascinating.

8

Examiner: What kind of books do you like reading yourself?

Student: I'd like to say the classics, but I really read paperbacks – you know stories I can read quickly and are not too heavy. I'm a huge fan of Stephen King. I think I've read nearly all his …

Track 95
Unit 9 Speaking 2

Pronunciation check
Listen again to the exchanges and focus on the speakers' pronunciation.
[Play Track 94 again]

Track 96
Unit 9 Listening 1

B   Listen to the introduction of a talk and check your answers.

Voice: Over the next term, we're going to be looking especially at great female writers and where better to start – certainly for me anyway – than with the Brontës? I'm quite sure you all know something – perhaps quite a lot – about the Brontës, so forgive me if I tell you things you already know. I hope my introduction will help you enjoy the four novels that we'll be working on. So, the Brontë family lived in Hawarth, a village in West Yorkshire, in the 19th century. The environment was hugely instrumental as you'll come to appreciate. The literary sisters were Charlotte, born in 1816 – the best-known of her stories is, of course, *Jane Eyre*, but *Shirley* and *Villette* are also major works. Emily, born in 1818, known for her one astonishing novel *Wuthering Heights* and Anne, born in 1820, perhaps less known than her two sisters, but known for perhaps the most controversial of all the Brontë sisters' novels, *The Tenant of Wildfell Hall*. The sisters and their brother, Branwell, were very close and they developed vivid childhood imaginations through the collaborative writing of poems and stories. There were also two older sisters, but they died in childhood and this, together with the early death of their mother in 1821, had a huge impact on Charlotte, Emily and Anne's future work.

Track 97
Unit 9 Listening 2

A   Look at statements 1–8. Listen and match each statement with the correct sister A, B or C.

Voice: So … Charlotte was the eldest of the surviving sisters and probably the most successful in terms of the amount of writing actually published. Like her two sisters, she used a male pseudonym rather than her real name. At the time, it was not considered appropriate for women to be writers, and it was assumed that success was far more likely if readers thought that the story had been written by a man. Charlotte wrote mainly under the pseudonym of Currer Bell. After the death of their mother – as I've said, that was in 1821 – Charlotte was sent with three of her sisters, Emily, Maria and Elizabeth, to the Clergy Daughters' School in Lancashire. This was later the model for the school in *Jane Eyre*. Charlotte claimed that the dreadful conditions at the school were a major contribution to her own poor health and physical development, and the early death of her two elder sisters, Maria and Elizabeth. Back at home – their father took them out of the school when the girls died – Charlotte became the guardian and a mother figure to her two younger sisters despite their aunt, their mother's sister, living almost permanently at the house, as a carer. This is when the children began narrating the lives and struggles of characters from their imaginary worlds. Charlotte wrote tales of imperfect heroes, while Emily and Anne wrote articles and poems. At the end of her education, Charlotte worked briefly as a teacher and then as a governess to the children of wealthy Yorkshire families. This latter experience greatly influenced her writing. Around this time, together with Emily and Anne, Charlotte published a collection of poetry under the assumed names of Currer, Ellis and Acton Bell. Although only a handful of copies were sold, the inspiration to write for publication was born and just a little while later, Charlotte completed *The Professor*. Though this was rejected for publication, it was only a year later that the masterpiece *Jane Eyre* became an instantly popular phenomenon. Emily, the second sister, known really for her one novel *Wuthering Heights*, but what a novel! Emily, as I've said, was removed from school when her older sisters died and was educated at home. During this period, she and her younger sister Anne spent hours creating stories and poems about an imaginary island, Gondal. The girls even enacted scenes from their stories. Surviving diary pages show clearly that the extraordinary imagination and originality responsible for *Wuthering Heights* blossomed at this time. When she was 17, Emily attended the girls school where Charlotte was a teacher, but managed to stay only three months before being overcome by extreme homesickness. She tried working as a teacher herself for a while, but the 17-hour day was too much and she returned home, becoming the housekeeper of the family. It was in 1845 that Charlotte discovered how much poetry Emily and Anne had written and she insisted that the work be published. Emily was at first furious that her privacy had been invaded and refused to allow her work to be shared. She relented when she realized that Anne too had been so prolific. As previously suggested, it was this, despite the commercial failure of the collection, that drove the sisters to keep writing, and Emily was compelled to write her masterpiece.

The youngest sister, Anne, certainly isn't a household name like Charlotte and Emily, but nonetheless, her contribution to literature is notable and, as I previously suggested, *The Tenant of Wildfell*

Hall is possibly the bravest … certainly for its time … of all the Brontë novels. Anne spent most of her life with her family in Haworth. She was only a year old when her mother died, and while the older siblings found it difficult to establish a relationship with the rather stern aunt who now cared for them, Anne was shown real affection and was said to be her favourite. For a couple of years, Anne went to a boarding school, but when her older sisters were brought home, she was too and, as we've heard, the great period of creativity began. Anne and Emily were especially inseparable and started writing their tales and poems about Gondal. Anne worked, like her eldest sister, as a governess, but the children in Anne's charge were wild and spoilt and persistently disobeyed her. She had great difficulty controlling them and very little education was achieved. Anne was soon dismissed and returned home to join Charlotte and Emily. This episode was so traumatic for Anne that she reproduced it in almost perfect detail in her first novel, *Agnes Grey*. This first novel, though successful, was overshadowed by the epic *Jane Eyre* and dramatic *Wuthering Heights*. Anne's second novel, *The Tenant of Wildfell Hall*, was published in 1848 and was an instant phenomenal success, selling out within six weeks.

Track 98
Unit 9 Listening 3

A   Look at the statements 1–8 about four of the Brontë sisters' novels. Then listen to a continuation of the talk and match each statement with the correct title A, B, C or D.

Voice: Now, onto a quick overview of the Brontë novels we'll be focusing on this term. I'm sure from what I've already said that you can guess which novels those will be – well, at least three of them. *Jane Eyre* is Charlotte's gift to literature – one of the most important pieces of Victorian writing, perhaps most important of any time. It was described at the time as an influential feminist text because of its in-depth exploration of a strong female character. Apart from the intricate plot, there is a great deal of social criticism. The story has a strong sense of morality at its core and the actions of characters are so expertly depicted. It is in many respects a rites of passage novel, following Jane's development from abused child through to mature woman. The story of Jane's transformation from a poor, plain girl into a charming, confident, self-reliant lady was certainly ahead of its time. During Jane's childhood, she's emotionally and physically abused by her aunt and cousins. During her education at Lowood School, she makes friends and learns from role models, but also suffers oppression. During her time as a governess at Thornfield Hall, she falls in love with her charismatic

employer, Mr Rochester. All this is clearly influenced by Charlotte's background, which I described earlier. Charlotte's third novel, *Villette*, published in 1853, reworked ideas from her unsuccessful first novel, *The Professor*. The protagonist, Lucy Snowe, travels to the fictional city of Villette to teach at an all-girls school, where she is pulled into adventure and romance. The novel is celebrated more for its study of Lucy's character than for its plot. Earlier themes are revisited. Once again, there is a fiery male schoolmaster and, once again, there is no smooth passage to love. The final pages are ambiguous. Lucy – the story is told in the first person – says that she wants to allow the reader to imagine a happy ending, but she strongly implies that, in fact, the story ends in tragedy.

Emily's *Wuthering Heights* – and once more I should stress that this was her only major work – is one of the best-loved and frequently studied stories of all. The novel met with mixed reviews when it first appeared, mainly because of its dark description of mental and physical cruelty. Though Charlotte's *Jane Eyre* was generally considered the best of the sisters' works for most of the 19th century, more recent critics of *Wuthering Heights* have claimed that it was a superior achievement. Interestingly, the second edition of *Wuthering Heights* was edited by Charlotte after Emily's death. The narrative tells the tale of the passionate, but tragically thwarted love between the protagonist Catherine Earnshaw and Heathcliff, an abandoned boy who is adopted into her family. The unresolved passion eventually destroys them and people around them. For many people, it seems incredible that Emily Brontë, a young sheltered girl, who spent her time looking after the family home, could write a story of such intense emotion.

And finally, Anne's second novel, *The Tenant of Wildfell Hall*, published in 1848 under the pseudonym Acton Bell. As I've said, perhaps the bravest, even the most shocking of the Brontës' novels. It had an instant phenomenal success and sold out. After Anne's death, however, Charlotte prevented its republication. The novel, like Anne's first, is written in a sharper, more realistic style than the romantic style of her two sisters. It tells the story of a mysterious widow, Helen, who arrives with her young son at Wildfell Hall, a country mansion that has been empty for many years. She lives there under an assumed name and soon finds herself the victim of cruel gossip. In her diary, Helen writes about her husband's physical and moral decline through alcohol, and the world of cruelty and shame from which she has escaped. The novel is considered to be one of the first sustained feminist novels. Aspects of the story caused great controversy in Victorian Britain, where, by fleeing from her husband, Helen violates not only social conventions, but also English law at the time.

Track 99
Unit 9 Listening 3

B Listen to the part of the talk about *Jane Eyre* again.
   Complete the sentences below.

   Voice: *Jane Eyre* is Charlotte's gift to literature – one of
   the most important pieces of Victorian writing,
   perhaps most important of any time. It was
   described at the time as an influential feminist text
   because of its in-depth exploration of a strong female
   character. Apart from the intricate plot, there is a
   great deal of social criticism. The story has a strong
   sense of morality at its core and the actions of
   characters are so expertly depicted. It is in many
   respects a rites of passage novel, following Jane's
   development from abused child through to mature
   woman. The story of Jane's transformation from a
   poor, plain girl into a charming, confident, self-reliant
   lady was certainly ahead of its time. During Jane's
   childhood, she's emotionally and physically abused
   by her aunt and cousins. During her education at
   Lowood School, she makes friends and learns from
   role models, but also suffers oppression. During her
   time as a governess at Thornfield Hall, she falls in
   love with her charismatic employer, Mr Rochester. All
   this is clearly influenced by Charlotte's background,
   which I described earlier.

Track 100
Workbook Unit 9 Listening

B Listen and Label each picture with the name of the
   movement it is an example of.

   Interviewer: So, do you feel that there have been any
   significant developments in art over the last 20 or so
   years, or is it a case of simply redefining and dressing
   something up as new?

   Speaker: Well, that's a good question because, of
   course, so many so-called art movements really are
   all about rehashing – I mean rather pretentiously
   claiming that something is fresh and innovative when
   actually it's very little different to what's come before.
   For that reason, I want to concentrate on three
   movements that I really do believe are innovative.
   They may not be totally new in terms of the images
   created, but they are certainly fresh in the way that
   the work is available – I mean how and where people
   access the work.

   Interviewer: And you're going to concentrate on
   developments or movements, if you like, that have
   emerged since the domination of conceptual art that
   defined the art world during the 70s and 80s.

   Speaker: Yes, I am. Let me start in the 1980s, in fact,
   with sound art. Now, sound art was really a direct
   step on from conceptualism – I mean the idea that
   anything could be art. Personally, I'm not a huge fan
   of sound art, but I do think it's challenging and

interesting. Many people might argue that it's actually
more about music than art, but I think that's short-
sighted. The aim of the artist isn't to make music. It's
to make a statement through the medium of sound,
often combined with visual imagery – paintings or
sculpture – and very frequently with an environment
or installation of some kind. The relationship between
the sound and the other features of the art is the
essential element. It's also different from music in that
acoustics are more important than notes or melodies
– I mean the way the sound travels and interacts with
physical objects.

Interviewer: Isn't that what experimental music is
supposed to be about?

Speaker: Yes, I admit there's still debate about whether
sound art can really be categorized as art or whether
it would be better labelled as experimental music. In
2010 – it took a long time to catch on! – the Turner
Prize was won by an artist who sang various
overlapping versions of an ancient Scottish song
played back through loudspeakers. There was no
visual element at all and the honour was seen as an
important boost for this relatively new genre.

Interviewer: Mm, interesting. I know you want to talk
about the Internet now and how that's changed art,
or at least where people look at it.

Speaker: Yes, now I'm a bit sceptical about all the
different labels and movements that are supposed to
exist. In the 90s, we had new media art and Internet
art. Now, we have video game art and virtual art.
Frankly, they're all a slight twist on what's ultimately
the same basic concept. Internet art, or net art, as
it's often called, is digital artwork distributed over the
Internet. For me, the interesting thing is that this form
of art has bypassed the traditional dominance of the
gallery system, delivering aesthetic experiences
directly to the viewer – that may be at home or while
they're at work. The viewer is often drawn into some
kind of interaction and messages – just like many
forms of art over the centuries – are frequently social
and political in nature.

Interviewer: So, I assume that a Van Gogh painting
downloaded and sent as an attachment is not net art.

Speaker: No, certainly not. Simply digitalizing existing
images is not the point. Lots of traditional artists now
exhibit their work in online galleries. That doesn't
mean they're net artists. Net art relies intrinsically on
the Internet to exist, taking advantage of interactive
interface and connectivity to multiple social and
economic cultures. Net art can be created through
websites, e-mail collaborations, original software
projects and the creation of games. It may also
include video and audio elements.

Interviewer: It sounds to me as though you're saying
that the Internet itself is art – I mean, that almost any
feature of the net can be seen as an art form.

Couldn't this have been said about all sorts of previous aspects of design, like packaging?

Speaker: I think it was.

Interviewer: Mm. You're going to tell us about street art now. I don't know a great deal about it, but I'd like to. I sense that there's something a bit more substantial here – something really a bit different.

Speaker: Well, perhaps, though, as I said, it's the where the art exists that is different – not necessarily the imagery itself. Street art is any art created in public spaces – that is, usually in the streets. Street art typically refers to unsanctioned art rather than government or local authority-sponsored art. Very much as with graffiti, once it is allowed and people accept it, it loses some of its purpose and appeal.

Interviewer: So, is street art really graffiti, then?

Speaker: No, definitely not. While traditional graffiti artists used free-hand aerosol paints, street art encompasses a range of media and techniques, including mosaic and tiling, murals and stencils. Street installations are popular, as is video projection. A new angle is sticker art, where art is produced and then stuck onto walls or other surfaces in public places.

Interviewer: So, in many respects, it's traditional art that's been taken out of the studio and gallery and onto the street?

Speaker: Absolutely. Street artists claim that they don't aspire to change the definition of art, but rather to question the environment in which it exists.

Interviewer: So, what are the legal implications? I mean, graffiti was and still is often just vandalism. Is street art more acceptable?

Speaker: Some street artists have become very popular very quickly, and have sold work to well-known collectors or commissioned to create work for advertisers. Street art has a veneer of respectability that graffiti didn't. However, most street artists create their work in order to spread a social or political message and some of it is still quite simple and very subversive. For this reason, street art is sometimes referred to as post-graffiti. I'd say that most street artists don't wish to become part of the establishment.

Interviewer: Yes, I'd be interested to know how exactly a collector goes about buying a painting on the wall of a city centre building or a video projected onto a bridge in the middle of the night. It does seem that once …

Track 101

Workbook Unit 9 Listening

C   Look at the statements 1–8. Listen and match each statement with the correct movement A, B or C.
[Play Track 100 again]

Track 102

Workbook Unit 9 Listening

D   Read the tapescript as you listen again. Make a note of any new words and phrases that you think are useful.
[Play Track 100 again]

Track 103
Unit 10 Vocabulary 1

Pronunciation check
Listen to these words that contain the sound. Then practise saying them.
1   lightning
2   frightening
3   frightened
4   certainly
5   important

Track 104
Unit 10 Speaking 1

A   Listen to some interview exchanges. Make notes about what each student says.
    1
Examiner: Do you have four seasons, like in European countries?
Student: No, we don't. We have a rainy season and a dry season. It's the rainy season now, so we expect some rain most days. Sometimes it's just overcast or there are a few showers, but on other days there are severe storms and very heavy rain. It can be very humid – muggy, I think you say.
    2
Examiner: Would you say the weather influences the Spanish lifestyle?
Student: Definitely – probably like in all countries where there is a lot of sunshine. We can depend on the weather to be good for several months of the year and this allows us to enjoy an outdoor lifestyle. People drive to the coast at the weekend or arrange parties in their gardens. You see people sitting outside restaurants to have dinner – not like in the north of Europe, where everyone eats inside.
    3
Examiner: So, what do you think of our English weather?
Student: Um, I don't want to sound too negative, but I get a bit fed up of it. I have to carry an umbrella all the time, but I still get soaked on the way to college most mornings. I think the frequent bad weather stops people doing a lot of outdoor activities and it discourages them from arranging to meet friends for a picnic or barbecue. In Brazil, we have social events like that very often.

Track 105
Unit 10 Speaking 1

C   Listen again and complete the sentences.
    [Play Track 104 again]

Track 106
Unit 10 Speaking 2

C   Listen and match each student with a question in Exercise B.
Student A
Student: That's a very difficult question. I think it's possibly a bit of both. Of course, we know that glaciers and ice caps are melting and there have been extreme heatwaves in some countries, but the winters are still very cold – maybe even colder than before. It seems more a case of the weather becoming more extreme, rather than it just getting hotter. I think there are some reports that spread panic.

Student B
Student: Well, many people say it is and sometimes I think it is. It seems that summer days are hotter each year and winters go on for longer. Now, it seems there's no spring at all – one day it's cold and then it's summer! However, when I think back to when I was little, it was just the same. I remember at least two winters when there was lots of snow and summers when it was too hot to go out.

Student C
Student: It's a good question. I think some events like hurricanes probably have always happened and will always happen, but there are other events like floods and mudslides that people cause. I don't understand completely, but I heard that we cut down too many trees and then they don't hold the rainwater. This results in floods that we say are 'acts of God' even though we made them happen. Also, we build towns and villages in places where we know there are extreme conditions. I think we must say then that we are partly to blame if there's a catastrophe.

Track 107
Unit 10 Speaking 2

D   Listen again as you read the tapescript. Notice that you do not need to be an expert to give a good extended answer.
    [Play Track 106 again]

Track 108
Unit 10 Listening 1

B   Listen to the first part of a lecture about how deforestation can cause mudslides. Check your ideas in Exercise A.
Voice: So, we've been looking at global warming and this week we've been focusing on deforestation and thinking about some of the consequences of that. If you remember, I told you that an area something like the size of Panama is cut down in various parts of the globe each year – a huge rate of destruction. We've seen how deforestation deprives wildlife – not to mention the very few indigenous tribes that still reside in the rainforest – of natural habitat and how the loss of unique plants may mean losing opportunities to find the natural remedies for disease – we may be wiping out future cures of cancer in our haste to build roads and infrastructure. Today, we're going to concentrate on the so-called natural disasters that can be a direct cause of deforestation – how mudslides occur on steep slopes stripped of vegetation when torrential rain or earthquakes destabilize them. Mud can flow down the slopes, sometimes at high speeds, gathering rocks and debris, and can completely destroy buildings and bury villages.

Track 109
Unit 10 Listening 1

C   Listen again and write down some of the other effects of deforestation that were mentioned.
    [Play Track 108 again]

Track 110
Unit 10 Listening 2

A   Listen to the next part of the lecture and complete the first part of a flow chart.
Voice: So, what are the reasons for deforestation in the first place? Let's go back over the causes before we move on. First of all, *ranching* – that is, clearing land so that cattle can feed. Of course, this is not the cattle of local farmers, but ranching on a huge scale that provides produce for international markets. Secondly, *logging* – that's cutting down the trees for timber – not simply burning the rainforest to clear it, but to use the wood the trees provide. Thirdly, *construction* – this is more often than not road building as parts of countries are linked. It may also be the construction of new residential areas as populations increase. Finally, forests are cleared for *mining* – gold and silver mining are common in areas where rainforest exists and new sources of precious metals are exploited wherever they may be.

Track 111
Unit 10 Listening 3

A Listen to the rest of the lecture and complete the flow chart.

Voice: Onto the specific theme of today's lecture then – mudslides. You've probably heard the term *landslide* before – that's pretty much the same thing, but we use *mudslide* when the soil and debris that slides consists of a lot of water – it's wet – it's mud! To illustrate how serious an event a mudslide can be, let me say that in 1999, a mudslide in Venezuela was responsible for taking 20,000 human lives when torrential rain pounded down onto deforested hillsides. The trees in the rainforest stop soil eroding in various ways. Most importantly, underground, their tight-knit root systems keep soil in place and hold it to the bedrock below. Tree litter – that's fallen leaves, branches and twigs – slows water runoff which occurs when it rains. Obviously, when the rain is torrential, this water runoff is far more evident and causes far more damage. It carries away topsoil, weakening the foundation that lies below. When land, especially land on slopes and hillsides, is stripped of vegetation, this whole layer of protection disappears. When there are storms and rain is especially heavy, often during the rainy season, in many areas where mudslides occur the chances of a catastrophe are far higher. Large areas of hillside or chunks of rock give way and start sliding downwards. In some cases, a single relatively small chunk of hillside can cause untold damage if close to an area of residence – perhaps just an isolated farmhouse or a tiny mountain village. Generally speaking, however, the area of land that slides is high up on the hillside and the potential for catastrophe is even greater. By the time the original breakaway chunk arrives at the foot of the slope, it may be far, far bigger. As the land slides – and let's remember that we're talking about thick wet mud, so perhaps we should say *flows* rather than *slides* – it picks up more soil as well as rocks and any other debris in its path. If the slide has already destroyed one or two hillside homes, it will have picked up and be carrying substantial amounts of solid matter – perhaps even cars and other large pieces of machinery. When the mudslide arrives at the bottom of the slope, it can completely destroy whatever is in its path and bury whole villages. In 2006, a mudslide completely covered a village in the Philippines, killing 57 people in just two minutes. As deforestation accelerates – and remember, we've said that an area of rainforest the size of Panama is cleared annually – catastrophic mudslides increase in frequency. The most pessimistic estimates conclude that our rainforests could vanish within 100 years. Fortunately, there's now awareness and a realization that destruction cannot continue and governments in many of the countries which …

Track 112
Unit 10 Listening 3

Key vocabulary in context

C Listen and mark the main stress on the words from the lecture.
1 indigenous
2 precious
3 accelerate
4 catastrophe
5 catastrophic

Track 113
Unit 10 Exam Practice – Listening

C Listen to the talk and answer the questions.

Voice: Now, I'm sure you're all here to find out what to do to stop your water pipes freezing and bursting, but first let me say something about why pipes burst and why here in the south, where it's warmer than in many parts of the country, you're actually more at risk. Most people assume that in cold northern climates there's more risk of pipes freezing up, but in fact, houses in northern climates are generally built with the water pipes located on the inside of the building insulation and that, of course, protects them from sub-zero temperatures.

Houses in slightly warmer climates are more vulnerable to winter cold spells. Water pipes are more likely to be located in unprotected areas outside of the building insulation, and homeowners are very often not as aware of freezing problems, which probably only occur once or twice a year. Pipes in lofts and attics, pipes in basements and crawl spaces and pipes in outside walls are all vulnerable to freezing, especially if there are cracks or openings that allow cold, outside air to flow across them. Holes in an outside wall where a television cable or telephone lines enter can also provide access for cold air that can affect water pipes.

So, water pipes freeze and burst because cold air gets to them – remember that when you're warm inside, temperatures outside might be far lower and water pipes that are exposed might be getting much colder than you realize. I don't want to alarm you though – the majority of burst pipes occur when homes are left empty for a while or when the heating inside is simply not sufficient to keep the whole house warm enough. Now, water expands when it freezes – have you ever put a can of soda or a bottle of wine in the freezer to chill it quickly, but then forgotten about it? What happened? It exploded and you spent an hour clearing up the mess! Well, when water freezes in a pipe, it expands in the same way. If it expands sufficiently, the pipe bursts, water escapes and there's some serious damage to contend with. Now, what surprises people is that it isn't ice forming in a pipe that directly causes a break – the split doesn't occur where the ice blockage is. The expansion of the ice against the wall of the pipe isn't the issue. What actually happens is that when a pipe is completely blocked by ice, the water pressure increases downstream – that is, between the blockage and a closed tap at the end. Upstream from the ice blockage there's no danger as water can always retreat back towards its source – there's no build-up of pressure. A water pipe usually bursts where little or no ice has actually formed. This doesn't really matter much to the homeowner, though, as he or she is faced with a clean-up and repair bill when water escapes.

So, what can homeowners do to stop water pipes freezing? Well, quite a lot in fact – pipes that are protected along their entire length by placement within the building's insulation, insulation on the pipe itself or by a sufficient level of heating within the building, are safe. The ideal solution is to place water pipes only in heated parts of the house and to keep them out of the vulnerable areas we've mentioned – lofts, attics, basements and so on. Of course, in modern buildings this is taken for granted and there's really not an issue. In existing houses, it's sometimes possible, though not always practical, to re-route pipes to protected areas. A more realistic and common solution is proper insulation. Vulnerable pipes that are accessible should be fitted with insulation sleeves or wrapped with insulation – the more the better. It's important not to leave gaps that expose the pipe to cold air. Hardware stores and DIY centres will have the necessary materials – sleeves are usually made of foam rubber or fibreglass. Specialist plumbing supply stores will have pipe sleeves with extra-thick insulation and you may feel that the added protection's worth the extra cost. Even if your pipes are well-insulated, it's important to seal cracks and holes on outside walls as these allow cold air in. Another simple solution is to allow taps to drip – this won't guarantee that pipes don't freeze, but it makes it less likely. If there's a spell of extremely cold weather, allow taps to drip. It's not that a small flow of water prevents freezing – this helps, but water can freeze even with a slow flow. It works because opening a tap slightly prevents the build-up of pressure that we've said actually causes the burst in the pipe. If there's no excessive pressure, a pipe won't burst, even if the water inside the pipe freezes.

So, this brings me to what to do if a pipe does freeze and if you suspect that you have a frozen pipe somewhere in the house. If you open a tap and no water comes out …

Track 114

A   Listen to a news report about an unusual weather event and answer the questions.

Newsreader: People in parts of the UK woke up this morning to find their houses and cars coated in a layer of yellowy-brown dust. The cause was sand, which had been carried on the wind all the way from the Sahara Desert. Meteorologists quickly allayed any fears, saying that the settled dust was harmless and posed no health risk. The sand, which was blown at high altitude from North Africa, fell overnight during showers of light rain, while most people were in bed, so any possible disruption was limited.

The event is very rare – the last time something similar was reported was nearly 15 years ago. Airstreams that affect the UK usually arrive from the Atlantic, but, recently, winds have been blowing in from the desert region of Africa. Areas of Spain and France were also affected. In France, drivers reported reduced visibility, though the majority of journeys were completed. Spain was harder hit, and a number of flights from airports in the south were delayed due to conditions deemed to be unsafe. I'm joined now by Tim Atkins from our weather team, who's going to explain what probably happened. Tim.

Weather forecaster: Yes, well, as the wind blows across the Sahara every day, it lifts off particles of sand – huge amounts of it in fact. When there are sandstorms – and that's quite common in the Sahara – greater quantities of sand are picked up and carried over long distances. A light wind starts a sandstorm by lifting the top layer of very fine particles. These particles start vibrating and then saltate – that means jump around. As the particles swirl around, they loosen more sand, which also saltates. Before long, the sand is travelling in suspension and a sandstorm is underway. Large sandstorms can cover a huge area and it's little wonder that some of this sand is then carried over long distances. As you said, the unusual wind direction meant that, on this occasion, sand was carried all the way to Europe.

Newsreader: Thanks Tim. I'll finish by saying that though people here may have been inconvenienced, what they experienced is nothing compared to one of the most notorious cases of Sahara sand over Europe. In 1947, many parts of the Swiss Alps were turned pink and remained pink for several days after red dust was carried on winds from Algeria after a severe sandstorm.

Track 115

B   Listen again and answer the questions.
[Play Track 114 again]

Track 116
Unit 11 Speaking 1

D Listen to somebody describing a situation and answer each of the questions she poses. Then discuss the situation in your pair.

Voice: Imagine you are waiting for the results of a test or exam that you've just done at school or university. You go into class and your teacher or tutor tells you that you scored 95% in the test. How do you feel – proud, delighted? Are you looking forward to comparing your result with the other students when they arrive? The other students start to arrive and the teacher tells them their scores. All of the other students have scored between 97% and 100% – half of the class, in fact, have scored full marks. Your score is actually the lowest in the class! Does this change the way you feel? Can you explain why? What's important to you – doing well and fulfilling your potential or doing better than other people?

Track 117
Unit 11 Vocabulary 1

Pronunciation check
Listen to the words and phrases carefully and then practise saying them in pairs.
1 my big break
2 set goals
3 last chance
4 make plans
5 don't hold back
6 take good care

Track 118
Unit 11 Speaking 2

B Listen to some students answering the questions.
1
Examiner: Does succeeding mean doing better than other people?
Student: No, I don't think so.
Examiner: … So, what do you think success really means …
2
Examiner: Why do you think some people succeed while others fail?
Student: Mm, that's a good question. For me, succeeding is all about achieving what you set out to achieve and perhaps even becoming well-known for doing that – somebody who writes a novel or an athlete who wins a gold medal in the Olympics, for example.
3
Examiner: Is it easier for people from certain backgrounds to succeed?
Student: Yes, I think you have to say that it is. Of course, there are many examples of people from poor backgrounds who do great things – they

succeed against all the odds, if you like – but in reality, people who have a good education and are surrounded by successful people are much more likely to do well in life.
4
Examiner: Do you think success brings happiness or that happiness equals success?
Student: I think both of these can be true and depends on the person. If somebody achieves his … erm … his …, you know, it will make him happy. But also, somebody what is very … err …. contended with his life can say he is successful. It goes both ways, I think.

Track 119
Unit 11 Speaking 2

C Look at the tapescript and listen again.
[Play Track 118 again]

Track 120
Unit 11 Listening 1

B Listen to extracts from each section of the Listening test. Identify which section you think each extract comes from.
Extract A
Father: Look, what we're saying is that we moved heaven and earth to get you onto this course and now you're just not making the most of the opportunity.
Lucas: What do you mean, moved heaven and earth?
Father: You know exactly what I mean. Your exam results weren't that good and we had to persuade the college to accept you. We talked about the fact that there would be other students on the course who'd find it less challenging and you promised to make an effort.
Mother: Yes – that's all we ask – make an effort – do your best. We don't expect miracles and we're not asking for super high marks or anything.
Lucas: So, why do you assume I'm not making an effort?
Father: Oh, come on Lucas. We've read the report – you've read the report. It's just like all those school reports we fell out about, isn't it? The bottom line is there's always something you'd rather be doing than working towards a future.

Extract B
Voice: It's interesting that the Russian anarchist philosopher, Peter Kropotkin, viewed the concept of survival of the fittest not as competition or in any way the modem perception of people climbing over one another to succeed, but as supporting co-operation. He coined the phrase 'mutual aid', having concluded that the fittest was not necessarily the best at competing individually, but often the community consisting of those best at operating together. In the animal kingdom, the vast majority of

species live in societies – association is the best strategy in the struggle for survival. Struggle for survival understood, of course, in its wide Darwinian sense – not as a struggle for the sheer means of existence, but as a struggle against all natural conditions unfavourable to the species. The animal species, in which individual struggle has been reduced to a minimum, and the practice of mutual aid has attained the greatest development, are invariably the most numerous, the most prosperous and the most likely to make further progress.

Extract C

Voice: Secondly, those who run successful businesses develop a business blueprint. It's what we often refer to as a strategic business plan. This describes clearly their business concept, their mission and their overall philosophy of business. It sets out personal and corporate goals and draws up specific timelines and a set of strategies that will ensure these goals are achieved.

Owners of a successful business develop a structure that functions as a well-oiled machine. This structure – including all its policies and procedures – will encourage staff and associates to perform to their maximum capabilities. It'll aim to reward people who shine in proportion to the contribution they make. It'll probably also describe how to discipline anyone who deviates from acceptable behaviour – what the organization expects of them. Positions, duties and responsibilities are defined and communicated and performance is assessed on a regular basis.

Extract D

Interviewer: And what do you consider to be your greatest strength?

Speaker: I think I have a number of strengths. I especially pride myself on my customer service skills. I think I'm good at resolving problems and making sure that difficult situations are not allowed to develop. That applies both when dealing with customers and other members of staff, I think.

Interviewer: And do you have any weaknesses?

Speaker: Mm, I suppose I have to admit that I can be too much of a perfectionist – I mean, perhaps unrealistic in terms of how well something needs to be done. I sometimes spend too long on a project or task, or accept a job that could easily be delegated to somebody else. I never miss deadlines, but I do need to improve in terms of knowing when to say a job is complete and to move on to the next. I guess I need to be more trusting about handing tasks over to other people. I tend to feel that if a job needs doing, I should do it myself.

Track 121
Unit 11 Listening 1

D   Listen again and note examples of formal and informal use of language.
[Play Track 120 again]

Track 122
Unit 11 Listening 2

A   Listen to longer versions of each extract and answer the questions.
Section 1 extract

Interviewer: And what do you consider to be your greatest strength?

Speaker: I think I have a number of strengths. I especially pride myself on my customer service skills. I think I'm good at resolving problems and making sure that difficult situations are not allowed to develop. That applies both when dealing with customers and other members of staff, I think.

Interviewer: And do you have any weaknesses?

Speaker: Mm, I suppose I have to admit that I can be too much of a perfectionist – I mean, perhaps unrealistic in terms of how well something needs to be done. I sometimes spend too long on a project or task, or accept a job that could easily be delegated to somebody else. I never miss deadlines, but I do need to improve in terms of knowing when to say a job is complete and to move on to the next. I guess I need to be more trusting about handing tasks over to other people. I tend to feel that if a job needs doing, I should do it myself.

Interviewer: So, can you describe one particular challenge and how you dealt with it?

Speaker: Well, last year we were having a few issues with one particular client. They were threatening to take their business elsewhere. I felt that some people on our side were not being … how shall I put it? – as diplomatic as they could be. I met personally with representatives of the client and managed to persuade them that we could handle their account in a way that suited them better. It all ended up very amicably.

Interviewer: Good. Now, if I asked somebody who knows you well why you should be offered this position, what would he or she say?

Speaker: I think they'd say I possess the skills outlined in the job description and I bring seven years of expertise with me. I've heard people describe me as hard-working, professional and trustworthy and everyone knows me as a team player.

Interviewer: OK – that's good to hear. And, what about your expectations of salary? Is that something …

Section 2 extract

Voice: Businesses that succeed must have something that sets them apart from businesses that fail. First of all, successful businesses – or the people who run them – generally have a very positive attitude towards their business and a positive outlook on life in general. Successful business owners will see opportunities rather than obstacles, for example. They'll take risks and accept failure – I've heard so many people say that they regret not having tried something far more than they regret trying something that didn't work out. Again, it's that sense of a chance not seized – a fish that got away!

Secondly, those who run successful businesses develop a business blueprint. It's what we often refer to as a strategic business plan. This describes clearly their business concept, their mission and their overall philosophy of business. It sets out personal and corporate goals and draws up specific timelines and a set of strategies that will ensure these goals are achieved.

Owners of a successful business develop a structure that functions as a well-oiled machine. This structure – including all its policies and procedures – will encourage staff and associates to perform to their maximum capabilities. It'll aim to reward people who shine in proportion to the contribution they make. It'll probably also describe how to discipline anyone who deviates from acceptable behaviour – what the organization expects of them. Positions, duties and responsibilities are defined and communicated and performance is assessed on a regular basis.

Finally, the owners of successful businesses develop support systems. The objective is to support and make efficient all the activities carried out by the organization, relieving management of irksome routine tasks and giving owners more time to think and plan ahead. These tracking systems provide critical information about sales, cash flow and various financial performance data, so that senior management can take action as soon as change occurs. Problems are flagged before they have a chance to become unmanageable.

So, in summary, before I move on, the four areas I've outlined are …

Section 3 extract

Mother: Lucas, can we have a chat about college? You know we've been looking at the report, don't you?

Lucas: Oh, all right, I guess so.

Father: Don't you want to talk about it, then?

Lucas: Well, no, not really. I know what you're going to say.

Mother: Which is?

Lucas: That you're disappointed and I should've done better.

Father: Yes, you're right that we're disappointed, but it's not really that you should've done better – though that would be nice – it's the lack of commitment.

Lucas: Look, how is it that everyone seems to know that I've got no commitment? Maybe I just think …

Mother: Because we can all see that you're not making an effort. The report isn't just about the grades. Every one of those tutors has commented that you're not trying.

Father: Look, what we're saying is that we moved heaven and earth to get you onto this course and now you're just not making the most of the opportunity.

Lucas: What do you mean, moved heaven and earth?

Father: You know exactly what I mean. Your exam results weren't that good and we had to persuade the college to accept you. We talked about the fact that there would be other students on the course who'd find it less challenging and you promised to make an effort.

Mother: Yes – that's all we ask – make an effort – do your best. We don't expect miracles and we're not asking for super high marks or anything.

Lucas: So, why do you assume I'm not making an effort?

Father: Oh, come on, Lucas. We've read the report – you've read the report. It's just like all those school reports we fell out about, isn't it? The bottom line is there's always something you'd rather be doing than working towards a future.

Lucas: Look, maybe I just don't see my future sitting at a keyboard in some stuffy office.

Mother: So, what exactly does inspire you, then? Could you share it with us? Times are getting harder for everyone and if you have no qualifications, it'll be almost impossible.

Father: I suppose you think you think you're going to make a fortune playing those dreadful drums, don't you? Well, let me tell you, it doesn't work like that – not for the vast majority of …

Section 4 extract

Voice: So, we have seen that the term *survival of the fittest* has been rather misused over the years and, in fact, has probably been misunderstood by the vast majority of people who have used it. I think we can certainly say that it isn't a direct synonym for *natural selection,* which, as I've said, was what Darwin first used the term in relation to.

It's interesting that the Russian anarchist philosopher, Peter Kropotkin, viewed the concept of survival of the fittest not as competition or in any way the modem perception of people climbing over one another to succeed, but as supporting co-operation. He coined the phrase 'mutual aid', having concluded that the fittest was not necessarily the best at competing individually, but often the community consisting of those best at operating together. In the animal kingdom, the vast majority of species live in societies – association is the best strategy in the struggle for survival. Struggle for survival understood, of course, in its wide Darwinian sense – not as a struggle for the sheer means of existence, but as a struggle against all natural conditions unfavourable to the species. The animal species, in which individual struggle has been reduced to a minimum, and the practice of mutual aid has attained the greatest development, are invariably the most numerous, the most prosperous and the most likely to make further progress.

Applying this concept to human society, Kropotkin presented mutual aid as one of the dominant factors of evolution. He claimed that that we can retrace co-operation to the earliest stages of our development and in it find the origin of our ethical values. In the progress of man, mutual support rather than mutual struggle has had the upper hand. He also believed that despite the obvious conflict between people in modern society, mutual aid is the only way we can hope to continue to evolve.

Track 123
Unit 11 Consolidation – Speaking

B **Listen to some students answering the questions. For each question, tick the student that you think gives the better answer.**
Question 1 – Student A
Examiner: Give me an example of somebody who you think has been very successful.
Student: Mm, there are so many people I could choose. I prefer to say someone who has triumphed over adversity as it means more to succeed when you started with nothing. For me, Barack Obama is the perfect example. I know he didn't start exactly with nothing, but he was born into a normal family. To become the first black president of the USA was an incredible achievement.
Question 1 – Student B
Examiner: Give me an example of somebody who you think has been very successful.
Student: I think my father has been very successful and I have a lot of respect for him. He worked hard to start his own business and it grew into a very big business. I work for him and I want to be so successful as he.

Question 2 – Student A
Examiner: What has been your biggest achievement so far?
Student: Oh, that's difficult – I'm still young. Maybe, to be the captain of my football team in school was it. I was very proud and my father was very proud too.
Question 2 – Student B
Examiner: What has been your biggest achievement so far?
Student: Mm, I am not sure – I have to think. Last year, I ran in the marathon. It was not a full marathon, but a shorter one – 10 km. I felt it was an achievement not just because I finished, but because I did it for the right reason – for a good cause. I raised about 500 euros for orphan children in my country.

Question 3 – Student A
Examiner: Is it important to persevere or is it best to give up if you know that something is bound to fail?
Student: Yes, it's very important not to give up. I think you say if you don't succeed first time, you must try

again or something like that. To give up is the failure in my mind.
Question 3 – Student B
Examiner: Is it important to persevere or is it best to give up if you know that something is bound to fail?
Student: It's a good question. People say you should never give up or that you must keep on trying, but I'm not sure that's true. You can't be good at everything. I knew, for example, that I would never be a singer even though I had some singing lessons. I was happier when I gave up.

Question 4 – Student A
Examiner: What have you failed to achieve recently and how did that make you feel?
Student: That's easy – my driving test. It made me feel really bad because I thought I would pass easily – maybe I was too confident. Now I must take it again next month.
Question 4 – Student B
Examiner: What have you failed to achieve recently and how did that make you feel?
Student: Mm, recently, I'm not sure. I think everyday there's something that is a little success and something that's a little failure. Maybe a specific example is not getting a job I applied for last year. I thought I did OK in the interview, but they gave the job to someone else. I wasn't too disappointed because I know there were many people who wanted this job. I had to pick up myself and try again.

Track 124
Unit 11 Consolidation – Speaking

C **Listen again to the students' answers. In pairs, discuss why you feel that one student's answer was better in Exercise B.**
[Play Track 123 again]

Track 125
Workbook Unit 11 Listening

A **Listen to two extracts from a Listening test, one from Section 2 and the other from Section 3. What is the common theme of both extracts?**
Section 2 extract
Voice: During any recession, small businesses are more dramatically affected than larger, more established businesses. Of course, we read about the giant high-street stores going to the wall, but we rarely hear about the small concerns that are folding every day. So, what can a small business do? The simple answer is that they must adapt and diversify, but what does that really mean? Well, the most common tactics are pretty obvious – launch new product ranges and trade at weekends – if, of course, you

weren't doing that previously. More than half of all small business owners admit that they've adapted in order to survive the downturn. Everywhere we see businesses diversifying and offering new products or services that target new customer groups.

Now, this might mean that some businesses are no longer operating within their specific area of expertise – in their comfort zone, so to speak. Diversification is potentially risky, as I'm sure you can appreciate. Of course, it's essential that managers and thinkers remain entrepreneurial and that they can anticipate market change. They have to be versatile and ready to respond to any opportunity that presents itself. However, it's also vital that they remain focused on their original business plan and retain a very clear image of what their original objectives were when they set up in the first place.

Now, there are other options that businesses are taking – perhaps more drastic options – and they involve paring down the workforce. Many companies have been forced to make staff redundant, even though it's the last step they want to take. An alternative is cutting …

Section 3 extract

Student 1: Well, as business students, we ought to be able to suggest some solutions quite easily, don't you think?

Student 2: Yeah, I don't think it's too difficult. What was the exact brief again?

Student 1: Let's see. Here we are. To make a list of some of the measures that small businesses are taking in order to survive the recession. It's just a brainstorming task really – we're going to go into it more deeply in tomorrow's lecture.

Student 3: OK, well to start with, let's establish why we're focusing on small businesses. Have they been hit harder than bigger businesses?

Student 1: Yeah, I think so. Businesses that have been around for a while can weather the storm – you know, they already have loyal customers and probably more to fall back on. Smaller, newer businesses are more vulnerable and find it harder to stay afloat.

Student 2: OK, so they need to branch out.

Student 3: What does that mean exactly?

Student 2: Well, they need to find new products to offer.

Student 3: Or services.

Student 2: OK – and they need to aim them at new customers.

Student 1: True – but doesn't that mean that businesses lose sight of their original business plan? I mean they become a sort of Jack-of-all-trades. Every business ends up selling the same thing as everyone else.

Student 2: Mm, a bit of an exaggeration, but I take your point. There are certainly pros and cons to diversification.

Student 3: I think in the current climate, one of the ways that business people need to adapt is to become

more of an all-rounder. I mean, no, they shouldn't start trying to operate within markets they know nothing about, but they need to be adaptable.

Student 2: OK, I think we've said that now. What else is there?

Student 1: Well, I'm not sure if it's really an adaptation, but I guess quite a few businesses have had to lay people off.

Student 3: Or cut their pay. I think it's always a last resort, but …

Track 126

Workbook Unit 11 Listening

B Listen again. Can you identify any examples where the same idea is expressed formally in one extract and informally in the other?
[Play Track 125 again]

Track 127

Workbook Unit 11 Listening

C Listen to the Section 2 extract and for each question choose a, b or c as your answer.
[Play **Section 2 extract** of Track 125]

Track 128

Workbook Unit 11 Listening

D Listen to the Section 3 extract and complete the notes.
[Play **Section 3 extract** of Track 125]

Track 129

Unit 12 – Speaking 1

B Listen to two students talking with an examiner.
Speaker 1

Examiner: So, are you ready?

Student: Yes, I think so. Well, I want to talk about a crime that is very typical nowadays. Of course, in many big cities, it's not always safe to walk around, especially after dark. Street robbery – I think you call it mugging – is common, and for women there are specific dangers too. However, people think they're safe if they drive – at least they used to. Now, that's maybe not so true. Carjacking is happening more and more. It's like hijacking, but it's not a plane – it's a car waiting at traffic lights or at a busy junction. The people who do – no, commit – this crime are usually young men – often just boys. They are poor and probably quite desperate, but that doesn't make it OK. The victims are very frightened and feel violated – sometimes there's violence if the car driver tries to hold on to a bag or a jacket, for example.

Examiner: So, do you mind if I ask if you've personally ever been the victim of this kind …

Speaker 2

Examiner: So, are you ready?

Student: Yes, I think so. I think the most obvious crime of the modern age is online crime – I mean theft of bank details and so on, and even identity theft, though I'm not sure exactly how that works. Online crime is becoming more and more common and it seems that the criminals are always one step ahead of the programmers who make the online safety software. Um, oh yes, the people who commit this crime I guess are getting more clever though I heard many are still very young. I read that now they are better organized – you know, not just one person vandalizing a site, but groups working together to steal money from accounts. They are cracking even secure sites.

Examiner: … And how do the victims of online crime feel?

Student: Oh yes. Well, I can say from experience. When I was shopping online, I suddenly had a message about a big offer to save money. Stupidly, I clicked it and the next thing I had a virus. It was a fake – you know, it said that my credit card details had been stolen and I must download this program to protect myself – they try to make you panic. If I'd run the program, then they would have asked for my details to pay for the protection and then I would have really been in trouble. As it was, I had to pay a lot for my computer to be cleaned – you know, put back to normal. It made me feel really bad, like somebody had burgled my house – they were in my computer. Also, I felt it was my fault – if I hadn't clicked the window with the offer, it wouldn't have happened.

Track 130
Unit 12 – Speaking 2

B Listen to some students answering the questions. Do you agree with any of the points they make?

1

Examiner: Should prisoners be released early if they show remorse or seem to be rehabilitated?

Student: Mm, I'm not sure. I guess you could say that there must be some incentive to behave well in prison. I mean, if you feel there's no hope of getting out before 20 years, say, is up, there's no reason to improve yourself. On the other hand, criminals that commit terrible crimes really shouldn't be released until they've served their whole sentence.

2

Examiner: Would there be so much crime if people were more equal?

Student: I think there'd still be crime – I mean, certain crimes are committed by people from any background. But, perhaps, there would be less crime and certainly less crimes that are driven by need – you know, like theft, robbery and so on. I'm quite

sure there are prisoners everywhere who are thinking that if they'd had a few more opportunities when they were younger, they wouldn't be behind bars now.

3

Examiner: Is crime ever acceptable if driven by extreme poverty?

Student: I don't think you can say a crime is acceptable or that you condone it, but you might say it becomes more understandable or forgivable. You know, if your children were hungry, you might decide to steal some food from a shop for them.

4

Examiner: Is the main role of prison to punish or to rehabilitate offenders?

Student: I don't think prison should be just a punishment – that's like an eye for an eye philosophy. I'm against the death penalty because it's so clearly just a punishment. Prison should also be a deterrent – I mean it should discourage people from committing crime. That's why prisons must be places that people are afraid of – not too soft. As for rehabilitation, I don't know. Yes – a period in prison should rehabilitate the offender, but I'm not convinced that really happens very often. I read that most people released from prison commit more crime.

Track 131
Unit 12 Speaking 2

Pronunciation check

Listen to some native speakers saying the sentences from the *Grammar check*.

1 If you feel there's no hope of getting out before 20 years, say, is up, there's no reason to improve yourself.

2 Would there be so much crime if people were more equal?

3 If I hadn't clicked the window with the offer, it wouldn't have happened.

4 There are prisoners everywhere who are thinking that if they'd had a few more opportunities when they were younger, they wouldn't be behind bars now.

Track 132
Unit 12 – Listening 1

B Listen and match the Extracts 1–3 with the pictures a–c.

Extract 1

Police officer: Hello, what can I do for you?

Student: I've just had my purse stolen.

Police officer: Oh dear – I'm sorry. Where was this?

Student: In the High Street. I didn't phone from there as somebody told me the police station was so close.

Police officer: OK, well, how long ago did this happen?

Student: Just now – I came straight here.

Police officer: I'll put 2:20, then, shall I? That's ten minutes ago.

Student: Yes, OK – I don't really mind. Is there anything you can do? I mean, is there any chance of finding whoever stole it?

Police officer: Well, tell me what happened first and then we'll see. Did somebody grab the purse from you? Did you see the person?

Student: No, it was a pickpocket. The purse was in a loose bag that I was carrying over my shoulder. I didn't realize it was missing until I was in a shop buying something.

Police officer: Ah, so it could've been stolen longer than ten minutes ago.

Student: No – well certainly not much longer than ten minutes – I had it just before that when I bought something in another shop.

Police officer: I'll be honest. If you didn't see anybody and you're not sure exactly when this happened, there's not much chance of catching anybody – we don't know who we're looking for. The best thing now is if you give me some details and describe the purse. Very often, thieves take what they want and then throw a bag or purse away. You might get it back and some of whatever was in it. Now, what's your name?

Student: Joanna – Joanna Moore.

Police officer: Is that double *o* and an *e* on the end?

Student: Yes.

Police officer: Is that name on anything in the purse?

Student: Erm, I don't know – yes, it'll be on debit cards – if they're still in the purse. It'll be on my student ID card too.

Police officer: OK, I'll take an address and so on in a moment. Tell me what the purse looked like first.

Student: It's silver with a golden clasp.

Police officer: Gold clasp?

Student: No, just coloured gold I mean. It's not an especially expensive purse. It has a sort of checked design. I mean checks sort of in the leather – not different coloured checks.

Police officer: OK, and what was in it?

Student: There was about £70 cash, two debit cards and a credit card. As I say, my student ID was in there and probably my student bus pass too.

Police officer: And nothing else was taken from the bag on your shoulder?

Student: No, thankfully no – I think they just reached in and …

Extract 2

Voice: Now, this may seem really obvious, but always lock before you leave. In an average year, over 5,000 houses are burgled because the occupier fails to lock their front door. It's easy to forget to lock the front door, especially when you're in a hurry or distracted, and you'd be amazed how many people just don't bother if they're popping out to the local shop or on a school pick-up. It only takes five minutes to get in and make off with a DVD player, laptop or iPod when the occupier makes it so easy. Leaving the front door unlocked on just one occasion is enough. The vast majority of burglars are opportunists – they look for an easy way to get in that won't take long and won't arouse suspicion. The front door is often the first thing they try.

Burglars choose a target that presents them with the fewest obstacles. Again, this may seem obvious, but a building that appears to be unoccupied and insecure is far more likely to be targeted than one which is properly secured. Access to open windows, even at the top of the building, are an invitation, as are unlocked gates to the rear of a property and high fences or trees that obscure a natural view. Needless to say, leaving ladders out where they can be used to assist a break-in is asking for trouble. People who live in multi-occupancy blocks should be mindful not to grant entry to people they don't know via an intercom system and to be suspicious of anyone who appears to be trying to follow them into the building.

Extract 3

Police officer: Police.

Man: Oh, hello. I want to report a car theft.

Police officer: Your car's been stolen?

Man: No, no – my car's been broken into. Some little … somebody's smashed the back windscreen and stolen quite a few bits and pieces. Can you send somebody here?

Police officer: Well, probably yes, but tell me what's been stolen first.

Man: A briefcase and a jacket – there were quite a few valuable items in the case too.

Police officer: Such as?

Man: My mobile and iPod – oh, and two flight tickets as well – I'd forgotten about them. Urgh, it makes me so …

Police officer: Yes, I understand. Can I ask why you left the items in the car? I mean, presumably they were in easy reach if they deliberately targeted the back windscreen.

Man: I only stopped for a few minutes to nip into a restaurant to give somebody a message. I was double parked for goodness sake. I can't believe that nobody saw, or heard, it happen. It's a busy enough street.

Police officer: OK, so where are you exactly?

Man: In Upper Street about 30 m down the road from La Fourchette.

Police officer: How do you spell that?

Man: La – L-A and then F-O-U-R-C-H-E double T-E.

Police officer: Thirty metres north or south?

Man: Towards the tube station – that's north, isn't it?

Police officer: Yes. And what's the name?

Man: Brian. Brian Rafferty. That's R-A double F-E-R-T-Y.

Police officer: OK, I'll get a patrol car to you as soon as possible and they'll take further details. I can't promise it'll be immediate, but it'll be in the next 15 minutes or so.

Man: OK, thanks.

Track 133

Unit 12 Listening 2

A   Listen to the first extract again complete the police report.

[Play **Extract 1** of Track 132 again]

Track 134

Unit 12 Listening 3

A   Listen to the second and third extracts again and answer the questions.

[Play **Extracts 2 and 3** of Track 132 again]

Track 135

Workbook Unit 12 Listening

B   Listen and answer the questions.

Voice: Rehabilitating an offender once he or she has become involved in crime, and especially once he or she has served a prison sentence, is a massive challenge. The vast majority of people simply have no idea of the difficulties and disadvantages that most convicted criminals have had to deal with in the past and still have to cope with on a daily basis.

To start with, many prisoners lack the most basic qualifications and have little or no experience of employment. Few have what we all consider to be social contacts or meaningful friendships and most have housing problems of one kind or another. These practical difficulties are often compounded by drug, alcohol and mental health issues. In short, most members of the prison population have experienced a lifetime of social exclusion.

Here are some disturbing statistics. Prisoners are more than ten times as likely to have been in care as a child than the average person and more than ten times as likely to have been a regular truant from school. They're far more likely to be unemployed and far more likely to be or have been a young parent. Prisoners are almost three times as likely as the average person to have had a family member convicted of a criminal offence.

The level of a typical prisoner's basic skills will shock many of you – 80% have the writing skills, 65% the numeracy skills and 50% the reading skills of a child under 11 years old. And the situation is deteriorating – prisoners under 20 years of age have an unemployment rate and school exclusion background far worse than older prisoners.

It's generally now accepted that handing out a prison sentence actually exacerbates the factors associated with offending and reoffending. A third of prisoners, for example, lose their home while in prison. Two-thirds lose their job and a fifth face increased financial problems. Nearly half lose contact with their family. There's also the likelihood of mental and physical health deteriorating further and exposure to drugs – whether they're already using them or not.

Let me tell you about a real case. Annette lost her accommodation as a result of being in prison. Nobody talked to her when she arrived or during the following months about how she could keep her house or what she could do to ensure that she had somewhere to live on release. Her rent arrears accumulated and she was evicted. Her request for early release was rejected because of the absence of an approved address. When she was finally released, her local authority refused to provide accommodation because of her previous rent arrears. You may find this story incredible, but it happens over and over. So, is there a solution? Well, I want to …

Acknowledgements

Page 11, audio for Exercises B and C, Extract 4 reproduced with kind permission of Rhett A. Butler, Mongabay, www.mongabay.com. Copyright Rhett Butler 2010.

Page 12, Extract A reproduced with kind permission of *Scientific American*. © 2013 Scientific American, a Division of Nature America, Inc. All Rights Reserved.

Page 12, Extract B reproduced with kind permission of The Royal College of Midwives, © RCM.

Page 12, Extract C reproduced with kind permission of *Science 2.0*.

Page 14, text from www.liveboldandbloom.com. Reproduced with kind permission of Barrie Davenport.

Page 16, line graph data taken from *Life Tables for the United States Social Security*, Area 1900–2100, Actuarial Study no. 120, www.ssa.gov.

Page 16, pie charts reproduced with kind permission of the *UC Atlas of Global Inequality*.

Page 17, graphs and table adapted from European Union data. © European Union 2005–2011.

Page 21, text reproduced with kind permission of Leo Babauta, www.zenhabits.net.

Page 25, audio for Exercises B and C. © Pamela Prindle Fierro and About.com. Used with permission of About Inc., which can be found online at www.about.com. All rights reserved. Additional information in this text reproduced with permission of *The Tech Museum of Innovation* and Stanford University's Dr Barry Starr from http://genetics.thetech.org.

Page 26, text © Kimberly Powell. Used with permission of About Inc., which can be found online at www.about.com. All rights reserved.

Pages 27 and 28, text taken from an article by Wilson Wayne Grant, MD: "Nature or Nurture: Products but not Prisoners of Our Past, "Oates Journal, January, 2010. Published by the Wayne Oates Institute. Louisville, Kentucky. USA.

Page 35, text reproduced with kind permission of *MedIndia Network for Health*, © MedIndia 2008. All rights reserved.

Page 40, audio Extract 1 taken from www.grand-national.me.uk. Reproduced with kind permission of Eddison Media, www.eddison-media.com.

Page 40, audio Extract 3 taken from Wikipedia, http://en.wikipedia.org/wiki/Danica_Patrick. Text has been modified and used under the CC-BA-SA 3.0 license, http://creativecommons.org/licenses/by-sa/3.0/legalcode.

Page 42, Extract B, taken from an article from the Calgary Herald, a division of Postmedia Network Inc. Reprinted by permission.

Page 42, Extract D and pages 218–219 taken from *USA Today Magazine*, www.usatodaymagazine.net © The Society for the Advancement of Education. All rights reserved.

Pages 43 and 44, text reprinted with permission of *Psychiatric News*, (Copyright ©2002). American Psychiatric Association.

Pages 46–48, graphs taken from the *Bureau of Labor Statistics*.

Page 51, graph taken from the *National Center for Health Statistics*.

Page 55, audio for Exercise A taken from Wikipedia, http://en.wikipedia.org/wiki/Penny-farthing. Text has been modified and used under the CC-BA-SA 3.0 license, http://creativecommons.org/licenses/by-sa/3.0/legalcode.

Page 56, text adapted and reproduced with author's permission from "Sweet Remembrance," Psychology Today, May 2006.

Pages 57 and 58, text taken from Wikipedia, http://en.wikipedia.org/wiki/Nostalgia. Text has been modified and used under the CC-BA-SA 3.0 license, http://creativecommons.org/licenses/by-sa/3.0/legalcode.

Additional information in this text taken from *Integral Options Cafe*, http://integral-options.blogspot.co.uk.

Pages 75 and 76, text reproduced with kind permission of *Business Lexington*. Taken from the edition on the 16th May 2008 of *Business Lexington*, www.bizlex.com.

Page 78, graph data taken from OECD (2012), "Average annual working time", *Employment and Labour Markets: Key Tables from OECD*, No. 8. doi: 10.1787/annual-work-table-2012-1-en, 14th February 2013.

Page 80, graph adapted from Office for National Statistics data and licensed under the Open Government License v.1.0.

Pages 83 and 84, text reproduced with kind permission of the University of Illinois at Urbana-Champaign. Taken from, 'All work and no play makes for troubling trend in early education' (February 12, 2009), *ScienceDaily*, http://www.sciencedaily.com.

Pages 92 and 93, text reproduced with kind permission of Jane Meighan, www.RunawayJane.com.

Pages 102 and 103, audio for Listening 1–3, taken from Wikipedia, http://en.wikipedia.org/wiki/Organ_transplantation, http://en.wikipedia.org/wiki/Kidney_transplantation, http://en.wikipedia.org/wiki/Pancreas_transplantation,

Page 223, Extracts A and B, Perdikogianni M., Anastassiou-Hadjicharalambous X.: Infantile Amnesia. In: Goldstein S., Naglieri J. (Ed.) *Encyclopedia of Child Behavior and Development: SpringerReference* (www.springerreference.com). Springer-Verlag Berlin Heidelberg, 2011. DOI: 10.1007/SpringerReference_180186 2011-05-09 09:18:39 UTC.

Additional information in these texts taken from Wikipedia, http://en.wikipedia.org/wiki/Childhood_amnesia. Text has been modified and used under the CC-BA-SA 3.0 license, http://creativecommons.org/licenses/by-sa/3.0/legalcode.

Pages 226 and 227, text reproduced with kind permission of Mark Shead, www.productivity501.com, *The Futurist* magazine and the University of Maryland's Americans' Use of Time Project.

Page 228, graph adapted from Crown Copyright data from *The Taking Part Survey*, Department for Culture, Media and Sport. From the Office for National Statistics and licensed under the Open Government License v.1.0.

Page 231, text taken from Just the Flight, www.justtheflight.co.uk.

Pages 234 and 235, text reproduced with kind permission of Historic UK, © Historic UK 2013.

Pages 239 and 240, text reproduced with kind permission of NFU Mutual.

Page 243, audio taken from Wikipedia, http://en.wikipedia.org/wiki/Street_art. Text has been modified and used under the CC-BA-SA 3.0 license, http://creativecommons.org/licenses/by-sa/3.0/legalcode.

Page 253, from Forbes, May 24th © 2007 Forbes. All rights reserved. Used by permission and protected by the Copyright Laws of the United States. The printing, copying, redistribution, or retransmission of this Content without express written permission is prohibited.

Page 255, graph taken from Database sports, www.databasesports.com. © 2002–2011 databasesports.com.

Pages 257 and 258, audio for Exercise B © Crown Copyright 2002. Contains public sector information licensed under the Open Government Licence v1.0, www.nationalarchives.gov.uk/doc/open-government-licence/open-government-licence.htm.

Pages 258 and 259, text reproduced with kind permission of the *Metropolitan Police*. © Mayor's Office for Policing and Crime 2013. Additional information and diagrams reproduced with kind permission of *Virtual Science Fair Inc*.

IELTS Target 5.0

CEF LEVELS A2 TO B1/IELTS 3.5–5.0

Preparation for IELTS General Training – Leading to IELTS Academic

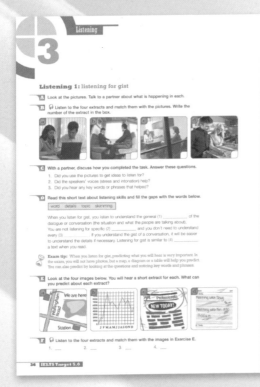

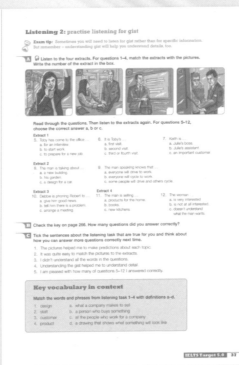

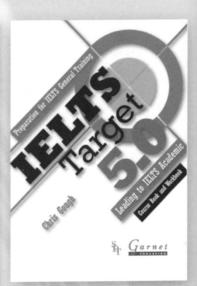

IELTS Target 5.0 is for students who are entering IELTS study between Band 3 (extremely limited user) and Band 4 (limited user). Such students might need to raise their IELTS score to:

- satisfy criteria set by the institution where they study
- work towards a score of 5.0
- lay the foundation for further study of the Academic Module

KEY FEATURES

- Comprehensive 240-hour course
- IELTS General Training ideal for students on lower band scores
- Provides foundation for further General Training or Academic study
- Four sections provide flexibility of use

- Clear, scaffolded activities
- Focus on real student needs
- Interactive Course Book CD-ROM
- Teacher's Book provides vocabulary development

IELTS Target 5.0
Course Book and Workbook, sample tests,
audio DVD 978 1 90861 493 3
Teacher's Book 978 1 90861 494 0
Interactive Course Book CD-ROM 978 1 85964 578 9

www.garneteducation.com

EDUCATION

IELTS Target 6.5 & 7.0

CEF LEVELS B1 TO C1/IELTS 5.0–7.0

Preparation for IELTS Academic

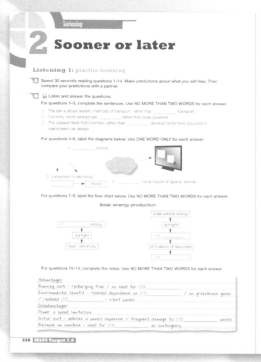

IELTS Target 7.0 **is included with the existing** *IELTS Target 6.5* **material** and addresses the increasing trend of institutions demanding higher language competence from students. This level provides less pre-skills guidance and scaffolding, and more post-skills practice and analysis. It aims to develop core language skills and improve scores through more challenging topics and tasks.

UNITS

- Life and death
- Nature or nurture
- Boys and girls
- Past and present
- Work and play
- Home and away
- Kill or cure
- Bricks and mortar

- Words and pictures
- Rain or shine
- Sink or swim
- Crime and punishment
- Live and learn
- Sooner or later
- Haves and have-nots
- Man and beast

IELTS Target 6.5 & 7.0
Course Book and Workbook
with audio DVD 978 1 90861 491 9
Teacher's Book 978 1 90861 492 6

www.garneteducation.com

Garnet
EDUCATION

Passport to Academic Presentations

CEF LEVELS B2 TO C2/IELTS 5.0–7.5+

A course for students giving oral academic presentations in colleges and universities

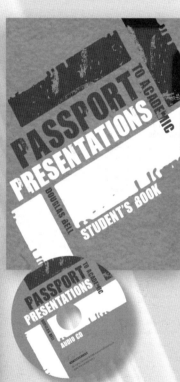

A course book specifically designed for students who need to give presentations in English as part of their university study. *Passport to Academic Presentations* provides students with the tools to speak with confidence and fluency.

KEY FEATURES

- Audio CD for further self-study and listening practice
- Tips for successful presentations
- Step-by-step coverage of the oral presentation process
- Focus on key language and pronunciation areas
- DVD includes extended learning through filmed presentations

UNITS

- Getting started
- Organizing your material
- Dealing with questions and answers
- Creating more impact
- Using visual aids
- Giving persuasive presentations

Passport to Academic Presentations
Student's Book & audio CD 978 1 85964 400 3
DVD (includes audio CD material) 978 1 85964 416 4
Teacher's Book 978 1 85964 415 7

www.garneteducation.com

Garnet
EDUCATION

English Practice Grammar

CEF LEVELS A2 TO B1/IELTS 3.0–4.0

A reference and practice book for classroom or self-study use

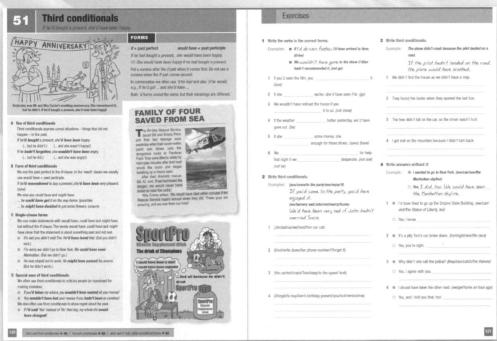

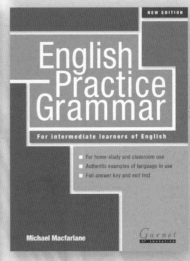

English Practice Grammar contains the essential grammar for successful communication in English up to and including Upper Intermediate level. It is designed as a complete reference grammar for all students of English studying at this level.

English Practice Grammar is a reference and practice book in one. It is perfect both for self-study and for use in the classroom.

KEY FEATURES

- Brand-new, full-colour layout
- Twelve new units, making a total of 100 units
- Clear layout enables students to find information quickly
- Grammatical points illustrated by authentic examples from everyday life
- A new cross-referencing system takes students quickly to related units
- Now includes Checkpoint, a test for either diagnostic or exit use
- The Appendix includes irregular verbs, pronunciation and spelling tips, for both British and American English
- Includes a full answer key

English Practice Grammar
International edition (with answers) ... 978 1 85964 688 5

www.garneteducation.com